Spectacular Passions

Spectacular Passions

CINEMA, FANTASY, GAY MALE SPECTATORSHIPS

BRETT FARMER ᔐ

Duke University Press DURHAM AND LONDON 2000

© 2000 Duke University Press
All rights reserved
Printed in the United States of
America on acid-free paper ⊗
Typeset in Janson by Tseng
Information Systems, Inc.
Library of Congress Cataloging-in-
Publication Data appear on the last
printed page of this book.

For Peter

Contents

Acknowledgments

Like many happy things in life, this book is the result of an advantageous combination of good fortune, enabling opportunity, and considerable personal and institutional assistance. It started as a doctoral dissertation at Griffith University, where it benefited enormously from the careful guidance and expert advice offered by my supervisors, Gillian Swanson and Dugald Williamson, and the warm encouragement extended by the members of the examination committee: Jane Crisp, Alexander Doty, Barbara Creed, and Edward Baron Turk. I thank them all for the kind enthusiasm and generosity with which they read and responded to my work.

At Duke University Press, Richard Morrison provided diligent editorial support for the project, and two anonymous readers gave invaluable feedback on ways to hone and strengthen the book's major arguments and claims.

The Department of English at the University of Melbourne furnished an accommodating and intellectually stimulating context within which to achieve the often arduous tasks of redevelopment and rewriting. I owe particular thanks to my Heads of Department, Simon During and Ken Ruthven, for their unflagging commitment to the value of my research work. I would also like to extend special thanks to two of my colleagues in the Cultural Studies Program, Chris Healy and Annamarie Jagose, for their guidance and support through what has been an enormously steep learning curve and for their personal and professional magnanimity.

Many others contributed both directly and indirectly to the realization of this project. I would like to thank Nick Adams, Steven Angelides, Annita Boyd, Jodi Brooks, Marion Campbell, Melissa Connell, Frank Davies, Emma Felton, John Hirsch, Nichole Matthews, Sue Strong, Andrew Surrey, and Chris Tennant. I am also grateful to the many gay men who shared their views on film and film viewing with me: Mark Adams, George Anastasiou, Richard Anderson, Andrew Batt, Greg Bell, Wally Cowin, Devon Clayton, Tony Donnelly, Keith Ellis, Mark Findlay, Andrew Gallagher, Peter Hall, Samuel King, David W. Kinnick, Michael Lambert, Paul Lawrence, John Lestrange, Graeme Loyer, Romano Lunghi, Ian McGregor, Raymond Ng, Tommy Nguyen, Donald Olsen, Phillip Pang, Will Porter, David J. Quinn, Stuart Rawe, Sol Rosen, Peter Rudd, Jonah Satoa, Tom Saunders, Ken Schessler, Christopher Stone, Carmello Strollo, Harrison Tate, Mark Thompson, Phillip Tjoeng, Ed Torres, Ken Turner, Raul Valenta, Sacha Vujovic, Samuel Walker, Gregory Wallis, Neil Weiss, Paul Yau, and Barry Young.

Parts of this book were presented as conference or seminar papers at various events or institutions, including Queer Collaborations, the Institute for Psychoanalytic Research, Australian Teachers of Media, the American Film Institute, Griffith University, the University of Queensland, and the University of Melbourne. Thanks to organizers and respondents for the chance to discuss my ideas and to receive useful feedback. A section of chapter 4 was previously published as "I Remember Mama: Cinema, Memory, Gay Male Matrocentrism," *Screen* 39.4 (winter 1998).

I offer my final and deepest thanks to Peter Lowings, who has been at my side throughout this project, providing the type of steadfast emotional support and unquestioning affirmation that only ever comes from sincere devotion. For this—and because I think he'll be chuffed—I dedicate this book to him with love.

Introduction ᴄ᷍ AT FIRST SIGHT: DEFINITIONS,

CLARIFICATIONS, AND ASSORTED PROLEGOMENA

I'm uncomfortable generalizing about people who do queer writing and teaching, . . . but some effects do seem widespread. I think many adults (and I am among them) are trying, in our work, to keep faith with vividly remembered promises made to ourselves in childhood: promises to make invisible possibilities and desires visible; to make the tacit things explicit; to smuggle queer representation in where it must be smuggled and, with the relative freedom of adulthood, to challenge queer-eradicating impulses frontally where they are to be so challenged.
—Eve Kosofsky Sedgwick, *Tendencies*

When I was ten years old, my grandmother gave me a book about the films of Judy Garland.[1] This book quickly became one of my most cherished possessions, and I would spend countless hours poring over it, scrutinizing each photograph and reading the text so often that I virtually memorized it by heart. I recall that there was one particular part that held a special fascination for me. It was an addendum at the very end of the book about Garland's "number one fan," Wayne Martin. According to the piece, Martin took movie fandom to "new extremes," going so far as to turn his modest-looking apartment into a veritable Garland shrine, which he dubbed "Judyland." My fascination with this particular section came from a pressing sense that Wayne Martin and I shared something more than just an interest in Judy Garland. Though it was never stated, I "recognized" that Martin was gay, in much the same way— and using many of the same hermeneutical signs—that I was coming to "recognize" my own gayness. I could see it, for example, in the carefully structured references to Martin as "strange," "peculiar," "gentle," and "lonely." I could see it in the accompanying photographs of Martin where he stands near but never really with Garland, looking ill-fitting, sidelined, different, an outsider. But more than anything I could see it in the "obsessive," "fanatical" way Martin took up and lived out his film spectatorship.

I understood very early on that a certain connection existed between an intense, overinvested film spectatorship and male homosexuality. This knowledge came no doubt from numerous sources, but by age ten it was so entrenched that I could instantly interpret Martin's "movie madness" as a sign of gayness. I was not alone in this knowledge. Those around me were equally privy to it and were thus quick to interpret my own filmic obsessions as a symptom of social and sexual dissonance. Yet despite the conviction that I and others may have had about this correlation between an excessive cinephilia and male homosexuality, it was something that was never formally recognized. Like so many signs of gayness, this was one that, in my childhood at least, could only circulate as an "open secret," relegated to the shadowy realm of unspoken, if not unspeakable, knowledge.[2]

Some recent scholarship has suggested that there may in fact be something "unspeakable" about the figure of the "fan-atical" spectator in general. Henry Jenkins argues that "fandom" functions as "a scandalous category in contemporary culture, one alternately the target of ridicule and anxiety, of dread and desire." Because fans "transgress . . . bourgeois taste and disrupt . . . dominant cultural hierarchies," they are seen "as abnormal and threatening" and must, therefore, "be represented as 'other,' . . . held at a distance so [as] . . . not [to] pollute sanctioned culture."[3] This argument helps draw into sharper focus two of the issues raised by my autobiographical anecdote. The first is how the gay spectator functions as "the figure of a certain discursive unease" in contemporary culture.[4] Like fandom in general, gay spectatorship poses a scandalous affront to dominant sensibilities. It represents a cultural perversion, an abnormal deviation, an outrageous refusal of "appropriate" modes of conduct and taste. In fact, the popularity and marked receptivity of the image of the gay spectator as fan-atic is a direct result of the way male homosexuality and fandom already share fundamental discursive equivalences. Both function as points of otherness, a troubling excess in the social order. Much of the rhetoric of contagion employed to characterize the status of the fan, for example, is strikingly similar to that used by dominant discourses to represent male homosexuality. This is one reason why gay spectatorship is so representable/readable in terms of an over-invested fanaticism.

The second issue is that because gay spectatorship signals such a scandalous affront to mainstream sensibilities, it must, to repeat Jenkins's formulation, be "held at a distance so [as] . . . not [to] pollute sanctioned culture"—it must, in other words, be marginalized and contained. As a child reading my book on Judy Garland, I realized that there was a very good reason why the piece on Wayne Martin was relegated to the appendix, and I used its peripheral status as further evidence to surmise that something was "not quite right" about Mr. Martin and his passions. Just as quickly, I learned that the only proper, not to mention safe, place for my own filmic obsessions was in the secretive margins of my private world, far away from public scrutiny and ridicule. The demonizing cast of dominant discursive representations encodes gay spectatorship with a sense of social impropriety, even shamefulness, ensuring that, again like so many other forms of queerness, it remains largely sequestered, repressed, closeted.

The pressure, if not the demand, for the marginalization of gay spectatorship resides in more specialized discourses as well. Academic film theory also promotes a central suppression of gay spectatorial possibilities. Judith Mayne writes:

> For the longest time, I think I naively accepted that [film] theorists weren't addressing the kinds of issues I addressed because they weren't personally interested in them—you know a basic liberal approach to the field. But [now] . . . it's obvious that [these silences] . . . are in a sense . . . [the result] of conscious refusals within film theory to acknowledge the lesbian or gay other.[5]

I can still recall the sense of incredulous frustration I experienced when, as an undergraduate student, I first came to film studies with the hopeful expectation of having my queer cinematic desires and pleasures accounted for. What I found instead was a complex of critical discourses that informed me, however eruditely, that those desires were once again unrepresentable, those pleasures unknowable. In addition to being disappointed, I was extremely perplexed, because much of the work I was reading—indeed, much of the work that has dominated film theory for the better part of the past three decades—was explicitly concerned with the interrelations between cinema and sexuality, analyzing how and why the former functions as a privileged forum for the production, incitement, and regulation of the latter. However, because this work was, almost to a critic, cast and recast in emphatically heterocentrist terms, it effectively excluded questions of the interrelations between homosexualities and film. Whether it was Raymond Bellour declaring that the heterosexual couple "organizes, indeed constitutes, the classical American cinema as a whole," or Laura Mulvey asserting that cinema enforces a heterosexual masculinization of spectatorship, "regardless of the actual sex (or possible deviance) of any real live movie-goer," the message was the same: heterosexuality is the inalienable condition and effect of film, and everything else must be disallowed.[6] As far as film theory was concerned, gay spectatorship was all but a conceptual impossibility.

Ironically, even the little work available in film studies that has attempted to address issues of homosexuality and film has tended to close off with equal dogmatism questions of gay spectatorial pleasure. Until recently, most of this work was situated within certain political traditions of representational analysis, aimed primarily at identifying and castigating the deformative effects of Hollywood's heterocentric agenda on filmic constructions of homosexuality. The resulting theory of cinematic homophobia has been of undoubted critical value, but with its exhaustive taxonomies of pernicious stereotypes and its impassioned diatribes against an allegedly universal filmic heterocentrism, it has effectively marginalized gay spectatorial desires out of existence. "In decrying Hollywood homophobia," writes Ellis Hanson, this work concerns itself "with only one gaze: the ubiquitous, prefabricated, gullible, voyeuristic gaze of homophobia. . . . Meanwhile, our own pleasure, that elusive gaze of delight, is left curiously undertheorized and at times inadmissible."[7] How can one conceive, let alone account for, an active or pleasurable gay spectatorship when mainstream cinema is deemed to be, as one of the more popular and broadly influential works of this tradition puts it, a wholly homophobic enterprise "incapable of giving [gays and lesbians] the kinds of films that truly touch their lives and experiences?"[8] What does this say—indeed, what can it say—about the many gays and lesbians, myself included, who have not only had Hollywood cinema "touch their lives" but have made it an integral, even foundational, component of those lives, and whose most intense and pleasurable experiences have often been provided by the very films that this critical work seeks so vehemently to condemn?

Recent work has, however, increasingly challenged the occlusion of gay and lesbian spectatorships in film theory and criticism. Some writers have started to insist on not only the possibility but the validity of gay/lesbian/queer spectatorship as a formation of cinematic reception and a category of critical analysis. Although they frequently write from divergent theoretical positions and employ different methodological approaches, these critics agree that, given the centrality of sexual difference, subjectivity, and identification to theories of spectatorship, the question of the role of *homosexual* difference, subjectivity, and identification is vital. As the editors of one recent collection put it, it is high time to "challeng[e] cultural readings which overlook the dynamic of sexual preference . . . [and] explor[e] how lesbians and gay men might position themselves as spectators of popular culture."[9] Much of the work proceeds from the relatively simple but critically indispensable proposition that mainstream cinema and its receptions are substantially more polyvalent and capacious than film studies has traditionally seemed prepared to acknowledge. Although Hollywood's role as an institution of heteronormativity is indisputable and its representational strategies of homophobic abuse glaringly evident, this in no way exhausts the vast range of cinema's signifying effects or the dynamic ways in which it is often used and interpreted within the contexts of gay and lesbian reception. As Ellis Hanson asserts with delightful camp flourish, "Hollywood, despite its history of censorship and its pretense to heterocentrism, is one of the queerest institutions ever invented."[10]

This study is intended to contribute to and develop this nascent (counter)tradition of queer spectatorial studies. In this book I explore one central question: How is cinematic spectatorship articulated, practiced, and experienced in the contexts of gay male subjectivity? I argue that the cultural, historical, and psychic frameworks of gay subjectivity furnish gay-identifying spectators with certain positions and references that fundamentally inflect their cinematic engagements. In particular, the psychocultural specificities of gay subjectivity motivate gay spectators to forge distinctive investments in and readings of cinematic texts. In short,

I argue that gay identification functions as a "difference that makes a difference" in filmic reception, and it is possible, therefore, to speak of gay spectatorship as a specific—if inevitably complex and contingent—configuration of cinematic meaning production and exchange.

Such a project is fraught with epistemological dangers and vulnerabilities. The very notion of gay spectatorship may seem to many theoretically misguided and epistemologically indefensible. To adapt an argument mounted by Diana Fuss in relation to notions of female spectatorship: is it really possible to "speak so simply of ['gay male spectatorship,' 'gay subjectivity'] as if these categories were not transgressed, not already constituted by other axes of difference (class, culture, ethnicity, nationality . . .)? Moreover, are our reading responses really so easily predictable, so readily interpretable?"[11] Caroline Evans and Lorraine Gamman clearly think not. They argue that the notion of gay spectatorship is rooted in and promotes the unacceptably "essentialist idea that relations of looking are determined by the biological sex of the individual/s you choose to fornicate with" and that it therefore reduces the multiple differences of spectatorship to the single issue of sexuality. "It seems far too simplistic," they assert, "to argue that who you sleep with may determine how you identify with cinematic images."[12]

Gayness or homosexuality is, however, much more than just a question of "who you sleep with." In a culture in which, as Foucault has famously demonstrated, sexuality is deployed as the privileged locus of individual truth and knowledge, homosexuality has assumed a veritable excess of social significances, an ever expanding range of meanings and effects that exceed those of simple sexual acts. Indeed, the injunction enforced by modern Western cultures to "place ourselves under" and know ourselves through "the sign of sex" means that, again as Foucault has demonstrated, homosexuality operates as the grounds for a specification of identities and that it takes on therefore all the various capacities and properties this entails.[13] To identify as homosexual is to be situated in a particular network of sociodiscursive relations that, though undeniably complex and multivalent, occasions specific, if not specified, identity effects. Homosexuality thus functions in modern Western cultures as what Teresa de Lauretis terms "a sociosymbolic form," "a form of psychosocial subjectivity that entails a different production of reference and meaning."[14] It is within this context that I place the claim for a notion of gay spectatorship as a particular configuration of cinematic reading relations. If gay-identifying subjects inhabit different sites or frames of psychosocial discursivity, then this will affect processes of meaning production and exchange in certain ways. As a site of subjective specification, homosexuality provides identifications, desires, and knowledges that, though not entirely predictable or even knowable, make for specific forms of cinematic engagement and reading.

This may seem simply to be gilding the lily. Is not the crux of the problem precisely the deployment of homosexuality as the grounds for a specification of identity? By assuming and asserting the category of gay identity, am I not simply buying into a dominant discursive system of sexual personhood that enforces an essentializing and, therefore, oppressive binarism of hetero/homo sexual definition? This is the pith of the argument mounted by Evans and Gamman in their critique of theories of gay reception referred to above, in which notions of gay and lesbian spectatorship and the categories of gay and lesbian identity on which such notions depend are defined as "essentialist fictions" that need to be recognized and repudiated as "instruments of regulatory regimes." [15]

Apart from its problematical supposition that sexual identities are optional, this type of argument assumes that gay identity is always represented and mobilized in an essentializing and, thus, disabling manner. Yet the idea of gay identity is rarely quite so homogeneous or self-identical, referencing and producing diverse, even contradictory meanings and effects. In fact, formations of gay identity are largely taken up and articulated contradictorily by gay subjects themselves. Jonathan Keane argues that

> excluded identities such as gays, blacks and lesbians . . . do not often live in an Imaginary realm of coherence but are more likely to be only too painfully aware of identity as incoherence. . . . those marginalized by cultural hegemony find it almost impossible to experience identity as self-presence, as they are constantly positioned by that culture as its negative element while they are simultaneously constructed through other discourses to aim for mastery and positivity. [16]

Certainly, my understanding and mobilization of gay identity in this study is not a unified, stable essence but a complicated field of subjective articulation that is provisional and shifting. For this reason, I prefer to use the term *gay subjectivity* rather than *gay identity*, for it imparts a greater sense of conceptual heterogeneity. The term *subjectivity* encompasses a much broader definitional sweep than *identity*, taking in the full range of subjective articulations across the social, the cultural, and the psychic. As Robert Stam, Robert Burgoyne, and Sandy Flitterman-Lewis argue, the term *subjectivity* "suggests a whole range of determinations (social, political, linguistic, ideological, psychological) that intersect to define it. Refusing the notion of self as a stable entity, . . . subject[ivity] implies a process of construction by signifying practices that are both unconscious and culturally specific."[17]

In particular, because of its psychoanalytic provenance, the term *subjectivity* helps restore the psychic as an integral component of gay identity formations. In discussions of homosexual definition the notion of gay identity is often used as little more than an expanded version of the sociological concept of role. This is particularly true of neo-Foucauldian social constructionist paradigms, which have in many ways come to dominate discussions of gay identity and which, with their central emphasis on reading homosexuality as an effect of sociodiscursive disciplinarity, have made the social the primary if not exclusive field of homosexual articulation. I write from the conviction, however, that homosexual definition is played out not simply at the level of social and institutional discursivity but at the level of psychic organization as well and that this must be acknowledged in critical analyses. Given the centrality of issues of desire to the definitions, representations, and performances of gay subjectivities, any analysis that ignores the role and specificity of the psychic in and for those subjectivities is both conceptually impoverished and analytically restricted.

A critical reassertion of the psychic dimensions of gay subjectivities also resists any simplistic reification of gayness as a fixed essence, for it forces a recognition of the fundamental heterogeneity of psychic life and the destabilizing presence of the unconscious in all subjective forms. As Jacqueline Rose writes, "The unconscious constantly reveals the 'failure' of identity. Because there is no continuity of psychic life, so there is no stability of sexual identity, no position . . . which is ever simply achieved."[18] This does not mean, as sometimes is suggested, that sexual identity is, from the point of view of psychoanalysis, an impossible fiction that must be abjured. Some form of identity or structuration is crucial for a psychosexual subject to exist in the first place; without it there could only be psychosis or what Jane Gallop refers to as "the oceanic passivity of undifferentiation." [19] However, the conflicting dynamics of psychic life and the destabilizations of the unconscious mean that, to repeat Rose's formulation, "no position . . . is ever *simply* achieved." For my discussion, this means that the "gayness" of gay subjectivity is never self-identical or absolute but, rather, polyvalent, conditional, and mobile.

Because the concept of subjectivity encompasses a greater degree of relational diversity, its deployment as a definitional frame for discussions of gay identity-formations foregrounds the irreducible heterogeneity of those formations. No gay subject—or, for that matter, no gay spectator—is ever *just* gay; that gayness is always cut across and inflected both by the heterogeneous fluidity of unconscious desire and by the real world dissymmetries of race, ethnicity, class, age, nationality, and so forth. The notion of gay subjectivity helps accommodate a recognition of this by insisting on the fundamentally contingent nature of (homo)sexual identifications and thus referring those identifications to the full range of competing discourses, psychic and social, through which individual, material subjectivities are always produced and experienced.

I am aware, however, that to speak of *gay* subjectivity or *gay* spectatorship as I do is still to claim a certain coherence for gayness as a critical term. No matter how much I may seek to complicate, pluralize, attenuate its definition, the very concept of gay subjectivity/gay spectatorship means that I am still effecting, even if only implicitly, a conceptual reification of gayness as a separable category, still expropriating gayness from the wider field of differences within which subjectivity and spectatorship are always located. In that respect, the project I propose here is still open to charges of abstraction and essentialism. To a certain extent, this is unavoidable, for there is, as Mary Ann Doane notes, no "realm in the production of knowledge which escapes abstraction." [20] In the case of critical writing, a degree of abstraction is both necessary and desirable. To write critically and productively, one must be able to generalize, to identify patterns and typicalities, and to construct heuristic models with which to read and make sense of these things. The theoretical construction of gayness as a relatively coherent and therefore potentially abstracted category is itself a response to and acknowledgment of the specificity and productivity of gayness as a structuring term. Homosexuality *is* a central determining paradigm in modern, Western cultures, and many subjects articulate their desires, make their meanings, and live their lives, whether in part or whole, whether centrally or peripherally, through it. Thus it is valid to speak of gayness as an identifiable category of subjective organization, to recognize that it has a specific force and function, even if its realization in material contexts, its performance so to speak, will always be contingent and variable.

Furthermore, the production of a formal figure of gay spectatorship can be a powerful and enabling strategy to combat heteronormative presumption, and this more than justifies any putative risks of abstraction and essentialism. Not only does the construction of a theoretical image of gay spectatorship refuse the pervasive demands to silence and marginality that circulate around the very idea of gay spectatorship in dominant culture, making visible the invisible, speaking the unspeakable; such a theory also provides important opportunities for the production of new, gay-identified sites of discourse and knowledge. An argument mounted by D. N. Rodowick in reference to the concept of female spectatorship has equal significance for a theorization of gay spectatorship:

> The very question of the female spectator presents certain political and theoretical risks. Even when employed in arguments that critique . . . essentialism, locating a female spectatorship always implies an ontology. The singularity and self-identity of this concept—*the* female spectator—can only be preserved by a binary logic that opposes it to what it is not or what it must negate. . . . There are, however, advantages to envisioning "femaleness" as an ontological category, best represented by Gayatri Spivak's suggestion that feminist theory might have to accept the risk of essentialism. . . . I take this to mean that it is incumbent upon feminist theory—and in fact all critiques of domination—to attempt to *create* new positions of interpretation, meaning, desire and subjectivity even while acknowledging they sometimes stand on shaky philosophical legs.[21]

It is, however, also incumbent on "critiques of domination" to make their shaky philosophical legs as stable as possible. Gayness may be a central category in Western technologies of the subject, and the deployment of gayness by gay-identifying subjects may also be a potent tactic of antiheteronormativity, but unproblematized reifications of gayness as an overly homogenizing abstraction only reinscribe further forms of discursive domination and exclusion. Any notion of gay subjectivity/spectatorship is at best a speculative fiction, a heuristic construct designed to help us think about the nature of gay cinematic receptions. As Rodowick puts it: "Despite the achievements of psychoanalytic film theory and textual analysis in the past twenty years, I would insist that all claims made about processes of identification [and reading] in actual spectators, powerful and important as they may be, are speculative. . . . To assert that film theory describes positions of identification that are ultimately undecidable with respect to any given spectator is . . . an indispensable political *a priori*" (269).

To keep this sense of "ultimate undecidability" at the forefront of this book, I frame my theorizations of gay spectatorships within the psychoanalytic concept of "the fantasmatic." As I argue in the next chapter, the fantasmatic is a post-Lacanian concept that refers to the variable networks of fantasy and desire that subtend and structure subjectivity. Different subjectivities are sites of different fantasmatic organizations. Thus one may speak of the gay male fantasmatic, meaning the various formations of psychocultural fantasy, desire, and identification specific to and constitutive of male homosexual subjectivities. In terms of the present discussion, the organizational effects of the fantasmatic are understood in psychoanalysis to be simultaneously structural and contingent. The fantasmatic functions not only structurally, in that it positions the subject within preexisting paradigms of desire and meaning, but also contingently, in that the realization of fantasmatic imperatives always depends on the determinate conditions of the subject's cultural and historical particularity. In other words, the fantasmatic may be the site of general, transindividual formations of fantasy and desire, but how those formations are actually played out at the punctual level of the subject is always directly determined/shaped by the full range of that subject's material individuality.

In relation to gay spectatorship, the fantasmatic provides a conceptual framework within which to speculate about possible formations of gay subjective and spectatorial specificity while avowing the contingency of those formations. It forces a recognition that any potential features of gay spectatorial specificity identified at the structural level may be articulated by individual spectators—if in fact they are at all—in diverse and often unpredictable ways.

My project here is primarily theoretical. To open up a space within film theory for the construction and exploration of questions of gay spectatorial specificity, I engage with and interrogate critical paradigms that have been central to discussions of spectatorship in film studies. In particular, I work across what I see as the three major approaches to spectatorship in contemporary film theory: the text-centered readings of apparatus theory; the contextual models of social spectatorship drawn from cultural studies; and recent cine-psychoanalytic theories of spectatorial fantasy. Although I ultimately argue for a fantasy-based model of gay spectatorship, I also assert that these approaches share important points of continuity and overlap and that it is possible therefore to use arguments and insights from all three. I champion the fantasy-based model because it accommodates readings of spectatorship across the interrelated registers of institutional, textual, social, and psychic determination.

My mobilization of fantasy theory as a governing paradigm, does, however, entail an undeniable prioritization of psychoanalysis as an epistemological and methodological approach to questions of gay spectatorship. This is both willful and, I hope, strategic. I believe that psychoanalysis provides an unparalleled framework within which to pursue questions of subjectivity, sexuality, and cultural identification. In particular, for gay and lesbian theory, psychoanalysis can be invaluable for analyzing homosexual desires and their complex effects on both psychic and social life. I am, nevertheless, cognizant that psychoanalysis is plagued with pitfalls, that, as its critics proclaim, it is frequently universalizing, ahistorical, and reductive. I am also well aware that psychoanalysis is, particularly in its institutionalized forms, a powerful tool of heteronormativity and that its instrumental role in producing and promoting pathological readings of homosexuality cannot be ignored. For some, this all but invalidates the utility of psychoanalysis for any gay-identified critical enterprise. Eve Kosofsky Sedgwick, for example, has mounted a sustained and broadly influential critique of psychoanalysis in her work as so "profoundly . . . shaped by homophobic and heterosexist assumptions and histories" to be irreparably "damaged at its origin."[22] More recently—and in specific relation to film—Ellis Hanson explicitly questions the efficacy of psychoanalysis as a framework for analyses of gay spectatorships. Although he concedes that psychoanalytic theory might provide a "nuanced analysis of queer desire and spectatorship," its heteronormative presumptions pose "severe problems," rendering it incapable of thinking gay spectatorial specificity outside the dominant fictions of heterosexuality. Because "the definition of homosexuality in [psychoanalysis] almost always relies on dubious Freudian conceptions of same-sex desire as a narcissistic crisis in gender identification, . . . homosexuality becomes the return, or perhaps merely the persistence, of the repressed in an otherwise anxious and heterosexual narrative."[23] This is an important critique and, to the extent that it advocates a cautious reflexiveness for gay deployments of psychoanalysis, it is well taken. I am not so certain, however, that the alleged heteronormativity of psychoanalysis nullifies its use-value for gay/lesbian or queer theory.

If psychoanalysis does promote a critical imaging of sexuality in which certain heterosexual fictions—sexual difference, oedipality, phallic desire, to cite the usual suspects—are accorded theoretical centrality, one must ask how much of this is heterocentric prejudice and how much simply analytic recognition of the importance these fictions assume in contemporary culture. This hoary issue of "description versus prescription" has long been bandied about in relation to psychoanalysis. Although the debate is tired and, in many respects, irresolvable, it remains vitally significant. For better or worse, heterosexuality is encoded in almost all the dominant discourses and institutions of contemporary Western culture as the normative ideal, which affects all forms of human desire, homosexuality included. To the extent that psychoanalysis theorizes the psychocultural ramifications of this, it offers an important critical mapping of how the social imperatives of heterocentrism are translated—or not—into a psychic reality for the sexual subject. For gay or queer sexualities, the psychoanalytic referral of these to cultural scenarios of compulsory heterosexuality is simply a recognition of the fact that these sexualities never occur outside the sociosymbolic networks through which they are constructed. All of us learn to desire from within the narratives of sexuality made available by the culture at large, which is not to say that desire is simply preprogrammed but that it is psychoculturally determined and governed. Homosexualities undoubtedly can produce and pursue possibilities of desire not contained or even understood by the available scripts of heterosexuality—and psychoanalysis avers as much, addressing both the particularities and the complexities of homosexuality as a dynamic configuration of desire—but this is never absolute, and it would be the worst type of naive utopianism to assume a homosexuality somehow outside or free from the dominant psychosocial discourses (discourses of compulsory heterosexuality, gender, oedipality, and so forth) that frame and regulate, however variably, the field of contemporary sexuality.

It would also be erroneous to assume that psychoanalysis simply trades on and installs an unproblematical heteronormativity. The foundational psychoanalytic concept of the unconscious necessarily undercuts any assumption of a straightforward or absolute sexual fixity. Because sexuality is always understood in psychoanalysis in relation to the unconscious, it cannot be assumed as coherent or guaranteed but as shifting and mobile, constantly prone to lapses, excesses, and conflicting impulses. The centrality of the unconscious to sexuality means that, as Freud contends in the "Three Essays," all desire is ultimately perverse, irreducible to either conscious aim, zone, or object-choice. The most resolutely heterosexual-identified subject is, according to Freud, "capable of making a homosexual object-choice and ha[s] in fact made one in [the] unconscious," just as the most resolutely gay-identified subject could and would incorporate important unconscious heterosexual cathexes.[24] By thus insisting on the inherent "queerness" and wayward heterogeneity of desire, psychoanalysis is in many respects profoundly antinormative, pitting sexuality against the normalizing efforts of sociosymbolic discourses of identity, even as it also recognizes and theorizes the juridical operations and psychic effects of those discourses. Therein can be identified perhaps both the difficult radicalism of psychoanalysis and its extraordinary fecundity for gay criticism. "In its understanding of sexuality as unconscious," writes Tim Dean, psychoanalytic theory "invalidates the distinction between normal and pathological" and "reveals sexuality in its full complexity, opening up queer possibilities."[25]

Undeniably, profound dynamics of heteronormative conservatism course through the psychoanalytic project, and histories of homophobia have plagued—and, in some cases, continue to plague—psychoanalytic discourse and practice. Nonetheless, psychoanalysis is never entirely coincident with or reducible to these dynamics and histories, and the values of psychoanalytic theory are, in the words of Stephen Heath, "vastly more important than the positions [it is] led to develop, the worst stereotypes [it] grotesquely rejoins and repeats."[26] Thus, though aware of its many failings and dangers, I remain committed in this study to the epistemological value and political worth of psychoanalysis and use it—carefully, respectfully, and, I hope, productively—as a strategic tool to theorize gay spectatorial possibilities.

It has become almost mandatory to preface discussions of gay issues with a brief clarification of terminology. It frequently goes along the lines of: "I use *homosexual* to refer to mainstream representations, *gay* to refer to politicized, self-identified representations, and *queer* to refer to everything that exceeds these two." I am not quite so systematic, however, in my writing. I tend to use all three terms in different ways. In some contexts, I do use *homosexual* to refer to hegemonic or otherwise traditional definitions, *gay* to refer to modern or subcultural definitions, and *queer* to refer to wider notions of antiheteronormative desire; yet in others, I use the three terms interchangeably, almost as synonyms. In part, this is a result of a need for stylistic variety—there are only so many times you can use the same word in the one paragraph. But it is also a result of a very real desire to acknowledge and hopefully replicate the sense of definitional heterogeneity that I argued earlier was vital for a reasoned analysis of gay subjectivities and/or spectatorships. By shifting references between gay, homosexual, and, sometimes, queer, I hope to avoid any oversimplified stabilization of these terms while imparting a sense of how "gay subjectivity"—or indeed any form of subjectivity—necessarily exceeds the limits of its categorization.

This is, of course, precisely what is claimed for the notion of queer. My own response to queer tends to be rather ambivalent, however, and this comes through in my use of the term. When I first started researching this book, queer was more-or-less in its infancy. Over the past few years, though, it has developed at a breathtaking rate. One has only to look at the explosion of books, articles, and even university courses with the term *queer* in their titles to evidence the meteoric rise of queer as a category in both academic and popular discourses.[27] Proponents of queer claim it provides a new category "beyond" the limits of received heterosexist notions of gender and sexuality and that it is therefore a strategic term for deconstructing and displacing heteronormativity. They also claim that, because of its mercurial status, queer is a far more inclusive term than gay/lesbian, capable of representing sexual differences other than just homosexual, as well as the social differences that cut across and, in many instances, refigure sexualities. This is an exciting and enabling development, and in this respect I value queer as a term and a concept. However, in its desire to transcend the "limits" of received notions of gay and lesbian identity, queer incurs the possibility of devalorizing and/or displacing gay and lesbian specificity.

One problem I have with queer is that it frequently encourages an acritical pluralism wherein the differences that structure sexual subjectivities are all flattened out into a postmodern vision of democratic pansexuality. Although this may represent an appealing type of libidinal utopianism, it runs the risk of ignoring the specificities of sexual subjectivities, as well as the very real disymmetries of power that govern and work through those subjectivities. Thus, though it certainly provides an important and suggestive paradigm within which to extend the signifying range of homosexualities, speaking to the differences and silences elided in and by received notions of gay and lesbian identity, queer is itself frequently in danger of being reduced to some sort of megalithic ur-category that circumscribes and subsumes the unique particularities of its various constituencies.

I think queer is at its most valuable (and this is largely how I deploy it) when it is seen not as an alternative to gay or lesbian—as a wider umbrella-term that incorporates these categories—but as an adjunct to them, an additional way to reconceive and extend the terms of gay and lesbian sexualities and identities that still respects and upholds the organizational force and political primacy of these terms. Eve Kosofsky Sedgwick presents this point with characteristic eloquence when she argues that queer "can never and must never stand outside of the province of gay and lesbian meanings from which it arises. For to disavow those meanings, or to displace them from the term's definitional center, would be to dematerialize any possibility of queerness itself."[28]

In chapter 1 I explore in detail some of the foundational issues flagged here in the introduction, arguing for a theoretical recognition of the specificity of gay spectatorship and developing a critical framework for its analysis. Through a series of arguments about identity and sexuality, I develop a broad reading of gay spectatorship as a site of performativity in which the queer spectator articulates and cathects a discourse of gay difference, producing and confirming gay identifications, desires, and meanings. In a survey of existing analyses of gay and lesbian spectatorship, I examine how and where they provide support for such a reading, exploring in particular the use of cultural studies models of social spectatorship. Although their insistence on reading spectatorship as a site of struggle between competing frames of textual and social determination is invaluable for theorizing gay cinematic reception, these models are frequently limited by a prioritization of the social dynamics of spectatorship at the expense of other equally vital dynamics, notably the psychic. As a corrective, I turn to the psychoanalytic concept of fantasy, which has recently been popularized by certain theorists precisely because of its perceived capacity to support a combined sociopsychic reading of spectatorship. In particular, I mobilize the post-Lacanian notion of the fantasmatic, defined as the specific network of libidinal organization that undergirds and determines our psychocultural identities, as an ideal framework for such an exploration. I argue that it is possible to theorize a gay fantasmatic as the network of fantasy and desire that subtends and works through gay subjectivities and that this can then be used as a framework to analyze the processual performativities of gay spectatorship.

Chapter 2 initiates my theoretical exploration of potential exchanges between gay fantasmatic specificity and cinematic spectatorship by focusing on gay subcultural receptions of the Hollywood musical. One aim of this chapter is to establish a model of gay spectatorial reading that may then be developed and complicated in subsequent chapters. In particular, I demonstrate how gay spectators can engage in queer fantasmatic negotiations of mainstream film. I suggest that, in their readings of the Hollywood musical, gay spectators latch on to those points of rupture or excess to which the musical is so spectacularly prone and mobilize them to construct patently queer forms of fantasmatic desire.

Chapter 3 develops this analysis of gay cinematic negotiation further by addressing the celebrated discourse of camp as a particular mode of gay cultural taste widely deployed in gay spectatorships to produce disruptive, antinaturalist readings of mainstream film. In particular, I focus on gay camp engagements with the excessive female star-image, arguing that such readings subvert heteropatriarchal apparatuses of gender and sexuality. Such readings are both effects of the gay subject's own "experiences" of gender/sexual dissonance as well as an "articulation" of queer psychic ambivalence vis-à-vis normative discourses of (hetero)sexual difference. I pursue this argument through an analysis of gay subcultural readings of a classic Hollywood star, Mae West.

Chapter 4 attempts a slightly more specific analysis of the exchange between gay fantasmatic economies and cinematic reception by focusing on matrocentrism and its potential role in the constitution and performance of gay spectatorships. Psychoanalysis accords a central role to maternal identification in the fantasmatic organization of male homosexualities; this has, however, been largely construed and mobilized in homophobic and misogynous ways. The issue of maternal identification needs to be reclaimed as a potential site for the articulation of gay specificity, and I work through and beyond Freudian theories of mother fixation to theorize the identificatory bonds between gay subjectivities and the maternal. I explore how the maternal may function as a key organizational category in gay spectatorial forms, looking at, for example, gay male fascination with vintage Hollywood film and the gay cult of female star worship as variable configurations of gay male matrocentrism, as well as gay subcultural popularizations of the Hollywood maternal melodrama.

The final chapter addresses gay male relations to paternal desire and phallic masculinity. I argue that gay relations to and uses of masculinity are underscored by a logic of refusal and destabilization and focus on how this can translate into gay cinematic readings. In particular, I concentrate on how gay spectators appropriate and transform some of the figures of masculinity offered by mainstream film. To this end, I look at gay male reconstructions of the cinematic male image as an insistently erotic spectacle and the potential destabilizations this generates for the phallocentric economies of meaning on which mainstream film is based. I also develop an analysis of gay identifications with the cinematic male image, arguing that gay spectators frequently cathect those male images that provide aberrant or marginal types of male gender signification. These arguments are referenced and developed through an ex-

tended case study of gay subcultural engagements with the star-image of
Montgomery Clift.

As should be evident from its title, *Spectacular Passions: Cinema, Fantasy, Gay Male Spectatorships*, this book is essentially an exploration and celebration of desire. Most specifically, it is an attempt to trace and account for the production of gay male spectatorial desire in mainstream cinema. For over a century now, cinema has been an influential "dream factory," furnishing contemporary cultures with an arena for collective fantasmatic escape and libidinal tutelage. The dazzling images, sounds, and narratives of cinema that entertain, astonish, and seduce us into returning again and again to the dark of the movie house do not merely reveal desire in some sort of simple representational mimesis, they actively teach desire, interpellating us into the psychocultural discourses of sexuality and providing us with a luxuriant lexicon through which to speak and hear our own libidinal utterances. Gay men have been no exceptions to this process. Although mainstream cinema may have studiously sought to excise homosexuality from the screen—at least, in manifest terms—this has not prevented gay-identifying men from mobilizing film as a significant site for the investment and production of their own queer desires, fantasies, and meanings. The aim of this study is to affirm and theorize how this production of gay spectatorial desire can and does occur. It seeks to bring gay spectatorship out from the tenebrous margins to which it has been relegated and provide it with some theoretical recognition and (virtual) existence. Consequently, this book is unavoidably political in design and, I hope, effect. It seeks to make a direct gay intervention into dominant discourse—especially the "discourse" of film studies—and claim a space there for gay spectatorial specificity.

However, as should also be evident from its title, this book is not intended to provide or even aspire to a single model of gay spectatorship. Even if such a model were possible, it would be entirely counterproductive, for it would repeat the exact type of homogenizing universalism that has marginalized critical questions of gay spectatorial specificity for so long. Instead, this book provides speculations, hypotheses, and fictions that address themselves to the possibilities of gay spectatorship. I see and offer this study as a theoretical logbook, a plotting of certain coordinates across the complex field of gay cinematic reception. On their own or even together as a group, these coordinates do not constitute a definitive overview of that field or exhaust its ever shifting range of potentialities, but they do provide a possible route through it and, I hope, ways to begin to think about the question(s)—and passions—of gay spectatorship.

Chapter One ∿ SOMETHING A LITTLE STRANGE:

THEORIZING GAY MALE SPECTATORSHIPS

When director Hector Babenco approached the major Hollywood studios with his plans to make a film version of Manuel Puig's celebrated novel, *Kiss of the Spider Woman*, he encountered fierce opposition. The production executives he consulted gave him a long list of reasons why he should not make the film, ranging from the difficulties of adapting Puig's fractured, modernist narrative to an alleged public disinterest in "social message" films. Not surprisingly, the most widespread and insistent objections that were raised concerned the fact that the protagonist was what critic Leonard Maltin describes as "a gay man whose only food for survival is . . . tacky Hollywood movies."[1] It seemed that the prospect of a film about a flaming movie queen proved to be just a little too much to contemplate for the studios' top brass. As one executive bluntly opined, "Who is going to want to see a story about a movie-mad faggot? I mean, the guy's a bit of a freak."[2]

It is impossible to know how or even if these responses influenced the film's final production, but it is interesting to note that the gay protagonist in *Kiss of the Spider Woman* is in fact represented as "a bit of a freak." From the outset, the character of Molina (William Hurt) is explicitly defined as eccentric, even grotesque. Our introduction to him occurs in the opening sequence through a long, rather ambiguous mobile shot that crawls across the shadowy interior of a prison cell to reveal the figure of Molina, standing divalike in a floral-print kimono with a towel wrapped around his head as an improvised turban, passionately recounting the plot of an unidentified film he has seen. Taking on the role of the glamorous female star, Molina acts out entire scenes from the film while his straight cell mate, Valentin (Raul Julia), looks on with incredulous disdain. "Something a little strange," Molina whispers with breathless ex-

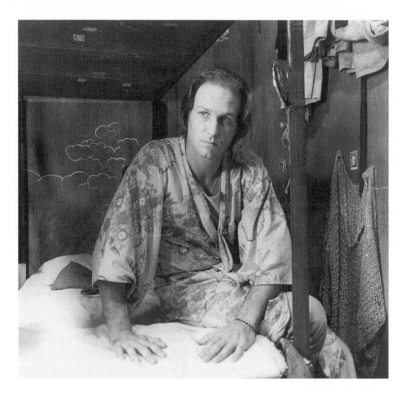

The eccentric gay male spectator: William Hurt in *Kiss of the Spider Woman* (1985) (author's collection)

citement, "that's what you notice . . . that she's not a woman like all the others. She seems all wrapped up, lost in a world she carries deep inside her." As he continues his extravagant performance, descriptions of the female star's "glistening skin," "sensuous legs," and "petite feet" are all correlated with a vertical pan down Molina's solid, hirsute torso.

The primary objective of this opening sequence is clearly to produce a sense of uncanniness that the film directs toward and attributes to the figure of the homosexual Molina. The diegetic ambiguity of the establishing tracking shot situates Molina within a semiotic economy of mystery and foreboding while the juxtaposition of contrasting visual and aural signifiers across his body encodes him as a freakish figure who disrupts, even perverts, the gendered categories of hegemonic meaning. Should these formal cues be lost on the viewer, the film offers the character of Valentin, whose intercut looks of scornful disgust and periodic critical interjections support and fix in no uncertain terms the sequence's construction of Molina as perverse spectacle. That *Kiss of the Spider Woman* should refer this economy of semiotic and sexual uncanniness to a formation of gay spectatorship is significant and more than a little revealing. Cinema has long functioned as a vital forum for the production of gay male meanings and identifications to the point that a certain type of film spectatorship has become a veritable shorthand for male homosexuality in various cultural discourses. Molina's extraordinarily intense spectatorship functions in *Kiss of the Spider Woman* as one of the more spectacular and readily legible signs of that character's homosexuality. If, as his opening voice-over promises, we are to notice "something a little strange" about Molina, that strangeness is nowhere more manifest than in the peculiar nature of his spectatorial passions.

Routinely characterized in terms of an "uncanny" strangeness, gay spectatorship is something that exceeds and, by so doing, disturbs mainstream categories and protocols. To think of the gay male spectator is to conjure up, almost automatically, an image of someone who, like Molina, cultivates an intense fascination with film, especially classical Hollywood film; who surrenders totally to the lure of cinema and its escapist fantasies; and who engages and relates to film in a manner that, to borrow J. P. Telotte's description of the cult film spectator, goes "beyond reason, beyond the usual ways of seeing, caring about, and identifying with film."[3] That this popularly conceived image of the excessive gay spectator is little more than a mythological fiction that could never be assumed as in any simple way "true" or "real" almost goes without saying. In empirical terms, few gay-identifying men would engage their spectatorships with anything like the operatic extravagance or all-consuming intensity suggested by a fictional character like Molina. Furthermore, in its status as a myth, this image also fundamentally services heteronormative hegemony. Roland Barthes has famously taught that the primary aim of any popular myth is the naturalization of ideological meaning and the ratification of the social status quo. One need not look too hard to discern the normalizing operations of the "myth" of an excessive gay spectatorship. Its coding of gay cinematic reception as deviant and extreme openly inscribes gayness in a regulatory structure of visible and thus delimitable difference while devaluing it as the obscene other of an implied, stable, heterosexual norm.

Nevertheless, precisely in its status as a myth, the popular image of the obsessive or eccentric gay male spectator does provide a starting point from which to begin to think about the question of gay spectatorial specificity, of how and where gay-identification frames, shapes, affects the relations of cinematic reception or, vice versa, how cinematic reception frames and affects gay-identification. As Barthes observes, "any myth with generality" will, at some level, "represent . . . the humanity" of those it depicts and "of those who . . . borrow it."[4] In the mythologies of the excessive gay spectator, these widely circulating images seize on and articulate the broad significances that cinema has played and continues to play in gay male cultures while also offering insight into some of the values and functions of spectatorship for gay-identifying men. At the very least, these myths attest to the multivalent fertility of spectatorship as a site for producing gay male meanings and pleasures.

As one of the dominant mass cultural forms of contemporary society, cinema plays a potentially important role in the cultural practices of many subjectivities and/or social groups. Gay men have, however, forged what critic Richard Dyer terms "a special relationship with the cinema," a relationship in which film and its attendant forms have been mobilized as a vital arena for gay self-definition.[5] Generations of gay men have used film to produce their sexual and social subjectivities with the result that spectatorship has, as Judith Mayne notes, developed as a fundamental "component of the various narratives that constitute the very notion of a gay/lesbian identity."[6]

A Special Relationship: Gay Men and Cinema

Even the most cursory overview of gay cultural history reveals that homosexuality and film have become imbricated in integral, mutually productive ways. Historically, cinema and identity-based homosexuality are more or less coterminous, both emerging out of the massive sociodiscursive transformations of nineteenth-century, Euro-American modernity. It was thus inevitable, perhaps, that the two should have developed such significant interrelations. For its part, cinema has long been a forum for the circulation of sexual meanings and pleasures. With its congregation of bodies in close, darkened spaces; its simulation of patently voyeuristic structures; and its lush supply of erotic visual spectacles, cinema has, from the beginning, been marked as a profoundly sexualized form. And the long history of homophobic film censorship notwithstanding, homosexuality has always been an integral part of cinema's erotic allure. As Mark Finch notes:

> It is part of popular cultural mythology that homosexuals are meant to be obsessed with Hollywood. . . . What is much less remarked upon is precisely the reverse: Hollywood's obsession with homosexuality. . . . In films as different as *Adam's Rib* (1949) and *American Gigolo* (1980), *A Florida Enchantment* (1914) and *The Hunger* (1980)—from Laurel and Hardy to lesbian vampires—since cinema began, Hollywood has been fascinated with . . . gayness.[7]

In return, gay men have used cinema as an important arena for the production of their own homosexual desires and meanings. Quite literally, in certain respects, movie theaters have long functioned as important venues for male homosexual encounters. In his history of "gay New York," George Chauncey details how the city's movie theaters, for example, emerged very early in the century as popular homosexual cruising areas, noting that in the first six months of 1921 alone, "at least sixty-seven men were arrested for homosexual solicitation in movie theaters in Manhattan, including an astonishing forty-five men at a single theater." Importantly, these encounters were not merely sexual but often assumed a strong social function as well, so much so that some movie theaters quickly developed the reputation as a place where, in the words of one disapproving magistrate of the time, "men of a certain class . . . [could] meet congenial spirits."[8]

In more abstract but equally crucial ways, movies themselves emerged quite early in the century as important sites for homosexual identification. Some critics have suggested that, because of their experiences of social marginalization and alienation, gay-identifying men have been particularly responsive to the escapist potentials and fantasmatic largesse of film. Dyer argues, "Because, as gays, we grew up isolated not only from our heterosexual peers but also from each other, we turned to [film] for information and ideas about ourselves. . . . This isolation . . . perhaps also made the need to escape more keen for us than for some other social groups—so, once again, we went to the pictures."[9] Although obviously speculative and thus impossible to determine with any precision, this reading does key in suggestively with arguments made about the special historical appeal of cinema to other marginalized or disempowered social subjects such as women, people of color, and immigrants. For many of these subjects, cinema has long provided what Miriam Hansen terms "an alternative horizon of experience," a relatively accommodating space within which they could access formations of meaning, pleasure, and consumption not readily available to them elsewhere in the realm of public culture.[10]

The special appeal and significance of cinema for many gay men is evident in the way film has developed as a particularly privileged source of and for gay subcultural production. In his pioneering study of subcultural logic, Dick Hebdige contends that subcultures turn on a constitutive process of stylistic bricolage in which they appropriate various objects, texts, and signs from the "dominant" culture and refigure them so as to produce alternative, "subcultural" meanings.[11] As Hebdige sees it, this constitutive process of social articulation allows subcultures to produce and reproduce themselves as "different" from the dominant or "parent" culture through their aberrant modes of cultural consumption. The varied practices of bricolage in subcultures become both the site and the currency of subcultural definition, the space for and tools with which a subculture produces and displays its cultural difference(s). Developing this reading further, Sarah Thornton coins the term "subcultural capital" to refer to the extensive and often highly developed systems of tastes, knowledges, and competences developed and used by subcultures as marks of distinction and group affiliation.[12] By possessing and exhibiting the requisite forms of subcultural capital, a given subject expresses and ratifies his or her membership in a subcultural group.

Homosexual subcultures first started to develop in larger Euro-American urban centers in the late nineteenth and early twentieth century, and almost from the start cinema provided a rich font of material for gay subcultural capital. In her study of lesbian audiences of the 1930s, Andrea Weiss argues that Hollywood cinema was widely deployed in lesbian subcultures as an important tool for communal identification. She contends that "cinema's contribution toward the formation of lesbian identity in the early-twentieth century should not be underestimated."[13] Certain films and, particularly, film stars were routinely used by many lesbians as texts to express and confirm their homosexual identity, both to themselves and to other lesbian women. As Weiss writes: "Aspects of certain star images were appropriated by the growing number of women who began to participate in the emerging urban gay subculture, and played an influential role in defining the distinctive qualities of that subculture. . . . For a people striving toward self-knowledge, Hollywood stars became important models in the formation of gay identity" (35–36).

The case was similar for early gay male subcultures. Indeed, because their gender status furnished them with a much greater degree of social and economic independence, it was perhaps even easier for many gay men of the early twentieth century to develop extensive practices of subcultural cinematic consumption.[14] By midcentury, Euro-American gay male subcultures had mobilized Hollywood film into quite elaborate formations of subcultural capital, with certain genres and stars possessing special significances for and devoted followings among gay men. From the forties through the sixties, Hollywood film and its products became a veritable lingua franca within urban gay male subcultures, providing a rich source of material for subcultural appropriation and a capacious reference system for gay subcultural codings. As Michael Bronski notes, "Eight-by-ten signed glossies of movie stars were standard . . . decor" in gay subcultural venues of the time.[15] A discreet reference to a particular film star with a strong gay following was often used by gay men during this era as a coded way to declare their homosexuality.[16] One gay man recalls:

> I first came out onto the gay scene in the early-sixties and movies were a huge part of the scene in those days. It wasn't that we went to the movies so much—though we certainly did go frequently—it was more that movies provided common reference points for us. They were like a shared passion. You could tell whether someone was gay or not simply by the types of films they liked and how seriously they treated them. We all had our favourite stars and would discuss them endlessly. Many of the bars had Hollywood-related themes and the drag shows nearly always had some type of movie star reference.[17]

With the massive expansion and increased legitimization of gay subcultural formations in the post-Stonewall period, cinema has continued to play a crucial role in the production and circulation of gay subcultural capital. In line with broader sociohistorical shifts in contemporary culture such as the diversification of leisure markets and the emergence of new entertainment forms, cinema has inevitably lost the position of unrivaled predominance it enjoyed in gay subcultures in earlier decades; today it competes with other media such as popular music and television as privileged sources of gay subcultural capital. Nevertheless, film remains a vital forum of and for collective gay investment and definition. The "older" traditions of gay cinematic capital are regularly maintained and passed on through repertory screenings, television broadcasts, gay video stores, and endless references/discussions in gay publications; while more recent screen-based practices such as independent gay/queer cinema and gay/lesbian film festivals have expanded and enlivened gay cinematic capital with a wealth of new texts and pleasures.[18] Writing in 1985, Al LaValley provided the following snapshot of (then) contemporary gay cinematic tastes that, though somewhat caricatural, highlights the important role of cinema in recent gay subcultural productions:

> It's no secret to patrons of urban repertory film houses that for years a large part of the audience has been gay men. To the "gay rep" of Hollywood classics—films like *All About Eve*, *The Women*, *Sunset Boulevard*, *A Star Is Born*, *Now, Voyager*, and the star vehicles of Greta Garbo, Joan

Crawford, Bette Davis, Judy Garland, and Marilyn Monroe—have been added newer gay cult favorites (*Cabaret, Mahagonny, The Rose, American Gigolo*), as well as the more openly gay films (*Victor/Victoria, Making Love, Taxi zum Klo*), and even occasionally a few of the more political gay-produced documentaries (*Word Is Out, Track Two*). A soupçon of gay porn often completes this varied menu.[19]

In sketching this broad and inevitably reductive overview of the "history" of gay subcultural relations to and uses of cinema, I am not trying to advance a homogeneous or neatly linear reading of that history. Obviously, gay subcultural formations of cinematic reception are marked by all sorts of diachronic and synchronic discontinuities and differences. My aim, rather, is to indicate the historical significance and productivities of cinema for gay cultures and, by extension, to the lives of gay-identifying subjects. If, as Elizabeth Ellsworth contends, "social groups use cultural forms in the process of defining themselves," then in the case of gay male subcultures and the gay men who inhabit them, cinema has played a key role.[20]

That cinema can be and often is used by gay men in their gay (self)definitions and identifications is a pivotal and theoretically productive idea. Earlier I evoked a passing comparison between gay spectatorship and cult spectatorship when I borrowed J. P. Telotte's memorable description of the cult spectator as someone who engages film "beyond all reason." The correlation between gay male and cult spectatorships is possibly more instructive than the casual nature of my earlier reference might suggest, for though there is often something of the cultish about certain forms of gay cinematic reception, both gay and cult spectatorships share what may be termed an *identificatory performativity.* Several critics have suggested that cult spectatorship is essentially performative in nature, that it is a practice through which the cultist performs his or her "difference" from the mainstream, as well as his or her commonality with other, fellow cultists. Cult spectatorship provides the framework for producing and declaring one's identification with a discourse of difference—a discourse variably articulated either in terms of the film itself, the time and space of its exhibition, the nature of its consumption, or a combination of all three. As Telotte puts it, cult spectatorship evokes and speaks a desire or "longing to express the self, to express difference." He continues: "It effectively constructs a culture in small, and thus an island of meaning for an audience that senses an absence of meaningful social structures or coherence in life outside the theater. In essence, therefore, every cult constitutes a community, a group that 'worships' similarly and regularly, and finds a strength in that shared experience."[21]

Spectatorship assumes a similarly performative function within gay contexts. For many gay men, spectatorship offers a privileged forum in which to define and express their identifications with discourses of gayness. Daniel Harris claims that, for gay men, film has "served a deeply psychological and political function" because it has provided "a vehicle for expressing alienation from our surroundings and linking up with the utopic homosexual community of our dreams." Gay spectatorship, he asserts, has developed historically as "an emphatic political assertion of ethnic camaraderie," "a way of achieving a collective subcultural identity."[22] This is most obvious in those subcultural contexts of reception referred to above in which individual spectators literally become part of a self-identified gay and/or queer audience. Gay subcultural cinematic practices such as film festivals and the like openly engage and bind spectators together in an "imagined community." Audiences at these events are, as Samantha Searle notes, "actualised in what could be described as queer public spheres, taking part in *social* events of off-screen visibility, of subcultural affirmation and pride."[23] Much of the efficacy and appeal of these "community" events lie precisely in the scope they offer for the performative production of gay/lesbian/queer collective identifications, and, as anyone who has ever attended these events can attest, the experience of queer affirmation they provide can be empowering and immensely pleasurable.

However, the performative identifications of gay spectatorial relations are equally and just as importantly played out in other, more privatized contexts of reception. Given how cinematic reception is by nature simultaneously public and private, communal and individual, many of the most fundamental functions and pleasures of any spectatorship will obviously occur beyond the immediate level of public sociability. The "extra public" or private dynamics of film viewing are especially vital, however, in the case of gay spectatorship, in which the privileged tropology of interiority, privacy, and secrecy that underwrites and shapes modern constructions of homosexuality—what Eve Kosofsky Sedgwick has famously dubbed "the epistemology of the closet"—seems to sensitize and orient gay-identifying subjects more than most to the lure of the private and cinema's capacity to reproduce that lure.[24] Indeed, one cannot help but wonder how much of the fertile productivity of spectatorship as a site of gay identificatory investment comes from the way in which cinema and homosexuality alike share a fundamental investment in discourses of the personal and the private. With its constant negotiations between seeing and not seeing, secrecy and disclosure, knowledge and ignorance and its central promises of visibility, escapism, and emotional discharge, film spectatorship seems perfectly suited to the articulations of a homosexuality understood—and, more often than not, experienced—as privatized interiority.

More specifically, gay spectatorship often results in an alienating preclusion from the public components of film reception, an enforced retreat into a privatized space of difference. Given the overwhelmingly heterocentrist and frequently homophobic nature of most mainstream film, gay/lesbian/queer spectators regularly experience what Tamsin Wilton terms "sudden recoil" in the cinema, in which the heteronormative significations of the text or the responses of the audience suddenly make us aware of our (sexual) difference from the dominant social bodies in which we are physically and discursively located.[25]

Even apart from these structuring experiences of privacy and marginalization, much of the force of spectatorship as a site for gay identificatory performativity necessarily takes effect in profoundly personal ways. For example, one gay man recalls this particularly memorable moment of (gay) spectatorship:

> I can remember Susan Hayward and Dana Andrews in *My Foolish Heart* and it is always tied up with the fact that I was sitting next to a sailor at the Trans-Lux. He was groping me and I was groping him and I was watching Susan Hayward pregnant in *My Foolish Heart*. That is part of my whole sexual experience. . . . I'm sitting there, identifying with Susan Hayward, of course, and she is in love with Dana Andrews and suffering these trials, and the song is "My Love, My Foolish Heart" and here I am with a stiff cock in my hand. I mean, that's just heaven.[26]

This moment clearly functions for its subject as an especially resonant site to performatively declare his homosexuality, a site within which he both produces and cathects a striking identification with (homo)sexual difference. Although that identification is constitutively framed by the "public," or social, dynamics of the spectatorial experience—the presence of the sailor, for example, is vital to the codification of this moment as explicitly gay—it is not necessarily dependent on or exhausted by them. In fact, many of this moment's "queerest" dynamics occur at the profoundly private level of psychic interiority—the fantasmatic internalization of the homosexual encounter, the transgressive cross-gendered identification with the female star (a pregnant Susan Hayward, no less), the engagement of a perverse scenario of pleasurable masochism ("suffering these trials"). More generally, the fact that the gay subject has fetishized this particular moment and turned it into a treasured memory demonstrates both the significance of it to the personal narratives of his (homo)sexual identity and the fact that, decades after its original historical instantiation, this moment of spectatorship continues to function psychically for him as an endlessly renewable site of gay identification and pleasure. I will say more about the psychic dimensions of gay spectatorship later; for the moment, I draw attention to the complex, multileveled ways in which spectatorship operates as a site for the performative production of gay identifications. If spectatorship is routinely mobilized in gay contexts as a forum for gay identificatory performativity, the functions and effects of that process cannot be limited to the realm of public, subcultural sociability alone.

This is where gay spectatorship differs perhaps from the more ritualized, communal-dependent cult spectatorship. Unlike cult spectatorship, which requires some type of public or ritual validation to produce its performative identifications with difference—a requirement that, as Telotte and others contend, ultimately makes cult spectatorship a conservative practice, an identification with "a *safe* difference that is . . . nearly not difference at all"—gay spectatorship performs its identifications with (homosexual) difference in all sorts of contexts and at all sorts of levels.[27] In contrast to the containment of the performative practices of cult spectatorship within the carnivalesque of the cult screening, the performative identifications operative in gay spectatorship feed out of—and back into—the identificatory discourses through which the spectator defines and produces his gay identity outside the theater.

It is precisely this notion—that the discourses of gay identity that structure subjective relations "outside the theater" affect and help structure spectatorial relations "inside the theater"—that grounds the very concept of gay spectatorship in the first place. To speak of gay spectatorship is to speak of a formation that, by definition, reaches beyond the immediate moment of film viewing to the wider contexts of subjectivity within which that moment occurs. As both a theoretical concept and a cultural formation, gay spectatorship necessarily refers to the complex and wide-ranging networks of interaction and exchange that web between gayness as a space of subjective identification and cinematic reception/reading. But what is meant by gayness in this context? How is it defined? If spectatorship has developed as an important site for the performance of gay identifications, what exactly is it that is being performed here? What is being identified with?

The Specificity of Gay Spectatorship

It was mentioned in the introduction that for some the very concept of gay spectatorship is a problematical, even dangerous one. Certain critics contend that any notion of gay spectatorship as a specific or distinct form is, by definition, essentialist and turns on a deformative logic of exclusion and normalization. To speak of gay spectatorship is to buy into and ratify the disciplinary pretensions of the hegemonic hetero/homosexual binarism and, by so doing, to refuse the multiple differences that inevitably frame and work through social practices and experiences like cinematic reception.

Anyone familiar with contemporary cultural theory will recognize that these contentions feed out of and form part of a much wider network of debates inspired by what may be broadly termed the poststructuralist critique of identity. The history and nature of these debates is extraordinarily complex, and a detailed survey of them is not possible here. In essence, however, the primary argument advanced by poststructuralists is that the dominant Western conception of identity as unitary, coherent, and self-present is an ideological fiction that works through inequitable processes of exclusion and hierarchization. Identity, it is argued, always functions at the expense of difference and alterity, enforcing socially constructed and policed categories of being that devalue, if not repudiate, all that is outside their taxonomic boundaries. As Diana Fuss puts it: "To the extent that identity always contains the specter of non-identity within it, the subject is always divided and identity is always purchased at the price of the exclusion of the Other, the repression or repudiation of non-identity."[28]

In the case of sexuality, where much of the robust energy of the poststructuralist critique of identity has been invested, these arguments have inspired trenchant and broadly influential criticisms of identity-based formations of sexuality and identitarian sexual politics. One central claim has been that the dominant discursive organization of Western sexuality in terms of a hetero/homo binarism is an ideological technology designed for the disciplinary regulation of bodies and pleasures. The binarism locks subjects into a normalizing structure that ensures, through the hierarchical primacy of its first term, heteronormativity, and, through its assumption of gendered object-choice as the primary axis of sexual definition, reduces and regulates the otherwise limitless field of sexual possibilities and differences. Within this context, to assert an affirmative sexual identity, even an apparently antihegemonic one such as gay or lesbian, is to buy into and maintain the dominant juridical system of sexual regulation. "From a poststructural perspective," writes Steven Seidman, "gay identity constructions maintain the dominant hetero/homosexual code, including its normative heterosexuality. If homosexuality and heterosexuality are a coupling in which each presupposes the other, each being present in the invocation of the other, and in which this coupling inevitably assumes hierarchical forms, then the epistemic and political project of affirming a gay subject reinforces and reproduces this hierarchical figure."[29] Add to this the interrelated claim that gayness as a category of identity is exclusionary, that it marginalizes and devalues, if not refuses, those forms of sexuality outside its narrow representational capacities, as well as those axes of subjective difference other than sexuality (race, ethnicity, class, age, etc.), and it becomes difficult not to conclude, as David Herkt does, that "gay identity is observably a conservative construct."[30]

Many of these same issues and arguments attend theoretical debates around questions of gay spectatorship. To the degree that the concept of gay spectatorship definitionally depends on identitarian categories of homosexuality, it has been subjected to charges of essentialism, exclusion, and epistemological conservatism. Caroline Evans and Lorraine Gamman, for example, argue that "work which has addressed gay and lesbian spectators . . . is flawed by the essentialism of the terms that frame the debate."[31] They contend that

> because identity itself is not fixed, it is inappropriate to posit any single identification with images. If we deconstruct the subject we must by implication also deconstruct the subject's reading/viewing position. . . . anti-essentialist discussion of identificatory processes actually challenges the fixity of notions about gay, lesbian or straight identities. It also challenges essentialist ideas that relations of looking are determined by the biological sex of the individual/s you choose to fornicate with. (39–40)

In line with some of the broader theoretical moves developed in the wake of anti-identitarian poststructuralism—moves that generally seek to deconstruct, denaturalize, and reconceive sexual identity as incoherent and plural—many film critics argue that, rather than pursue what they take to be the essentializing, exclusionary project of theorizing gay spectatorship as a specific, delimitable reading formation, it would be wiser and more productive to foreground how spectatorship actually traverses and thus destabilizes regulatory fictions such as gay identity. Instead of starting with predefined categories of sexual identity and looking for how those categories accord with or influence spectatorship, these critics suggest we would do better to look to how the pleasures and forms of spectatorship effect a displacement of sexual identity, a rupture of its disciplinary regime. Judith Mayne offers an eloquent representation of this argument:

> Film theory has been so bound by the heterosexual symmetry that supposedly governs Hollywood cinema that it has ignored the possibility, for instance, that one of the distinct pleasures of the cinema may well be a "safe zone" in which homosexual as well as heterosexual desires can be fantasized and acted out. I am not speaking here of an innate capacity to "read against the grain," but rather of the way in which desire and pleasure in the cinema may well function to problematize the categories of heterosexual versus homosexual.[32]

Not surprisingly, *queer* has been widely promoted in this context as a productive term through which to theorize the sexual displacements and ambivalences of spectatorship. As mentioned in the introduction, queer has emerged as a powerful discursive tool within both cultural theory and political activism for enabling precisely those moves beyond the limits of received categories of (homo)sexual identity called for by poststructuralist theory. Because queer is explicitly relational in nature—it is almost always defined in terms of its oppositionality to normative economies—it is assumed to lack any fixed or positive content. Queer, writes David Halperin, "demarcates not a positivity but a positionality vis-à-vis the normative—a positionality that is not restricted to lesbians and gay men but is in fact available to anyone who is or who feels marginalized."[33] Within film studies, many critics have enthusiastically embraced queer as the ideal antidote to the perceived limitations of theorizing spectatorship through categories of sexual identity. Evans and Gamman explicitly advocate queer as a corrective to what they see as the unavoidable essentialism of notions of gay/lesbian spectatorship, asserting that queer "gives us the space to start to rethink difficulties with cohesion of identity or identification through viewing, and to look for greater fluidity in terms of explanation." As heterosexual-identified women, they argue, "we are as perverse in our looking habits as many 'essentially' gay or lesbian spectators, and only by introducing some queer notions can we begin to explain our experiences beyond the dogma of ideas associated with the meaning of specific sexual orientations."[34]

Alexander Doty mounts a similar argument for queer as the perfect discursive tool for rethinking spectatorial engagements outside the pincers of sexual identity. Unlike Evans and Gamman, Doty does not reject the utility of sexual identity categories altogether; in fact, he retains a central reading of gay and lesbian identities as relatively meaningful forms of social and sexual subjectivity. Yet his primary interest is in theorizing how spectatorship moves beyond and confounds "the traditional opposition of hetero and homo" and thus produces "queer" pleasures and effects.

> The danger of making essentializing statements about both audiences and their reception practices lurks behind any uncritical use of [identity] categories. . . . Further, conducting reception studies on the basis of conventional audience categories can also lead to critical blindness about how certain reception strategies are shared by otherwise disparate individuals and groups. I would like to propose "queerness" as a

mass culture reception practice that is shared by all sorts of people in varying degrees of consistency and intensity. . . . I am using the term "queer" to mark a flexible space for the expression of all aspects of non- (anti-, contra-) straight cultural production and reception. As such, this cultural "queer space" recognizes the possibility that various and fluctuating queer positions might be occupied whenever *anyone* produces or responds to culture.[35]

The deployment of queerness as a term through which to (re)think cinematic reception is both exciting and productive. It offers a timely challenge to many of the orthodox assumptions and categories of reception studies and enables the theorization of spectatorial possibilities that would otherwise remain overlooked, if not wholly unidentified. However, I do not believe, as some of its more enthusiastic proponents suggest, that the turn to queerness in recent film studies necessarily offers a better or more authentic reading of spectatorship than that provided by other categories of subjective organization such as sexual identity or gayness. Nor do I believe that it supersedes the need for or utility of thinking spectatorship through these categories. Although queerness undoubtedly opens up many possibilities and avenues for theorizing spectatorship in new contexts, it also threatens to close others down.

One criticism often made of the concept of queer—as of the broader discourses of anti-identitarian critique from which it stems—is that it erases gay and lesbian specificity. With its constitutive deconstruction of sexual identity categories and its celebratory promotion of a broadly inclusive antinormativity, queer runs the risk of despecifying or, as David Halperin puts it, "degaying gayness." Developing this argument further, Halperin writes that "the lack of specifically homosexual content built into the meaning of 'queer' has made that term all too handy—not for generating a de-essentialized identity or defining a marginal positionality so much as for multiplying the opportunities for disidentification, denial, and disavowal."[36]

Queer and anti-identitarian discourses more generally have also been widely criticized for delegitimizing gayness and its status as a productive, material site of subjective definition. The critical representation of gay identity within these discourses as an instrument of regulatory regimes that inadvertently makes those who assume it complicit in their own oppression tends to demonize gay identity as a disabling category of ideo-logical subjugation and to represent gay-identifying subjects as unen-lightened dupes. As a result, the positive, enabling dynamics of gay iden-tity as a site of subjective production and political agency are neutralized, if not entirely denied. Some critics suggest that because anti-identitarian critical discourses deconstruct gay identity virtually out of existence, they erase the conditions of possibility for antihomophobic action. "In reject-ing the essentializing identities derived from sexual preference," protests Leo Bersani, anti-identitarian theory "mount[s] a resistance to homo-phobia in which the agent of resistance has been erased: there is no longer any homosexual subject to oppose the homophobic subject."[37] This era-sure of gayness as a space of agency not only problematizes possibilities for political resistance and change but, as Bersani, perhaps melodramati-cally but nevertheless compellingly, declares, "it accomplishes in its own way the principal aim of homophobia: the elimination of gays" (5).

By outlining these criticisms, I do not want to seem antagonistic to-ward or dismissive of poststructuralist critiques of sexual identity or anti-identitarian formations of queer—both of which I hold to be enormously valuable, if not indispensable for contemporary sexual theory and poli-tics. Nor do I want to suggest that the despecification of gayness is a struc-tural effect of every deployment of queer—as mentioned above, a critic like Doty, for example, is careful to retain at least some notion of gay par-ticularity. Nevertheless, the delegitimization or erasure of gayness is one of the more problematical potentials of these critical moves. The produc-tive particularities of gay spectatorship often go unrecognized in many queer-based readings of spectatorship that refute identity as a basis for spectatorial organization and promote instead universalizing accounts of film reception in which homosexuality and perverse desire more gener-ally are presented as omnipresent, readily available modes of identifica-tory engagement. Because gayness is largely subsumed within these read-ings as part of a wider, pansexual queerness that, in turn, is represented as a positionality or dynamic available, even if only potentially, to all spec-tators regardless of sexuality, the question—even, the possibility—of gay spectatorial specificity is more or less foreclosed.

Although I agree with queer-based readings that cinematic spectator-ship operates through many different libidinal configurations and offers a range of shifting desires, identifications, and pleasures, I do not agree that this supplants the structuring force of sexual identities or obviates the need for theorizing spectatorship in terms of those identities. I write from the conviction that spectatorship inevitably operates in and through the variable psychosocial systems, networks, and patterns that constitute the spectator's subjective specificity and that these determine (even if only partially) how, where, and to what extent the libidinal potentials and identificatory relations of cinema are realized—or not, as the case may be. Without a recognition of this, one is left with an acritical, utopian reading of spectatorship as unbounded and voluntarist, with subjects gleefully partaking of a panerotic smorgasbord with no regard for the structuring materialities of social, sexual, and psychic organization. To the extent that gayness is an integral site of subjective structuration in contemporary Euro-American cultures, producing subjectivities, desires, social roles, and meanings, it inevitably functions as an important, if variable, determinant in spectatorial relations. Any model or reading of spectatorship that would displace or erase this fact is both theoretically flawed and analytically naive.

The sticking point in this debate is not so much categories of gay identity per se, but how those categories are defined and assumed. Despite the dogmatic certainty with which some critics dismiss it, I am not convinced that gay identity is, to repeat David Herkt's assessment, "an observably conservative construct." Although it is true that every assertion of identity produces systems of exclusion and operates as a normalizing, regulatory force, this does not circumscribe or exhaust the functions and effects of identificatory practices. As Foucault's celebrated "reverse discourse" neatly reveals, even the most seemingly hegemonic identificatory category can generate meanings and possibilities far in excess of the mechanisms and terms of its discursive construction. Gay identities can and do function in competing and often contradictory ways that confound simple assessments of them as wholly reactionary or, for that matter, as wholly progressive. Identity constructions are not, as Steven Seidman notes, "disciplining and regulatory only in a self-limiting and oppressive way; they are also personally, socially and politically enabling." [38] To engage gay identity is to engage a complex psychosocial web of discourses, knowledges, desires, and practices that have competing effects—oppressive and subversive, hegemonic and resistant, disabling and enabling.

However, even if gay identity were nothing more than a regulatory category of heterosexist hegemony, it is far from certain that those whose desiring subjectivities are nominated through that category could so readily escape its juridical hold or move beyond its constitutive boundaries. Simply because identity categories are discursive and thus fictional does not mean they are voluntary. The pull of identity is strong and ingrained and is more often than not experienced as an inescapable compulsion. In terms of sexual identities, the modern epistemic demand to produce the self through sexuality is so pervasive in Western cultures as to make identification with categories of sexual subjectivity all but inevitable. The psychocultural narratives of sexuality into which we are interpellated and through which we learn to desire are not discrete options that one can take up or not at will—they are, quite simply, the very conditions of possibility by which we exist as sexed subjects. Furthermore, because these narratives are "implanted" in us as subjects and constantly reproduced at an unconscious level—which is precisely the central claim of psychoanalysis—they are seldom even amenable to conscious recognition, let alone voluntarist manipulation. This does not mean that we should simply acquiesce in the dominant formations of sexual identity, or that we shouldn't work to critique and resist their disciplinary functions, but it does mean that we need to take those identities seriously and to analyze how and where they affect subjective formations and productions of cultural meaning—spectatorship included. "Since deconstructing an imposed identity will not erase the habit of desire," asserts Leo Bersani, "it might be more profitable to test the resistance of that identity from *within* the desire."[39]

Let there be no confusion, this is not an attempt to revive some type of naive gay identitarian essentialism. To claim that gayness functions as a material, structuring force in the lives of gay-identifying subjects and the cultural practices they engage in and that this is worth investigating is not a rallying call to essentializing definitions of gay identity. It is simply to claim that gayness has a *specificity*, that it designates a space for the constitution of subjectivity, the arrangement of desire, and the productions of meaning in specific or particular ways. This is a very different proposition from claiming gayness as an expressive, self-identical essence. In many respects, the assertion of gay specificity is perhaps incongruent with essentializing constructions of homosexual identity and may even run counter to them. Not only is it the case that, in its status as a position of sociodiscursive alterity, gayness is invariably marked by negativity and is thus rarely assumed and experienced by those who engage it as a self-present site of identity, but the assertion of gayness as, precisely, a specificity produces and re-presents gayness not as some type of ontological essence expressed uniformly and coherently but as a contingent space of identificatory production that is provisional and changing. Shane Phelan argues that "specificity" is the most advantageous conceptual framework for theorizing (homo)sexual identities and the most apposite for representing the diverse ways in which those identities are produced and experienced in shifting, material contexts. Because specificity contains a combined emphasis on questions of both difference and particularity, it helps guard against essentialist reifications. "One of the virtues" of specificity, Phelan writes,

> is its redefinition of the important categories for recognition and analysis. . . . We need structural analyses of particular differences to show us how our various positions within these structures limit and guide our ideas and actions. . . . We cannot and should not, however, hope to build theories that will completely explain each of us. . . . Specificity demands the simultaneous exploration of categories of social marks and orders and attention to the unique or the individual.[40]

This same emphasis on the simultaneous pull of general and particular, macro and micro, structure and instance, is also at the heart of what might be seen as a theoretical corollary of specificity, the notion of performativity. Much of the extraordinary popularity of performativity as a critical precept in recent cultural theory stems precisely from how it is seen to enable the type of simultaneous reading of general and particular that Phelan suggests a recognition of sexual specificity demands. Judith Butler, the critic with whom recent theories of sexual performativity are most closely associated, claims that performativity provides a more relational understanding of identity categories without erasing the material efficacy of their structural work, redefining sexual identity as "neither fatally determined nor fully artificial and arbitrary."[41] Because it conceives of sexual identity as an effect constituted in and through the reiterative enactment of specified norms, gestures, and desires, performativity represents sexual identity more as a processual production than an expressive essence. Within the context of performative theory, one does not so much *have* an identity as one *does* identity—a process of doing that is re-iterative, multiple, and constant. Identity categories exist in this reading, and they have a determinative force, functioning as what Butler terms "generative structures," but that force and function remain tied to the variable, multiplicitous instances of discursive production through which sexual identities are performatively constituted in, for, and by the individual subject. Like specificity, then, performativity works against the reification of an identificatory category such as gayness as a unified, self-identical essence and toward a representation of it as a contingent site of diverse productions. It acknowledges gayness as a "generative structure" or, to use another Butlerian term, a "constitutive constraint"—one that is, more often than not, engaged and experienced by the gay-identifying subject not as an external imposition or a willful assumption but as the very conditions of its sexual existence—however, it equally acknowledges and asserts that that structure is reproduced in often vastly different ways across the heterogeneous field of individual subjectivities.[42]

This was one reason why I suggested performativity may be a useful sign under which to commence a theoretical consideration of gay spectatorship. To think of gay spectatorship within the broad context of performativity is to think of it in terms that stress its processual, variable cast. It is to recognize the specificity of gayness as a structuring formation both in subjectivity and subject-based practices such as cinematic reception but also to recognize that the structural operations of gayness are not absolute givens with uniform functions and effects; they are produced and played out in variable ways in the performative spaces of specific moments of spectatorship and individual acts of cinematic engagement. To read gay spectatorship through the lens of performativity is to read it as a network of possibilities that is realized in different ways in the diverse citations, acts, or moments that constitute its reiterative productivity.

The Negotiations of Gay Spectatorship

This reading of gay spectatorship as a processual formation in which the structuring dynamics of gay specificity are performatively articulated in variable ways has broadly influenced critical studies of gay spectatorship. Although little work exists within film studies on questions of gay and/or lesbian cinematic reception, the limited work that has been done has pursued at least some variant of this reading of gay spectatorship as a space for the diverse reproduction of gay identifications. Not surprisingly, much of this work has been situated within the interdisciplinary traditions of cultural studies, particularly the subfield of subcultural theory.

As is well known, cultural studies has developed a rather different set of theoretical models and analytic tools from those of the collective traditions of mainstream film studies, and it has been widely championed by some critics as an alternative paradigm within which to rethink questions of film spectatorship. Broadly speaking, film studies pursues a high structuralist, text-oriented theorization of cinema as a massively functioning institution of sociosymbolic production, whereas cultural studies takes a more pluralist, socially-oriented approach that emphasizes the localized, polysemous nature of cultural production and exchange.[43] The distinctive casts of mainstream film and cultural studies can, perhaps, be neatly illustrated by the differing models of ideology that they have generally deployed and promoted. In line with its structuralist ideals, film studies has largely advanced an Althusserian reading of ideology as an interpellatory system of subjection in which individuals are sutured into predefined positions and relations of meaning. This has of course been at the heart of the influential notion in contemporary film theory of the cinematic apparatus in which film is theorized as a multileveled institution designed to enjoin subjects to dominant ideological discourses. Through the privileged figure of the cinematic apparatus, contemporary film studies has developed a complex body of scholarship whose primary aim has been to show how film as both institution and text places individuals into ideologically circumscribed positions of reading and desire.[44]

Cultural studies, on the other hand, has mobilized the less mechanistic model of ideological reproduction provided by Gramsci's theory of hegemony. In this theory, ideology is seen less as a structure of interpellatory domination than as an interactive process of negotiation through which individuals are coaxed to assent to their own social subjection; a process that, importantly, is never guaranteed, but must constantly struggle to maintain its effectivity and to renew subjective assent against the myriad points of resistance and failure that inevitably beset it. The deployment of a Gramscian model of hegemony has impelled cultural studies to develop a more relational reading of culture and cultural reception as polysemous sites of struggle in which, to quote Tony Bennett, "dominant, subordinate and oppositional cultural and ideological values and elements are "mixed" in different permutations."[45] This latter formulation provides a working definition of one of the fundamental premises of cultural studies: that culture and cultural subjects are the complex sites of diverse, even contradictory, discursive processes. The project of much cultural studies has been to show how these diverse processes interact and thereby articulate variable meanings. In particular, cultural studies has, as Simon During notes, "been . . . most interested in how groups with least power practically develop their own readings of, and uses for, cultural products—in fun, in resistance, or to articulate their own identity."[46] The social marginality of subaltern or disempowered groups exemplifies the reading of culture as a site of struggle. These groups are not readily addressed or accommodated by dominant cultural forms, and as such they often function as points of resistance in the cultural field, forced to rework dominant texts and meanings in order to align them with their own nonhegemonic positions. There is, thus, a long and influential tradition within cultural studies of analyzing how marginalized cultural groups—especially working-class groups, youth subcultures, and minority ethnic communities—appropriate and refigure cultural forms for their own purposes.

Even though much of the work carried out in the tradition of cultural studies has concentrated on television and the popular press and, until recently, has not really addressed film or cinematic practices in a sustained manner, the appeal and applicability of many of its arguments for analyses of film spectatorship has not gone unnoticed. This is perhaps particularly true of those film critics wanting to address the possibility of alternative or nonhegemonic spectatorships. These writers often assume the stress on diversity and struggle in cultural readings as a way to address the possibilities of spectatorial difference and resistance generally seen to be closed off by the more traditional text-centered models of film theory. As early as 1978, Christine Gledhill was arguing that "the general lack in film theory of a means to conceptualize the social relations [rather than just the textual relations] in which a specific audience is constituted can lead to severe limitations on proposals for subversive cultural activity."[47]

Gledhill has in fact been a central proponent of and active agent in the appropriation of cultural studies–based models for film theory. Her

1988 essay "Pleasurable Negotiations" provides one of the more rigorous and influential attempts to use cultural studies in discussions of film spectatorships. In this essay, Gledhill mobilizes the emphasis of cultural studies on "socio-culturally differentiated modes of meaning production and reading" to pose the possibilities of nonhegemonic or resistant spectatorships.[48] As the title of her essay suggests, Gledhill pays particular attention to the model of reading as a process of "negotiation" between textual and extratextual discourses. This model was first introduced by Stuart Hall, a pioneering figure within the field of cultural studies, in his important essay "Encoding/Decoding" and was used by him to assert that the act of reading or "decoding" is never a case of the text imposing its message on a passive receiver but is rather a negotiation between both text and receiver and the variable discourses that constitute them.[49] In her essay, Gledhill describes this argument in the following terms: "As a model of meaning production, negotiation conceives cultural exchange as the intersection of processes of production and reception, in which overlapping but non-matching determinations operate. Meaning is neither imposed, nor passively imbibed, but arises out of a struggle or negotiation between competing frames of reference, motivation or experience."[50]

In other words, the model of negotiation reconceives cultural exchange as a bi- or even multilateral process in which textual and extratextual discourses play equal and interrelated roles of determination. In many instances, these discourses will be perfectly compatible and, in such cases, meaning production is a relatively simple, harmonious affair. In others, however, there will be a gap or a misfit of varying degrees between the dominant discourses promoted by the text and those espoused by the spectator in his or her cultural and historical particularity. And it is in these cases that a process of negotiation occurs whereby the spectator shifts or modifies the dominant discursive register set up by the text in such a way that it might accommodate his or her social identity and frames of reference more comfortably. "The viewing or reading situation affects the meanings and pleasures of a work," writes Gledhill, "by introducing into the cultural exchange a range of determinations, potentially resistant or contradictory, arising from the different social and cultural constitution of readers or viewers—by class, gender, race, age, personal history, and so on" (68).

It is precisely this accent on spectatorship as a processual site of struggle between nonmatching frames of reference that has been mobilized by several critics in their attempts to pose and theorize questions of gay spectatorial specificity. Following the emphasis in cultural studies on addressing spectators' diverse social positionings, these critics have analyzed how the social discourses of gay and lesbian identities and their frames of reference might be seen to affect and help shape spectatorial relations.

One of the earliest and most influential pieces to emerge out of this context is Elizabeth Ellsworth's 1986 essay on lesbian responses to the film *Personal Best*.[51] Ellsworth studies the film's reception by contrasting reviews of it, which she classifies as either "mainstream," "liberal feminist," or "lesbian feminist," depending on the type of publication in which the review appeared. Ellsworth discovered that each category produced fairly different readings of the film, negotiating between what the text had to offer and the various frames of reference from within which the particular reviewer was writing. Interestingly, Ellsworth found that the lesbian reviewers seemed to take the greatest liberties with their interpretations. They actively intervened in the text, altering many textual features and rearranging conventional or received patterns to produce readings that more fully matched their own subject positions as lesbian women. For example, the lesbian reviewers focused almost entirely on the film's first half, which deals with the protagonist's lesbian relationship, and ignored much of the later narrative material that deals with her heterosexual romance—even though the text clearly attempts to mark out the heterosexual relationship as "more important." Similarly, Ellsworth notes that many of the lesbian reviewers redefined the conventional roles of "main character" and "supporting character" to elevate Tory, the fully lesbian character played by Patrice Donnelly, to the position of the film's main star, despite promotion of Mariel Hemingway as the star and the significantly greater amount of screen time devoted to her character, Chris. The lesbian reviewers consistently refused the film's attempts at heterosexist closure (i.e., its attempts at providing a "safe" heterosexual ending) by either refocusing attention on Tory rather than Chris at the close of the film—thereby producing a validation of lesbian sexuality over heterosexuality by making the lesbian character the final image of narrative meaning and not the heterosexual character, as the film's ending

seems to encourage—or by simply rejecting the text's "reheterosexual-
ization" of Chris and imagining that Chris would one day "see the light"
and come back to Tory. Indeed, one lesbian reviewer cited by Ellsworth
even goes so far as to offer a fantasized description of a romantic reunion
between the two female stars.

Richard Dyer develops a similar reading of gay male spectatorship in
his influential account of gay subcultural readings of the star-image of
Judy Garland. Dyer attempts to explain why Garland has been such an
iconic figure in postwar gay subcultures, as well as to look at how gay-
identifying spectators produce variant meanings in their specific engagements with the Garland image and texts. In reference to the latter, Dyer
focuses on how the specific frames of reference brought by gay men to
their readings of Garland affect the meanings they derive. He suggests
that gay receptions of Garland turn on a negotiation wherein gay spectators latch on to certain salient features of the Garland star-image and
associate these features with their own positions and experiences as gay
men. Gay spectators use their "knowledges" of social difference and marginalization, he asserts, to forge specifically gay identifications with the
scenarios of "emotional difference" or "extraordinariness" that characterize so many Garland films, as well as the Garland biography itself.[52]
This incorporation of gay-specific social knowledges into readings of
Garland texts also results in frequently aberrant interpretations. Drawing
on film reviews, memoirs, and personal correspondence, Dyer demonstrates that gay male readings of the Garland image and films often differ
from mainstream or dominant readings in both the types of textual features they privilege and how they evaluate and interpret such features. In
the case of *The Wizard of Oz*, for example, which has emerged as something of a canonical text in and for postwar gay male subcultures, Dyer
suggests that it is widely read by gay audiences not as the wholesome validation of heterosexual family values for which it is generally remembered
but as a celebratory affirmation of homosexual difference. The film's representation of the Garland character as a social misfit who escapes from a
world of ordinariness into one of extraordinariness in which she encounters all manner of "queer" creations—"friends of Dorothy"—has been
read and feted in gay male subcultures as a symbolic narrative of gay experiences and biographies. By relating these various textual elements to
their own frames of reference and positions of social difference, gay audi-

ences (re)produce *The Wizard of Oz* as an affirmatory production of gay identification.

In a way that relates nicely to and actually draws on the Dyer piece, Janet Staiger devotes a chapter of her book *Interpreting Films* to gay male receptions of Garland's 1954 film, *A Star Is Born*. Staiger challenges existing text-centered models of spectatorship by demonstrating that "the contextual discourses derived from our social formation are critical in the reading strategies available to individuals. . . . Furthermore, inequities that unfortunately still exist in all social formations produce not merely diversity but conflict among interpreters."[53] Through case studies, Staiger highlights how these "inequities," or differences, in interpreters' social and historical positions give rise to different forms of spectatorial investment and meaning production. In her chapter on *A Star Is Born*, she pursues this in relation to how the specific conditions of gay- or homosexual-identifying spectators in the mid-fifties affected and shaped both the way these spectators engaged *A Star Is Born* and the interpretations they produced. Like both Dyer and Ellsworth, Staiger draws on such material as film reviews and memoirs and then compares them with correlative material from more "mainstream" sources to show that gay spectators of *A Star Is Born* often used alternative interpretive strategies in their readings of this film to produce meanings that accorded more fully with their social and historical positions of gay identification. In particular, she asserts that gay spectators frequently mobilized extratextual references from their own socially constructed "experiences" to draw homologies between themselves and various textual elements. Using their own knowledges of social marginalization, for example, as well as subcultural gossip about Garland's private life, gay spectators of *A Star Is Born* interpreted the film, she suggests, "not so much [as] the making of a star" as "the comeback of a performer who had been oppressed" (174).

I shall return to these examples and discuss others at various points throughout this study. However, the work outlined here should suffice to give a sense of the way a cultural studies–based model of spectatorial negotiation has been used in critical discussions of gay or lesbian spectatorship. All the writers mentioned here take up the retheorization of spectatorship by cultural studies as a processual exchange to raise the question of gay and lesbian spectatorial specificity. In particular, they claim that the "differences" of gay/lesbian spectators' social and historical conditions play a crucial role in determining how they engage with and read film. As Staiger puts it: if "receptions are dependent upon specific historical configurations . . . [then] defining one's self as homosexual [must] count much in th[at] contextual interaction" (158).

This work clearly attests to the productive capacities offered by cultural studies models of negotiated reading to analyses of gay spectatorships. The assumption of film reception as a site of struggle between competing frames of reference comes closest perhaps to theorizing the processual dynamics that I have argued structure gay spectatorship as a site of gay identificatory performativity. The general reading of gay spectatorship that emerges from this collective work is of a complex formation that is played out in the determinative pull of various discourses of gay identity and the contingent frames of text, culture, and history that shape specific moments of reception. As such, it offers a solid foundation from which the specificities of gay spectatorship can begin to be theorized. I say begin to be, because, as much as these readings go further than most in recognizing the determinative potentials of gay particularities, they are also hampered by what I think is a rather restrictive conceptualization of the forms and functions of both gay subjectivity and spectatorship.

As should be apparent even on the basis of this brief discussion, negotiational models of spectatorship concentrate almost exclusively on questions of *social* difference and positioning. They turn on a conceptualization of the subject-spectator in which the realm of the social and its constituent discourses assume center stage. Although this centralization of the social aspects of reading has clearly enabled the recognition and theorization of spectatorial differences, it gives rise to an analytic framework in which determinative dynamics other than the social are marginalized or displaced altogether. This is particularly true of the psychic dynamics of spectatorship, for, as is widely recognized, the major traditions of cultural studies have avoided, if not purposely rejected, issues or questions of the psychic with an almost fervent zeal.[54] In large part, the reluctance to address the psychic is a direct result of the "enemy territory" status that psychoanalysis has come to assume in much cultural studies. In the so-called *Screen* debates of the eighties, for example, many cultural studies critics explicitly attacked the widespread use of psychoanalysis in film theory, arguing that it was homogenizing, ahistorical, and phallo-centric and that it only impeded the development of a properly material-ist theory of cinematic production and reception.[55] By rejecting psycho-analysis point-blank, however, cultural studies not only runs the risk of "tossing out a powerful theory of the subject, as well as explanations of some types of affect and pleasure," as Janet Staiger claims; it also imposes profound limitations on the theories of subjectivity it does work with, curtailing their ability to engage and analyze the full range of subjective forms and processes.[56] The almost exclusive prioritization of the social, and the concomitant refusal of the psychic, in much cultural studies fos-ters what Constance Penley, in a different though not unrelated context, refers to as an "economical" theory of subjectivity wherein the subject and its "entire range of differences . . . are . . . all seen to be historically determined *social* [forms and] differences."[57]

Psychoanalysis claims, on the other hand, that the subject always ex-ceeds its definition in the social. It argues that the subject is also sub-ject of and to a register of psychic organization that, though fundamen-tally imbricated with the social, is irreducible to it. This is of course the argument behind the Freudian postulation of "psychic reality" in which the subject's psychic structures are claimed to have an order of their own, relatively autonomous of the structures of physical reality. Freud's "discovery" of the unconscious impelled him to recognize that subjec-tivity is fundamentally fractured and heterogeneous, that it is produced and reproduced through constitutive processes of division and repression across interacting fields. To say we are subjects in psychoanalytic terms is to say we are subject to forces and dynamics beyond our individual consciousness that both exceed and, in many ways, undercut the social self. There is nothing that demands we must accept the "truth" of this argument. However, if we do, or even if we only concede that the theo-ries of psychic organization proposed by Freud offer some useful insights into contemporary forms of subjectivity, then the register of the psychic needs to be acknowledged and addressed in our readings.[58]

This is particularly true in relation to analyses of spectatorship in which the constitutive centrality of such emphatically psychic dynam-ics as fantasy, pleasure, identification, and desire seem to all but demand some measure of psychoanalytic address; becoming even more impera-tive, perhaps, in the specific case of gay spectatorships that are so obviously grounded, both in terms of their definitions and performances, in the psychocultural categories of the sexual. From the point of view of psychoanalysis—in which sexuality is, as John Fletcher writes, "always psychosexuality," always "formed as a set of psychical representations"— gayness as both a formation of (homo)sexual desire and a category of sexual identification obtains fundamental and irreducible psychic dynamics.[59] Any attempt, therefore, to analyze homosexual subjectivities or cultural practices such as gay spectatorship that fails to attend to their psychic dynamics will also fail to understand the full range of their functions and effects.

One does need to exercise caution here, however, to avoid hasty or simplistic incorporation of theories of the social and the psychic. Although I would contend that a combined sociopsychic analysis is the only way to apprehend the complexity of gay spectatorial specificities, I am mindful that such a call can easily lead to what Judith Mayne terms a naive, "happy integration," "whereby it is assumed that all one needs to do is to take what is most attractive from supposedly opposing theoretical claims and mix them together."[60] Some critics openly question the feasibility of linking psychoanalytic theory to socially oriented traditions of analysis such as cultural studies because, as they see it, the two are incommensurate. Janet Bergstrom and Mary Ann Doane argue that the difference between psychoanalytic film theory and cultural studies "is not simply a difference between text based and audience based analysis, but a profound divergence in epistemological premises and theories of subjectivity." They assert that, unlike psychoanalytic film theory, "the unconscious is not a pertinent factor" for cultural studies and that, consequently, the two traditions work with "conflicting and incompatible frameworks" that construct "entirely different objects of study (e.g., the 'spectator' vs. the 'audience')."[61]

Bergstrom and Doane are right to suggest that psychoanalysis and cultural studies inhabit different theoretical landscapes. As argued, cultural studies has traditionally worked within a sociocentric framework of analysis, so its epistemological moorings are bound to differ from those of psychoanalysis. Bergstrom and Doane are also right to point out that, because of this, psychoanalysis and cultural studies frequently construct and work with different objects of analysis. However, difference is not incompatibility, and to suggest that psychoanalysis and cultural studies are incommensurable because one works with a psychic-based and the other with a social-based theory of subjectivity is to imply that the areas of the psychic and the social have no forms of correspondence or exchange. This stance not only leads to the type of ahistorical psychic idealism that opponents of psychoanalysis love to lampoon, it also misrepresents Freud's own arguments about the nature of psychic-social relationality. For though Freud accords the order of the psychic a strong degree of autonomy, arguing that it functions with a logic and a reality of its own, he also emphasizes that the psychic is tied to the social in fundamental and mutually interactive ways. As Stephen Frosh contends, "The entire heritage of social psychoanalysis has demonstrated exactly how much the structure of the individual psyche is infiltrated by the structure of society."[62] It would thus be untenable from a psychoanalytic perspective to suggest that there is no possible point of congruence or exchange between social and psychic registers or analyses.

Admittedly, the question of relations between the social and the psychic is a notoriously thorny one, especially because of Freud's emphasis on the psychic as both tied to and relatively autonomous of social structures. The answer, however, cannot be a blanket rejection of attempts to combine social-based and psychic-based readings. Rather, such alliances must be carefully staged to take up cultural studies' and psychoanalysis' accents on social and psychic specificity respectively, highlighting the intersections between these two registers but still acknowledging their differences. What is needed, in other words, is a dialogic analysis that, as James Donald puts it, "can hang onto both the operations of the unconscious and the opacity of the social at the same time."[63] This is undoubtedly a tall order, but it is one that remains necessary for an effective reading of the full range of subjective and/or spectatorial forms.

The framework for just such a dialogic sociopsychic analysis may be found in the recent work in film theory on the psychoanalytic concept of fantasy. Like the cultural studies model of negotiation, the concept of fantasy has been used in film studies to fundamentally reconceptualize spectatorship as a processual production shaped by competing relations of determination. However, unlike cultural studies, this work on fantasy does not limit its reading of the extratextual dynamics of spectatorship to the social alone but places a strong emphasis on questions of the psychic. Many of the theorists working in this area champion the concept of fantasy precisely because they see it as opening up theories of cinematic reception to both the social and the psychic dimensions of subjectivity/spectatorship without compromising the specificity of either. The great advantage of the notion of fantasy, asserts James Donald, is that it "makes it possible to focus on the translation of the social into a psychic reality, the articulation of history and the unconscious, without reducing either to the other or assuming that either term provides a sufficient explanation of the forms taken by the other" (6–7).

Theories of Fantasy, Theories of Spectatorship

Reading film in terms of fantasy is hardly new. From the technological prehistory of the "magic lantern" to popular characterizations of Hollywood as the "dream factory," cinema has long been aligned with fantasy-related forms. The so-called turn to fantasy in film theory referred to here, however, works with and promotes a rather different reading of the cinema-fantasy equation because it draws specialized concepts from psychoanalysis. In particular, much of this work takes its understanding of fantasy from an essay written by the French psychoanalysts Jean Laplanche and Jean-Bertrand Pontalis, "Fantasy and the Origins of Sexuality." First published in 1964, this essay did not receive widespread attention in Anglo-American film studies until the mid-eighties, when it was "rediscovered" by cultural theorists and subsequently translated into English for the 1986 anthology *Formations of Fantasy*.[64] Ostensibly an exegetical overview on Freud's writings on fantasy, Laplanche and Pontalis's essay also retheorizes these writings in light of Jacques Lacan's structuralist rereadings of Freudian psychoanalysis. It thus seeks to not only draw out a theory of fantasy from the varied, even contradictory, writings of Freud on the subject but also restore to this theory a dimension of epistemological radicality through a structuralist reworking.

Laplanche and Pontalis assert that fantasy is "the fundamental object of psychoanalysis," providing both the material for its analytic regime and the mark of its theoretical particularity. They point out that it was only when Freud rejected the seduction theory (i.e., his initial theory that hysteria resulted from a real seduction) for an understanding of hysteria as an effect of seduction in fantasy (which may or may not have "really" occurred) that he was led to posit the existence of the unconscious, and psychoanalysis proper came into being. Furthermore, with this shift away from the grounding of psychical processes in phenomenological causality to fantasmatic causality, Freud effectively redefined fantasy as the elementary field of the subject's "inner life," or psyche, and thereby set the psychoanalytic notion of fantasy apart from conventional understandings of it as simple illusion, the definitional antithesis of reality. By making fantasy the arena or language of the psyche, Freud suggests that fantasy is as much a reality for the subject as the material world, that it shapes his or her existence as fully as any "external" force.

Laplanche and Pontalis contend that in Freudian theory fantasy assumes a structural function, that it plays a determinative role in psychical processes. In opposition to "commonsense" readings of fantasy as simple wish fulfillment, the imaginary space in which the intentional subject lives out or stages its desire, in psychoanalysis the reverse is in fact the case—it is fantasy that stages the subject's desire by giving that desire its form. This point is elegantly expressed in what is undoubtedly the most frequently cited phrase in the whole essay: "Fantasy is . . . not the object of desire, but its setting," "its *mise-en-scène*" (26). That is, fantasy is the mechanism through which desire is constituted and played out. For psychoanalysis there is not first a desiring subject who then produces fantasy to satisfy his or her desires; rather, fantasy produces the desire and the subject's relations within that desire. This difficult thesis is explained by Slavoj Žižek as follows: "The fundamental point of psychoanalysis is that desire is not something given in advance, but something that has to be constructed—and it is precisely the role of fantasy to give the coordinates of the subject's desire, to specify its object, to locate the position the subject assumes in it. It is only through fantasy that the subject is constituted as desiring: *through fantasy we learn how to desire*." [65]

The structuring role of fantasy is most evident in the Freudian notion of the primal fantasies, or *Urphantasein*. Freud was struck from an early stage by the repetition of certain fantasy scenarios recounted to him in analysis, which led him to speculate that, behind the myriad narratives woven from an individual's mnemonic traces, there might lie a finite number of privileged unconscious fantasy structures that organize and motivate the subject's fantasmatic production. He termed these "primal," or "original," fantasies and argued that they provided fantasmatic "explanations" to some of the fundamental enigmas of subjective existence. Freud outlined three original fantasies in particular—fantasies of the primal scene, seduction, and castration. Each fantasy structure seeks to represent an "origin" to the subject; thus, fantasies of the primal scene picture the origins of the subject itself in parental coitus, fantasies of seduction figure the origins of sexuality, and fantasies of castration represent the origins of sexual difference. It is important to note that Freud believed these fantasy structures to be prototypical, to precede and determine the subject and his or her fantasy life. Through the originary fantasies, the subject receives and takes up certain key libidinal scenarios that then help form the matrices of his or her desire.

If the primal fantasies precede and shape the subject's own fantasmatic production, they do so, however, not as an autonomous structure in dominance, a transcendental absolute, but as a "*prestructure* which is actualized and transmitted by the parental fantasies."[66] As Laplanche and Pontalis argue, the original fantasies are always constructed and generated culturally; they come to us through the cultural discourses of history—most specifically, through "the history or the legends of parents, grandparents and the ancestors: . . . this spoken or secret discourse, going on prior to the subject's arrival, within which he [*sic*] must find his way" (18). The structures of fantasy theorized by Freud as primal thus preexist the "instance" of the individual subject or fantasy—inasmuch as they already circulate in the culture into which the human subject is born—but are themselves dependent on and shaped by the variable contexts of those "instances" and their specific historical articulations. As Laplanche and Pontalis put it, the "original fantasy is first and foremost fantasy—it lies beyond the history of the subject but nevertheless in history—a kind of language and a symbolic sequence, but loaded with elements of imagination; a structure, but activated by contingent elements" (18).

To theorize this more fully, Laplanche and Pontalis mobilize the Freudian notion of deferred action, or retroactivity (*Nachträglichkeit*). This is one of those curious concepts in Freudian thought, absolutely pivotal, yet never really explicated in substantive terms. Its full significance was only fully apprehended "retroactively" itself in Lacan's recuperative rereadings.[67] It is, however, crucial to the Freudian theory of fantasy wherein it describes both the temporal and causal relations of fantasmatic production. Briefly, *Nachträglichkeit* refers to how a secondary figure or scene recalls and thus revises an earlier scene for the subject, resulting in either new meaning for the earlier scene or providing it with psychical effectivity for the first time. This is not, it must be stressed, simply retrospection, where the latter scene or figure is transferred back onto an earlier site; both scenes "exist" and have a specificity of their own. However, in deferred action, or retroactivity, the latter scene reactivates the earlier scene, constitutes it precisely *as* a scene, a figure of psychical significance.[68] Laplanche and Pontalis take this notion of deferred action as the organizing "logic" of fantasy to mean that the scenarios of fantasy theorized by Freud as primal do not function as a priori structures in toto with a given content or set of contents but as culturally motivated potentialities that are only ever constituted "retroactively" within the variable frames of the individual fantasy event.

This dialectical understanding of fantasy as a product of both the transindividual (pre)structures of primal fantasy and the contextual contingency of the individual fantasizing subject helps refine even further Laplanche and Pontalis's assertion that fantasy represents "the *mise-en-scène* of desire," for it suggests that fantasy is the product neither simply of the subject's "internal" imagination nor of culture's "external" impositions but the negotiational coarticulation, or "setting," of both. It represents fantasy as a scene that is spoken by the subject's desire, but that also and simultaneously speaks that desire, producing it within a prestructured regime of symbolic meaning. In this way, fantasy can be seen as a psychical performance of the subject in which all the various strands, elements, signifiers of his or her individual sociohistorical position are processed and replayed through a system governed by laws antecedent to but only ever constituted in the individual fantasmatic moment.[69]

On the grounds of this fertile (re)conceptualization, Laplanche and Pontalis outline fantasy's distinctive features. They argue that the logic of retroactive determination operative in fantasy puts in question the traditional practice of differentiating between unconscious and conscious, or primary and secondary, levels of fantasy—where the latter are generally regarded as symptomatic effects of the former—because it demonstrates that both levels determine the organization of fantasmatic production. Indeed, they contend that "the unity of the fantasy whole depends . . . on [its] mixed nature, in which both the structural and the imaginary can be found, although to different degrees."[70]

They also suggest that the "mixed" nature of fantasy—its construction in the variable pull of primal prestructure and contingent particularity or, shifting the terms slightly, primary and secondary levels—means that the role of the fantasizing subject itself is equally prone to structural variability. Following Freud's famous analysis of the fantasy "a child is being beaten," they argue that the subject in fantasy is not always represented in stable terms but can frequently be dispersed across shifting, even contradictory, points of identification. "In fantasy," they write, "the subject does not pursue the object or its sign: he appears caught up himself in the sequence of images. He forms no representation of the desired object, but is himself represented as participating in the scene. . . . As a result, the subject, although always present in the fantasy, may be so in a desubjectivized form, that is to say, in the very syntax of the sequence in question" (26). By way of example, Laplanche and Pontalis argue, somewhat polemically perhaps, that the "typical" scenarization of the seduction fantasy, "a father seduces a daughter," constitutes a "scenario with multiple entries, in which nothing shows whether the subject will be immediately located as *daughter*; it can as well be fixed as *father*, or even in the term *seduces*" (22).

With its radical retheorization of the interrelations between identification, desire, and representation and its use of explicitly cinematic tropes such as visualization and mise-en-scène, the psychoanalytic theory of fantasy schematized by Laplanche and Pontalis offers obvious and wide-ranging potential for applications to film. As mentioned, this potential has not gone unrecognized with some film critics turning in recent years to this theory of fantasy and using it in their work. Most of them start from the premise that film is itself a central form of fantasy; that in the dark of the movie house we engage libidinal scenarios and articulate desires that are, "for the most part, [ordinarily] only ever admitted on the couch."[71] Significantly, many critics who have mobilized psychoanalytic theories of fantasy have done so in the context of explicit attempts to theorize spectatorial diversity. Much like the appropriation of cultural studies discussed earlier, fantasy theory has been widely promoted as a way to move beyond the homogenizing limitations of structuralist film theory to a recognition of spectatorship as plural and heterogeneous. Although not all critics use and interpret psychoanalytic readings of fantasy in the same way, most develop their analyses of spectatorial diversity on the basis of two interrelated key points in those readings: the multiple and shifting nature of subjective identification in fantasy, and the active role of the subject and his or her personal history in the determination of fantasmatic forms.

The first point about the multiple nature of fantasmatic identification has emerged as arguably the most influential component of the entire "turn to fantasy" in film studies. For many, the accent on pluriposition- ality in fantasy theory provides the greatest rejoinder to traditional theo- ries of spectatorship by showing that, far from being "interpellated" into fixed, unitary positions of desire/identification, spectators are capable of taking up multiple positions in their engagements with film. In her in- fluential essay "Fantasia," Elizabeth Cowie makes this a primary claim in her promotion of fantasy theory as an alternative paradigm for criti- cal analyses of spectatorship. Following Laplanche and Pontalis's argu- ments about the transactional, mobile nature of fantasmatic identifica- tion, Cowie contends that film, as a form of fantasy, "present[s] a varying of subject position[s] so that the subject takes up more than one posi- tion and thus is not fixed."[72] She illustrates this with detailed analyses of several classic films in which she focuses on the variety of identificatory positions potentially available to spectators. In an analysis of the 1949 film *The Reckless Moment*, for instance, Cowie highlights how the film presents an "unstoppable sliding of positions" for the spectator; a slid- ing that "involve[s] the diverse positions father, mother, child, lover, wife, husband, each of which are never finally contained by any one charac- ter.... The film thus illustrates the way in which at its most radical ... the staging of desire has multiple entries, where the subject is both present *in* the scene and interchangeable with any other character" (101). The significance of this argument for theories of spectatorship is enormous. Within the terms set up by fantasmatic pluripositionality, spectatorship is understood almost necessarily to move across and incorporate differ- ent, even disparate, positions—many of which directly compete with, if not counteract, the hegemonic positions "preferred" by dominant textual and cultural forms. As Donald Greig puts it in his assessment of fantasy theory, with "its stress upon the interchangeability of roles, for spectator and character," fantasy theory opens up "the possibility for the spectator, ultimately, of positions, rather than the one (male) subject position that the text seems to favour. This is to assert not only multiple entries into the text, but also multiple identities within the text."[73]

In certain respects, this argument sounds similar to claims about shifting identifications and libidinal investments made by proponents of theories of queer spectatorship discussed earlier. Just as I counseled the need for caution there to avoid falling into the utopic trap of reading spectatorship as unstructured and identityless, so, too, a certain degree of vigilance is required in relation to the arguments about spectatorial plurality in fantasy-based film theory. Some critics have openly attacked this accent on fantasmatic pluripositionality, arguing that it can lead to "the optimistically silly notion of an unbounded mobility of identities for the spectator-subject."[74] These critics point out that the notion of identificatory fluidity outlined by psychoanalysis is largely based on unconscious fantasies that are, by definition, unstructured and that this is very different from cinema, in which fantasmatic scenarios and the subject's access to them are far more coded and contained. Most fantasy-based readings are careful, however, to account for this, asserting that, though spectatorial identification in film may be more complex and diverse than previously thought, it is hardly "unstructured" and certainly not "limitless." Cowie, for example, is quick to point out that because film is a public form of fantasy, it is inevitably more "censored" than many of the private fantasy forms discussed by psychoanalysis. She notes that the conventions of film, especially those associated witn narrative, impose "a relative coherence and continuity" on the "heterogeneous assortment" of a given film's fantasmatic scenes and that they thereby "seek to *find* (produce) a proper place for the subject." However—and this is the crucial point— these attempts at organization/censorship cannot be seen in isolation; they cannot be separated from the potentials of identificatory plurality that they seek to structure/contain. Following Laplanche and Pontalis's arguments about the structural inmixing of original/secondary or unconscious/conscious modes in fantasy, Cowie claims that it is "the form of tension and play between the fixing of narrative—the secondary elaboration—and the lack of fixity of the subject" in fantasy, "which would seem to be important, and not any already-given privileging of one over the other." She also stresses that the "fixing" of positions at the level of form does not necessarily translate into an automatic fixing at the level of spectatorial engagement. At the very close of her essay, Cowie asserts, "While the terms of [fantasy might be] fixed, the places of . . . spectators in relation to those terms are not." What "moves" finally in film for fantasy theory is not so much the text or the fantasy scenario itself but the spectator, "the only place in which all the terms of the fantasy come to rest."[75]

This provides a bridge into the second important feature of fantasy-based film theory: the active role of spectators in determining fantasmatic forms and relations. The distinction between the formal terms of film qua fantasy and the position(s) of spectators in relation to those terms is itself underwritten by an implicit assumption that spectators are not passive pawns of a discursive or cinematic system in dominance but that they play a pivotal and active role in determining which positions will be taken up in film, as well as what meanings and pleasures will be articulated. In their wide-ranging history of film theory, Lapsley and Westlake argue that the greatest contribution made by fantasy theory to critical understandings of spectatorship is its restoration of a much needed agential dimension to the spectator-subject, a demonstration that the spectator is not just "constituted" but is also "constituting."[76] This restoration of agency is not, of course, a restoration of intentionality in the sense of humanist conceptions of the subject as self-present agent of free will. It will be noted that the spectator-subject is still referred to as "constituted." However, the way in which fantasy theory understands the "constituted" nature of the spectator-subject is such that it allows a certain room for agency. The concept of the spectator mobilized in fantasy theory is not limited to the site of the film-text alone; it encompasses and addresses the productions of the spectator in wider systems of meaning and desire. The spectator of fantasy theory is understood as "always already" a constituted psychosocial subject, "always already" positioned within diverse, but determinate, networks of sociosymbolic organization; and it is precisely because of this that the spectator is seen to play an active role in the determination of the cinematic experience, adopting positions and constructing meanings in accordance with those networks and the variable patterns of his or her own desire. Spectatorship is defined in fantasy theory as a site of continuous interaction between the potential fantasmatic scenarios signaled by the text and the shifting psychosocial frames inhabited by the individual spectator. Different configurations of psychosocial organization will affect spectatorship in decisive ways, determining how meaning is produced, what pleasures are derived, and which positions of identification on offer in film will be taken up and which will be refused. Fantasy theory, thus, enforces a radical reconceptualization of spectatorship in terms of absolute difference both in recognition of the shifting mobility of film's fantasmatic potentials and "in recognition of the uniquely determined complexity of the psychic economy of each spectator. Fantasy means diversity of response to the same film, with . . . spectator[s] enunciating their own economy of desire through it" (94–95).

It is here that the full potential of fantasy theory for a theorization of gay spectatorships becomes apparent. By redefining cinematic reception as a localized practice contingent on the framing psychosocial discourses of the spectator's subjectivity, fantasy theory asserts that the libidinal coding of spectatorship—its organization into particular patterns of desire—is itself a contingent and, thus, variable effect of these same discourses. As a modality of subjectivity, gayness emerges in this context as a significant frame of spectatorial determination that can be seen, even if only theoretically, to fundamentally shape cinematic engagement, not only generating particular formations of desire in reading but also governing the diverse receptions and uses of cinema by gay-identified subjects.

The receptivity of fantasy theory for analyses of gay spectatorship is in fact noted and partially explored by Teresa de Lauretis in *The Practice of Love: Lesbian Sexuality and Perverse Desire,* in which she uses the psychoanalytic concept of fantasy to mount a wide-ranging theorization of lesbian sexuality and subjectivity. In particular, she seeks to chart how the libidinal and fantasy formations of lesbian subjectivity affect practices or forms of "lesbian sexual structuring and self-representation."[77] In one section, de Lauretis develops this theoretical matrix in relation to cinema by posing and addressing the "subjective and self-reflexive question: How do I [as a lesbian] look [in film]?" This question clearly operates on several levels:

How do I see—what are the modes, constraints, and possibilities of my seeing, the terms of vision for me? How am I seen—what are the ways in which I'm seen or can be seen, the conditions of my visibility? And more—how do I look *on,* as the film unrolls from reel to reel in the projector, as the images appear and the story unfolds up on the screen, as the fantasy scenario unveils and the soundtrack plays on in my head? (85)

Although she focuses predominantly on the circulation of fantasy in cinematic relations of lesbian representation, de Lauretis does look at—albeit intermittently—how fantasy functions in and influences lesbian spectatorship. Here she takes up the fantasy-based argument that "spectatorial desire and identification . . . rest less on cinematic conventions or forms . . . than on the spectator's subjectivity . . . or subjecthood" and uses it to suggest that the specific frameworks of lesbian subjectivity give rise to equally specific formations of spectatorship.

In keeping with fantasy theory's combined psychosocial accent, de Lauretis defines these frameworks of subjectivity as including both "the spectator's psychic and fantasmatic configuration, the places or positions that she or he may be able to assume in the structure of desire" and the spectator's social configurations, "the ways in which she or he is located in social relations of sexuality, race, class, gender, etc., the places she or he may be able to assume as subject in the social." Together "these complex subject processes" work to shape cinematic reading, "engag[ing] or *prevent[ing]* spectatorial identification" and desire in different ways (129). In the case of lesbian subjectivity, its interdependent social and psychic configurations provide the lesbian-identifying spectator with a unique set of perspectives on and entry points into the fantasy scenarios of film that in turn give rise to potentially different formations of meaning and desire. To recast an assertion made in an earlier section of her book, de Lauretis suggests that "lesbianism . . . is a form of psychosocial subjectivity that entails a different production of reference and meaning" for the lesbian spectator (xvii). Although it remains frustratingly underdeveloped, de Lauretis's argument here highlights the considerable potential opened up by fantasy theory for an exploration of gay spectatorships, as well as providing some exemplary guidelines for such an exploration. It suggests that the reconceptualization of spectatorship in fantasy theory as contingent on the psychosocial formations of the spectator's subjectivity provides an ideal conceptual paradigm within which to address questions of gay spectatorial specificity, enabling a critical recognition and analysis of the determinative role played by the variable psychosocial discourses of gay subjectivities on cinematic desire, identification, and reading.

Another way to approach this issue—one that provides a slightly more formalized framework within which to locate the type of analysis that these comments point to—may be through the psychoanalytic notion of the "fantasmatic." Although I have largely been using the term *fantasmatic* in its more pedestrian form as an adjective, it also has a more specialized meaning in psychoanalytic theory—if not yet film theory—as a noun that refers to precisely those organizations of fantasy and desire discussed by de Lauretis that subtend and structure subjectivities and subjective relations. The term *fantasmatic*—or *phantasmatic* as it is sometimes written—was first used in this sense by Laplanche and Pontalis in their collobarative "dictionary," *The Language of Psychoanalysis*, to formalize Freud's insight that every aspect of subjective behavior is governed in some way by the unconscious structures of fantasy and desire that we, as subjects in the symbolic, all take up in various and variable ways. In his 1912 paper, "The Dynamics of Transference," Freud refers to this underlying complex of unconscious fantasy and desire as a "stereotype plate . . . which is constantly repeated—constantly reprinted afresh—in the course of the person's life." [78] Laplanche and Pontalis develop this argument by forwarding the notion of the fantasmatic, which they suggest highlights more forcefully the "structuring action" of fantasy on subjective life. They define the fantasmatic as the particular network of fantasy and desire that subtends and motivates not only the more immediately recognizable manifestations of the unconscious such as "dreams, symptoms, acting out, repetitive behaviour" but "even [those] aspects of behaviour that are far removed from imaginative activity, and which appear at first glance to be governed solely by the demands of reality." As they write, it is "the subject's life as a whole which is . . . shaped and ordered by" the fantasmatic. [79]

In her expository discussion of this argument, Kaja Silverman describes the fantasmatic as "the 'blueprint' for each subject's desire." [80] Every subject, she explains, "lives its desire from *someplace*, and the fantasmatic is the mechanism through which that subject-position is articulated" (5). The libidinal scenarios and identificatory positions that each subject takes up at the level of unconscious fantasy in the fantasmatic "map . . . out a symbolic position for the subject," "regulating [not only his or her] erotic investment[s]" but his or her social and cultural investments as well (355). The notion of the fantasmatic as an unconscious "blueprint of desire" is used by Silverman as a theoretical model with which to speculate about the possible psychosocial dynamics of diverse subjectivities. Different subjectivities, she contends, are frequently grounded in and produced by different fantasmatic organizations. In her study *Male Subjectivity at the Margins*, Silverman explicitly theorizes the fantasmatic properties of "deviant" or marginal male subjectivities such as masochistic, traumatized, and, significantly for my purposes, homosexual male subjectivities. She argues that these diverse subjectivities are framed by an unconventional pattern of desire and identification at the level of fantasmatic organization—that is, at the level of unconscious fantasy and desire—that sets them apart from hegemonic forms of male subjectivity. Thus, in the case of masochistic male subjectivities, Silverman argues for the presence of an unconscious scenario of feminization and paternal deposition at the fantasmatic level. In relation to male homosexual subjectivities, she speculates that the fantasmatic organizations of these subjectivities are potentially marked by shifting psychic scenarios of maternal identification. I discuss these and other aspects of Silverman's important work in fuller detail in subsequent chapters. My interest here is to highlight how the notion of the fantasmatic can be used to frame theoretical discussions about the *psychosocial* specificity of various subjectivities.

I stress the term *psychosocial* here, for on the surface of this overview it may seem that the notion of the fantasmatic is predominantly psychic in nature. However, given the way psychoanalysis conceives of fantasy as the very process by which social realities are internalized by and for the subject, the fantasmatic necessarily encompasses the social in primary terms. As Silverman notes, "the images [and fantasies of the fantasmatic] within which the subject "finds" itself always *come to it from outside*," from the networks of language and culture, and, as such, the fantasmatic is itself inevitably "marked by historicity," produced in and by the determinate relations of culture and history (6–7). Furthermore, the fantasmatic is never static, never fixed in some mythological moment of infantile psychic constitution but, as Laplanche and Pontalis assert, is "constantly [changing and] drawing in new material" according to the shifting demands of the subject's social contexts.[81] The fantasmatic thus continues to respond to and is directly shaped by sociocultural forces throughout the subject's life. This latter assertion clearly emanates out of the general theorization of fantasy discussed earlier as simultaneously structural and contingent and suggests that the fantasmatic needs to be understood in similar terms. Like fantasy itself, the fantasmatic functions structurally to produce and position the subject within paradigms of desire and meaning that preexist and transcend the individual subject. However, the realization of the fantasmatic, its coming-into-being as well as its continued effectivity in the subject's life, is itself wholly contingent, dependent on the determinate conditions that frame the subject in his or her cultural and historical particularity.

The notion of the fantasmatic, thus defined, is useful within discussions of gay spectatorship, for it provides a productive paradigm for formalizing theoretical analyses of the structuring effects of gay specificity on spectatorial engagements. The fantasmatic understood as the *combinatoire* of unconscious fantasies and desires that subtends the subject's psychic, erotic, and cultural investments allows critical speculation about both the types of psychosocial organizations that may be specific to gay subjectivities and the possible implications they may generate for spectatorship. As a conceptual paradigm, the fantasmatic condenses and upholds many of the various critical issues I have been flagging in this chapter. The fact that the fantasmatic is located and understood at the interface of both psychic and social registers allows for the type of combined psychosocial analysis that is required for a sustained exploration of gay spectatorial forms. A theory of the fantasmatic enables multi-leveled analyses of gay spectatorial specificity, focusing, whether together or separately, simultaneously or consecutively, on the full and complex range of psychic, social, and historical determinants that constitute gayness as a site of identification and that frame gay cinematic reading relations.

Further, because the fantasmatic is seen in its organizational effects to be simultaneously structural and contingent, it upholds the principles of specificity that were identified earlier as indispensable for a theory of gay spectatorship. The logic of *Nachträglichkeit*, or retroactive constitution, that governs the psychoanalytic reading of fantasy and that signifies that fantasmatic production always and only occurs in the simultaneous pull of transindividual psychocultural narratives and the contingencies of individual instances instates the same dual focus on structural and local axes prescribed by critical arguments about specificity and performativity. To suggest that a particular fantasy scenario or psychosocial configuration may form part of a general gay fantasmatic in no way predicts or preempts how that may be realized (or not) by individual gay-identifying subjects. The most that can be targeted and offered in a fantasy-based reading of gay spectatorship is a theoretical imaging of certain potentialities of gay sexualities/subjectivities and their effects on cinematic reception. This in turn helps guard against any simplistic understanding of the types of psychosocial formations outlined in and by a formal model of the gay fantasmatic as exhaustive of the gay subjectivities it purports to describe. As stressed earlier, no subject is ever defined solely in terms of his or her gayness, and it is crucial to bear in mind that the discourses of gay subjectivity will always be inflected and, in some cases, totally recast by the wide range of competing social and psychic discourses through and across which individual subjects are always positioned. With its built-in accent on contingency, the notion of the fantasmatic helps keep this fundamental principle at the forefront of critical attention.

I propose, therefore, to mobilize the notion of the fantasmatic as a frame for my own theoretical readings and analyses of gay spectatorial specificity. As a broad conceptual paradigm, this notion enables a critical theorization of the general dynamics of gay spectatorship—the patterns, tendencies, and repetitions that cohere across diverse spectatorial relations and that index the structuring operations of gayness in and on those relations—without hypostatizing those dynamics or reifying them as prescriptive structures in dominance. Such a framework also allows for a heuristic abstraction of the specificities of gayness from the wider field of social, historical, and psychical differences without diminishing the determinative force of those differences or denying the transformative effects they can and do have on sexual identities and meanings. Put simply, the fantasmatic represents gay spectatorship as a processual activity in which the forms of gayness (the fantasies, desires, discourses, relations, practices, and knowledges that constitute gayness as a site of psychocultural subjectivity) figure as determinative categories but in ways that are wholly provisional. How those categories function in material instances and how their determinative effects are played out by individual figures cannot be guaranteed in advance but will depend on the full range of variables that frame and constitute those particular moments.

Using the concept of the fantasmatic thus defined, I explore in the following chapters some potential points of intersection and exchange between the psychosocial specificities of gay male subjectivity and relations of film spectatorship. Spectatorship is a vital but exceedingly complex site for the production and performance of gay male identifications. It has assumed a vast range of productive functions and effects for gay subjectivities/cultures, enabling articulations of gay subcultural identity, fostering formations of gay desire, and providing an endless source of material for the production of gay meanings. The value of fantasy theory lies in its capacity to recognize and analyze the structuring dynamics of these processes without denying their heterogeneity or reducing the almost endless variability of their unpredictable effects.

The Hollywood musical as queer spectacle: poster art for *The Pirate* (1948)
(author's collection)

Chapter Two ⌒ FANTASMATIC ESCAPADES:

GAY SPECTATORSHIPS AND QUEER NEGOTIATIONS

OF THE HOLLYWOOD MUSICAL

He could hear his own running feet, and he could feel cobbles underfoot through the soles of his shoes. The bricks were bright yellow, so bright that it hurt his eyes. "Wait for me!" he called. And they all turned, Judy Garland, and the Scarecrow and the Lion. He caught up with them.

"Can I come too? Can I come too?" he asked them, panting. The fields were bright red, and the sky was full of a white smiling face, and it was snowing too, flowers and snow together, and there was music, grand and happy at the same time.

"Why of course you can," said Judy Garland.

—Geoff Ryman, *Was*

To begin "fleshing out" the theoretical arguments I have been advancing about film, fantasy, and gay spectatorial specificity, I focus in this chapter on gay male engagements with the Hollywood musical. Gay subcultural fascinations with the Hollywood musical are arguably the most visible, certainly the most frequently cited, facet of gay spectatorial formations, yet they remain curiously undertheorized, even unacknowledged, in contemporary film and cultural studies. Alexander Doty notes that "of the articles and books written about film musicals only the revised edition of Jane Feuer's *Hollywood Musicals* [*sic*] goes beyond a passing remark in considering . . . gay and lesbian reception practices. . . . While there has been a rich history of queers producing and reading th[is] genre . . . , surprisingly little has been done to formally express this cultural history."[1]

The musical is also an important genre of classical Hollywood cinema. As a category of textual organization, metacritical discourse, and cinematic reception, genre provides a useful context within which to pursue questions of spectatorial diversity. Genres are exceedingly complex signifying formations, made up of literally thousands of texts and intertexts, including most obviously the films themselves and their myriad structural interrelations as well as the wide range of interreferential discourses that circulate around and help constitute genre films—advertisements, studio publicity, critical reviews, popular and academic studies, fan discourses, and so on. This (over)abundant intertextuality means that genres are sites of a radical semiotic polysemy, a plurality of meanings, replete with all the complexities, discrepancies, contradictions, and possibilities for variable interpretation that this entails. In this respect, genre is similar to that other major reference point of popular cinematic reception, stardom, for both are complex intertextual systems with multivalent functions. And just as "cinematic spectatorship take[s] on a different cast when perceived through the phenomenon of stardom understood intertextually," so too spectatorship "looks" differently in the context of an analysis of genre, since the polysemic nature of genre foregrounds possibilities of spectatorial difference and negotiation.[2]

To delineate a broad-based model of gay spectatorial reading that may then be expanded and refined in subsequent discussions, much of this chapter focuses on questions of reading practice. What are the procedures of queer reading? What are some of the possible strategies used by gay audiences in their receptions and reconstructions of the musical? How do gay spectators use texts to articulate gay fantasies and meanings? At first glance these issues may seem rather mechanical, especially in comparison with the broad focus and theoretical timbre of the preceding chapter. However, these discussions of gay reading practices are still firmly informed by and will make important contributions to the theoretical complex that I have been advancing. In particular, these discussions will take up the fantasy-based argument that spectatorship is a process of coconstitution played out between text, spectator, and the psychosocial dynamics of both.

At its most extreme, and perhaps its most important, fantasy theory radically retheorizes cinematic textuality and interpretation, turning around many of the most ingrained assumptions of film and cultural studies. In their study of the shifting receptions of the fictional figure of James Bond, Tony Bennett and Janet Woollacott assert that cultural theory has long been burdened by a persistent metaphysical conceptualization of the text as possessing some form of existence of its own that is either outside or antecedent to the readings and interpretations it generates. They argue that this has resulted in a reductive, ahistoricizing abstraction of textual meanings from the material frames of their constitution. Because texts can have "no existence prior to or independently of the varying 'reading formations' in which they have been constituted as objects-to-be-read," it is absurd and misleading, they suggest, to ascribe an ontological integrity to the text or to speak of it as if it remained constant outside its always variable (re)production in specific instances of reading.[3] Even the cultural studies model of negotiation that, they concede, provides one of the most nuanced, "socially oriented approach[es] to the question of reading" still promotes a metaphysical view of the text as something that has a virtual identity of its own. The model of negotiation may provide for "a variability of reader response," but "when all is said and done, such variations are conceived as merely different responses to 'the same text'" (62). Bennett and Woollacott claim, on the other hand, that different readers produce not only different readings of the same text, they produce in effect different texts. Consequently, it is necessary to recognize the fundamental contingency of textual reading: that neither texts nor readers can exist independently of the other and "the processes through which the struggle for textual meanings is socially enacted" (65).

Such a recognition is in fact already operating within fantasy theory, particularly in its central notion of *Nachträglichkeit*, or retroactive constitution—a notion that, if carried over into cultural analysis, problematizes, if not collapses, any attempt to treat texts, readers, and readings as discrete entities. The logic of *Nachträglichkeit* is used in psychoanalysis to argue for the simultaneous constitution of fantasy across both structural and specific axes. According to this logic, fantasy is always determined in the simultaneous pull of both the transindividual scenarios of desire to which the subject as cultural product is heir and the frames of reference inhabited by the fantasizing subject in his or her psychocultural particularity. Neither side can exist without the other and, because of this, both need to be understood in their mutual interdependence.

In relation to film this can be taken to mean that both poles of constitution in spectatorship—textual and contextual—play equal, interdependent roles and that, therefore, it is impossible to define the two individually. Although the text clearly functions structurally, determining the spectator's desire by providing it with a scenario, a mise-en-scène, the particular form that the film-text assumes, its realization, as it were, is itself dependent on and determined by the practice of its reading and the highly variable social, historical, and psychical discourses that frame that practice. Following the logic of simultaneous coconstitution, fantasy theory suggests that there can be no text outside the contingent framework of its specific realization, that the text is always produced—and variably so—in the determinate conditions of the specific reading instance. In this way, fantasy theory goes further than almost any other critical paradigm in stressing the absolute contingency of the text on its contextual particularity. Because fantasy theory asserts that the text can only ever exist in the cultural, historical, and psychic situatedness—not to mention variability—of its particular reading, it problematizes any attempt to mark out certain elements as fixed features of some essential intratextuality. Even in the case of so-called dominant textual features, they can never be seen as intrinsic attributes of a text divorced from its actualization in reading because notions of what is dominant in terms of either textual, aesthetic, ideological, or libidinal codes are themselves entirely relational, dependent on the proclivities, knowledges, and frames of reference espoused by the spectator in his or her specificity. This does not mean that the text ceases to have any power in fantasy theory. Obviously, the text will always play a central role in the determination of cinematic meanings, providing the very grounds of possibility of reading/spectatorship, as well as limiting the range of potential readings through its orchestration of codes and its location in particular traditions of representation and reception. However, according to the logic of simultaneous coconstitution proposed by fantasy theory, the determinative role and effects of the text can never be known outside that text's articulation in specific reading contexts, its situatedness in variable histories and practices of spectatorship, and therefore they can never be defined as essential properties of the text in dominance. Any similarities or continuities that exist between readings of a given text are, according to this schema, more the result of shared psychocultural frames and perspectives among audiences than of a putative essential constancy within the text itself.

Fantasy theory thus lays the grounds for a radical retheorization of textual reading that blurs and collapses the distinctions between texts, readers, and readings. It suggests that, far from being stable "containers" of meaning that have an existence of their own, texts are in fact inherently relational, dependent on and determined by the shifting conditions of their specific readings. This in turn redefines the whole issue of meaning construction in film—suggesting that it is never simply a question of a text imposing its meaning on a passive spectator or, it must be said, of a spectator imposing its meaning on a text; rather, it is a relational process in which meaning arises through the *simultaneous enunciation of text and subjective fantasy.* The radical implications held out by this argument for reception studies are summarily identified by Teresa de Lauretis:

> What this means for theories of spectatorship is that only subjective readings can be given, however many other spectators may share them, and thus share in the fantasy that each reading subtends; and that no one spectator's reading of, or identification in, a film can be generalized as a property of the film (its fantasy) or merely an effect of *its* narration. In other words, . . . when it comes to engaging the spectator's fantasy and identification, a film's effects are neither structural (if structural is equated with universal) nor totally structured by the film (by its fantasy, narration, or form); rather, they are contingent on the spectator's subjectivity and subjecthood.[4]

In this chapter I explore and analyze this process of fantasmatic coconstitution in terms of gay spectatorial receptions of the Hollywood film musical. Gay readings of the Hollywood musical are produced in and through a structural process of negotiation between the variable potentials for queer meaning on offer in the musical text and the psychosocial or fantasmatic formations of gay specificity.

Gay Spectatorships and the Hollywood Musical

The gay male celebration of the Hollywood musical is one of the most widely noted aspects of gay spectatorial relations. As Al LaValley matter-of-factly puts it: "At the heart of gaycult, the aesthetically stylized genre of the musical reigns supreme."[5] The affinity between gay men and the musical is so intense as to have produced at times marked metaphoric associations. In gay subcultural argot, the term *musical* has long been used as a coded reference to homosexuality; to describe someone as "musical" or "into musicals" is to describe them as homosexual. "It is surely no coincidence," writes Phillip Brett, "that among the many code words and phrases for a homosexual man before Stonewall (and even since), 'musical' . . . ranked with others such as 'friend of Dorothy' [a reference to the 1939 MGM musical, *The Wizard of Oz*] as safe insider euphemisms."[6] In a more personal vein, Wayne Koestenbaum describes how as a child in the sixties and seventies his first incipient gay identifications were made not through a conscious recognition of same-sex erotic attractions but via his fondness for musical comedy: "I worried, listening to records of *Darling Lili, Oklahoma!, The Music Man, Company* and *No, No, Nanette*, that I would end up gay: I didn't know the word "gay" . . . but I had a clear impression (picked up from where?) that gays liked musical comedy."[7]

Even today, long after the demise of the musical as a central form of popular culture, the symbolic associations between musicals and male homosexuality seem to have lost little of their signifying resonances for gay subcultures. A glance through almost any of the scores of English-language gay magazines will attest to this. For example, a recent copy of *Outrage*, an Australian gay lifestyle "glossy," features two articles on musical-related themes, an essay on "show queens" and an interview with a local musical comedy star, Judi Connelli, as well as laudatory reviews of two new musical recordings. As John Thurfitt writes in one article, "in a culture which sometimes seems dominated by dance floor divas like Kylie and Madonna, it is interesting that musical theatre has lost none of its hold over gay men, and musical icons like Merman, Minnelli [and] Streisand . . . are perennial."[8]

It would, of course, be naive to assume that all gay men take the same pleasures in musicals or that these pleasures have somehow remained constant and unchanged over time. The historical marginalization of the musical—especially, perhaps, the Hollywood musical—has meant that it has become an increasingly rarefied taste, even within gay male subcultures. Younger gay or queer men tend not to respond to the musical with the same degree of devotion and personal attachment that often characterizes the receptions of this genre among (some) older gay men. The latter's receptions of the musical have invariably shifted in time, waxing and waning as the musical has moved from mass cultural form to nostalgic object. Even in its heyday during the midcentury, enthusiasms for the musical would not have been universal among gay men, being largely associated with—though, by no means, limited to—those white, middle-class men who composed the most affluent and, therefore, most visible constituency in urban gay subcultures. Nevertheless, the musical has exercised and continues to exercise considerable fascination for gay men with the result that, more than any other cinematic genre, it has developed as a singularly privileged site of and for gay subcultural investments. So much so that, even those gay-identifying men who claim no particular interest in or taste for the musical remain fundamentally subject to its gay associations. As D. A. Miller notes in his recent meditation on the cultural relations between gay men and the Broadway musical, "though not all gay men—nor even most—are in love with Broadway, those who aren't are hardly quit of the stereotype that insists they are, which appropriates their musical taste nonetheless by imposing on it the burden of *having to take a position* vis-à-vis the mythos of male homosexuality for which . . . an extreme devotion to the musical theatre is a chief token."[9]

Yet what is it about the musical that has made it such a resonant form for gay male discourses and identifications? One of the most common explanations for the enduring affinity between gay audiences and the musical is the genre's widely recognized status as "escapist entertainment." As Richard Dyer writes, musicals are generally seen to offer "the image of 'something better' to escape into, or something we want deeply that our day-to-day lives don't provide. Alternatives, hopes, wishes—these are the stuff of utopia, the sense that things could be better, that something other than what is can be imagined and maybe realized."[10] For many commentators this is the precise source of gay fascination with the musical. LaValley, for example, asserts categorically that gay men have been drawn to the musical because of its "utopian level of wish fulfillment, charged with bold colors, elegant style, dance, costume, and song." He extends this reading to gay spectatorship in general, arguing that "movies have always held a particular attraction" for gays because "here they found hints of a utopian and alternate world, one more congenial to their sexuality and repressed emotions."[11] More recently, Peter Kemp has argued that the reason the musical has proven "such a compelling source of endless appeal for gay men" is the genre's construction of "a stylised non-naturalism, a formal out-of-this-world-ness that would particularly attract the culturally unconventional, the socially unacceptable."

> From the multi-populated, kaleidoscopic fantasies of visionary cine-choreographer, Busby Berkeley through to those "three cocks in a frock on a rock" in *The Adventures of Priscilla, Queen of the Desert* (1994), the narrative worlds of movie musicals have been decidedly surreal, unreal and escapist. . . . If you feel yourself to be "different", then filmusicals [*sic*] can take you out of yourself, can transport you on the wings of song or through the charge of dance on to somewhere else, some place better that's both different and familiar.[12]

Significantly, a number of the men who wrote to me as part of the preliminary background research I did for this project made similar use of a certain notion of escapism to explain their own personal commitments to the Hollywood musical. One gay man recounts:

> For me, growing up in the "safe" manicured sterility of Sacramento in the fifties, movie musicals were an escape into a different world of glamor and excitement. It was a world where anything could happen and often did. In so many ways, the world on the screen was the exact opposite to the straight world of suburban middle America in which I found myself, but that was *my* world, that was where I belonged and once a week on Saturdays I got to go home.[13]

Another younger gay man writes:

> My favourite type of film has always been the musical, especially the classic MGM musicals. I used to love watching these films on television as a kid. I used to think I was the only person my age to like these films but as I got older I recognised that there was a long tradition among gay men of loving the musical. . . . I've often wondered why this is so. I guess it's because musicals are out of the ordinary and they offer a form of escape.[14]

These attempts to represent and make sense of gay male fascinations with the Hollywood musical in terms of escapism are widespread, and in many ways the argument they advance is both persuasive and appealing. What I find particularly captivating about these readings is the way they define cinematic spectatorship as a privileged space of fantasmatic expression for gay-identifying subjects. These accounts explicitly suggest that gay men use their spectatorships of the Hollywood musical to articulate and shape their innermost fantasies and desires. As such, they provide a solid entry point for the type of fantasy-based inquiry into gay spectatorships that I am promoting. However, these accounts of gay fascinations with the musical in terms of escapism also present potential difficulties or limitations for a critical analysis.

For a start, these characterizations sound similar to pathologizing descriptions of homosexuality as a flight from reality that circulate with such enduring force in mainstream culture. One cannot help but wonder how much of the widespread popularity and resonance of these characterizations of gay spectatorship as pure escapism stems from how the trope of escapism already figures centrally in dominant constructions of male homosexuality. "The popular view of homosexuality," notes Michael Bronski, "is that it is a flight . . . , variously from women, from masculinity, from the 'responsibilities' of heterosexuality (i.e., wife, children, and a house in the suburbs), from male competition, or from the 'self.' "[15] This discursive tradition provides ample scope for the devaluation of gay spectatorial escapism, whether in relation to Hollywood film, in general, or the musical, in particular. Although most of the writers cited above are careful to avoid this type of reading, other critics have been less cautious and have explicitly interpreted gay subcultural obsessions with so-called escapist forms of entertainment like the musical as an indication of what they see as the vacuousness of much gay culture.[16]

Furthermore, though a reading of gay fascinations with the musical in terms of escapism or utopianism goes some of the way toward explaining the broad-based appeal this genre can hold for marginalized or disempowered groups such as gay men, it does not really tell us very much about the particularity of gay pleasures in the musical. What exactly is it within the musical that has spoken and continues to speak so powerfully to gay spectators? Nor do these accounts allow for a recognition and adequate appreciation of the dynamic, active nature of gay engagements with the Hollywood musical. In fact, these accounts tend to portray gay receptions of the musical as a largely abstract, passive affair. They imply that gay spectators simply and effortlessly escape into a fantasy world that is waiting tailor-made for them in the musical film. This reading ignores the rather obvious fact that, like most forms of mainstream cinema, the Hollywood musical is produced in, by, and for a culture that insists on the definitional primacy of heterosexuality and that, as a result, the utopian idylls it presents are almost universally heterosexual. One need only look at the enshrinement of heterosexuality in the titles of many Hollywood musicals like *Twenty Million Sweethearts* (1934), *For Me and My Gal* (1942), *Royal Wedding* (1951), *The Farmer Takes a Wife* (1953), and *Seven Brides for Seven Brothers* (1954) to gauge the extent to which the musical as a genre is predicated on an assumption of heterosexuality as celebratory ideal.

Some scholars have suggested that the musical may in fact be the most heterosexist of all Hollywood film forms. Patricia Mellencamp argues that the musical plays out and celebrates "the ritual of re-creation/procreation of the privileged heterosexual couple"; Steve Neale asserts that, in the musical, "heterosexual desire occupies a central . . . place . . . , its presence is a necessity, not a variable option." [17] The most influential version of this argument is presented by Rick Altman in his detailed 1987 study, *The American Film Musical*, in which he defines heterosexuality as the veritable sine qua non of the musical's entire structural organization. Altman argues that, unlike most classical films, which focus largely on the diegetic trajectory of a single character, the Hollywood musical follows a dual-focus structure of gendered parallelism in which a carefully balanced sequence of textual repetition and rhyme plays a masculine paradigm off a feminine one. This is generally represented by a leading male/female character couple—as Altman puts it, "in the musical *the couple is the plot*." [18] This basic sexual duality is overlaid by secondary competing oppositions, with each sex linked to "a particular attitude, value, desire, location, age or other characteristic attribute . . . [that] always begin diametrically opposed and mutually exclusive" but that end up reconciled in the grand utopian finale of hymeneal union. For Altman, the Hollywood musical serves an important ideological function by "fashion[ing] a myth out of the American courtship ritual" and naturalizing heterosexuality as compulsory norm. As he puts it: "The American film musical seems to suggest that the natural state of the adult human being is in the arms of an adult human being of the opposite sex" (24–32).

Such analyses highlight the inadequacy of simply reading off gay spectatorial passions for the musical as a direct effect of the utopian scenarios offered by the musical text, for they demonstrate the extent to which these scenarios assume and promote a heterocentrist economy of meaning/desire. If gay-identifying spectators do in fact use the Hollywood musical as a site to articulate their own utopian or escapist fantasies, then clearly they must engage in active and quite extensive processes of resistance and negotiation. This is not to say that gay spectators are somehow excluded from or incapable of making pleasurable psychocultural investments in a given fantasmatic scenario simply because it is coded as heterosexual. The gay male spectator's homosexuality does not endow him with an intrinsic aversion to or immunity against the appeals of a heterosexual fantasy; relations of desire and identification are never that clear-cut. Furthermore, as critics like Judith Mayne and Rhona Berenstein have argued, part of the appeal and fascination of cinema may actually lie in the very opportunities it provides for assuming sexual identifications different from those ordinarily assumed by the spectator in "real" life.[19] It could be entirely possible, therefore, that a pleasurable investment in and identification with heterosexuality is an integral component of gay receptions of the musical. Nevertheless, given the musical film's dominant tendencies toward supreme heterosexual idealization, there is a point at which one must acknowledge a fundamental misfit or incongruence between the (dominant) desires promoted by the musical text and the desires of the gay-identified spectator; and that, as a result, if the gay spectator is to appropriate the musical film for the construction and exploration of gay-identified fantasies and meanings, then this will require at least some form of textual disruption and refiguration.

For such processes of textual negotiation to work, they would need to open up a space within the musical film for alternative formations of (gay) fantasy and desire. In light of the arguments presented by theorists like Altman about the importance of textual closure in determining the musical film's dominant heteronormative agenda, the most effective strategy for any proposed practice of queer negotiation would be to refuse and undermine the musical's push toward closure. If the musical is structured to build up to a final, all-embracing moment of heterosexual union as utopian ideal, then a disruption of its linear trajectory toward closure would, perforce, also disrupt its textual path to heterosexual utopianization.

Several critics have suggested that such a resistance to clotural containment may in fact form a standard strategy of gay engagements with mainstream film in general. In her ethnographic-based study of lesbian receptions of *Personal Best*, Elizabeth Ellsworth argues that lesbian spectators consistently rejected that film's attempts at repressing the possibilities of lesbian desire opened up by the narrative within a safe, heterosexual ending.[20] She contends that they did this by focusing on the lesbian character at the close of the film rather than on the heterosexual couple, even though the film clearly defines the lesbian character as marginal and less important. At a more general level, Al LaValley claims that gay spectators habitually reject mainstream cinematic attempts to contain meaning within a heteronormative closure by disordering the dominant linear trajectory of filmic narrative in such a way as to give determinative supremacy not to the final moment of closure as is customary but to other textual features often repressed or marginalized by the recuperative processes of closure. He contends that gay spectators frequently

> shuck off last reel repentances, marriages, and moral condemnations as necessities of . . . the dominant heterosexual industry and audience. They treasure . . . film not so much for its narrative fulfillments as for its great moments, those interstices that [a]re often, ironically, the source of a film's real power. . . . These [moments] reveal the hidden and repressed facets of society, and gay audiences are apt to foreground them, whereas straight audiences, often oblivious to . . . or frightened by them, tend to repress them.[21]

This is a quite radical process of textual reconstruction by which gay spectators refute the functional power of closure to recontain signification within a heteronormative paradigm by prioritizing *other* moments — or moments of otherness — in the text, thereby opening the text up to the possibilities of alternative readings and desires.[22]

The issue here is not a reading practice that simply ignores the last ten minutes or so of a film. What the particular practice of gay spectatorial reading suggested here entails, rather, is an active reordering of the text that is both a refusal and a redefinition of the preferred meanings of a film's given clotural scenario. By making certain marginal textual features the organizational pivot of narrative meaning construction, this style of negotiational reading practice produces a radically restructured semiotic economy in which the "earlier" textual features thus privileged come to inflect a text's clotural scenario in such a way as to undermine its dominant significatory agenda and open it up to alternative interpretations. In the case of the musical, this may mean that, by latching on to certain moments or features that are marginal or oblique vis-à-vis the demands and concerns of the dominant (straight) narrative and making them central to the organization of their own textual engagements, gay spectators can redefine the clotural scenario of idealized heterosexual union promoted by the musical and refashion it to support the articulation of gay-identified fantasies and desires.

These gay negotiational reading practices are similar to those forms of critical reading "against the grain" proposed by certain film theorists as a way to expose and subvert a film's dominant ideological paradigm. Both forms of reading strategically locate and extend points of disruption in the text, points at which the control of the dominant narrative seems to falter and other potential meanings emerge. Within film theory, these points of textual fracture have largely been theorized in terms of a disruptive "excess"—marks of a signifying surplus that exceed the needs or demands of the dominant filmic narrative.[23] The concept of cinematic excess is based on the proposition that the film-text is the site of a complex semiotic heterogeneity that can never be totally reduced to or exhausted by a film's dominant narrative structures, and this heterogeneity is evident whenever the smooth functioning of the dominant representational conventions breaks down and permits a momentary outburst of diegetically unaccommodated signification. These moments of excess appear as a deviation from or a going beyond the motivations of dominant narrative demands either at the level of narrative content, such as certain scenes, shots, characters, or actions that have no apparent narrative function and bear little if any relation to dominant diegetic foci, or at the level of textual form, such as unconventional camera work, obtrusive editing styles, extravagant mise-en-scène, and the like. The concept of excess, then, allows one to gain greater analytical purchase on some of the specific strategies involved in gay negotiational readings of the musical text. If the moment of textual excess is understood as a symptomatic point of failure, a gap or rip in the fabric of dominant textual homogeneity, then it seems to recommend itself as a fertile point of reference for gay spectatorial resistances to and reconstructions of the heteronormative dynamics of mainstream film.

The Hollywood musical has in fact long been theorized as a privileged genre of excess. Stephen Heath, one of the leading theorists of filmic excess, argues that "the musical is an obvious and extreme example [of excess] with its systematic 'freedom' of space . . . and its shifting balances of narrative and spectacle."[24] As this might suggest, many arguments about cinematic excess and the musical film focus on what is perhaps the genre's defining feature—the deployment of both realist and nonrealist textual modes in its characteristic combination of spoken narrative and musical number—as the primary structure enabling this disruptive excess. With its characteristic "breaks" from linear narrative flow into spectacular song-and-dance sequences, the musical constructs a multileveled system of textual enunciation unique in mainstream film. The admixture of markedly different textual modes employed by the musical is something normally associated with avant-garde and experimental film forms. As a result of this unusual discursive pluralism, the Hollywood musical provides unprecedented scope for the articulation of some of the more heterogeneous dimensions of filmic signification. Jane Feuer, for example, argues that the narrative/number split produces a singular system of "multiple diegesis," a plurality of narrative forms. "The narrative with its third-person mode seems to represent a primary level. . . . But unlike other kinds of movies, a secondary level, presented in direct address and made up of singing and dancing, emerges from the primary level . . . [and] disturbs the equilibrium of the unitary flow of the narrative." Feuer points to the example of backstage musicals directed or, at least, partially directed by Busby Berkeley for Warner Brothers during the 1930s—*42nd Street* (1933), *Gold Diggers of 1933*, *Footlight Parade* (1933)—in which the musical numbers signal a radically different mode from that of the conventional narrative: "a separate universe, a world of cinematic excess and voyeuristic pleasure . . . an absolutely unfettered play of the imagination."[25]

Significantly, these moments of cinematic excess in the musical are frequently understood to signal an anarchic disruption of not only the dominant structures of classical narrative film form but the structures of textual and spectatorial desire as well. In this argument, the subversion of linear narrative form produced by the musical's "break" into song-and-dance occasions a correlative subversion of the text's dominant libidinal forms, a metaphoric slippage into the unconscious that produces a disruptive effusion of ordinarily censored erotic material. Just as the camera in the musical number breaks out of the confines of classical film form into the implausible perspectives and frenetic mobility of crab dollies, crane shots, split-screen montage, and the like, desire—textual and spectatorial—undergoes a similar transformation and is released into a range of libidinal formations. Musical spectacles, argues Patricia Mellencamp, "are momentarily subversive fantasy breaks in the . . . narrative superstructure. These breaks displace the temporal advance of the narrative, providing immediate, regular doses of gratification rather than delaying the pressures until The End. . . . Through this play, the psychical energies of the spectator are granted freer movement and the signifiers are less repressed." [26]

Another way to look at this, one that helps relate this discussion more explicitly to questions of gay specificity, is to think of the libidinal "excessiveness" of the musical number in terms of its representation of non- or even anti-oedipal formations of desire. Indeed, if, as many critics contend, the linear trajectory of narrative represents a structural replaying of heterocentric, oedipal development, then the musical's insistent breaks, or deviations, from narrative progression into nonlinear spectacle seem to all but beg this type of reading.[27] Within such a schema, the move from a teleological structure of narrative into a spatial structure of spectacle signaled by the musical's breaks into song-and-dance numbers becomes readable as a correlative move from a linear, oedipal economy of straight desire into a de-oedipalized framework of perverse desire. This is something suggested by Dana Polan when he writes that the moment of spectacle in the musical number "brings male and female together, but this moment is a moment outside the forward propulsion of time, *outside the impulse of a domestic desire that drives oedipal narrative along.*" [28]

This reading of the musical number as the site of a perverse, de-oedipalized eruption offers some potentially interesting inroads into an analysis of gay engagements with the Hollywood musical film. Psychoanalysis has, of course, traditionally represented homosexuality as a certain "refusal" or disorganization of dominant oedipal relations. Although Freud argued that homosexual desire functions in different ways and assumes multiple forms, he consistently positioned it as an effect of the oedipal paradigms that, he argued, constitute and regulate sexuality. In "A Child Is Being Beaten," for example, Freud posits "the derivation of all perversions from the Oedipus complex," arguing that homosexuality, in particular, "forces the Oedipus complex in a particular direction." In "A Case of Homosexuality in a Woman" he describes homosexuality as the result of "forces which le[a]d the . . . libido from the normal Oedipus attitude into that of homosexuality."[29] Although this reading of homosexuality as a failure or refusal of dominant oedipality has provided much of the motivational force behind the long pathologization of homosexuality within institutionalized psychoanalysis and other hegemonic practices, it need not be evaluated in such disempowering terms. There is an equally important tradition in psychoanalysis—starting with Freud himself—that refuses to pathologize the oedipal distinctions of homosexuality, arguing for them as simply a variable response to the dramas of subjectivization and sexual organization metaphorized within the psychocultural drama of the oedipus and castration complexes. Some critics even mobilize the psychoanalytic construction of homosexuality as a perversion of oedipal relations as the grounds for a radical retheorization of homosexuality as libidinally and politically progressive. Bracketing such issues for the present, however, the constitutive representation of homosexuality within psychoanalysis and beyond as an erotic formation that refuses or turns away from the dominant libidinal patterns of heteronormative oedipality suggests the potential for all sorts of isomorphic correlations and fantasmatic resonances between gay-identifying subjects and the de-oedipalized dynamics of the excessive musical number.

Thus, one could argue that much of the extraordinary force of gay-spectatorial receptions and popularizations of the Hollywood musical turns on a structure of engagement invested in what might be called *fantasies of perverse, de-oedipalized desire* or, to put it in another, slightly more user-friendly way, *fantasies of queerness*. By the latter, I mean the full sense of the term *queerness* as it has been defined in recent critical theory as a shifting space of antinormative difference that resonates profoundly with homosexualities but is not necessarily synonymous with them. Alexander Doty defines queerness as "a wide range of positions within culture that are non-, anti-, or contra-straight . . . a flexible space for the expression of all aspects of non- (anti-, contra-) straight cultural production and reception."[30] Queerness, thus defined, has strong associations with notions of homosexuality as de- or anti-oedipal in that both refer to positional structures of antinormativity. Indeed, in certain respects, queerness may be read as a reproduction of Freudian arguments about perverse desire and unconscious sexuality under a different name.[31] Reading gay receptions of the musical in terms of a broad fantasmatic structure of de-oedipalized desire, or queerness, has the advantage of highlighting the resonant fascination of the musical for gay spectators/gay readings while stressing the psychic complexities of that fascination. For what the musical number in its excess provides—and what, I would contend, is seized on by gay spectators in their engagements with the musical—is not simply representational formations of homosexual desire (though these do abound in the musical number and they provide important sites of fantasmatic engagement for gay spectators) but formations moreover of queer desire—desire let loose into positions that are aberrant, perverse, or just plain "nonstraight."

The musical number has long been recognized as providing "a covert method of conceiving normally undiscussed aspects of intersexual relationships."[32] Linda Williams correlates the Hollywood musical number to the sexual "number" in the pornographic film wherein, for example, she compares the musical's "solo song or dance of self-love or enjoyment" to masturbation, the trio to a sexual ménage à trois, "the choral love songs celebrating the sexual union of a whole community" to orgies, and so on.[33] Taken out of context in this way, such an analogy can seem contrived, but it nevertheless highlights how the excessive dimensions of the musical number can be seen to represent a "queer" libidinal heterogeneity—something that far exceeds the parameters of the domestic, oedipalized heterosexuality promoted by the narrative.

As suggested, the musical number frequently offers images and sequences that can be read as homosexual or, at the very least, homoerotic. Alexander Doty suggests that part of the appeal of musicals for gay men may be rooted in what he terms its "hidden cultural history of gay erotics."[34] He cites the homoerotic triangles of the "male trio" musicals such as *Take Me Out to the Ball Game* (1949) and *On the Town* (1949), as well as the representation of the male body as erotic spectacle in numbers such as "Is There Anyone Here for Love" in *Gentlemen Prefer Blondes* (1953) and "Y.M.C.A." in *Can't Stop the Music* (1980). To this list could be added the exuberant sexual duets of male stars such as Gene Kelly and Frank Sinatra in *Anchors Aweigh* (1945); the narcissistic displays of male solo dances such as the "I Like Myself" number by Gene Kelly in *It's Always Fair Weather* (1955); the athletic cowboy dancing routines in *Seven Brides for Seven Brothers* (1954), *Oklahoma!* (1955), and *The Best Little Whorehouse in Texas* (1982); the all-male, balletic gang dances in *West Side Story* (1961); and the orgasmic gyrations of Elvis Presley and his band of male prisoners in the "Jailhouse Rock" sequence from the 1957 film of the same name, or John Travolta and his fellow gang members in the "Greased Lightning" number in *Grease* (1978). These numbers all provide instances of a spectacular eroticization, if not homoeroticization, of the male image that is quite unusual in mainstream cinema. Several critics have claimed that the musical may in fact be "the only genre in which the male body has been unashamedly put on [erotic] display in mainstream cinema in any consistent way."[35] Significantly, these critics contend that this insistent eroticization of the male body in the musical destabilizes traditional gender structures. Both Steve Neale and Steven Cohan, for example, claim that the musical's eroticization of the male image serves to "feminize" that image because it places it in the conventionally "feminine" role of sexual object.[36] I deal with the question of gay spectatorships and male cinematic objectification at length in chapter 5, but it is worth noting that this "feminization" of the male image in the musical provides strong potentials for empathic identification on the part of gay-identifying spectators, as well as for the projection of gay fantasies of gender disorganization. Male homosexuality has developed strong, even constitutive associations with discourses of femininity in our culture; consequently, many gay spectators would be highly responsive to the musical's aberrant constructions of a spectacular, feminized masculinity and the potentials this extends for gay fantasmatic indulgence.[37] At the very least, the feminization of the male image in the musical film attests to the dynamics of antiheteronormative queerness that I am suggesting run through the excessive space of the musical number.

Further evidence for my claim that the musical number is frequently the site of a liminal breakdown of oedipalized desire and heterosexual normativity resides in the musical's extensive representation of various forms of gender or sexual subversion. The most obvious example here is the widespread use of cross-dressing in the musical number, such as Mickey Rooney's Carmen Miranda routine in *Babes on Broadway* (1941), or Garland and Astaire dressed as tramps for the "Couple of Swells" number in *Easter Parade* (1948), or the "Thanksgiving Follies" routine in *South Pacific* (1958). Other examples are the seemingly ubiquitous musical figure of the androgynous female performer in male tuxedo and tie such as Eleanor Powell in *Broadway Melody of 1936* (1935) and *Lady Be Good* (1941), Garland in *Summer Stock* (1950) and *A Star Is Born* (1954), and Vera-Ellen in *Three Little Words* (1950); the brash butchness of the eponymous female characters in *Annie Get Your Gun* (1950) and *Calamity Jane* (1953), or, conversely, the effeminacy of male characters like the Cowardly Lion in *The Wizard of Oz* (1939) and the long line of sissy boys played by Edward Everett Horton in musicals of the thirties and forties. More recent examples are the explicit celebrations of transvestism in such modern musicals as *Cabaret* (1972), *The Rocky Horror Picture Show* (1975), *Victor/Victoria* (1982), and *The Adventures of Priscilla, Queen of the Desert* (1994). These spectacular moments of gender transgression all point to a profound current of sexual subversion at play in the musical number. With their images of gender and sexual "otherness," they present what Annette Kuhn describes as "a vision of fluidity of gender options," "a utopian prospect of release from the ties of sexual difference that bind us into meaning, discourse, culture."[38] It should not be surprising, therefore, that many of these examples of gender transgression in the Hollywood musical have become privileged images of and for gay subcultural iconographies.

In a rather different vein, the musical number has frequently represented and explored not only sexual differences but racial differences. Altman argues that "from its very beginnings in the *Jazz Singer* (1927), the musical has been associated with black faces."[39] The most obvious example here is the presence of certain iconic African American actors and performers in the Hollywood musical such as Bill Robinson, Ethel Waters, Lena Horne, Louis Armstrong, Pearl Bailey, and Sammy Davis Jr. Significantly, one of the first films featuring an entirely African American cast to find widespread success at the U.S. box office was a musical, *Hallelujah* (1929). This was followed by several all-black film musicals including such notable successes as *Cabin in the Sky* (1943), *Stormy Weather* (1943), *Carmen Jones* (1954), *Porgy and Bess* (1959), and *The Wiz* (1978). Other examples in this context include the representation of Asians or, at least, "Asianness" in such musical films as *The King and I* (1956) and

Flower Drum Song (1961), or in numbers such as "Anything Goes" in the 1936 film of the same name and the "Limehouse Blues" routine in both *Ziegfeld Follies* (1946) and *Star!* (1968); the use of Middle Eastern locales and cultures in such films as *The Desert Song* (1953) and *Kismet* (1955); the celebration of Polynesian "exoticism" in the long line of South Seas musicals from *Waikiki Wedding* (1937) to *Pagan Love Song* (1950) to *Blue Hawaii* (1962); or the popularization of Latino motifs, locales, and actors (Carmen Miranda, Don Ameche, Fernando Lamas, Ricardo Montalban) in the range of South American musicals made during the forties such as *Down Argentine Way* (1940), *That Night in Rio* (1941), and *Week-end in Havana* (1941). Although many of these representations are undoubtedly racist—using ethnic difference in a patronizing and objectifying manner, as, quite literally, "added color" and, often, in accordance with the ideological fantasies of Western orientalism—they suggest that the exploration of *queerness* or, to use a slightly more appropriate term in this particular context, *otherness* in the musical number is not limited to sexual differences alone. And just as the formations of sexual queerness in the musical number exceed and disrupt narrative straightness, so, perhaps, this wide-ranging imagery of racial difference may also exceed and disrupt textual discourses of hegemonic "whiteness" in certain ways.

It has in fact been suggested that the musical as a genre turns on a foundational structure of racial mimicry that works in competing ways to both shore up and problematize the stability of hegemonic ideologies and identities. In her critical reading of *Singin' in the Rain*, Carol J. Clover argues that this film—and by extension the entire history of the Hollywood musical that the film knowingly references and represents—depends on an "uncredited" appropriation of African American cultural forms, most notably dance forms, which are subsequently attributed to and possessed by white performers. "The film musical," she writes, "drew heavily and variously on black art and talent. Only in the 'Negro musical' was that talent front and center. The more common pattern was to put it off to the side . . . or behind the scenes . . . or out of 'creditable' range altogether."[40] This act of negated cultural appropriation clearly supports relations of white dominance and black marginality as Clover details, but it potentially problematizes those relations as well. Not only does the most vehement negation of the musical's "black roots" fail to exorcize completely the disavowed "specter" of racial difference that, as the examples cited above suggest, remains to "haunt" and energize the genre in diverse and often spectacular ways, but the very act of racial/cultural appropriation that critics like Clover argue underpins its basic generic structures imbues the musical with an inescapable logic of identificatory masquerade that cuts against the grain of its normalizing operations. Although I in no way want to undercut the full acknowledgment of cross-racial appropriation and mimicry as violent strategies of racist oppression, the dynamics of boundary crossing that inevitably attend the transvestic operations of these practices make them potential agents of what Marjorie Garber terms "category crisis." By this she means "a failure of definitional distinction, a borderline that becomes permeable, that permits of border crossings from one (apparently distinct) category to another: black/white, Jew/Christian, noble/bourgeois, master/servant, . . . male/female."[41] Garber is careful to point out that cross-racial imitation can be mobilized for various political purposes and "signifies differently in different cases and contexts," but she asserts that, as with any instance of categorical transvestism, it contains a powerful potential "to disrupt, expose, and challenge, putting in question the very notion of 'the original' and of stable identity" (303, 16).

It is difficult to define the precise role these dynamics of racial otherness and exchange may play in gay readings of the musical, but Garber's emphasis on the interrelations between otherwise distinct forms of "category crisis"—"category crises can and do mark displacements from the axis of class as well as from race onto the axis of gender [and sexuality]"—suggests a possible homology or isomorphism between the musical's formations of sexual queerness and racial "otherness" that would be broadly appealing and responsive to gay investments (17).[42] The widespread celebration in gay male cultures of African American and Latina musical stars such as Carmen Miranda, Dolores del Rio, Lena Horne, Pearl Bailey, and Rita Moreno, to say nothing of more recent traditions of black disco/pop diva worship, suggests that many gay spectators strongly identify with figures and images of racial/ethnic difference. The resonances of these images of racial otherness would, of course, be further heightened—certainly, more overdetermined—in the case of gay men of color. It is also important not to overidealize the relations of white gay men to these images; such relations can never be entirely free from the discourses of racism and white privilege that frame the production, circulation, and evaluation of racial differences in white contexts. Nevertheless, the dynamics of alterity, marginality, and binaristic disruption that shape the representation and experiences of gayness and blackness alike provide, if not a metaphoric equivalence, then at least a potential affinity between gay spectators and the musical's formations of racial difference.[43]

The fantasmatic lure of the "excessive" musical number for gay audiences appears in other, more abstract ways as well. Recent work in musicology suggests that music itself may, in certain contexts, signify a space of "perverse" or queer desire. Much of this work takes up psychoanalytic arguments about the potential in music to reactivate and/or replicate pre-oedipal modalities and memories. The post-Lacanian analyst Guy Rosolato has argued famously that part of the pre-oedipal bond between mother and child is played out at an aural level. He argues that the mother's voice acts as a "sonorous envelope" surrounding the infant in a soothing and highly pleasurable blanket of sound and that it provides the subject with its "first model of auditory pleasure." Music, he suggests, "finds its roots and its nostalgia in [this] original atmosphere, which might be called a sonorous womb, a murmuring house, or music of the spheres."[44] In a similar vein, Julia Kristeva suggests that the rhythmic flow of music and some poetry has the potential to evoke memories of the maternal voice from the pre-oedipal phase or, what she terms, the "semiotic." She contends that the nonrepresentational properties of these forms replicate the prelinguistic sounds of mother-infant communication and that they, therefore, signal potential points of libidinal disruption, points where the pre-oedipal or semiotic erupts through the dominant discourse of symbolic signification.[45] Theories such as these have prompted some critics to suggest that music may signal a transgressive realm of feminine *jouissance*—in which maternal incantation triumphs over paternal logocentrism. This is why, it is suggested, music is largely coded and marginalized as "feminine" in patriarchal cultures. "Nonverbal even when linked to words, physically arousing in its function as initiator of dance, and resisting attempts to endow it with, or discern in it, precise meanings," writes Phillip Brett, music "represents that part of our culture which is constructed as feminine and therefore dangerous."[46] Although purely theoretical, these arguments provide interesting material for a further analysis of the queer potentials of the excessive musical number. They suggest that the "musicality" of the musical may be a form of de-oedipalizing queerness in and of itself. In particular, they suggest that the musical number may give rise to fantasies of pre-oedipal, maternal identification.

Some ramifications of these psychoanalytic arguments for readings of the Hollywood musical have been addressed by Edward Baron Turk in a fascinating essay on "song, sopranos and cinema." Turk suggests that much of the widespread derision of the film musical is a direct effect of its potential to evoke archaic memories of bodily fusion with the mother. Using singing film star Jeanette MacDonald as his focus, he claims that the musical film in general and the cinematic female soprano in particular reactivate "an imaginary, pre-Oedipal state of total identification with the mother's voice."[47] This is why male audiences and critics revile a screen soprano like MacDonald, he suggests; her voice reawakens male phallic anxieties about maternal authority and subjective insufficiency.

> For the moviegoer who is well-disposed to it, the intensity of sound MacDonald produces . . . reactivates the hallucinatory pleasures of acoustic omnipotence associated with prelinguistic, infantile narcissism. For moviegoers otherwise disposed, these same factors generate anxiety and embarrassment. At issue, in both dispositions, I suggest, is the moviegoer's willingness to accept or disavow the maternal voice as the agency of acoustic authority. (237–38)

Although Turk implies that this polarization in responses to the fantasy of the omnipotent maternal voice in the musical is largely gendered, with female spectators embracing the fantasy and male spectators refusing it, it is important to recognize that there may be significant exceptions. In particular, many gay male spectators would find such a fantasy compelling, even seductive. As I argue in more detail in chapter 4, maternal identification is represented in psychoanalysis as a central scenario of homosexual fantasmatic organization. According to Freudian theory, male homosexual desire is, in certain configurations at least, predicated on and governed by an unconscious fantasy of matrocentrism. Within the oedipalized narratives that constitute and legislate contemporary forms of bourgeois, Western sexuality, an imaginary assumption of the maternal position functions as a privileged fantasmatic route to and psychic framework for male homosexuality. Even if one refutes the legitimacy of psychoanalytic theories of homosexual psychic constitution, the fact that they are so ingrained in contemporary discourses of male homosexuality and, by implication, gay identity suggests that, at the very least, scenarios of maternal identification have an overdetermined significance for gay men. In this case, gay subjects are, perhaps, more responsive to and may even be psychically predisposed toward the lure and pleasure of the musical's potential for fantasies of maternal identification and pre-oedipal regression. Indeed, in his recent essay on gay men and the Broadway musical referred to earlier, D. A. Miller argues that the enduring passionate attachment between gay men and musical theater is underwritten by a fantasmatic logic of maternal identification. In its prototypical form, the Broadway musical, he contends, turns on a central scenario of feminine spectacularization in which the audience is invited into a fantasmatic identification with the central female performer, or what he terms "the Star-Mother." This is why the Broadway musical has become such an intensely gay genre, he opines, because it promotes a queer mode of fantasmatic engagement in which gay men can embrace an identification with the all-singing, all-dancing, all-powerful Star-Mother and, thus, indulge in the aberrant but spectacular "thrills of a femininity *become their own.*"[48]

In support of this argument, one could cite the much-noted veneration of the female singing diva in gay male subcultures. From Judy Garland, Maria Callas, and Patsy Cline to Barbra Streisand, Bette Midler, and Madonna, the powerful female voice has been cherished and celebrated in gay cult. That this celebration frequently assumes matrocentric forms is suggested evocatively by Wayne Koestenbaum when, in a discussion of the gay adulation of Maria Callas, he writes that, listening to the voice of the female diva, "we are the ideal mother ('mother' as idea) attending to the baby's cries, and we are the baby listening to the mother for signs of affection and attention, for reciprocity, for world."[49] As mentioned, the question of gay male matrocentrism and its effects on gay spectatorial relations is the primary focus of chapter 4; for the moment, I simply highlight how the matrocentric potentials of the musical may be cited as further evidence that the excessive musical number represents a space of de-oedipalized queerness, a space in which the dominant systems of (hetero)sexual organization are subverted and desire is refashioned into perverse/queer formations.

Even more abstractly, the musical number offers the potential for a fantasmatic staging of erotic reversibility in which desire becomes displaced from the conventional oedipal scenarios of subject-object relationality into a radical scenario of libidinal fluidity and fragmentation. The passage from Koestenbaum just cited implies the presence of precisely such a current of identificatory fluidity at work in gay engagements with the female musical star when it represents those engagements as oscillating between simultaneous identifications with positions of both mother and child. In their influential theorization of fantasy, Laplanche and Pontalis argue that, at a fundamental level, fantasy is marked by a certain logic of desubjectivization in which the fantasizing subject is dispersed across competing points and terms in a given fantasmatic scenario. Most critics advisedly point out that this argument is predicated on an assumption of fantasy at its most basic unconscious form, and, as such, it cannot be simply transposed to the context of cinema—or, indeed, any other form in the symbolic—in which the secondary processes of psychic and social censorship, textual representation, and filmic narrativization (to say nothing of the individual spectator's own psychosocial defenses) necessarily impose a structuring grid on the transactional mobility of fantasy. Yet inasmuch as the musical number is precisely characterized by a breakdown of many of these same structuring grids (narrative form, classical continuity style, oedipal heterosexuality), it can be argued that it represents one of the closest analogues in mainstream cinema to a desubjectivized fantasmatic fluidity. The unorthodox use of fragmenting formal techniques in the musical number such as jump cuts, split screens, multiple optical printing, crane shots, and so forth (techniques that, outside the musical, are seldom used in mainstream film precisely because of their perceived disruptions to textual and spectatorial coherency) seem to indicate that the musical number is governed by a logic of fragmentation and dispersal. The musical number may, thus, be seen to evoke a much more flexible erotico-identificatory system in which spectatorial investments are literally dispersed across competing positions that are interchangeable or simultaneous. How else could one describe the libidinal operations of the kaleidoscopic musical spectacles of Busby Berkeley, say, in which images and bodies are arrayed in such totally abstract formations that they rupture all spatial and realist constraints?[50] Or the "orgiastic" stagings of a number like "Once-A-Year Day" in *The Pajama Game* (1957), in which the camera cranes, pans, tracks, and all but performs cartwheels in and around the writhing bodies of dozens of dancers to the point that one loses any sense of perspective and textual coherency; or the split-screen montage of numbers like "Six Months Out of Every Year" in *Damn Yankees* (1958) and "Rhythm of Life" in *Sweet Charity* (1969), in which images and bodies are repeatedly spliced and multiplied in variable configurations within a single frame? In all these examples, cinematic vision and, by implication, spectatorial access to the image is so fractured that it becomes difficult to determine how and where libidinal investment would be placed. The sequences in question present such a fluid fetishization of bodies and their interchangeable parts that it would seem to encourage a diffusion of fantasmatic investment across a range of possibilities within the field of representation.

The various elements of de-oedipalized desire, or "queerness," that I have been briefly sketching here are not, of course, immutable properties of the musical number qua text. They are not hard and fast meanings imprinted on the celluloid of these films like some subtextual phantom that manifests itself for all to plainly see. Rather, they are potentialities of textual signification that may be realized or not by different spectators in accordance with the frames of their variable social, historical, and psychical positionings. Certainly, it is more than possible to ignore or suppress these potentialities and to read the musical number "straight," engaging and interpreting its erotic scenarios as exclusively heterosexual, if not heteronormative. However, it is also possible to read the musical number "otherwise," which is what I am suggesting gay spectators can— and often would—do. Gay spectators are not as invested in or constrained by the frameworks of compulsory heterosexuality, and thus they are more productively positioned to acknowledge and realize the shifting potentials for queer desire signaled in and by the excesses and unconventionalities of the musical number. Obviously, gay spectators are not the only ones to activate these potentialities, and not all gay spectators register or respond to them in the same way. Nevertheless, their psychical investment in formations of perverse desire and their identifications with variable discourses of queer difference make gay spectators particularly responsive to the musical number's possibilities for nonheteronormative, psychoerotic excess. Their assumption of a position of alterity in the social field and a sociosexual identity variously defined as alternative, marginal, and subcultural makes them ideal readers of the type of ambiguous, connotative signification through which these possibilities of queerness are encoded and circulated in the textual arena. As Harold Beaver asserts, gay subjects are nothing if not "prodigious consumer[s] . . . of hidden meanings, hidden systems, hidden potentiality."[51]

With its wide range of potential queer significations—of de-oedipalized desire, of homoeroticism, of cross-dressing and gender subversion, of racial and ethnic otherness, of imaginary matrocentrism, of erotic reversability and dispersion—the musical number provides ample scope for gay fantasmatic investment. The strong, multifaceted points of resonance that criss-cross between the potentials of queer excess in the musical number and the psychosocial dynamics of gay subjectivity establish a context within which the musical can be assumed as a particularly gay-receptive genre. The spectacular moments of queer excess in the musical function as ideal bases for gay receptions and readings, providing powerful "gaps" in the heteronormative text through which to insert gay desires and weave gay fantasies.

However, this assumption of the musical number as disruptive point of (queer) excess is but part of the negotiational process. These moments of excess need to be extended and amplified to combat dominant textual attempts to recontain and redomesticate the disruptions they pose. As any number of critics have pointed out, one defining feature of the carnivalesque moment of excess is its transience. It is by definition "momentary"; it never lasts, it comes to an end, and then order and stability is reasserted.[52] In the case of the musical, the spectacular number may very well represent a potential break from the heteronormative demands of an oedipal narrativity into a polymorphous space of libidinal queerness, but this is only ever temporary, and the film nearly always returns to the psychocultural stability of linear narrative. As Mellencamp writes in reference to what is quite possibly the paradigmatic example of libidinal excess in the Hollywood musical, the spectacles of the musical number "are ultimately contained by the process of narrativization. Just as the policeman must stop and censor Lockwood's sexual explosion in the cold shower spectacle, 'Singin' in the Rain', so does the narrative regulate, order, and contain the spectacles for the film's (and the spectator's) climax."[53] In a similar vein, Feuer argues that in "the Hollywood musical, heterogeneous levels are created so that they may be homogenized in the end through the union of the romantic couple. In the Hollywood musical, different levels are recognized in order that difference may be overcome, dual levels synthesized back into one."[54] These critics are primarily concerned, however, with dominant or preferred forms of spectatorial reading. Consequently, they presuppose a compliant acceptance on the part of the spectator of the text's recontainment of disruptive excess within the confines of hymeneal closure. In contrast, I have already suggested that gay spectators habitually reorder conventional patterns of textual organization to resist and reject such processes of narrative recuperation.

In the case of the musical, by privileging the excessive dynamics of the musical number, by making them the primary source of textual pleasure and, quite possibly, meaning, gay spectators are able to create a very different paradigm of interpretation in which hermeneutic primacy is granted to the disruptive, centrifugal dimensions of spectacle and excess over and against the homogenizing, centripetal forces of narrative ordinarily prioritized in and by conventional, "straight" (in both senses of the word) reading practices. This in turn provides a way to resist and refigure dominant textual attempts to repress and domesticate desire within the clotural frame of institutionalized heterosexual union.

Interestingly, in a recent postscript to the second edition of her study of Hollywood musicals, Jane Feuer concedes that one problem with her and other theorists' work on the musical is its presupposition of a monolithic audience and its consequent inability to "explain how resisting readers may transform musicals." As a preliminary step in redressing this situation, Feuer briefly discusses "cult audiences" for musicals, particularly those of the gay male urban subculture who, she contends, "used and continue to use classic Hollywood musicals" in a way "that must lead to a different reading of the genre than that . . . base[d] . . . on ideas of normative . . . heterosexual coupling" (123–24). Although Feuer does not develop a sustained analysis of gay readings of the musical, she suggests that gay spectators may transform the genre's heteronormative dynamics by refuting clotural supremacy and privileging other points or features in the text instead. In particular, she suggests that queer readings of the musical "shift the emphasis from narrative resolution as heterosexual coupling (an emphasis on the comic plot) and towards readings based on non-narrative, performative and spectacular elements (an emphasis on the numbers). Such readings might also reinterpret musical narratives away from an emphasis on the comic plot as a form of closure that re-confirms heterosexual norms" (141).

This process of clotural resistance and transformation may in fact be actively facilitated by the way the musical achieves narrative closure, not through a "straight" diegetic event but through a grand finale number. The moment of hymeneal closure is marked in nearly all musicals by a final song-and-dance sequence that in many cases is the most extravagant moment in the whole film. Most theorists suggest that this is the point at which the text actually co-opts the excessive space of the number and subordinates it to the demands of classic linear narrative by using it for the teleological enshrinement of domestic heterosexual stability. However, it could also be argued that this final combination of number and nar-rative in the musical's grand finale creates a potential dynamic in which the excesses of spectacle affect and possibly undermine the homogenizing designs of hymeneal diegetic closure—or, at least, provide the potential for such a reading.

Consider, for example, the finale of *Rosalie* (1937), in which the film's stars, Eleanor Powell and Nelson Eddy, are married. The scene starts off in a fairly straightforward manner with a mid-shot of an organist play-ing the opening bars of "The Wedding March." But what one thinks is going to be a conventional wedding scene filmed according to the tra-ditions of classical Hollywood film form is very quickly transformed as the camera pans over to Powell and Eddy, who start singing a reprise of the film's theme song, and then pulls back in a diegetically unmotivated crane shot to reveal a panorama of outrageously wild extravagance—not one but dozens of organists, scores of angelic choristers, endless lines of bridal maids wrapped in a sea of organza and tulle and phalanxes of uni-formed soldiers all placed on an oversized white staircase set that seems to go on forever. The formal unconventionality and stylistic opulence of this sequence clearly problematize any reading of its signifying effects in terms of simple narrative recuperation. This final number introduces such marked elements of spectacular excess that it actively subverts any presumed attempt at recontaining meaning and desire within a clotural frame of domestic heterosexuality—or, once again, that is the way it could be read.

Admittedly, this is a rather extreme example, but it highlights the potential for polyvocal conflict and tension signaled by the musical film's attempts to co-opt the spectacular space of the musical number for the function of a conservative narrative closure. These potentials for conflict and tension are evident in many other musical finales as well. The celebrated closing number of *Easter Parade* is a good case in point. In this scene, Garland and Astaire, who have finally confessed their love for each other, step out to walk in the Easter parade of the title. As the song progresses, the camera slowly draws away in a continuous pull-back shot until Garland and Astaire are lost in a sea of singing, milling people. Like the *Rosalie* finale, the final number of *Easter Parade* creates a conflicting dynamic in which spectacle threatens to overtake and, quite literally, engulf the dominant text's attempts to reharness meaning and desire to the stable vehicle of heterosexual narrative closure. Strikingly similar scenes occur in the grand finales of other musical films as diverse as *Royal Wedding* (1951), *My Sister Eileen* (1955), *Oklahoma!* (1955), *The Music Man* (1962), and *Hello Dolly!* (1969), in which the narrative couples are again literally subsumed as the camera pulls back to reveal the greater space of excessive spectacle.

The potential of the grand finale to overwhelm and destabilize the operations of heterosexual closure may explain why so many musicals employ the rather bizarre technical conceit of featuring a dislocated image of the diegetic couple superimposed over the film at the end of the final number, such as the close-up of a beaming Garland and Rooney at the end of both *Strike Up the Band* (1940) and *Babes on Broadway* (1942); the extraordinary superimposed cut-out shot of Keel and Grayson hovering, somewhat eerily, over the wildly applauding audience at the close of *Kiss Me Kate* (1953); the final image of Streisand and Montand floating through the clouds in *On a Clear Day You Can See Forever* (1970); or the patently ludicrous shot of John Travolta and Olivia Newton-John flying heavenward in their automobile at the end of *Grease* (1978). It is almost as if these films were making one last valiant attempt to impose some semblance of narrative stability and hegemonic or straight psychocultural order over the excessive dynamics of the spectacular number by refocusing attention on the culturally legitimated figure of the heterosexual couple. In all of these examples profound currents of tension and contradiction potentially underlie the musical's attempts to achieve heterosexual closure by marrying off not only the diegetic couple but also the disparate textual modes of narrative and spectacle.

It is this predilection toward polyvocal conflict—to say nothing of polyvalent sensation—that has made the musical so amenable to the types of negotiational reading practices that I have been suggesting are frequently used by gay spectators in their engagements with mainstream film. By assuming the disruptive dimensions of textual excess that are so extravagantly on offer in the musical, especially in its spectacular numbers, and mobilizing these as the bases for their readings, gay spectators are able to subvert dominant textual tendencies to heteronormative idealization and thereby create a space within which to articulate and explore variant formations of pleasure, fantasy, and desire.

Although it would be helpful to look at how some of these issues operate in relation to a specific example, not much has been written about gay spectatorships and individual musical films. Because most commentators tend to speak of gay audiences and the musical in fairly broad terms, discussing a whole range of musical styles, texts, and stars that have been popular in and for gay subcultures, it is difficult to single out any one text for special consideration.

In his article on gays and film, Al LaValley does make special mention of the films directed by Vincente Minnelli for the Arthur Freed Unit at MGM during the forties and fifties. With "the largest following" of any particular group of musicals among gay men, LaValley suggests that Minnelli's films appeal to gay audiences because they take the stylistic excesses of the musical to exaggerated, or "camp," extremes. By way of example, he cites the 1948 Minnelli/Freed film, *The Pirate*, starring Judy Garland and Gene Kelly, in which, he argues, "the narrative, as well as the musical numbers is . . . stylized."[55] Jane Feuer also cites *The Pirate*, along with Minnelli's 1945 musical *Yolanda and the Thief*, as iconic texts for gay male audiences. She asserts that "a gay subcultural reading would elevate these two Minnelli masterpieces of the 1940s above the currently more esteemed Freed Unit musicals of the 1950s—*Singin' in the Rain* and *The Bandwagon*, whose sophistication stems more from their smart Comden and Green scripts than from elements of excess in their *mise-en-scène*."[56]

Significantly, both *The Pirate* and *Yolanda and the Thief* are often singled out by critics as the best, or worst, as the case may be, examples of the wild excessiveness of the Minnelli/Freed style of musical. Ted Sennett points to both these films as "perfect examples" of what he sees as Minnelli's trademark "penchant for running riot (and occasionally to excess) with color and design." He finds *The Pirate*, in particular, "too extravagant," "florid," "gaudy," "strain[ing] a little too hard," "never tak[ing] itself seriously"—in short, it's a "hothouse flower, beautiful to look at and admire but also too delicate to survive the years."[57] Although such stylistic extravagance makes *The Pirate* problematical for some critics, it is precisely this extravagance that has made it such an enduringly popular film for gay audiences.

Its popularity is enhanced, no doubt, by Judy Garland. Her appeal was widespread among gay men during the postwar era when *The Pirate* was released in 1948. Two years later the gay popularization of Garland intensified, according to Richard Dyer, as news of her first suicide attempt became public. For Dyer, this initiated a series of significations (a rupture between public persona and private self, a battle against oppression, a relationship with emotional suffering) that redefined Garland as an eminently receptive figure for gay cult engagement and identification.[58] Some commentators have queried the artificiality of such a precise dating. Janet Staiger argues that "it is difficult for me to believe that Garland was suddenly perceived after her suicide attempt as a figure for cult status," claiming that Garland was already privileged within gay subcultures before this time, albeit in a less consolidated, less visible form, and that this provided the "groundwork for the 'sudden' arrival of the cult after her attempt on her life."[59] Either way, as a Garland film, *The Pirate* would have had important gay appeal at its release and would have been assumed as a privileged text of and for gay investment.

Gay receptions and popularizations of *The Pirate* are not limited to the historical context of the film's initial theatrical release, however. It continues to enjoy cult success within urban, Anglo-American gay subcultures. Revival screenings at repertory theaters, broadcasts on television, and, more recently, its release on home video have made *The Pirate* accessible to contemporary gay audiences, and promotions of it as "a treasured classic of gaycult" in the plethora of recent gay-oriented publications have ensured its continued significance in contemporary formations of gay subcultural capital and cinematic taste. This is not to say that gay subcultural receptions of *The Pirate* are simply continuous or one-of-a-piece. Although it is impossible to recover a full account of the shifting history of gay receptions of *The Pirate* or, indeed, any film, it is important to recognize that those receptions do have a history and that the significance and popularity of this text within gay subcultures, as well as the uses and readings made of it, are plural and changing. Any attempt to delineate a potential gay reading of *The Pirate*, therefore, will only ever be just that, a potential reading.

Within this context I would like to address *The Pirate* and analyze it as a gay cult text. In particular, I look briefly at how some of the issues I have been discussing about potential patterns of gay negotiational readings of the Hollywood musical may operate in relation to *The Pirate*, paying special attention to how the excessive dimensions of this film, especially as they are presented in its musical numbers, may be used by gay spectators to open up the text and create spaces for gay fantasmatic productions.

Queer Readings of The Pirate

At first glance, *The Pirate* seems incompatible with gay male fantasy and desire; like most musicals, it is primarily concerned with heterosexual romance and marriage. Indeed, the film could well function as a textbook example of Rick Altman's contention that the Hollywood musical is organized entirely around heterosexual courting. Set in an unidentified Caribbean country sometime during the height of Spanish colonial rule, the film tells the story of Manuela (Judy Garland), a young woman who dreams of a life of romance and passion on the high seas with the notorious pirate, Macoco, but who is forced to accept an arranged betrothal to Don Vargas (Walter Slezak), the wealthy, boorish mayor of the small village in which she lives. While visiting the neighboring seaport of San Sebastian to pick up her trousseau, Manuela encounters the rakish actor, Serafin (Gene Kelly) whose amorous advances she at first resists, but after he pursues her back to her village and seduces her by pretending to be Macoco, she quickly falls for his charms. Their inevitable union is enabled when, following a series of narrative twists, it is revealed that Don Vargas, the mayor, and not Serafin, is in fact Macoco, gone to seed and living in disguise. He is duly imprisoned as a criminal by the governor, and the film ends with Manuela and Serafin joined as lovers, performing euphorically on stage.

To construct and legitimate the heterosexual couple, the film exploits every element to create the mythos of idyllic heterosexuality, which the text defines and offers, to Manuela and spectator alike, as narrative telos and libidinal reward. Promoted on its initial release as "a musical romance," *The Pirate* traded centrally on the spectacle of Garland and Kelly —reteamed by MGM for the first time since their earlier hit, *For Me and My Gal* (1942)—as heterosexual star couple. Yet as the film's poster— with its central graphic of the heterosexual couple surrounded by smaller images of various spectacular scenes—reveals, *The Pirate* is also traversed by alternative currents of signification that undermine and, in many instances, overtake this dominant push to idealized heterosexuality, currents that are privileged in and by gay receptions of this film.

In many ways, *The Pirate* is a text riven by contradictory impulses, both toward and against heteronormative idealization, toward and against socially sanctioned desire. Proponents of an author-based approach to film criticism have suggested that all the musical films of Vincente Minnelli display such contradictions. Bruce Babington and Peter William Evans contend that Minnelli's musical films are nearly always centered on a plot structure in which an "imaginative, artistic self" who has "alternative visions of a different order of being . . . struggles to match the outer world to their inner desires."[60] Whether such a description applies to Minnelli's films as an oeuvre, it certainly sums up one of the chief thematic concerns of *The Pirate*. The young Manuela dreams of a life of romance and sexual adventure far removed from her mundane, smalltown existence. Faced with the prospect of a future of routinized domesticity, she fears that her deepest passions are doomed to remain unexpressed and unrealized. From the start, then, *The Pirate* opposes Manuela's innermost desires to an inimical external world that seems to offer no place for them. As she says in sullen resignation to her aunt in an early scene after learning of her arranged betrothal, "I realize there's a practical world and a dream world. I know which is which, I shan't mix them."

Even on its own this thematic opposition signals strong grounds for queer spectatorial investment, for it mirrors the sociodiscursive binarisms of public/private and inside/outside that ground modern gay identities, as well as the experiences of enforced secrecy that are often an integral component of those identities. In his analysis of gay subcultural receptions of Judy Garland, Richard Dyer argues that much of the intensity of these receptions stems from the way the Garland persona and texts embody a complex negotiation of dualisms such as ordinariness/extraordinariness and sameness/difference that gay men have been able to assume and interpret as broadly homologous to their own gay knowledges and experiences.[61] The queer resonances of these dualistic negotiations would have been more acute, no doubt, for gay audiences in the fifties and sixties, when the gay cult of Garland was at its historical peak and when the social pressures on gay men for discretion made duality an almost universal feature of gay life; but given how the demands of the closet continue to frame and determine gay subjectivities to this very day, *The Pirate*'s thematic oppositions of inside/outside, secrecy/disclosure, repression/expression still resonate profoundly in and for contemporary gay spectatorships.

Significantly, though perhaps not surprisingly, these thematic oppositions are played out in *The Pirate* across the musical's formal polarities of narrative and number and the stylistic/cinematographic differences of each. If the narrative is understood to be the place in which Manuela's desires are disavowed and contained in and for the text's teleological march to institutionalized heterosexual union—"the practical world"—then the space of the spectacle or the number is Manuela's "dream world," the forbidden place in which those desires are set free.

The opening scene explicitly introduces the conflict between the expression and repression of desire through a parallel conflict between spectacle and narrative.[62] Although not starting with a musical number per se, the film opens firmly within the space of spectacle with an extreme close-up on a stylized image of a pirate from the pages of a picture book Manuela is reading. The extradiegetic music from the opening credits continues into this shot, thereby underlining its spectacular dimensions. Manuela reads in high melodramatic voice-over: "The history of the Pirate, Mack, the black Macoco: Macoco the dazzling, Macoco the fabulous, the hawk of the seas, the Prince of Pirates . . . staggering to the imagination and ravishing the sensibilities with tales of wealth, of gold and silver beyond dreams of avarice, of stolen treasures, of maidens captured, of villages destroyed, of cities decimated for a whim or a caress." On this last line, the camera pulls back to reveal Manuela standing on a balcony clutching the book to her breast as she dreamily gazes offscreen. "Macoco, where are you now?" she cries, "What seas do you traverse? Is it sunrise or sunset where you are?" That this visual shift from the picture book to Manuela is achieved through a continuous pull-back tracking shot rather than a cut places Manuela firmly within the continued space of cinematic spectacle. In this space, defined explicitly in terms of erotic expression, Manuela's desire is seen to run wild. Yet this spectacle of fantasy and desire is interrupted by the arrival of Manuela's aunt, who announces the news of Manuela's arranged marriage to Don Vargas. The interruption breaks the moment of spectacle—quite literally in that it occasions the film's first full cut and shot-reverse shot sequence—and resets the textual economy on a "proper" form of linear, narrative progression through, significantly enough, the pronouncement of an impending marriage. Thus right from the very start *The Pirate* contrasts spectacle defined as the place of desire with narrative defined as the place of the repression or, at least, containment of that desire.

The following scene underscores the contrast, as Aunt Inez scolds Manuela for looking so glum about the prospect of wedded life with Don Vargas. Manuela explains that if she seems a little apprehensive, "It's just that I shan't know what to say." To which her aunt replies, "Oh, say nothing! He's not marrying you to listen to you!" Don Vargas, who represents the narrative and its primary goal of the hymeneal containment of disruptive desire, is not interested, we are told, in listening to Manuela, not interested, in other words, in listening to the expression of Manuela's desire, which, we know from the opening scene, as well as from the fact that this is a musical film starring Judy Garland, can only mean that he is not interested in listening to Manuela sing in the spectacular space of the number. This implication is confirmed in the ensuing sequence when Manuela closes the door to her room and looks around despondently. The music begins to swell, obviously leading up to a musical number, but just when we expect, and hope for, a song, the film cuts to a shot of Don Vargas pulling up in his carriage, looking pompous and self-important. In a visual confirmation of the preceding exchange between Manuela and her aunt, Don Vargas as symbolic agent of narrative progression intervenes here to repress the articulation of Manuela's desire in the spectacular space of the musical number by literally cutting off her chance to sing.

It is not until a third of the way into the film that we actually get to see and hear Manuela/Garland perform in the vibrant "Mack the Black" number. Following the division foreshadowed earlier, narrative:libidinal repression versus number:libidinal liberation, this sequence is emphatically cast in terms of a dynamic eruption of repressed desires. In this scene, Manuela has snuck into Serafin's street circus, but, unbeknownst to her, she has been spied from backstage by Serafin, who conspires to secretly hypnotize her as part of his act. After she has fallen into a deep trance, Serafin declares to the hushed audience, "I am now about to release her spirit from its earthly bonds." He proceeds to question the entranced Manuela about her secret desires and passions in the hope that he may get her to confess her love for him. He does, however, get more than he bargained for. Jumping out of her chair, Manuela literally lets her hair down and starts singing a fast-paced number about the pirate, "Mack the Black," while dancing rumbustiously around the arena. The sense of wild abandon conveyed in this scene is underscored by unconventional cinematographic techniques such as crane shots, canted angles, and extensive mobile framing that counterpoint the highly formal, evenly paced structure of the preceding narrative scenes.

In some ways, this sequence can be read as simply another cinematic representation of an excessive and unstoppable female sexuality, one designed to play out and to male heterosexual fears and anxieties. The insert shots of a marginalized Serafin watching in horrified disbelief from the wings supports such a reading. Nevertheless, it is also possible to read Manuela's libidinal explosion not as something sinister or uncomfortable but as something celebratory, as she reclaims the spectacular space of the musical number to articulate her own pleasures and fantasies. In the context of queer readings, this sequence showing the liberation and expression of a previously repressed desire has readily recognizable, overdetermined significances for gay-identifying spectators. It is a scenario that strongly resonates with contemporary gay discourses and experiences of "coming out," the public declaration of one's (homo)sexual desire and identity, and thus allows for specifically gay investments.

The potential resonances of this sequence for gay spectatorships are further heightened by the metaphorical coding of Manuela's libidinal liberation within a queer paradigm. I have already suggested that the shift from narrative into spectacular number in the musical film often signals a shift from hegemonic, oedipalized desire into de-oedipalized queerness. The "Mack the Black" sequence spells this out with particular clarity. It starts off with a standard representation of phallic heterosexuality, in which Serafin dupes, manipulates, and commands Manuela. Yet as the sequence progresses, Serafin loses control over Manuela as she approaches the space of the number. Finally, Manuela pushes Serafin away and bursts into song, an act repeated several times throughout the first part of the sequence as Manuela wards off Serafin again as well as men in the audience who try to grab her and stifle her libidinal expression. Manuela is gradually joined in her singing and dancing by other members of the audience, both male and female, who begin to press around her. By the end of the number, Manuela has been engulfed in and by a polymorphous mass of writhing bodies. What started as a fairly traditional structure of heterosexual relationality ends up as a frenetic, almost orgiastic, celebration of queer desire that defies the conventional "laws" of oedipal sexual/gender positions.

In regard to earlier comments about the potential in the musical number to reactivate scenarios of pre-oedipal matrocentrism, it is also possible in the "Mack the Black" number to discern a celebration of the omnipotent maternal voice. Full, strong, and authoritative, the voice of Manuela/Garland commands the libidinal economy of the whole number. It is the voice that we have been waiting for, the primordial voice of the imaginary mother that the film has been promising but coyly withholding. When Manuela/Garland finally sings, her voice saturates the space of fantasmatic desire. The climax of the number, with a triumphant Manuela belting out full-throated notes as the crowd pushes in tightly around her, presents a scenario of fantasized fusion with the maternal body/voice. Memories of prelinguistic mother-infant communication are evoked in the libidinal *jouissance* of the climax as Manuela vocalizes several prolonged syllables: "Mac-Mac-Mac-Mac-co-co." This may be stretching interpretation to its absolute limits, but it does help highlight how the "Mack the Black" number can be read as the site of a deoedipalized or otherwise perverse libidinal queerness.

Another example of the progressive move into a utopian formation of queer desire that transcends the polarized divisions of oedipal gender systems is the earlier "Niña" number performed by Serafin/Kelly when he first arrives in San Sebastian. In this sequence, Serafin brags to a couple of men that when he arrives in a new town there are so many beautiful women with so many different names that he makes things easier by simply calling them all "Niña" ("little girl"). He then dances around the town square flirting with and singing to an array of different women whom he calls "Niña." Although on the surface this number appears to reduce women to homogeneous objects by and for male heterosexual desire, it is possible to read a gradual subversion and displacement of the dominant phallic heterosexual scenario. The narrative preamble and the number's early scenes suggest a more protean scenario of queerly (re)gendered desire through a reversal of erotic relations. What starts as a conventional specularization of the female image by a male character ends up objectifying and dephallicizing the male figure.

At the beginning of the number, as Serafin sings, he dances from woman to woman across the town square and even up into surrounding buildings. Most of the women respond with "appropriately" demure and coquettish behavior, but at one point Serafin goes over to a table of three women who, through their costume, makeup, and general appearance, are clearly coded as figures of illicit female sexuality. As he sings to them, they actively respond, returning his gaze and leaning toward him in defiant postures of sexual aggression. Serafin makes a frightened grimace and retreats quickly. However, he later returns to the three women, snatches the cigarette from the mouth of one of them and kisses her hard on the mouth. She grabs her cigarette back, and the other two women steal Serafin's hat and cane and dance around him. There then ensues an extended ballet sequence that builds on a struggle over possession of Serafin's hat, involving Serafin alone or together with one, two, or all three of the women. Freud famously quipped that often a cigar is just a cigar, and a hat, therefore, may also be just a hat, but, given the curious obsession in this sequence with detachable objects — cigarette, cane, hat — and the intense struggles over their possession, loss, and repossession, something a little more critical is being explored here. The struggle over possession of Serafin's hat is, in other words, a metaphoric struggle over possession of the phallus, which echoes the shifting balances of power and desire in the sequence, especially as they are codified in and through cinematic vision.

At the start, Serafin is the primary subject of desire. He dominates the frame and is firmly in control of the gaze, swaggering around with his hat firmly perched on his head, freely ogling the women. Midway through the number, he encounters a return gaze in the same frame from the equally active sexual advances of the three prostitutes, who challenge and steadily subvert his initial position of singular, heterosexual mastery. The encounter signals a shift in the specular dynamics of the sequence from an initial focus on Serafin's gaze of desire to a directly inverted emphasis on the women's gaze of desire. After the encounter with the three women, the forward tracking shots and pans used in the first part of the number give way to a reverse structure of backward tracks and pans. This shift in specular dynamics is also played out metaphorically in the balletic struggle over the hat. Serafin's increasing loss of control over the gaze in this sequence and, therefore, his loss of control over its circuits of desire is mirrored in the loss of his hat. Deprived of his hat, Serafin is no longer able to maintain his previous pose of phallic authority, becoming a passive object himself in and for the field of erotic vision. Serafin breaks away from the dancing and leads the women over to a small rotunda stage where he proceeds to dance provocatively for the congregating audience made up almost entirely of the very same women who had earlier been subjected to the erotic objectification of his own phallic gaze. Serafin no longer imposes his desire onto the women; the women now claim control of the gaze, scrutinizing and objectifying Serafin.[63]

What happens next in the sequence extends the hat metaphor. After Serafin assumes a "feminine" position of erotic objectification with his solo dance in the rotunda, a brief reprise of the earlier struggle over the hat follows, with each dancer, Serafin included, taking the hat and then passing it on. Given the shift in erotic power relations signaled by the increasing objectification/feminization of Serafin, this rapid circulation of the hat seems to symbolize a newly emergent fluidity in the number's economy of desire. The hat qua phallus is passed from dancer to dancer with such ease that its ability to regulate, let alone fix, a position of desire for any one gender is thoroughly undermined. Consequently, when Serafin finally regains possession of the hat, he simply tosses it off to one side of the stage and continues to dance. The phallus has lost its power to dictate relations of erotic exchange, and the number, as in "Mack the Black," unleashes a wild eruption of communal desire. Serafin moves back down into the audience, and everybody starts singing and dancing together in a single group; phallic heterosexuality and heterosexual gender structures are exchanged for blurred, diffused eroticism.

Both the "Mack the Black" and "Niña" numbers represent important moments of alternative signification in the text, as the control of the straight narrative falters and desire is let loose into aberrant, perverse, or otherwise queer libidinal formations. Although other spectacular moments in the film provide similar opportunities for textual and libidinal perversion, these two numbers suffice to give a sense of how the musical sequences in *The Pirate* may be read queerly. By offering markedly different scenarios of desire to the heteronormative paradigms constructed and maintained by the dominant straight narrative, which locates pleasure and fulfillment in the relatively stable space of heterosexual union, these numbers suggest an alternative possibility in which desire is allowed to move with relative freedom into various interchangeable configurations.

Yet the finale of *The Pirate* does reinstate and relegitimate an image of a single heterosexual couple as the ultimate form of intersubjective desire. Manuela may very well reject Don Vargas and the routinized domesticity of life with him, but she nonetheless falls into the waiting arms of Serafin and another form of heterosexual containment. However, the potentials offered by the earlier numbers make it possible to accept the final union of Manuela and Serafin without necessarily reading it as a simple reinstatement of heteronormative hegemony. If we focus on how the earlier numbers set up the spectacle as the space of a relatively diffuse de-oedipalized or dephallicized desire, the film's coda sequence allows a reading that goes beyond the containment of Manuela and Serafin's desire within institutionalized heterosexuality, opening out of that desire into what Dana Polan terms the "endless nonfinality" of the spectacle.[64] In fact, the somewhat extraordinary nature of the clotural finale with Serafin and Manuela dressed as clowns singing and dancing together to the joyous strains of Cole Porter's "Be a Clown" actively facilitates such a rereading, for it provides a symbolic representation of the couple as quite literally caught up in a frenzied chain of spectacular moments. The mise-en-scène of desire offered in this final sequence does not simply revalidate the heterosexual couple; it celebrates the libidinal mobility of the musical spectacle.

With this possible set of meanings, gay spectators of *The Pirate* seeking to clear a space for the articulation of queer fantasies—or fantasies of queerness—can refuse any simple notion of heterosexual containment. Taking their cue from some of the earlier numbers in which the arena of spectacle is defined through de-oedipalized excess, they can (re)interpret the film's finale as a utopian moment of queer carnivalesque, a moment beyond the limits and regulations of straight sexual/gender norms.

Female stardom as camp excess: publicity shot of Mae West at age seventy-six
for *Myra Breckinridge* (1970) (author's collection)

Chapter Three ∽ CAMPING UNDER THE STARS:

GAY SPECTATORSHIPS, CAMP, AND THE EXCESSIVE

FEMALE STAR IMAGE

How resplendent seems the art of acting! It is all impersonation, whether the sex underneath is true or not.
— Parker Tyler, in *Mother Camp: The Female Impersonator in America*

To continue my exploration of the variable exchanges between cinematic spectatorships and gay fantasmatic specificity requires a look at the celebrated discourse of "camp." As a transgressive mode of cultural engagement, camp disrupts and refigures dominant cultural forms, especially sexual forms. Traditionally popular with gay-identifying subjects, camp has also been widely used in gay subcultural contexts to read cinematic and extracinematic texts queerly, to open these texts up to gay or gay-resonant meanings and pleasures.

I want to make an argument for camp as a particular form or discourse of gay cultural *taste* in the sense given the term by Pierre Bourdieu: "an acquired disposition [used] . . . to establish and mark differences by a process of distinction."[1] For Bourdieu, taste is not "a gift of nature," an innate given, but the constructed and variable effect of systems of social organization. We acquire particular tastes because of our position as determined by the networks of history, culture, and society. Consequently, taste functions as an important means for the production and legitimation of social distinctions. Certain forms of taste become associated with particular sociocultural groups and are evaluated accordingly. The discourse of camp is a form of cultural taste produced by and is, therefore, emblematic of the particular frameworks of gay male subjectivity. Although Bourdieu articulates his notion of cultural taste primarily in reference to social dynamics, I look at how camp taste may be seen as a response to the psychic frameworks of gay subjectivity. In particular, I argue that camp is a discourse of taste that, in its gay configurations at least, is underwritten by a fantasmatic logic of gender ambivalence and sexual transgression.

It is not my intention, however, to claim an essential link between camp and gay subjectivities. Many non-gay-identifying subjects can and frequently do engage/express camp tastes; conversely, many gay men do not.[2] Nevertheless, the way in which camp functions as a taste of and for gay-identifying subjects is, I would argue, constitutively bound to the specific psychosocial contexts inhabited by these subjects. The specificity of these contexts means that camp frequently assumes a particular set of functions and effects for gay men that it does not always assume in nongay contexts.

Camp and/as Gay Taste

To analyze gay camp requires a working definition of what exactly camp is. This task is made all the more difficult by the seemingly antinomic status of a "serious," academic discussion of a discourse like camp that openly lampoons pretenses to truth, depth, and authenticity. As Susan Sontag quips, "serious" analyses of camp often "run the risk of having produced a very inferior piece of Camp."[3] This may explain why so many studies of camp resort to the use of illustrative lists. If the structures of camp prove so resistant to discursive definition, exemplification may be the most effective solution.[4] In many ways, however, this strategy of definition through exemplification has further compounded the problem of defining camp. It has tended to raise a question mark over the very conceptual status of camp, confounding camp as a property of objects and camp as an effect of readings. Andrew Britton argues that this is "the dilemma in which all apologists of camp eventually find themselves: is camp an attribute *of* something or is it attributed *to* something?"[5] Susan Sontag's pioneering essay, "Notes on Camp," offers a prime—and highly influential—example of this conceptual confusion at work. On the one hand, Sontag defines camp as a particular "sensibility," a "way of looking at things." Yet, on the other, she asserts that camp is not simply "*all* in the eye of the beholder," that it is also "a quality discoverable in objects and . . . persons," and she proceeds to list a series of "campy" items, including "movies, clothes, furniture, popular songs, novels, people, buildings," and the like.[6]

For some critics the confusion over whether camp is a property of objects or a property of readings "speaks volumes about the vacant nature of the concept [of camp] itself."[7] However, I suggest that, far from being a sign of camp's epistemological failure, this confusion over the conceptual status of camp may actually be a sign of camp's epistemological success, a sign that camp is actually working; for like most modes of cultural taste, camp is primarily performative in nature. Constituted in and through its very performance, it has little or no status (certainly no substance) apart from the various illocutionary acts—or, more appropriately for this context, textual readings—through which it is constituted. It is this central axiom that is reflected—if not always identified—in the constant slippage between seeing camp as an effect of texts and seeing it as an effect of reading.[8] What the endless lists of camp objects are responding to, and what they are attempting to replicate, is the performative logic of camp itself, the way it works and produces its effects through various acts of camp consumption.

In many ways, camp is a discourse of performativity par excellence, for it is first and foremost a discourse about performance and performative reiteration. Sontag defines camp as "the farthest extension, in sensibility, of the metaphor of life as theater." Camp, she contends, is suffused with a logic of theatricality, of "being-as-playing-a-role." This is why she argues for camp as the modern variant of the nineteenth-century "sensibility" of dandyism championed by Oscar Wilde and the late-Victorian aesthetes. Just as Wilde and his associates pursued a philosophy predicated on the evaluation and classification of the world and its objects according to wholly aesthetic criteria, so camp is a way of seeing the world as "aesthetic phenomena." For Sontag, camp "is the consistently aesthetic experience of the world. It incarnates a victory of 'style' over 'content', 'aesthetics' over 'morality', of irony over tragedy."[9]

Camp is a mode of ironic reading that engages texts in terms of surface and style rather than depth and content. Indeed, the camp deployment of style as the primary guarantor of meaning actively displaces content as the "natural" site of signifying production, inverting the claims of traditional hermeneutics for meaning as substantive, expressive, and essential.

For camp, the value and significance of a text or object lies wholly in its formal properties, its style and appearance, and not in any substance or content that it may be seen to possess. The more stylized or artificial a text or object is, the more amenable it becomes to camp appropriation and use. "Camp is a vision of the world in terms of style—but a particular kind of style," writes Sontag. "It is the love of the exaggerated, the 'off,' of things-being-what-they-are-not. . . . Camp sees everything in quotation marks. It's not a lamp, but a 'lamp'; not a woman, but a 'woman.' To perceive Camp in objects and persons is to understand Being-as-Playing-a-Role" (109).

The exemplary shift in this passage from "lamp" to "woman," from objects to (gendered) persons, is instructive, for camp has long mobilized gender as a privileged arena within which to pursue its formalist credo of "travesty, impersonation, theatricality." In many ways, camp prioritizes gender as the ultimate site of stylistic performativity. "The spirit of camp," writes George Burnett, "lies in its assault on dominant sex roles. . . . Camp is obsessed with [gender] . . . but it is a particular understanding of gender as all fancy-dress and masquerade."[10] As this may suggest, camp shifts the emphasis from seeing gender as an essentialized ontology, a fixed expression of an inner truth, to seeing it as a performative production. It rereads gender not as a biological essence but as "a question of aesthetics . . . , an effect of convention, genre, form, or some other kind of artifice."[11] To this end, camp is drawn to and privileges those images or figures in which the "conventionality" of gender is foregrounded, in which sexual traits and aesthetics are in some way exaggerated or overtly stylized. The best and certainly most frequently cited examples are movie stars. In her essay, Sontag compiles a long list of Hollywood stars who, she contends, are celebrated by camp discourses because of their perceived gender hyperbolization: the "corny flamboyant femaleness of Jayne Mansfield, Gina Lollobrigida, Jane Russell, Virginia Mayo; the exaggerated he-manness of Steve Reeves, Victor Mature. The great stylists of temperament and mannerism, like Bette Davis, Barbara Stanwyck, Tallulah Bankhead, Edwige Feuillère."[12]

Before exploring the dynamics of this privileged nexus of camp discourse, gender performativity, and stardom, I want to highlight how camp readings of gender as conventionalized style are often identified as the major point of attraction and exchange between camp and gay subjectivities/cultures. Sontag claims that, with its stress on the artificiality and thus "the convertibility of 'man' and 'woman,'" camp readings of gender represent a "triumph of the epicene [read: homosexual] style" (109). More directly, Jack Babuscio argues that, as a response to gender performance, camp "springs from the gay sensibility." [13] For Michael Bronski, camp readings of gender as masquerade are an "*essential* part of gay male living." [14]

Many of these arguments work from the general premise that gay and lesbian subjects have what can only be termed a relationship of profound ambivalence to dominant gender structures. According to hegemonic discourses in which compulsory heterosexuality is made the very grounds of sexual difference, homosexuality is invariably defined and represented as a site of gender dissonance or failure. To be gay or lesbian in our culture is to be outside or askew the categories of hegemonic masculinity and femininity, to be not-quite-man or not-quite-woman. As a result, the relationship between gays and gender is fraught with tensions and ambiguities. Like everyone, gays and lesbians are still subject to hegemonic gender, still interpellated into identificatory positions of masculinity and femininity, but those processes of gendered interpellation are often difficult and uneasy in a way that often does not occur for (many) heterosexual-identified subjects.

It is this profound ambivalence apropos dominant systems of sexual difference that is seen to underwrite the celebration of gender denaturalization in practices of gay camp. Because they do not automatically or effortlessly assume the positions of gender normatively prescribed as inevitable or natural expressions of self by the dominant culture, gays and lesbians tend to "experience" these gender positions as cultural roles or imperatives imposed externally and performed with varying degrees of conviction and effectivity. The gay practice of "passing for straight"— the performance of heterosexual gender usually to escape homophobic castigation—is frequently offered as a prime example of this. "The art of passing is an acting art," writes Babuscio, "to pass is to be 'on stage', to impersonate heterosexual citizenry, to pretend to be a 'real' (*i.e.* straight) man or woman." The structuring experience of gender dissimulation furnishes gays with a "heightened awareness and appreciation for disguise, impersonation, the projection of personality," which in turn motivates and "finds voice" in the denaturalizing readings of gender in gay camp as theatrical performance. "To appreciate camp in things or persons," claims Babuscio,

> is to perceive the notion of life-as-theatre, being versus role-playing, reality and appearance. If "role" is defined as the appropriate behaviour associated with a given position in society, then gays do not conform to socially expected ways of behaving as men and women. Camp, by focusing on the outward appearance of role, implies that roles, and, in particular, sex roles, are superficial—a matter of style. Indeed, life itself is role and theatre, appearance and impersonation.[15]

Gay camp is defined in this reading as both an effect and an expression of the ambivalent relations between gay subjects and dominant heterosexual gender structures. What is exhibited in gay camp, what gets articulated through its ironizing discourses is the experience—specifically, though not uniquely, gay/lesbian—of gender disidentification, of failing to recognize oneself or an image of one's desire in the dominant fiction of heterosexual gender categories.[16] This is why Cynthia Morrill argues for gay subcultural camp as "an *affective* response of the queer subject." Camp, she contends, "results from the uncanny experience of looking into a nonreflective mirror and falling outside of the essentialized ontology of heterosexuality, a queer experience indeed."[17]

By describing gay camp in these terms—as something constitutively imbricated within gay subjectivities, especially as they are organized around relations of gender dissonance—these arguments highlight two key, interrelated points. The first pertains to what I described earlier as the productive role of camp as a performative discourse of gay taste. These arguments about gay camp and queer knowledges/experiences represent camp as a discourse that, to co-opt Bourdieu's formulation, arises out of the gay subject's "place in social space" while "guiding the occupants of [that] place . . . towards the social positions adjusted to their properties, and towards the practices . . . which befit the[ir] . . . knowledge[s] and . . . conditions of existence."[18] That is to say, they represent camp as a discourse that articulates gay subjective specificity (gay experiences, gay knowledges, gay competences) and, by so doing, formalizes and concretizes that specificity into a particular sociodiscursive position. The determinative imbrications of camp and gayness are especially evident in those accounts that suggest that, because it emerges out of and responds to the gay subject's specific frames of reference, camp provides an important discursive space within which to articulate and affirm gay identifications. Richard Dyer, for example, asserts that camp provides gay subjects with "a tremendous sense of identification and belonging"; it is a subcultural discourse "that expresses and confirms being a gay man." [19]

Second, by positioning camp in constitutive relations to gay subjectivities, these arguments effectively refer camp to the whole range of registers and forms, social and psychic, across which those subjectivities are produced. Thus, even though most discussions of gay camp concentrate on the social dynamics of the productive relations between camp and gay subjectivities, they nevertheless help define camp as a discourse of taste that assumes important psychic capacities and effects as well. This potential is highlighted, I submit, by the widespread characterizations of gay camp in these arguments as an expression of the gay subject's ambivalent attitudes to (hetero)sexual difference.

Ambivalence is, of course, a fundamental concept of psychoanalytic theory that is used to describe the coexistence of opposing psychic attitudes or feelings toward an object. For Freud, ambivalence was a structuring dynamic of most psychic formations in which the basic dualism of psychic life and the resistance of the unconscious inevitably inscribe oscillation and reversibility as structural conditions of the psychoanalytic subject. However, as Laplanche and Pontalis argue, the notion of ambivalence may be more productively used to describe those specific psychic formations "in which the positive and negative components of the emotional attitude are simultaneously in evidence and inseparable, and where they constitute a non-dialectical opposition which the subject, saying 'yes' and 'no' at the same time, is incapable of transcending." [20] This description speaks profitably in several respects to arguments about the ambivalent relation of gay subjectivities to (hetero)sexual difference. Indeed, some psychoanalytic critics have explicitly mobilized the concept of ambivalence to describe and analyze the gendered relationalities of gayness.

Freud himself nominates ambivalence as a structural tendency of gay psychic organization when he defines homosexuality as a perverse revision of the psychocultural scenario of castration. As mentioned in the last chapter, Freud located homosexuality as a variable response to the constitutive narrativization of desire in the oedipus complex. The theory of the oedipus and castration complexes was developed by Freud to account for the production of sexuality in the subject. In its most basic form, the oedipus complex refers to prototypical patterns of intersubjective relationality played out across parental difference in which the infantile subject learns to desire according to the dictates of phallic supremacy and compulsory heterosexuality. Through the oedipus complex and its dissolution with the threat of castration, the subject is interpellated into a cultural structure of patriarchal sexual differentiation in which desire and identification are split and regulated along inequitable gendered lines: male-phallic-active versus female-castrated-passive. John Fletcher refers to this heterosexual bifurcation of identification and desire as the "law of Oedipal polarity," a law that in effect declares: "You cannot be what you desire; you cannot desire what you wish to be." [21] In the case of oedipal masculinity, this means renouncing attachment to the mother under the sign of castrated negativity and assuming an emulative identification with the idealized phallic father; for oedipal femininity, it means displacing the primary maternal cathexis into an identification with feminine passivity and transferring object-attachment to the polarized axis of patrocentric masculinity.

Although Freud developed several theories to account for the constitution of homosexual desire, he primarily attributed it to a foundational fantasmatic scenario of disavowed castration in which the subject refutes the entry of the symbolic father and the law of oedipal polarity that this entry is charged with instating. In the case of male homosexuality, Freud was particularly insistent that it turned on a fundamental refusal or failure (he uses the terms interchangeably despite their vastly different connotations) to acknowledge maternal castration and cede to a patrocentric structure of libidinal organization. The male homosexual, he argues, refuses to give up the mother to castrated negativity and continues to identify with her in his unconscious while assuming the marks of castration in his own subjectivity. Thus in "Some Neurotic Mechanisms of Jealousy, Homosexuality, and Paranoia," Freud argues that "attachment to the mother [and] fear of castration" are "the factors . . . that we have hitherto found in the psychical aetiology of [male] homosexuality." [22] In "The Sexual Life of Human Beings," he describes homosexual subjectivities as having denied maternal castration and "struck the distinction between the sexes off their programme." [23] This is the one continuous thread throughout Freudian and post-Freudian theories of homosexual desire wherein homosexuality is invariably read and represented as an oppositional response to the critical drama of castration and the socio-symbolic apparatus of (hetero)sexual difference that it is charged with instating.

This is, however, the precise reading that is generally seen to endow psychoanalytic constructions of homosexuality with their most insidious pathological potentials. Kenneth Lewes argues that "many of the arguments about the 'unnaturalness' of homosexuality maintain that the persistence of homosexual object choice is prima facie evidence either that the Oedipus complex has not been worked through or that its experience was so traumatic that it caused a major psychosexual regression to a primitive preoedipal stage."[24] This interpretation has certainly been widespread within orthodox clinical psychoanalysis. In the benchmark 1962 study *Homosexuality: A Psychoanalytic Study of Male Homosexuals*, Irving Bieber asserts categorically that homosexuality represents "a psychopathological escape from [the] sexual realities of the Oedipus complex."[25] As recently as 1993, another American psychoanalyst, Mark J. Adair, writes that the male homosexual disavowal of maternal castration means that the homosexual lives in a borderline-psychotic state of "a false reality" and that he "must pass away the greater part of his existence in flight from oedipal conflicts."[26]

In a slightly different vein, the reading of homosexuality as "a disavowal of castration" has also been assumed by certain feminist psychoanalytic theorists to pathologize homosexuality. Julia Kristeva has made several vicious attacks on homosexuality, both male and female, for what she describes as its "perverse denial of the abyss that marks sexual difference." It is a denial that, she argues, results in a narcissistic and "fascistic" sexuality that admits no "other race" and that she suggests, somewhat peculiarly, has been the motivational psychic structure behind the great social terrors of our century: "anti-semitism and the totalitarian movements that embrace it."[27] Less grandiose but equally as dismissive are the arguments of Jane Gallop, who writes: "I am suspicious of . . . the [male homosexual] wish to deny sexual difference. Women have historically been associated with sexual difference, have been sexually differentiated from the generic so-called mankind. The wish to escape sexual difference might be but another mode of denying women. I distrust male homosexuals because they choose men over women just as do our social and political institutions."[28]

These arguments—both the "classic" psychoanalytic pathologizations of homosexuality and the later feminist examples—depend, however, on reading and assuming the oedipal paradigm, that is the construction of individuated, sexed subjects according to differentiating poles of heterosexual identification and object-choice, as possessing the status of an ontology. Either an ontology of subjective identity as in the earlier examples, in which case homosexuality is pathological because it is an incomplete subjective formation, or an ontology of difference as in the latter, in which case homosexuality refuses difference *tout court* and thus approaches a psychotic refusal of symbolization, or, at the very least, a complete disavowal of the existence of the other sex.

However, as Lacan, among others, has famously taught, Freud's theory of sexual production through the oedipus and castration complexes is not an ontological system of endogenous development but a sociodiscursive network of symbolic fantasies and conventions that is culturally generated and maintained. This means that the homosexual refusal of castration signals not a rejection or denial of sexual difference or anatomical particularity but a refusal of a fantasmatic structure in which that difference is mobilized to bear certain meanings and to produce certain economies of desire and relationality. It is, as John Fletcher argues, not "a blind refusal of an object . . . or a person" or "a disavowal of genital difference, but . . . an attempt to contest or displace the meanings" that sexual difference is charged with transmitting in a phallocentric regime.[29] In fact, in the terms laid out by psychoanalysis in which all forms of structured sexuality are conceived as "perverse" reaction formations to the oedipal crisis, homosexuality can be no more pathologized than any other erotic mode, for all are variations in the field of possibilities opened up by the oedipal drama.[30] No more or less than heterosexuality, homosexual desire is a valid and "intelligible response" to the dilemmas of castration, a "living through" of "its exactions, repudiations, seductions and demands" in a specific way.[31]

It would be absurd to read the Freudian theorization of homosexuality in terms of disavowed castration as an absolute denial or erasure of oedipality or its regimes of sexual difference in toto. Not only is it the case that, logically, one can only refuse what one already engages, but, in psychoanalytic terms, disavowal always contains the trace of its opposite, always presupposes an avowal or identification on another level. For the homosexual subject to disavow castration, he must also avow it, he must accept a place within the symbolic field of oedipal relations opened up by the cultural drama of castration. Rather than capitulate to that field entirely and submit to its libidinal regulations, however, the homosexual subject may be understood to mount a psychic resistance to it—a resistance still contained within the general paradigm of sociosymbolic, oedipal sexuality (for there is no escape from that paradigm, no outside to the regime of meanings that it produces) but that struggles against and disrupts its legislative productions. In this respect, homosexuality is not unlike hysteria in that both function as modes of ambivalent psychic protest, simultaneously assuming and refusing the oedipal laws of sexual difference.[32] Neither fully outside nor fully contained by the symbolic field of oedipal law, homosexuality represents an oscillating vicissitude that, to repeat Laplanche and Pontalis's description of psychic ambivalence, simultaneously says "yes" and "no" to oedipal sexual difference. Thus, rather than read the alleged oedipal ambivalence of homosexuality as a total refusal of sexual difference, it may be more to the point to read it as a disorganizational revision that disrupts the fixity of a certain production of sexual difference—namely, phallic heterosexuality—and displaces it into alternative configurations of regendered desire.

The reading of gay fantasmatic organization sketched here should not be assumed as fixed or essential to formations of homosexuality or homosexual subjectivities. There are many ways to produce and experience homosexual desire that would not be reducible to this scenario of refused castration.[33] In the same way equally ambivalent responses to castration and phallic economies of sexual difference are possible in the psychic organizations and performances of heterosexual desire. For the moment, however, I want to assume this heuristic construction of homosexuality as an ambivalent response to the oedipal polarities of sexual difference in order to further think through the psychosocial functions and effects of gay camp. In particular, I want to explore how this construction speaks to the dynamics of gender disorganization that are generally identified as central to the practices and pleasures of gay camp. With its spectacular deformations of (hetero)sexual difference and its ludic productions of regendered sexuality, camp provides a powerful representation of the scenarios of oedipal ambivalence that psychoanalysis suggests underwrite certain formations of homosexual desire while also allowing extensive scope for the articulation of queer fantasies of gender and sexual rearrangement.

In this context camp has been championed in recent years by some feminist critics precisely because of its perceived capacity for disrupting and reworking hegemonic structures of gender and sexuality. These critics see camp, particularly gay camp, as potentially "subversive" because its central re-presentation of gender as theatrical role-playing embodies a "crucial axiom of feminist theory—the claim that gender is a social construction rather than a natural or biological essence."[34] Camp is viewed in this context as a form of anti-essentialist feminism *avant la lettre*, a coded theory of gender as performative masquerade. Judith Butler, the critic whom David Bergman describes as having "done the most to revise the academic standing of camp and to suggest its politically subversive potential," claims that gay camp provides a powerful model to make "gender trouble."[35] She argues that the parodic remapping of gender as stylized artifice in gay camp "brings into relief the utterly constructed status" of heterosexual gender categories and, therefore, offers a potent "denaturalization" of hegemonic sexual forms. In particular, Butler invokes the queer camp practices of drag, cross-dressing, and lesbian butch/femme stylization as subversive (re)figurations of gender that "*implicitly reveal . . . the imitative structure of gender itself—as well as its contingency. . . .* In the place of the law of heterosexual coherence, we see sex and gender denaturalized by means of a performance which avows their distinctness and dramatizes the cultural mechanisms of their fabricated unity."[36] This disruptive repudiation of the "law" of (hetero)sexual difference in gay camp opens up a site for the articulation of alternative, queer formations of re-gendered desire. As Butler asserts in another context, because it actively foregrounds the constructed, artificial nature of gender, gay camp gives rise to a "proliferating plurality" of gender performances in which "all sorts of resignifying and parodic repetitions become possible."[37]

Camp emerges in this context as a gay psychosocial carnivalesque, a liminal mode of social transgression that uses parody and irony to upset the dominant order of gender and sexuality. Like the carnivalesque, camp is a "fictive, theatrical element . . . that serves to give critical perspectives on social reality, on 'things as they are.'"[38] And like the carnivalesque, camp is "a way of poking fun at the whole cosmology of restrictive sex roles and sexual identifications." [39] However, where the carnivalesque traditionally pursues its brand of social parody through simple hierarchical inversion and thus remains largely recuperable, a form of "licensed release," camp displaces the legislative stability of gender binarisms through queer re-formations—or at least provides the potential for this.

This final point is important, for it cuts to the question of the political status and effectivity of gay camp. Some critics maintain that gay camp is essentially "disengaged, depoliticized—or at least apolitical" because it simply parodies existing gender categories and thus remains within the terms and control of those categories.[40] For some this explains why camp has been so easily and readily "co-opted" by mainstream culture in recent years. However, as David Bergman writes, "a style can be destabilizing without being overtly oppositional." [41] Indeed, the very notion of "overt oppositionality" is, in relation to gender and sexuality at least, a highly problematical, even impossible one. We are all subjects of and subject to the demands and relations of sexual difference, all subject to the "injunction *to be* a given gender." Consequently, it is impossible to access a position outside or external to sexual difference. There can, as Butler puts it, only ever be "possibilities of doing gender [that] repeat and displace through hyperbole, dissonance, internal confusion and proliferation the very constructs [of gender] by which they are mobilized." [42] Gay camp provides just such a possibility and therein lies its unique political potential. By producing practices and readings that foreground the conventionality of gender through parodic imitation, gay camp exposes the performativity of gender itself in a way that destabilizes the naturalized categories of gender and sexuality and opens up new possibilities for queer desire.

To provide examples of how camp can work as a site of gay fantasmatic performance, I return to gay spectatorships; in particular, gay spectatorial engagements with the excessive female star-image. The centrality of cinematic star-images to camp readings of gender has already been noted. This is especially true of gay camp, which has a long and popular tradition of celebrating female Hollywood stars. As we shall see, this tradition has provided strong potential for the production of all sorts of queer fantasies and desires.

Gay Camp and the Female Star-Image

In many ways, the very status of cinema as a "performing art" makes it ideal for camp readings. The mimetic nature of film, its status as a representation of an always missing referent, marks it out from the start as a particularly effective form of illusion and pretence. Furthermore, the emphasis in film, especially Hollywood film, on artifice and extreme stylization, on costume, script, and performance, signals to what extent cinema as a cultural institution may be seen as saturated by a logic of masquerade. This is nowhere more apparent, perhaps, than in the Hollywood star-system, that complex network of industrial, cultural, and textual relations through which the signifying functions of Hollywood film actors are constructed, defined, and circulated.[43] Indeed, the very profession of acting on which the star-system rests powerfully enshrines the notion of subjective masquerade. As Annette Kuhn argues:

> Understood in its everyday sense, performance is allied with acting, and acting is regarded as an activity that involves pretence, dissimulation, an intent to seem to be something or someone one is, in reality, not. An actor's role is assumed like a mask, the mask concealing the performer's 'true self.' . . . In effecting a distance between assumed persona and real self, the practice of performance constructs a subject which is both fixed in the distinction between role and self and at the same time, paradoxically, called into question in the very act of performance. For over against the 'real self,' performance poses the possibility of a mutable self, of a fluidity of subjectivity.[44]

Importantly, and symptomatically perhaps, the structures of Hollywood stardom actively downplay the disruptive potentials of cinematic performance by forwarding the star-image itself as epistemological guarantor of the star's "reality." Richard Dyer argues that one primary ideological function of Hollywood stardom is to construct a coherent star-image with which to anchor and recontain the star's multifaceted performativity. The star-image, he suggests, functions as the ground on which the star's authenticity is established and affirmed. This recuperative process is, however, riven by paradox, for the discourses that define and make up the star-image as "real" and "continuous" are themselves insistently artifactual. As a result, the entire star phenomenon is "profoundly unstable," and, in many cases, "the sheer multiplicity of the images, the amount of hype, the different stories told become overwhelmingly contradictory."[45]

The radical instability of the structures of stardom means that a star's image can be interpreted in different ways. Significantly, Dyer points to camp as a powerful example of just such a "different" reading of stardom. Camp, he argues, plays on the instabilities and contradictions within the structured images of stardom in order to foreground their artifactual performativity. Camp reads stars

> not for any supposed inner essence revealed but for the way they jump through the hoops of social convention. The undulating contours of Mae West, the lumbering gait and drawling voice of John Wayne, the thin, spiky smile of Joan Fontaine—each can be taken as an emblem of social mores: the ploys of female seduction, the certainty of male American power, the brittle niceness of upper class manners. Seeing them that way is seeing them as appearance, as image, in no way asking them to be what they are, really. (16)

Although Dyer refers here to a broad range of cultural structures or what he terms "social mores," camp is a deconstructive way to read stars that, as noted earlier, is concerned most centrally with questions of gender/sexual performance. Sontag's argument that camp readings of movie stars are organized essentially around the camp "relish for the exaggeration of sexual characteristics," citing the "corny flamboyant femaleness of Jayne Mansfield" and "the exaggerated he-manness of Steve Reeves [and] Victor Mature,"[46] is particularly true of gay formations of camp, which are, as noted, typified largely by parodic rereadings of gender as stylistic impersonation. Gay camp plays on the structural instabilities of the Hollywood star-image as a way to highlight and articulate queer experiences of gender incoherence. In their work on gay camp, Jack Babuscio and Michael Bronski stress the importance of gender parody to gay camp readings of Hollywood stars. Like Sontag, they cite the hyperbolic gender performances of Mae West, Jayne Mansfield, Maria Montez, Johnny Weissmuller, and Victor Mature as exemplary while also pointing to the "androgynous" stylization of Greta Garbo and Marlene Dietrich; the highly mannered performance styles of Bette Davis and Joan Crawford; the strong-willed independence of Katharine Hepburn, Barbara Stanwyck, Rosalind Russell, Barbra Streisand, and Bette Midler; and the powerful sexual personae presented by Lana Turner and Marilyn Monroe.[47] The list is far-reaching, encompassing nearly every facet of Hollywood stardom. Yet the common link in this seemingly disparate group of Hollywood stars is the way their "performances," at the level of both general star-image and individual role, are read by gay camp as patently excessive in relation to hegemonic definitions of gender and sexuality. Gay camp readings of these stars stress and celebrate how "they acted out, acted around or acted against the grain of the sexually circumscribed stereotypes which they were contracted to dramatize."[48] As such, gay camp charges the performances of these stars with defamiliarizing and distancing dominant configurations of gender signification and, through this, providing a critical space within which to construct new formations of queer desire.

Notably, almost all the stars cited as exemplars of and for gay camp reading are female. Although most commentators on gay camp refer to certain male stars like Victor Mature or John Wayne as potential vehicles for gay camp readings of gender parody, the main focus of their discussions, as, indeed, of the structures of gay camp reading themselves, is primarily Hollywood's female stars.[49] As Paul Roen writes, "The great camp actresses seem to have become a fixed and immutable part of gay culture, whereas actors, on the other hand, come and go, fade, diminish, and are eventually forgotten. Women such as Bette Davis and Mae West, to give but two examples, have become gay traditions, their memory lovingly handed down from one generation to the next."[50]

The reasons for these intense affiliations between gay men, gay camp readings, and female stars are both complex and varied. Much of the affective resonance between gay camp and female stars has to do with the unique, highly charged status of the female star-image within mainstream narrative film. Given the masculinist moorings of dominant cinema, the female image is the site of a problematizing "otherness" and "excess" for mainstream film in ways that the male image, conventionally, is not. Although the structural otherness of the female image has, of course, resulted in a series of highly developed representational practices designed to repress its significatory volatilities, of which the star-system itself is often cited as a privileged example, it also introduces marked elements of conflict and contradiction into the significatory labors of the female star-text. This semiotic instability in turn allows for resistant or aberrant readings; and it is this keen capacity for subversive reconstructions on the part of female star-images that lies behind their prioritization in gay camp readings.

The gay camp celebration of female stars may also be seen to be motivated by and expressive of the many feminine identifications that circulate in and around male homosexual definitions and subjectivities. Because male homosexuality is widely represented in our culture as possessing strong, even constitutive ties with femininity, an active assumption of a male homosexual identity will potentially occasion marked identifications with the feminine at several different levels. "Because their object-choice defies the libidinal logic of conventional masculinity," writes Kaja Silverman, "gay men are frequently viewed through the alternative screen of femininity." Not only are gay men seen and defined by the general culture as feminine, "they themselves feel the pressure of that definition" personally and psychically.[51] The gay camp fascination with and celebration of spectacular female stars may be understood as a symptomatic effect of this definitional correlation between male homosexuality and femininity. It is a way perhaps for gay spectators to play out and affirm their own forms of feminine identification.

Many gay commentators do in fact describe and evaluate gay camp fascination with female stars in explicit terms of feminine identification. Alexander Doty argues that

> gay men who identify with some conception of "the feminine" through processes that could stem from conscious personal choice, or from internalizing long-standing straight imperatives that encourage gay men to think of themselves as "not men" (and therefore, by implication or by direct attribution, as being like "women"), or from some degree of negotiation between these two processes, are at the center of the gay culture cults built around the imposing, spectacular women stars of opera . . . , theater . . . , film . . . , popular music . . . , and television.[52]

More directly, Michael Bronski asserts:

> There are hosts of female actors, singers, and personalities with whom gay men have strongly identified. . . . While there are certainly male sex symbols in Hollywood movies, and many gay men lust after them as sexual objects, they identify with the women as emotional subjects. . . .

gay men's identification with women stars is a celebration of their own sexual feelings and a means of experiencing them in an exalted context.[53]

The question of gay feminine identification is complex. At this point, however, I highlight it both as a way to explain — or at least help explain — the primacy of female stars over and against male stars in gay camp, as well as a way to disarm some of the criticisms often brought to bear against gay camp. Although I have strategically avoided addressing it before now, gay camp in general and gay camp readings of female stars in particular have been widely criticized in some circles on the grounds that they constitute yet another instance of the misogynous colonization of the feminine by men. By reading an excessive or otherwise denaturalized femininity into the various performance modes of female stars, gay camp, it is alleged, engages in a particularly insidious form of misogyny that reduces all femininity to the unnatural and the grotesque.[54] Andrew Britton, for example, argues that "the infelicitous combination of self-contempt and misogyny which is always latent, and sometimes nastily explicit, in the camp use of [female stars] transforms a body of work which has great significance for feminism (and thus for gay men) into an opportunity for frivolity or self-oppression."[55]

One widely influential critique is made by Marilyn Frye, who, though not directly concerned with the specific issue of gay camp readings of female stars, addresses the broader framework of gay camp "uses" of femininity that she, like Britton, sees as misogynous. Indeed, Frye points to the celebration of an excessive, theatricalized femininity in gay camp as exemplary support for her foundational argument that "woman-hating is an obvious corollary of man-loving."

> One of the things which persuades the straight world that gay men are not really men is the effeminacy of style of some gay men and the gay institution of the impersonation of women. . . . But as I read it, gay men's effeminacy and donning of feminine apparel displays no love of or identification with women or the womanly.
>
> For the most part, this femininity is affected and is characterized by theatrical exaggeration. It is a casual and cynical mockery of women, for whom femininity is the trappings of oppression, but it is also a kind of play, a toying with that which is taboo. It is a naughtiness indulged

in, I suspect, more by those who believe in their immunity to contamination than by those with any doubts or fears. . . . What gay male affectation of femininity seems to me to be is a kind of serious sport in which men may exercise their power and control over the feminine. . . . But the mastery of the feminine is not feminine. It is masculine. It is not a manifestation of woman-loving but of woman-hating. Someone with such mastery may have the very first claim to manhood.[56]

I cite this passage at length not only because it offers a crystalline example of the arguments often brought to bear against gay camp readings of femininity/female stars but also because it starkly illustrates the problematical gender essentialism that undergirds many of these critiques of gay camp as misogynous phallic colonization in disguise. As is apparent, Frye assumes an absolute structure of gender binarism that is the fixed property of male and female subjects anatomically defined: the feminine is assumed to belong exclusively and "naturally" to women and, conversely, the masculine to men. As a result, the "appropriation" of femininity by gay male camp can only be defined as an improper act of transgressive gender violation.

Such an argument becomes untenable, however, when one recognizes that femininity is not an innate essence that is the unique biological property of a particular sex but a shifting discursive construction that figures variably in the psychosocial representations and day-to-day performances of several different subjectivities. Female subjectivities or women are of course the group for whom the category of "femininity" features most prominently and decisively; however, as suggested, femininity also plays an important role in the definitions of gay male subjectivities. Gay camp readings of female stars do not represent, therefore, an illegitimate colonization of femininity by a group that has no claim whatsoever to that category but an exploration by gay men of their own important psychocultural relations to the feminine. As Butler asserts in an argument that, again although specifically concerned with the gay camp practice of drag, may just as effectively be applied to all forms of gay camp "uses" of femininity:

Drag is not the putting on of a gender that belongs properly to some other group, i.e. an act of *ex*propriation or *ap*propriation that assumes that gender is the rightful property of sex, that "masculine" belongs to "male" and "feminine" belongs to "female." There is no "proper" gender, a gender proper to one sex rather than another, which is in some sense that sex's cultural property. Where that notion of the "proper" operates, it is always and only *improperly* installed as the effect of a compulsory system.[57]

Gay camp readings of femininity can and, indeed, need to be seen not as a (mis)representation of a fixed sexuality that belongs "naturally" to women but as a play on the performances of femininity in particular circumstances by subjects who have been culturally and psychically ascribed fundamental relations to such performances.

This is not to say that gay male camp is devoid of misogynous effects or that it might not, in certain instances, even be motivated by misogyny. Like all subjects, gay men are still products, however marginal or attenuated, of an insistently masculinist sociocultural formation. Consequently, gay men are just as susceptible to misogyny as anyone else. Yet, here again, the issue of gay men's own definitional ties to femininity, their identificatory alignments with the feminine, means that we need to read and account for gay male misogyny in very specific terms. "Men may have misogyny in common," writes Alexander Doty, "but gay men's misogyny, particularly that of feminine gay men, needs to be discussed with more attention to its specific queer psychological and cultural foundations and patterns."[58]

Because gay men are defined in and by the dominant culture as gender dysphoric and placed in constitutive relations to femininity, gay male misogyny takes on a distinctive cast. Gay male misogyny, where and when it exists, is, as Doty notes, more likely to be directed "inward" toward a femininity understood as the gay man's own rather than "outward" toward a femininity understood as external and totally other, that is, as belonging to women. In this way, gay male misogyny is "perhaps more comparable to straight women's misogyny than to that of straight men," manifesting itself both in negative forms such as self-loathing and masochism as well as potentially liberating forms of self-parody, masquerade, and deconstruction (86–87). To compare gay male and female relations to femininity does not imply a simple equivalence between the two. Comparability is not synonymity and, even though gay men and women might both be placed in definitional relations to femininity, the nature and functions of those relations, as of the cultural forms of femininity constructed and/or mobilized by those relations, are profoundly different.

The major structures of these differences accrue from the fundamental dissonances that exist in gay male configurations of femininity, dissonances created in and by the constitutive misfit between the "masculine" and "feminine" signifiers that traverse and help define cultural constructions of male homosexuality. In this context, it is somewhat misleading to speak of gay male "relations" to or "configurations" of femininity as if they simply provide a different incarnation of a stable, preexisting category. The residual essentialism implicit in these formulations works against an understanding of how gay male configurations of femininity radically reconstruct not only femininity but, in effect, the entire field of gender signification.

The polyvocal collision of transgender signs intrinsic to the very notion of gay male femininity signals in and of itself an excess apropos hegemonic formulations of femininity. It pushes the definitional parameters of femininity so far out that it puts into question, at least for queer subjects, the status of "femininity" as a coherent, self-identical category. The gay assumption of the feminine works, as Butler suggests, is "to multiply possible sites of application of the term, to reveal the arbitrary relation between the signifier and the signified, and to destabilize and mobilize the sign."[59] This semiotic disorganization in turn also throws the category of "masculinity" into turmoil. Given the binary cast of hegemonic heterosexual gender structures in which masculinity and femininity are defined through mutually constitutive relations of difference and exclusion, the destabilization of one always affects the other. In the case of gay camp, its mobilization of the category of femininity as a strategic site for gay *male* enunciation ruptures and confounds the definitional borders of sexual difference to the point that their juridical power is undercut and their legislative effects (i.e., separate masculine/feminine gender classes) are thrown into disarray.

This argument may further explain why female star-images have traditionally been privileged by gay male camp over and against male star-images: the "transgender" dynamics of gay male feminine identification offer greater possibilities for the types of deconstructive reading and transgressive sexual reconfiguration that gay camp engages. In a brief discussion of gay male obsessions with classic Hollywood female stars, Michael Moon writes:

> Not the least of the cultural constructs shattered by [identification with] the adorable (self-) image on the movie screen is the masculine gender identity of male fans of Montez or Lana Turner or Jayne Mansfield. For how many gay men of my own or the previous generation were our earliest intimations that there might be a gap between our received gender identity and our subjective or "felt" one the consequence not of noticing our own erotic attraction to another boy or man but of enthusiastically enjoying and identifying with the performative excesses of Maria Montez rather than Jon Hall, or Lana Turner rather than Burt Lancaster, or Jayne Mansfield rather than Mickey Hargitay?[60]

By promoting an insistently cross-gendered identification, gay male celebrations of the spectacular female star radically undercut the stability of heterosexual gender systems. As such, they articulate the logic of psychic ambivalence and gender dissonance that I have suggested structures both gay camp and gay psychocultural organization alike. Interestingly, Moon's description of the "shattering" effects of gay male identification with the female star resonates suggestively with psychoanalytic characterizations of homosexuality as a disordering of polarized sexual difference across the oedipal axes of identification and object-choice. Gay spectatorial identification with female stars may be interpreted in this context as an important site in which to engage and pursue this constitutive homosexual struggle against the polarized injunction of phallic, oedipal desire. This potential of gay camp identification with the female star image is also highlighted, albeit in a more personal vein, by Wayne Koestenbaum when he writes: "I spent much of my childhood trying to distinguish identification from desire, asking myself, 'Am I in love with Julie Andrews, or do I think I *am* Julie Andrews?' I knew that to love Julie Andrews placed me, however vaguely, in heterosexuality's domain; but to identify with Julie Andrews, to want to be the star of *Star!*, placed me under suspicion."[61]

Because it insists on and promotes a flagrant identification with the female image, gay camp confounds the heterosexual polarization of desire and identification along gender lines, claiming against oedipal law that, "yes, I can be what I desire *and* I can desire what I wish to be."[62] Within the terms of gay camp, the oedipal polarity between desire and identification, phallic and castrated, being and having ceases to function with any real coherence. This flagrant disruption of oedipal coherency may be one of the primary—certainly one of the more psychically thrilling—pleasures offered by camp to the gay spectator.

Gay Camp, Sexual Ambiguity, and the Subversion of Gender
in Female Star Performance: The Case of Mae West

Gay camp traditionally privileges those female stars who can be read as enacting an excessive or parodic performance of femininity that denaturalizes and "gives the lie" to dominant orchestrations of gender and desire. Examples range from the hypersimulation of patriarchal images of female sexuality in the performance styles of stars like Mae West, Jayne Mansfield, or Dolly Parton to the "androgynous" stylization of Greta Garbo or Marlene Dietrich and the aggressively controlled and self-determined performances of stars like Bette Davis, Joan Crawford, Katharine Hepburn, and Barbra Streisand. Gay camp readings stress the way these star-images present enactments of gender and sexuality that exceed the culturally legitimated script of "appropriate" femininity, thereby destabilizing the fragile performativity of heterosexual gender categories and opening up critical textual space within which gay readers can engage and articulate their own fantasy scenarios of sexual and social transgression.

In her study of female cinematic representation, *From Reverence to Rape*, Molly Haskell introduces the now-famous appellations "superfemale" and "superwoman" to refer to the gender disruptive potentials contained within the performances of these various star-images. Haskell uses superfemale to describe those stars who remain largely within received forms of feminine gender role behavior but exaggerate them to such an extent that they become potentially ridiculous. She employs superwoman to refer to the "androgynous" performances of those stars who actively resist the confines of traditional femininity, "adopt[ing] male characteristics in order to enjoy male prerogatives, or merely to survive."[63]

Although suggestive, Haskell's distinction is difficult to sustain in analysis. Not only can the same star incorporate features of both categories, even in the same textual performance, but the ostensible effect of both categories is to destabilize and confuse the very gender differences on which these distinctions are based in the first place. Thus the hyper-feminine style of a superfemale performance, for example, often incorporates conventionally masculine features such as aggressiveness, self-confidence, and determination just as emphatically as the superwoman performances. The superwoman, in turn, can just as easily deploy traditional forms of femininity in her performances. As a result, the signifying powers of these gendered terms are radically undermined. To distinguish between performative styles based on either a parodically exaggerated adherence to received gender definitions or a deviant amalgamation of differentiated gender conventions becomes less important than the fact that by exceeding traditional gender definitions in one way or another these performances disrupt and subvert the fixity of gender boundaries. Within the signifying frameworks of such performances, gender boundaries can become erased or, at the very least, blurred and confounded.

This helps explain why tropes like androgyny, transvestism, and perversion feature so frequently in descriptions of the excessive performance styles of these star-images. Haskell describes Mae West, who provides one of the clearest cinematic examples of the exaggerated feminine performance of the superfemale, as markedly "androgynous" in her signifying effects. "So complete was West's androgyny," Haskell writes, "that one hardly knows into which sex she belongs, and by any sexual-ideological standards of film criticism, she is an anomaly—too masculine to be a female impersonator, too gay in her taste to be a woman" (115). By exceeding appropriate structures of feminine behavior and representation, both "styles" of excessive gender performance confound the borders between feminine and masculine and, consequently, both possess the potential for androgynous effect.

Certainly, this is how these star performances are received, read, and evaluated in gay camp traditions. The fundamental appeal and value of these various star-images stem almost entirely from their perceived disorganizations of hegemonic gender. The gay camp reception of the extravagant female star-image turns on a primary structure of sexual incongruity in which the star is seen to cross and mix the codes or signs of (hetero)sexual difference in such entwined, hyberbolic configurations so as to throw off their semiotic effectivity. Camp is a discourse rooted in irony, and, as such, incongruity is one of its privileged modes. Andrew Ross famously asserts that camp depends on a foundational logic of historical incongruity in which "the products . . . of a much earlier mode of production, which has lost its power to dominate cultural meanings, become available, in the present, for redefinition, according to contemporary codes of taste."[64] Although this is true of a certain tradition of mass or commercialized camp—as seen in the retro comedies that have been such a staple of mainstream cinematic camp in the past three decades, from *Thoroughly Modern Millie* (1967), *Head* (1968), and *Silent Movie* (1976) to *Peggy Sue Got Married* (1986), *The Brady Bunch Movie* (1995), and *Pleasantville* (1998)—it is less so of traditions of gay camp, which are shaped by an even more fundamental logic of sexual incongruity. Historical anachronism is often mobilized in gay camp, but its status is largely secondary, functioning as a strategy for the production of gay camp's primary concern, which is sexual inconsonance and gender subversion.

To develop this argument, I focus on the specific case of Mae West. Not only is West one of the most prominent and enduring icons of gay cinematic camp, her reception in gay cultures has consistently turned on an explicit foundational structure of sexual incongruity and ambivalence. Indeed, West's privileged status within gay male traditions is almost always explained in terms that stress the perceived ambiguity, or androgyny, of her gender and sexual performances. As Paul Roen notes, gay men "have always adored" Mae West because of the "camp quality" of "the tension between her aggressively masculine sexuality and her opulently feminine, face, figure, and screen persona. Truly, she is like a gay man trapped inside a woman's body."[65]

More than any other figure, West represents the most consistent and sustained engagement between gay camp and Hollywood stardom, an engagement that was, significantly, interactive and mutually productive. It is widely acknowledged that during her early career in vaudeville and theater West was strongly influenced by the exposure she received to male homosexual subcultures, and she drew extensively from gay camp practices of female impersonation and sexual humor when developing her distinctive persona and acting style. West's interest in and engagement with gay cultures is evident from the fact that, during the 1920s, she wrote and produced for the New York stage several plays with explicit gay content, one of which, *The Pleasure Man*, became something of a cause célèbre when it was closed down by the vice squad, and West was arraigned on obscenity charges.[66] West even managed to work numerous subtle references or allusions to male homosexuality into many of her films through the use of coded gay argot, the representation of effeminate or otherwise "queer" supporting characters, and the casting of actors such as Cary Grant, Randolph Scott, and Edward Hearn who were widely rumored to be gay in the subcultural gossip of the time.

Not surprisingly, this explicit engagement with and assumption of gay practices and styles has made West an enduring figure of gay subcultural reception. During her short but stunningly spectacular cinematic career in the thirties and early forties, West was widely popularized as a cult star in Anglo-American urban gay subcultures. Marybeth Hamilton asserts that West was a firm favorite with gay audiences of this period, noting that West "charged her theatrics with special meaning for gay men" of the time, who assumed and "enjoyed West precisely as a skillful camp agent" (135). Although inevitably fluctuating in intensity and changing in meanings and effects, West's significance for gay subcultures continued long after the close of her cinematic career. Throughout the postwar period, West remained popular in gay subcultures. She was, for example, a standard persona for gay drag performances throughout the midcentury and beyond.[67] The nightclub revues West developed and performed in the mid-fifties, first in Las Vegas and then in cities across the United States, attracted strong and highly visible gay followings, functioning as what one commentator described as "obvious homosexual events."[68] Gay receptions of West were further reinvigorated—if inevitably redefined—in the late sixties and seventies when West was suddenly "rediscovered" as a popular cultural icon by the mainstream traditions of retro pop and mass camp that emerged with such force during this era. The latter-day repopularization of West in both mainstream and gay subcultural traditions was further strengthened with West's own spectacular—if highly controversial—attempts to make a cinematic comeback in the seventies. More recently, a spate of popular and academic readings that position West centrally in relation to gay subcultural histories or discourses of camp have helped reassert her continued significance as a figure of investment in contemporary gay cultures.[69]

From the beginning, West's enormous popularity stemmed from her perceived challenges to and subversions of hegemonic structures of gender and sexuality. Indeed, the central image in gay receptions and readings of West is inevitably that of the female female impersonator or what Ramona Curry describes as a "female displaying a male displaying a female."[70] As early as 1934, George Davis was openly declaring this queer reading of West in the pages of *Vanity Fair*, where he wrote, "I love you, Miss West, because YOU are the greatest female impersonator of all time."[71] In fact, rumors suggesting West may have literally been a "drag queen" (i.e., a man masquerading as a woman) circulated for a long time as an integral part of Anglo-American gay urban folklore.[72]

Many commentators have criticized this insistent construction of West as drag queen in gay cultures, arguing that it is nothing more than an instance of cruel misogyny. In one early example of these critiques, Joan Mellen claims that the gay male audiences "who applaud West's performances at the re-run houses on St Mark's Place" do so merely "because she seems to them to represent the ultimate of sexual degradation in a woman." For these men, she writes, West imparts "an aura of the transvestite, making a mockery of female sexuality by flaunting what are no more than ordinary female attributes."[73] More recently, in an otherwise nuanced and insightful study of feminist camp, Pamela Robertson also dismisses gay readings of West as drag queen as "generally partak[ing] of camp's misogyny; West seems like a female impersonator because she appears to be grotesque, a man in drag, a joke on women and not a woman."[74] Although misogyny may be an element of gay receptions of West as drag queen, I am not convinced that it is the only or even dominant dynamic at work in these readings. As I argued earlier, the specter of misogyny is used far too frequently to denounce gay camp readings with little or no regard to the specific conditions of gay male subjectivities and cultures. Gay receptions of West as drag queen can only be understood in terms of their gay contexts and the psychocultural traditions of gay gender ambivalence and disorganization within which they are situated. These receptions assume, and what I claim their construction of West as drag queen is designed to facilitate, a fantasmatic appropriation and reproduction of West as site of gay identification. Gay camp readings of West as drag queen do not distance her as a monstrous or ludicrous other or reduce her to the status of pathetic object for the camp subject's humor; they claim her as a figure of and for gay identification and self-representation. By engaging and recasting West as a drag queen, gay camp readings redefine her as a coded or symbolic homosexual—what Paul Roen describes in the passage cited earlier as "a gay man trapped in a woman's body"—and, by so doing, render her a figure of specifically gay resonance, appeal, and emulative identification.

For evidence one need look no further than what is perhaps the most celebrated, certainly most widely disseminated, historical example of a gay camp reading of West: Parker Tyler's *Screening the Sexes: Homosexuality in the Movies*. Tyler was a leading American film critic of the postwar era who, in over twenty books and countless articles and reviews, developed a substantial and broadly influential body of film theory and criticism. He was also homosexual and a longtime fan and camp devotee of Mae West. He came out spectacularly as both in 1972 with the publication of *Screening the Sexes*, his most enduringly popular work. Written explicitly under what Tyler's longtime gay partner, Charles Boultenhouse, describes in a recent reissue of the book as "the aegis of High Camp," *Screening the Sexes* is a witty, wide-ranging, and willfully eccentric tour through a variety of cinematic configurations of homosexual desire.[75] Fittingly, given Tyler's self-avowed fascination with West and the fact that the book was written at the peak of her latter-day repopularization, the opening chapter is an extended panegyric to West, whom Tyler dubs, with obvious camp extravagance, "Mother-Superior of the Faggots." Assuming the widespread reading of West as drag queen in gay cultures as his starting point, Tyler asserts that far from constituting "serious disrespect," the "camp gesture" of claiming West as a symbolic female impersonator is, in fact, born out of a profound, if perverse, adoration; it is an assumption and celebration of West as what in pre-Stonewall gay subcultures was known as the "auntie," "an older queen [who] would act as oracle, authority, and admonisher to a group of younger, less experienced members of the clan." Implicit in this honorific construction of West as oracular "older queen" is the equally honorific, but no less functional, construction of her as a figure of gay identification, a site for the projection and cathexis of gay self-representations. Tyler promotes this scenario of symbolic self-identification as foundational for gay engagements with West when he describes her status in gay cultures as that of a "touring queen" and "a certain style of homosexual." What "homo society" perceives in West, he writes,

> is the perfect assurance of . . . its Mother Superior, whose suavity is that of a candid diplomat and whose tacit authority is that of the Commander in Chief of the Armed Forces. . . . The ease and authority of Miss West as a homosexual camp symbol speaks aloud of her unique privilege: she is, after all, a woman. In many respects she behaves like a homo with a lifelong dedication to putting on the ritz, while undeniably being a good fellow through it all. (1–2)

Although clearly a product of its time and place, Tyler's reading helps explicate the reticulated elements of identification, respect, and genuine affection that have been so vital, historically, to gay camp receptions of West and that continue to inform her iconic status and uses in contemporary gay camp as well.[76] Tyler's dazzling metaphoric collocation of shifting sets of diametrically gendered images to describe those receptions ("Mother Superior"/"Commander in Chief of the Armed Forces," "woman"/"fellow"; elsewhere he refers to West as "the kingliest of queens") also helps explicate how gay camp readings of West work through a logic of sexual incongruity. If West is assumed and cast in gay camp readings as a symbolic site of gay identification, that is largely because her image and texts are supremely amenable to those scenarios of sexual incongruity and ambivalence that are central to discourses of gay camp and gay fantasmatic specificity alike.

The West persona and oeuvre are replete with tropes and figures that could be assumed and read by gay spectators as gender ambiguous, if not gender subversive. West's calculated performance of an excessive, parodic hyperfemininity was modeled on the camp parodies of homosexual drag, and the result is what Pamela Robertson terms a "deliberate and ironic female masquerade," a "double mimesis" that "exaggerate[s], burlesque[s], and expose[s] stereotypical female styles as impersonation."[77] The femininity that West produces is heavily stylized, reduced to broadly drawn conventions, poses, and gestures that denaturalize and disrupt hegemonic assumptions of gender as expressive essence.

That the West persona is itself so readily given to parodic imitation and caricatural representation—as precisely "the Mae West character"—

demonstrates how invested it is in camp traditions of gender theatricalization. Take, for example, the extreme stylization of the West look itself. More than any other star, West flaunts the patent artificiality of glamorous Hollywood femininity. The extravagant, bodice-hugging, hourglass dresses; the heavily powdered, alabaster complexion; the precisely painted lips and eyebrows; the peroxided and coiffed hair—all attest to the meticulously constructed nature of the West look. The open artificiality of the West look is even underscored in the films themselves, as West is frequently shown engaging in labors of cosmetic production—"doing" her face, her hair, her fingernails—and other characters are often depicted responding to or commenting on the "unnaturalness" of her appearance. As one of the moralizing wowsers in *Go West, Young Man* (1936) quips, "In my time, women with hair like that didn't come out in the day."

The flagrant sense of excessive gender performativity in the West persona is further strengthened by other interrelated elements. West typically plays the part of an actual performer in the narratives of her films—vaudeville showgirl, saloon chanteuse, stage actress, film star—thus accentuating the imitation and theatricality that pervade her textuality. Her films also feature at least two or three stock musical numbers in which West takes to the stage and performs a series of broadly sexual spectacles. Generally, the numbers are the most artificially orchestrated sequences in the whole film, with West donning her most outrageous costumes. In *Klondike Annie* (1936), she appears in one musical sequence dressed in full oriental fantasy fashion; in the infamous "My American Beauty" sequence in *Belle of the Nineties* (1934), West is transformed through costume into a butterfly, a rose, a bat, a spider, and, for the grand finale, Lady Liberty herself complete with crown and flaming torch.

In addition to the theatrical display, West's unusual performance style, which is generally broad, exaggerated, and superficial, is played more for surface than depth. In most of her films, West projects a carefully composed exterior that veils the nature of the woman inside. Describing West's performance in *Belle of the Nineties*, for example, Paul Roen writes, "She's supposed to be a vaudeville star, yet she does virtually nothing when she's onstage. She just stands there, striking poses and giving off vibrations. . . . It's like she's getting paid to breathe."[78] The odd aloofness of West's performance style imbues her persona with a sense of cool irony that inscribes a potential distance between West as performer and the roles of patriarchal femininity she is playing. She is an expert mimic of the codes and gestures of femininity, but her enactment of them is generally playful, and she comes across as a resistant performer who impersonates gender rather than embodies it.

This patently resistant performance of excessive femininity and sexuality tends, in turn, to produce a range of broad but nevertheless commanding connotations of sexual ambiguity and androgyny. For example, the aggressive dynamism with which West enacts her femininity endows her persona with traditionally masculine dimensions of power, control, and authority. Her production of an insistently active, even predatory female sexuality mixes and confounds the traditional polarities of phallic heterosexuality in all sorts of disruptive ways.

Within this context, one could cite the much noted (and imitated) singularity of Mae West's vocal style. In a brief aside within the context of a discussion of how classic Hollywood film traditionally uses vocal irregularities such as accent, speech, or impediment to "corporealize" or "deposit . . . the female body into the female voice" and thereby contain feminine desire, Kaja Silverman cites West, along with Marlene Dietrich and Lauren Bacall, as notable exceptions, since, as she writes, "in each of these . . . instances it is a 'male' rather than a 'female' body which is deposited in the voice. In other words, the lowness and the huskiness of each of these three voices connote masculinity rather than femininity, so that the voice seems to exceed the gender of the body from which it proceeds."[79]

In the case of West, the androgynizing potentials of her vocality are not simply the result of a low or husky register. They are also the result of her vocal delivery and how she uses her body to facilitate that delivery. Witness the meticulously paced, self-aware manner with which West handles her lines. It is a masterful style of vocal manipulation that allows her to infuse seemingly innocent lines with the type of ribald sexual allusions traditionally associated with male humor. Combined with this is the unique way West typically poses her body when delivering the characteristic pun or wisecrack—lips curled in a sneer, hand on her waist, hips swaggering rhythmically with the accent of each phrase. It is a defiant possession of the female body that infuses her performances with marked qualities of "masculine" aggressiveness and sexual predatoriness.

The widespread use of an 1890s frontier setting in many of her films also heightens the sense of gender transgression and confusion that is an integral effect of West's parodic sexual performances—at least within the context of gay camp readings. The frontier world of the 1890s within which West pursues her particular brand of brash gender performance is a world popularly represented as masculine. It is a rough-and-tumble, rambunctious world, far from the "feminine" gentilities of the civilized East and populated almost entirely by men. By thus inhabiting and, in many ways, mastering a cultural arena defined as obsessively masculine, West further underscores the extent to which her parodic enactments of an extravagant female sexuality cross and rupture the fragile divide between the genders.

Not surprisingly, the gender ambiguities of the West star-image profoundly affect the sexual economies of her films, destabilizing or even upturning received gender hierarchies. In many of her films, West assumes the conventionally masculine role of sexual aggressor, with the result that the male characters are often forced into the conventionally feminine role of object or prey. In what is possibly the quintessential Mae West scene, the celebrated "Come up and see me" sequence in *She Done Him Wrong* (1933), this troubling potential for gender inversion is quite apparent. As she stands on the stairway towering over and leering at an increasingly nervous Cary Grant, she propositions him in an exchange that clearly masculinizes her position while feminizing his.

> *West:* Why don't you come up sometime and see me? I'm home every evening.
> *Grant:* I'm busy every evening.
> *West:* What are you trying to do, insult me?
> *Grant:* I've met your kind before.
> *West:* Come up. I'll tell your fortune. You can be had.

In *Go West, Young Man*, West again plays the experienced sexual roué to Randolph Scott's shy and submissive ingenu(e). Indeed, this film contains one of the most blatant examples in classical cinema of an illicit, active female eroticization of the male image. The Randolph Scott character, Bud, is introduced through an extraordinary shot/reverse-shot sequence initiated and controlled by the active desiring gaze of West's character, Mavis Arden. Mavis first spies Bud through her hotel window as he stands hunched over the engine of a motorcar. She watches eagerly as he straightens up and turns to camera front, his crotch clearly highlighted through the strategic use of framing and key lighting. The film cuts to a reaction shot of Mavis, who, eyes widening with obvious delight, murmurs, "Mmmm! What large and sinewy muscles!" She then spends the better part of the film ogling, pawing, and pursuing Bud, who is reduced to awkward passivity and adolescent naïveté.

This persistent subversion of traditional patriarchal structures of gender and sexuality made West a highly controversial figure, both during her cinematic heyday in the thirties and after. As is well known, West provoked considerable outrage and moral indignation within certain sectors of American society, becoming, in the words of one contemporary commentator, "as hot an issue as Hitler."[80] She was attacked widely and viciously by many within the press of the time and was even represented by conservative members of the federal government as a symbol of all that was deemed to be wrong with modern America. Yet if the brash sexual transgressiveness of West raised the ire of some of her contemporary audiences, it is the precise source and fuel for much of her enduring iconicity in gay subcultures and gay traditions of camp. Gay subcultural readings of West seize the various dynamics of sexual transgression and gender subversion signaled in and by her extraordinary star performance and mobilize them as the bases for camp denaturalization and gay fantasmatic engagement. As William Stewart notes, "Much of West's fascination for a gay audience lay in the way she projected gender. In appearance she fulfilled the male stereotype of female desirability to the point of parody, but she had a pre-emptive wit and clear scorn for all sexual hypocrisy and repressiveness. Like gay people, she was aware of the shocking power that control of her sexuality could give, and she . . . affronted public decency."[81]

West maintained this tradition of sexual shock and moral provocation throughout her life. Although most critics tend to focus on the films she made in the thirties and early forties, West continued to enact her brash brand of camp performance and sexual transgression well into old age. She performed in theatrical and nightclub revues in the forties and fifties, and in the seventies waged a brief but highly publicized return to the screen in two final films, *Myra Breckinridge* (1970) and *Sextette* (1978), at the age of seventy-seven and eighty-four, respectively. Her later career, especially the final bid for a cinematic "comeback," is almost universally dismissed by critics as of little value to the West legacy or, worse, as tragic debasements of it. Pamela Robertson argues that as "a 1970s celebrity, West enacted and became a one-dimensional misogynist joke," "a burlesque of a woman, a grotesquerie, beloved for her ridiculous and narcissistic belief in her own sexual appeal."[82] The later films are, however, vital to the history of gay camp readings of West, which have taken up and celebrated them as equally as the earlier "classics." Ramona Curry notes that "it was primarily gay male critics and audiences who revived West's image" in the latter part of her life and who "were most openly addressed" by her later films and their construction as "self-conscious camp."[83] Inevitably, the gay prioritization of West's later films has added further fuel to the persistent critical evaluations of gay camp readings of West as patently misogynous. In a recent newspaper article written to mark the centenary of West's birth, Molly Haskell writes with thinly veiled contempt that West's "unfortunate valedictory films" turn her into "a truly grotesque parody of a parody" because they were made "at a time when she was much too old and her gay constituency had become more explicit and obtrusive."[84]

Once again, I am not so sure that the later films made by West or the gay camp celebration of them can be written off quite so simply. Although *Myra Breckinridge* and *Sextette* are undoubtedly less accomplished texts than many of West's earlier films, they are still situated within and continue the same traditions of gender denaturalization and sexual transgression that West established so spectacularly in her earlier performances. If anything, they are even more subversive, pushing the disruptive potentials of West's sexual performativity to their most outrageous and confronting extremes.

The central image seized on and rejected by critics like Robertson and Haskell in their evaluations of West's later performances is essentially that of the female grotesque. The later films—and by extension the gay camp celebration of them—are problematical for these critics because they appear to "diffuse West's transgression through her construction as a grotesque figure."[85] The image of the female grotesque has, however, been explicitly championed by other writers as an important point of displacement in patriarchal structures of sexual difference that, far from diffusing transgression, actively facilitates it. Mary Russo, for example, argues that the image of "the female body as grotesque (the pregnant body, the aging body, the irregular body)" has long been a cultural figure of the unruly carnivalesque, "the world turned upside down." Although attentive to how this figure repeats dominant misogynous representations of woman as monstrous, Russo contends that the female grotesque can function as the figural site for a liberatory cultural politics for women, one that "resist[s], exaggerate[s] and destabilize[s]" existing hegemonies of gender and desire. In particular, she suggests that the figure of the female grotesque signals a hyperbolic performance of feminine excess, an extravagant masquerade that provides the female performer with the representational distance necessary for a discursive practice of self-determined articulation.[86]

The female grotesque has long provided a privileged source for gay camp readings of sexual transgression and excessive performativity as well. On one level, gay camp celebrates the image of the "loud, somewhat obscene wom[a]n, who violate[s] the decorum one is taught to expect from women" in the personae of stars such as Ethel Merman, Martha Raye, Bette Midler, and Roseanne Barr.[87] On a more extreme level, gay camp venerates horror films, which have been long recognized as a privileged cinematic site for the representation of a grotesque femininity.[88] The image of the female grotesque most closely associated with gay camp readings, however, and the one at the heart of gay receptions of West's later films, is that of the aging female star who refuses to relinquish her power and acquiesce to an "appropriately" passive old age. *Sunset Boulevard* (1950), *What Ever Happened to Baby Jane?* (1962), and *Mommie Dearest* (1981) with their necromantic apparitions of aging Hollywood goddesses in physical and moral decay are almost canonical in this respect. Gloria Swanson as the "crazy" Norma Desmond, Bette Davis as the "hysterical" Baby Jane Hudson, and Faye Dunaway as a "maniacal" Joan Crawford present powerful performances of an aging cinematic female masquerade taken to grotesque (i.e., hyperbolic) extremes.

It is this tradition that informs and frames the gay reception of West's later films in which the outrageous spectacle of the septuagenarian West performing the roles and poses of a young female siren is celebrated precisely because of its denaturalizing and disorganizational dynamics.[89] West's performances of an aging female grotesque transgress and confound all manner of social conventions from notions of gender propriety and decorum to received dictates about erotic desirability and appropriate sexual relationality. When, as in *Myra Breckinridge*, the seventy-seven-year-old West vamps a room full of young male studs or, as in *Sextette*, she is serenaded for her legendary sexual prowess by a chorus of scantily clad male athletes sixty years her junior, the effect is undoubtedly camp but also profoundly transgressive. West's insistence on continuing to play the role of a sexually voracious maneater despite her advanced age may be, as Ramona Curry notes, "the star's ultimate transgression," for it "violates the strong proscription against clearly postmenopausal women displaying sexual vanity and lust."[90]

This blatant violation of sexual taboos is, in large part, why these films are so unsettling to watch and why they provoke such profound anxiety in many viewers. Commentaries on the two films regularly use a vehement mix of moralistic indignation and personal revulsion to condemn West's confronting performances. In his review of *Myra Breckinridge*, Joseph Morgenstern terms it a "horrifying movie," "a nightmare" that is "the perfect picture for an emasculated [film] industry." West, he writes, appears as "a ghastly travesty of the travesty of womanhood she once played"; she has "a Mae West face painted on the front of her head and moves to and fro like the Imperial Hotel during the 1923 Tokyo earthquake."[91] The reviewer for *Time* magazine calls *Myra Breckinridge* "as funny as a child molester," "an incoherent tale of sodomy, emasculation, autoeroticism and plain bad taste." West, it complains, grinds "her ancient hips in a grotesque parody of bygone eroticism" that will "set everyone's gorge agurgling."[92] Vincent Canby of the *New York Times* describes *Sextette* as "a disorienting freak show," in which West looks "like a plump sheep that's been stood on its hind legs, dressed in a drag queen's idea of chic, bewigged and then seared with pink plaster." "Granny," he writes, "should have her mouth washed out with soap, along with her teeth."[93] The blithe cruelty of these descriptions may be for these critics an intellectual protest against and repudiation of the provocative image of West as aging grotesque, but it cannot conceal the obvious sense of dread and outrage evoked by that image, nor can it hide how phobic responses to the aging West are so often motivated not only by misogyny and ageism but by an insistent homophobia, as well.

The latter point is vital, for it indicates the alliance between the spectacle of the aging West—indeed, the figure of the female grotesque more generally—and notions of male homosexuality, which, as argued, frequently possess marked definitional ties to cultural categories of the feminine. These ties are especially strong in relation to the more specific category of the female grotesque. With its associational lexicon of excess, social rupture, and sexual abnormality, the female grotesque has long been a resonant discursive complex within which to pose representational figures of male homosexuality.[94] In the case of West, the homosexual dynamics of her performance as aging female grotesque in *Myra Breckinridge* and *Sextette* provide the most blatant queer disruptions of heterosexual hegemony in the entire West oeuvre, taking the traditional tendencies of her persona toward sexual ambiguity and transgression to new extremes.

In an early attempt to think through the sexual destabilizations of cinematic figures of the female grotesque, Madonna Kolschenblag argues that such figures "are threatening and disruptive because they challenge conventional boundaries between male and female, sexed and sexless, animal and human, plant and animal, life and death." These images "disrupt the proper 'scale' of the universe," she contends, and "they disorder the basic 'distinctions' which constitute our sense of reality."[95] With uncompromising gusto, the spectacle of the aging West embodies and trades on this capacity of the grotesque for binarist disruption and displacement. Not only is there the obvious disorganization of the dichotomy of youth and age, there is also a transgression of the divide between natural and unnatural, normal and perverse, knowledge and ignorance, active and passive, parent and child. Working through all these dichotomous displacements is an even more fundamental disruption of the binarism of (hetero)sexual difference, of masculinity and femininity. West's outrageous performance of the aging grotesque aggressively mixes and confounds the signs of gender. At the beginning of *Sextette*, for example, the eighty-four-year-old West makes one of her typical grand entrances wearing an elaborate white wedding dress with full, flouncy skirt and sequin-embroidered bodice. Playing the part of Marlo Manners, a "world-famous movie star" who has just married for the sixth time—to a very young Timothy Dalton—West saunters into the lobby of the hotel where she is checking in for her honeymoon. She surveys the scene with an imperious sweep and forges her way through the paparazzi who have been awaiting her arrival, trading ribald quips with them and leering at any young men in eyeshot. Looking like a cross between a swan and a swaggering prizefighter, West has the appearance of wholly ambiguous gender: her costume is female but her comportment, behavior, and sexual authority are emphatically masculine while her advanced age and heavily cosmeticized face push her sexual masquerade toward the surreal. Furthermore, the androgynizing dynamics of West's grotesque performance in this scene produce a veritable transvestic contagion, rippling out to queer much of the surrounding diegetic syntagma. Her young husband trails sheepishly behind her, assuming the symbolic role of blushing, virginal bride, while the male reporters react with maidenish demureness to West's aggressive philandering. The scene climaxes with an outrageously camp spectacle of gender inversion as a chorus of high-kicking male bellboys surrounds West in full Busby Berkeley–style dance formations, belting out "Hooray for Hollywood" while she stands beaming and swinging her hips. It is a flagrant moment of disruptive sexual carnivalesque that spells out the film's status in gay traditions as what Paul Roen terms "a campy, corny, funny, smutty romp" with "all the suitably fruity trimmings." [96]

Of all West's incarnations, the aging female grotesque offers the most sustained potentials for specifically gay engagement and fantasmatic investment. Contrary to claims by critics that the grotesquerie of the aging West works simply to distance her as reviled object, in the context of gay camp it furnishes the representational means by which West is made an even more powerful subject of gay engagement and identification. In *Screening the Sexes*, Parker Tyler clearly revels in the opportunities for gay identification afforded by West's aging queer grotesquerie. For Tyler, West's spectacular turn as aging grotesque finally explicates the fantasmatic status of symbolic male homosexuality that she had always assumed in gay receptions but that had, up till then, been a largely implicit, coded affair. "It was not until *Myra Breckinridge*," he writes, "that the preoccupations peculiar to a certain style of homosexual became literally a part of Mae's acting routine." [97] As Tyler points out, there is even a scene in the film in which it is implied that West's character, Leticia Van Allen, has actually sodomized a young man who lies naked on a bed in front of her. At this moment, Tyler opines, West spells out the transvestic homosexuality that had always been integral to her gay appeal since the thirties and, finally, realizes her queer destiny as "a fairy godmother of fairy godmothers" (15). That this flagrantly gay reading is transgressive, an affront to straight, bourgeois sensibilities, is undoubtable, but then so is the extravagant performance that supports it, a performance that Tyler describes and fetes as "a calculatingly outrageous fantasy." For this gay spectator, at least, far from undercutting the subversive dynamics of the West persona and legacy, her audacious turn as aging grotesque at the end of her career evokes, through its sheer gall and spectacular perversity, West's campest and most radical potential.

In their academic homage to the gay drag star Divine, Michael Moon and Eve Kosofsky Sedgwick coin the term "divinity-effect" to describe the outrageous combination of "abjection and defiance" that they argue characterizes the excessive and fiercely aggressive camp style of a queer performer like Divine. Despite the rather mystical sounding resonances of this description, Moon and Sedgwick understand the divinity-effect as a rigorously materialist mode of self-articulation, or what they define as "a way of staking one's claims to insist on, and participate actively in, a renegotiation of *the representational contract* between one's body and one's world."[98] The divinity-effect thus defined speaks powerfully, Moon and Sedgwick suggest, to the disjunctive corporeal experiences of, especially though not uniquely, gay men and fat women; both of whom must, in various ways, renegotiate and resignify the culturally abjectified misfit between their bodies and their desires. Within this context, they read the star-persona of Divine, "a three-hundred-pound [gay] man not trapped in but scandalously and luxuriously corporeally cohabitating with the voluptuous body of a fantasy Mae West or Jayne Mansfield," as a powerful (sub)cultural figure through which the "divine" interface of defiance and abjection is expressed most insistently and most suggestively (15).

This boldly utopian evaluation of the potential signifying effects of camp drag succinctly captures the refigurative valences that organize gay camp readings of female star-images such as Mae West. Just as a drag performer like Divine deploys the disorganizational potentials of an excessive female star performativity to pursue his/her own outrageous fantasmatic productions, gay spectators similarly use camp readings of certain transgressive female star performances to articulate and explore their own fantasies of sexual disruption and queer self-representation.

A gay camp reading emphasizes how the excessive female star-image recodes the star performance *as a performance*, a masquerade that does not correspond to the subjectivity on which it is played. In relation to issues of gender and sexual categorization, the effects of this gay camp reading of the star performance as artifactual masquerade denaturalize and destabilize hegemonic visions of gender as anatomically fixed and instead instate a polysemic scenario of gender ambivalence and queer transgression. Such a reading allows gay spectators not only to project and affirm their own psychocultural "experiences" of sexual ambivalence and gender dissonance but also to articulate their own fantasmatic productions of regendered desire.

Chapter Four ∾ MOMMIE DEAREST:

GAY SPECTATORSHIPS AND FORMATIONS

OF MATERNAL-ORIENTED DESIRE

A poignant scene at the beginning of the 1988 British film *The Fruit Machine* symbolizes the central concerns of this chapter. In this scene, the young, gay male protagonist, Eddy (Emile Charles), returns to his family's rather modest, working-class home in Liverpool with a selection of videos that his mother has asked him to rent. In the living room, his mother sits on a sofa sobbing as she watches the 1945 female melodrama *Brief Encounter* on television. Eddy quietly moves in behind her and kisses her on the cheek. The two then continue to watch together, enraptured and in tears, as the final scene of this famous film, loved by generations of women and gay men alike, plays itself out.[1]

This sequence from *The Fruit Machine* offers a canny representation of many of the popularly conceived features of gay male spectatorship that have been highlighted in previous chapters: an intense, even obsessive cinephilia; an overinvestment in the cinematic image, in general, and an (over)identification with the female star-image, in particular; an obsession with classic Hollywood or vintage film; and an assumption of spectatorship as an avenue of utopian escapism. The character of Eddy functions as an emblem of and for cultural discourses of gay spectatorship; his homosexuality is articulated just as centrally and just as legibly through the excessive or "queer" nature of his cinematic obsessions as through his same-sex desires. Yet the film also elaborates its representation of gay male spectatorship through another trope that has been central to the construction of all sorts of images of male homosexual subjectivity: the "mummy's boy." In the sequence just described, Eddy engages and performs his own particular gay spectatorship in a structure of contiguous relationality to that of his mother. Eddy and his mother become

The thrilling aberrance of the phallic mother: Gloria Swanson in *Sunset Boulevard* (1950) (author's collection)

spectators "side by side," and the intense *jouissance* of their spectatorial engagements seems to come as much from the pleasures accorded by this symbiotic proximity as it does from the actual film that they are watching.

The image of the mother and the gay son is an especially resonant one in our post-Freudian culture. However, it is an image that has, more often than not, been mobilized in homophobic and misogynous ways. Consequently, many gay theorists have been reluctant to address the significances of this symbolic configuration of male homosexuality and the maternal. Given Eve Kosofsky Sedgwick's contention that "any account of the origin of sexual preference and identity in individuals" is "always already structured by an implicit, trans-individual Western project or fantasy of eradicating that identity," this reluctance to inquire into the figure of the mother-identified homosexual—a figure that is etiological with a vengeance—may be a sensible strategy of self-preservation.[2] Yet, by refusing this figure, by failing to address its role in the definitions, constructions, fantasies, and performances of male homosexualities, we leave its homophobic and misogynous meanings unchallenged and intact. In addition to recuperating the figure of the mother and the gay son from its long history of deformative uses and reclaiming it as a legitimate and valuable figure for gay-identified theory, I want to establish that this figure is potentially useful for theorizing gay male spectatorships. The trope of gay maternal relationality—or, what I call gay matrocentrism—plays a critical role in articulating and organizing gay spectatorial pleasures.

It is not my intention to claim gay matrocentrism as some type of essential or universal truth of gay male spectatorship; even less still as an ontology of gay psychosexuality. My aims in this chapter are considerably more modest. I deploy homosexual matrocentrism as a gay epistemological tactic, a strategy for thinking through and thinking out gay male knowledges and experiences; knowledges and experiences, most specifically, of cinematic engagement. That is, I assume gay matrocentrism as what Teresa de Lauretis terms a "passionate fiction," a fiction for reading desire that is itself produced and marked by desire.[3] As a passionate fiction, gay matrocentrism can be used to read and make sense of the field of gay desire in spectatorship, but its relation to that field can never be one of universal correspondence or neutral description. Rather, it is a relation that is partial, contingent, and, above all, transcriptive. It transcribes or translates the field of gay spectatorship according to the "passions," the desires and fantasies, of its own fictional logic. As a passionate fiction, gay matrocentrism—or at least my use of it here—is also framed by my own "passions," my own desires and fantasmatic projections. What is the stake of my investment in gay matrocentrism? How do my desires fuel the foundational fantasy in this chapter of rescuing the dyadic figure of mother and gay son? I cannot but concede that this figure resonates profoundly for me at a personal level, it maps neatly—perhaps, a little too neatly, at times—onto the identificatory coordinates of my own life, even as I recognize that those coordinates may in fact be produced by the discourses of matrocentrism in the first place. All of this simply underscores the ultimately provisional nature of the theoretical endeavor I am proposing here. My project of reading gay spectatorship through the lens of matrocentrism is both speculative and subjective, and my arguments are neither generalizable to nor exhaustive of the wide range of formations that gay spectatorships can and do assume.

Psychoanalysis and Gay Male Matrocentrism

They can keep their "Name of the Father": that's their business. I'll have the "Shadow of the Mother."
—Christiane Olivier, *Jocasta's Children: The Imprint of the Mother*

Psychoanalysis tells us that as subjects of sexuality we always desire from a particular position made available to us by the sociosymbolic networks in and through which we are interpellated. In postindustrial, Western social formations such as our own, these networks are largely dominated, though never entirely exhausted, by the structure of the bourgeois nuclear family. The familial paradigm provides the primary frame within which our libidinal desires are articulated and organized into preordained cultural subject-positions.

This process of sociosymbolic interpellation provides the focus, of course, for Freud's theory of the oedipus and castration complexes. Within psychoanalytic theories of oedipal development the child is understood to assume the difference between the parents as a psychocultural blueprint for the difference between the sexes, repatterning its libidinal investments and realigning its identificatory mechanisms in accordance with a culturally designated system of genital similarities and differences. The child is encouraged to realign its libidinal investments in such a way as to identify with the parent of the same anatomical sex and disidentify or "differentiate" itself from the parent of the opposite sex, thereby recasting the latter as a symbolic pre-figure for subsequent erotic object-choices. The process is achieved, however, through an inequitable and rather violent reconstruction of the young child's libidinal economy wherein the originary moment of plenitude and symbiotic union with the mother that characterizes the pre-oedipal or Imaginary field is ruptured and replaced by a symbolic orchestration in which the father assumes the role and function of normative psychocultural ideal and in which the mother—and, by extension, femininity itself—is "devalorized" and redefined as a culturally negative site of lack.

Psychoanalysis suggests that male homosexuality emerges as a particular effect of and response to this cultural drama of sexual differentiation, especially as it is articulated around the devalorization of the maternal site. Freud argues that the young protogay subject refuses to accept the deposition of the pre-oedipal or phallic mother and the subsequent symbolic reconstruction of her as castrated and that, as a result, the subject refuses to reorganize his libidinal economies according to the hegemonic systems of patrocentric sexual difference and compulsory heterosexuality. This is the motivational scenario behind the classic Freudian definition of homosexuality as a "disavowal of castration or (hetero)sexual difference," and I assumed this definition as a productive starting point for my explorations of gay fantasmatic specificity and spectatorship in the preceding chapters. At the heart of this broad theoretical scenario of disavowed castration lies, however, a much more specific scenario of maternal identification. For Freud—as for the majority of psychoanalytic theorists after him—male homosexuality is almost always understood to be grounded in an unconscious psychic tableau of maternal-centered—or matrocentric—desire in which the maternal, rather than the paternal, site is made the organizational pivot and figure of primary identification. Freud provides his first formal theorization of this scenario in the 1910 second edition of the "Three Essays," in which he asserts in a new footnote: "In all the cases we have examined, we have established the fact that future inverts, in the earliest years of their childhood, pass through a phase of very intense but short-lived fixation to a woman (usually their mother) and that, after leaving this behind, they identify themselves with this woman and take themselves to be their sexual object."[4] Just one year later, Freud develops this proposition into a fully fledged theory in his infamous 1911 monograph on Leonardo da Vinci. Here he repeats and extends his earlier speculation that "the [homosexual] boy represses his love for his mother: he puts himself in her place, identifies himself with her, and takes his own person as a model in whose likeness he chooses the new objects of his love."[5]

In the Leonardo monograph, Freud proceeds, however, to discuss the scenario of homosexual constitution through maternal identification in a patently disapproving manner. In fact, he paints such a negative picture of the maternal dynamics of homosexual etiology that, as Madelon Sprengnether notes, the Leonardo study virtually "assumes the character of a cautionary tale about the dangers inherent in mother love."[6] This is particularly evident in the psychobiographical sections of the monograph, in which Freud seeks to read Leonardo da Vinci as protohomosexual. In what has become something of a stock response on the part of institutionalized psychoanalysis, Freud lays the "blame" for Leonardo's homosexuality squarely at the feet of his mother. He accuses Leonardo's mother, Caterina, of causing his "perversion"—or, as Freud puts it, of "determin[ing] his destiny and the privations that were in store for him." She does this, he contends, through loving Leonardo too much, through subjecting him to the "sinister menace" of her "unbounded tenderness" and "imprisoning" him in a "perverse" structure of identificatory relationality with her that "robbed him of a part of his masculinity."[7] Elsewhere in the same study, Freud repeats this characterization, extending it to include all mothers of homosexual sons, whom he describes as "masculine women, women with energetic traits of character, who . . . push the father out of his proper place" (190).

It is not difficult to divine the source of Freud's disapproving stance here. The mother of the homosexual son is guilty in his eyes of usurping the father's "proper place" of primary psychosexual reference and of, thereby, "blocking" the child's access to a patrocentric order of desire and phallic (hetero)sexuality. As Monique Plaza puts it in Lacanian terms, "It is she who does not allow the Paternal Signifier to happen for the child: she did not yield to Symbolic Castration and kept the child for herself, not allowing it to be a [full, mature] subject."[8] That this devaluative reading should sound so familiar is evidence of the astonishing force with which it has been taken up and canonized by both psychoanalytic and popular discourses. Many of the most conservative psychological views on male homosexuality can be attributed directly to Freud's theorization of homosexual matrocentrism, which has played a vital role in the continued classification of male homosexuality as psychopathological in various psychoanalytic and psychiatric traditions.[9]

Such a pathologizing reading of the identificatory relations between male homosexuality and the maternal depends, however, on an unquestioned assumption of a paternal-oriented, or patrocentric, orchestration of desire as the "natural," or at least "ideal," paradigm for a healthy, mature subjectivity. That Freud himself ultimately subscribed to such an assumption comes as no surprise. As has been frequently noted, Freud's whole conceptualization of psychosexual development—a conceptualization articulated most fully in his theory of oedipality—rests on a teleological model in which the end result of that development, namely patrocentric heterosexuality, is defined as normative ideal. In the case of a maternal-identified homosexuality, this means that, within the Freudian schema, it can only be defined as less than ideal, as a "failure" to achieve complete, paternal-identified heterosexual masculinity. And thus are laid the grounds for the long history of pathologizing nosologies of male homosexuality in psychoanalysis in terms of arrested development, immature fixation, psychic infantilism, artificial blockage, and so on.

It is not my intention to vilify or demonize Freud by glossing his theory of male homosexual maternal identification in this way. My avowed interest in deploying and recuperating that theory bespeaks a strong critical commitment to the value of Freud's work. Furthermore, it is worth recalling in this context that Freud is also the writer who, contrary to the trends of his time, argued vehemently against seeing homosexuality as neurotic or as an illness and who, in 1915, declared that heterosexuality "is also a problem that needs elucidating and is not a self-evident fact."[10] But Freud's recalcitrant adherence to teleology, and his unreconstituted assumption of paternal-dominated heterosexuality as the ideal end result of sexual maturation, ultimately paved the way for generations of pathologizing evaluations of maternal-identified homosexuality.

More recently, some psychoanalysts and psychoanalytic critics have begun to rethink the question of matrocentric homosexuality. Most of these critics follow Jacques Lacan's influential reconstruction of the psychoanalytic project in terms of sociosymbolic discursivity. Where Freud tended to theorize sexuality as a clearly demarcated sequence of developmental stages endogenously unfolding from flux to phallic heterosexuality, Lacan casts sexuality as "a complex, wayward and indefinitely extendible dialectic" determined and played out largely in terms of exogenous, symbolic, or sociocultural imperatives.[11] Lacan explicitly criticized what he saw as the normalizing cast of Freud's patrocentric theory of developmental sexuality. In his reading of Freud's "failed" analysis of Dora, for example, Lacan takes Freud to task for his refusal to recognize a maternal-oriented female homosexuality as a viable paradigm through which to make sense of Dora's desire, imposing in its place his own heterosexual oedipal program. "We would say," he writes, "that this has to be ascribed to prejudice, exactly the same prejudice which falsifies the conception of the Oedipus complex from the start, by making it define as natural, rather than normative, the predominance of the paternal figure."[12]

Lacan's retheorization of patrocentric oedipality as a process of symbolic normativization rather than natural progression helps counter the devaluation and even pathologization of matrocentric homosexuality in psychoanalytic discourses. It suggests that gay maternal identification is neither inherently deficient nor structurally perverse, and is just as capable of providing a complete and healthy endopsychic economy as patrocentric structures of heterosexuality. Indeed, Lacan's reconstruction of oedipal heterosexuality as the installed effect of cultural normativity and not nature or biology not only depathologizes psychoanalytic readings of male homosexuality in terms of a primary maternal identification but recasts these readings in a patently idealizing light. If, as both Freud and Lacan assert, paternal identification is the primary psychic mechanism through which patriarchal masculinity and compulsory heterosexuality is reproduced in the male subject, then the homosexual refusal of this identification in preference for a continuous primary identification with the maternal may be (re)read as a politically resonant refusal, or at least disruption, of patriarchal hegemony.

This type of political rereading of gay matrocentrism has in fact been forwarded by several critics in recent years. John Fletcher claims that the male homosexual subject's retention of a primary identification with the mother may be interpreted as a "rebellious response" to patriarchal culture. "It is a transgressive attempt," he writes, "to refashion oneself or an image to one's desire *over against* the forms sanctioned by the paternal Law." Read in this way, gay matrocentrism emerges as a form of psychic protest; "a stubborn refusal to leave the side of the mother, to change sides, even if the price paid is symbolic castration. The retention of the loving mother-son relation as the scenario of desire is an attempt to preserve the lost phallic ego-ideal in one's object, while bearing the burden of maternal castration oneself." [13]

Leo Bersani offers a similarly appreciative reevaluation of gay matrocentrism in his recent work, *Homos*, in which he argues that the gay subject's continued identification with the phallic or imaginary mother—that is, the mother at full value—and his correlative refusal to accept the patriarchal reconstruction of the mother/femininity as castrated "may be a powerful weapon in the defeat of those defensive maneuvers that have defined sexual difference" in patriarchal culture. According to Bersani,

> recent psychoanalytically inspired studies have emphasized the defensive and traumatic nature of the so-called normative development of desire. An exclusively heterosexual orientation in men, for example, may depend on a misogynous identification with the father and a permanent equating of femininity with castration. The male homosexual's desire, to the extent that it depends on an identification with the mother, has already detraumatized sexual difference (by internalizing it) *and* set the stage for a relation to the father in which the latter would no longer have to be marked as the Law, the agent of castration. [14]

A third and final example of this type of critical rereading of homosexual matrocentrism is provided by Kaja Silverman in her study of "deviant" or nonhegemonic masculinities, *Male Subjectivities at the Margins*. Like Fletcher and Bersani, Silverman reads the gay subject's retention of a primary identification with the maternal as a potential site of patriarchal contestation and challenge. She argues that, by refusing the patriarchal equation of the maternal body with castration, male homosexuality may be seen to undercut the foundational logic of phallocentric structures of sexual difference, as well as the heterosexual disjunction of identification and object-choice that ensues from this. Indeed, Silverman goes so far as to argue that, by embracing matrocentrism as its privileged psychic scenario, male homosexuality may be said "to negate the most fundamental premise of male subjectivity — an identification with masculinity — and in so doing obstruct paternal lineality . . . and turn away from the phallic legacy."[15]

As should be apparent, even on the basis of this thumbnail sketch, these (re)readings of gay matrocentrism are willfully utopian. In one way or another, each critic just discussed is centrally concerned with producing a theoretical reimaging of gay maternal identification as an idealized and idealizing psychic formation. The utopic impulses of these readings should not be seen to diminish their epistemological validity or value. In many ways, the unabashed utopianism of this revisionist work serves as a much needed corrective to the largely dystopian strains of traditional accounts of gay matrocentrism. As Silverman puts it when summarizing her position, the classic psychoanalytic scenario of male homosexual maternal identification

> admits of two quite diverse political readings. On the one hand, it can be explained as the inability of the homosexual subject to assimilate the anatomical particularity of the mother — as a stubborn refusal of alterity. On the other hand, it can be understood as a resistance to the whole process of devaluation which is made to follow from woman's "difference" — as a refusal to accede to the equation of the mother with insufficiency. Although the first of these readings has a whole psychoanalytic tradition behind it, the second cannot be entirely ruled out of order. It may, indeed, be the more compelling. (372)

This revisionist work provides both a rejoinder to traditional interpretations of Freudian theories of male homosexual matrocentrism and a framework within which to rethink those theories. The readings developed by critics like Silverman, Bersani, and Fletcher suggest not only that psychoanalytic arguments about gay matrocentrism may be recuperable to and for a gay-identified and gay-affirmative project, but that they may even be an important asset in thinking through questions of gay fantasmatic specificity and psychic resistance.

The arguments also provide a suggestive framework within which to pose and think through questions about matrocentrism and gay spectatorships. In her essay "Something Else besides a Mother," Linda Williams forwards an influential argument for female spectatorial specificity on the basis of the primacy of maternal identification in certain forms of feminine psychic organization. Drawing from the psychoanalytic traditions of object-relations theory, Williams argues that the matrocentric orientation that these traditions claim as central to feminine psychic patterns makes the female subject "a very different kind of spectator"—a spectator with different investments in and different responses to the fantasy scenarios of cinema. Following the work of feminist psychoanalyst Nancy Chodorow, Williams claims that the female subject's "continuity of relationship" with the pre-oedipal mother endows her with a greater capacity for "connectedness" in terms of both endopsychic and intersubjective relations and that this capacity may be realized in cultural practices like spectatorship in terms of certain distinct affective and/or interpretive proclivities such as an increased identificatory fluidity, an ability to assume and empathize with divergent positions simultaneously, and so forth.[16] One obvious danger with this type of analysis is that it can easily lapse into a sterile psychic essentialism in which matrocentric scenarios are seen to give rise to a fixed set of psychic attributes of and for the fantasmatic subject. Clearly, this is not the case, and it is important to recognize that any discussion of the putative effects of psychic formations on spectatorial relations are entirely theoretical and speculative. Nevertheless, Williams's analysis does indicate the potential for determinative exchanges between fantasmatic scenarios of matrocentrism and spectatorship. Following Williams's claims for the female subject, then, I suggest that the specific formations of desire and meaning that accrue from gay male matrocentrism may make the gay subject "a very different kind of spectator" in certain formations. In the next two sections, I propose to explore how this "difference" may be articulated.

Gay Spectatorship, Personal Memory, and the Mother

What is realized in my history is not the past definite of what was, since it is no more, or even the present perfect of what has been in what I am, but the future anterior of what I shall have been for what I am in the process of becoming.
—Jacques Lacan, *Ecrits: A Selection*

I have always been aware of the considerable influence exerted by my mother on the early formation of my own spectatorial pleasures. For a long time I assumed this was simply an idiosyncratic feature of my personal history. I have, however, come to suspect that the influential role of the mother in determining cinematic pleasures and practices may in fact form a standard feature of many gay men's spectatorial histories—or, at least, the fantasmatic representation of those histories. I have already noted the image of gay spectatorship as maternally influenced and authorized in the 1988 film *The Fruit Machine*, but this image features as a structuring presence in other popular texts as well. Manuel Puig's novel *Kiss of the Spider Woman* and the 1985 film of the same name provide celebrated representations of the mother-identified gay spectator, as do such otherwise disparate films as the slasher movie *The Fan* (1981); the chilling psycho-thriller *Apartment Zero* (1988); the gay teen romance *Beautiful Thing* (1996); and Terence Davies's haunting ode to childhood movie-going, *The Long Day Closes* (1992). Other more explicitly gay-identified (sub)cultural texts make similar use of a discursive imagery of matrocentric homosexuality in their representations of gay spectatorships. The popular novel *The Movie Lover*, by Richard Friedel, depicts the cinephile of its title as devoted in equal measures to Mom and the movies, while Dick Scanlan's novel *Does Freddy Dance* represents its protagonist as a gay man obsessed with the films his mother took him to as a child.[17]

It may not be surprising, then, to discover that a certain imagery of maternal-oriented spectatorship is frequently reproduced by gay men themselves in their own discourses of and about cinematic reception. David Pendleton is a film academic who has produced an autobiographical meditation on the history of his own (gay) spectatorship titled, rather pointedly, "My Mother, the Cinema," in which he asserts, "For better or worse, my introduction to cinema, my apprenticeship in acquiring what Metz refers to as the mental machinery of cinema, occurred through the agency of my mother."[18] More recently, Patrick E. Horrigan, another gay academic, has published an autobiography of his "development as a gay man" and how that development was "determined in large measure by the movies." A central component of this process, he suggests, was the influential presence of his mother, who had an enormous bearing on the forms and pleasures of his childhood spectatorship. "In their distortive way," he writes, "Hollywood movies reflected crucial aspects of my world when I was growing up. . . . The movies were filled with happy families, like my family; unhappy families, also like mine; underdogs and queer heroes, which, in a variety of ways, I understood myself to be; [and] all embracing mother-figures, like my mother." [19]

In a slightly different vein, as part of my preliminary research for this study, I engaged in some modest ethnographic research in which I printed an open call to respondents in a number of Australian and U.S. gay publications asking gay men to write to me with their views on film. [20] This research was admittedly rudimentary, and, as a result, the response was far from overwhelming. Nevertheless, I did receive about fifty replies, in which many of the men made explicit recourse to an imagery of matrocentrism in describing their spectatorships. Like Pendleton and Horrigan, many of these men emphasized the influential role played by their mothers in the constitution and organization of their spectatorial relations, referring all sorts of cinematic experiences and pleasures back to the figure of the mother. One respondent, for example, notes that "my mother always loved the movies, so I guess it was inevitable that I would follow suit." [21] Another explains his particular fascination with Barbra Streisand in terms of maternal influence: "This probably sounds stupid but I think part of the reason I connected with Barbra is that she reminds me a lot of my mother." [22] Not surprisingly, given the dismissive attitudes to gay matrocentrism discussed earlier, many of these men were extremely cautious in terms of how they represented the connections between their spectatorships and their mothers. As one man warily wrote: "This may seem 'namby-pamby', but my strongest memories of filmgoing are nearly all to do with my mother." [23]

Not only do these various autobiographical accounts echo the scenarios of gay matrocentrism that I have been discussing, they explicitly, even self-consciously, claim those scenarios as a framework within which to represent and valorize the particularity of their gay spectatorships. Matrocentrism is promoted by these gay-identifying men as one of the primary pleasures of their spectatorships, as well as one of the elements that makes their spectatorships different. Take, for example, the following excerpts from letters written to me by three different gay men: [24]

> My most vivid memories are of going to the movies with my mother as a young boy. We must have seen hundreds of films together. The movies was [sic] like a special magic carpet ride that would take us both on wonderful journeys to faraway places.

The bulk of my filmgoing was done with my mother—at least twice a week—and often twice on Saturdays—especially in winter. We'd get all dressed up and make a real night of it—having an early dinner somewhere first and then we'd sit side by side in the dark of the moviehouse, our eyes both glued to the screen. Occasionally, we'd nudge each other at an especially thrilling moment but generally we'd sit there totally enthralled. Afterwards, we'd ride home on the bus and talk and talk about how wonderful the film was.

When I was young I nearly always went to the pictures with my Mum. We both loved the movies and spent many a happy hour together in our local picture theatre. We didn't have much money in those days and life could be pretty tough, especially for my mother who was a real "battler", so going to the movies was a treat for us. I even had a scrapbook that I made with cuttings about the films we had seen or about our favourite stars—so when we couldn't afford to go to the movies, we would sit together and go through the scrapbook. I still have that scrapbook today and sometimes I might leaf through it and all the wonderful memories come flooding back.

The spectatorial portraits painted here are clearly organized around a central paradigm of maternal relationality. Spectatorship is represented, much as in the film *The Fruit Machine*, as something that is shared and enjoyed by mother and (gay) child in a structure of pleasurable contiguity—"a special magic carpet ride that would take *us both* on wonderful journeys"; "We'd sit *together side by side* . . . our eyes *both* glued to the screen." Proximity to the mother is characterized by these accounts in such a way as to emerge as a source of psychic pleasure potentially equal to, if not greater than, that of the film-text itself. These accounts thus invite a reading of gay spectatorship as a matrocentric space within which the special character of these subjects' relationships to the mother may be both avowed and played out.

In saying this, however, am I simply subjecting this material to overinterpretation? It could be argued that the centrality of the mother in these various accounts represents little more than a reflection of the way the mother has, within patriarchal social formations such as our own, been charged with performing the tasks of primary acculturation. Traditionally, the mother is the one who introduces the child to the various signifying forms and practices of the dominant culture. If these gay men remember their mothers as pivotal agents in their spectatorial development, might it not simply be because she was the one in charge of their early period of cultural education? Although such an argument is undoubtedly valid, it still does not account for the psychic significances of the mother's performance of these tasks of cultural education. What are the psychosocial effects of having the mother introduce us to cultural institutions like the cinema? Nor does such an argument explain the particular emphasis placed by these various accounts on the continued importance of the mother to gay male spectatorial pleasures. Why should it be that *these* subjects continue to represent the mother as a privileged reference point for the organization of their particular (gay) spectatorships, when many other subjects, who were also, one would assume, "introduced" to the cinema by their mothers, do not? How and why, in other words, is the mother elevated to a position of centrality in gay men's "rememberings" and representations of spectatorship?

Freud provides a reading of the nature and function of personal memory that may be of some use in this context. He defines memory not as the immediate reflection of a historic reality but as a highly structured process of psychocultural signification in which various tableaux from the past are selected and re-presented within the space of psychic interiority in order to articulate formations of desire in the present. This reading of memory as the space of a continual process of selective psychic representation is most forcefully explored by Freud in his celebrated "Mystic Writing-Pad" essay, in which he likens the structure of memory to that of a palimpsest, a formation of divergent layers interacting with each other so as to produce variable configurations of meaning.[25] In a letter to Fliess written about the same time, Freud describes his thinking on this subject:

> I am working on the assumption that our psychical mechanism has come about by a process of stratification: the material present in the shape of memory-traces is from time to time subjected to a rearrangement in accordance with fresh circumstances—is, as it were, transcribed. Thus what is essentially new in my theory is the thesis that memory is present not once but several times over, that it is registered in various species of "signs."[26]

Memory, in other words, functions for Freud as a fantasmatic construction that continues to organize meanings of and for the subject within the space of his or her present. It is, as Michel de Certeau puts it, a redefinition of the "space of memory" as "the past *in* the present."[27]

This argument provides a rather different purchase on gay "recollections" of the influential role played by the mother in the constitution of (gay) spectatorships, for it allows us to read these recollections or memories as the representation of a fantasmatic structure. Following Freud, we might suggest that if these gay spectators "remember" the mother as a pivotal agent in the determination and organization of their cinematic relations, it might be because the mother plays this role, not only in the historical past of these subjects' infantile cultural education but, also and more importantly, in the psychic present of their fantasmatic.[28]

This reading is partially suggested by David Pendleton in his essay "My Mother, the Cinema," in which he writes:

> My father's not much of a movie buff, so my mother used to take me with her once I got old enough. The excitement of going to the movies was acute in those days when I was too young to go on my own. I can still remember the almost visceral thrill when I would come home from school and my mother would announce that we were going to the movies that night. She never asked, she told me—she knew as well as I that there was no need to ask—the answer would always be yes, Mom . . .
>
> By now [you are probably thinking]—Oedipus . . . I'm not so sure; I'm thinking more along the lines of the Imaginary—my mother, the cinema. This is not a relation to the law of the father so much as a verification of my mother's position, there with me before the mirror, holding me up to it.[29]

In this passage, Pendleton also offers a reading of his particular gay spectatorship as a space of shared pleasures between mother and gay son. Like the other gay writers, he identifies the presence of the mother as a pivotal source of his early spectatorial pleasures—something that elicits "acute . . . excitement" and "visceral thrill[s]." However, he also goes on to provide a more theoretical gloss on this reading by redefining gay spectatorship as the site of a fantasmatic reactivation of Imaginary or pre-oedipal structures of maternal bonding.

A reading of spectatorship in terms of a reactivation of the Imaginary is not all that new. Contemporary film theory has, from the early work of Baudry and Metz onward, long provided a theorization of the cinematic experience in terms of an artificial replication of an Imaginary or pre-oedipal mode of subjective relationality.[30] However, most of these arguments focus on how the cinema replays an Imaginary relationship of primary narcissism between the subject and its own spectral imago as ego ideal, especially as it has been described by Lacan in his account of the mirror phase; as such, they tend to downplay or marginalize the significance of the mother in the determination of that relationship. In her influential feminist reworking of these early arguments, Laura Mulvey explicitly contends that the replication of Imaginary spectral identification in cinema turns on an emphatically phallocentric economy in which the cinematic signifier as spectral ideal becomes the site of the spectator's phallic identification and his concomitant renunciation of the maternal or femininity as castrated other.[31] Consequently, the vision of spectatorial Imaginary replication offered by these arguments is considerably different to the maternal-oriented paradigm forwarded by Pendleton and other gay men in their recollective descriptions of gay spectatorial pleasures.

It is possible, however, to extend or redevelop these influential arguments about the cinema's potential for Imaginary reactivation in ways that may incorporate and support gay representations of spectatorship as maternally oriented. In many ways, these arguments demand a reappraisal of the role of the maternal in cinematic metapsychology; as Jacqueline Rose asserts, the theory of the mirror phase on which many of these early readings are predicated "only has meaning in relation to the presence and the look of the mother who guarantees its reality for the child."[32] This suggests that, if the cinema offers a fantasmatic replication of the Imaginary structure, especially as it is figured through the spectral economy of the mirror phase, then the mother must play a role in that fantasy. E. Ann Kaplan certainly suggests as much. In one of the more forceful attempts to assert the significance of the maternal to metapsychological theories of film, she writes that "the cinema is the closest analog in the realm of the Symbolic to access to the maternal body: it allows subjects to re-experience the pleasures of fusion with the maternal body in fact impossible after the pre-Oedipal period."[33]

If the cinema does occasion a psychic return to the maternal body or at least provides for fantasies of such a return, it becomes possible to suggest that spectators activate or respond to this potential in different ways, depending on the forms of maternal relationality operative within their own psychosexual economies. Thus those subjectivities that privilege a more continuous, identificatory bond with the pre-oedipal mother, for example, may take up the potential reactivation of Imaginary maternal fusion in the cinema with a greater enthusiasm than those subjectivities that do not. This explains perhaps why certain commentators like Metz, Baudry, and Mulvey, for example, displace or repress the role of the mother in their theories of spectatorship as Imaginary replication, whereas others, like Pendleton and Kaplan, foreground it. These theorists are dealing with patently different forms of spectatorial engagement, phallic male in the former and female and gay male in the latter, each producing different responses to the cinema's potentials for Imaginary regression owing to the different values accorded by each of these subjectivities to fantasies of the maternal body.

However, if cinematic spectatorship acts as a potential site for the playing out of, in this instance, gay psychic scenarios of matrocentrism, this cannot simply be in terms of a fantasized return to an oceanic oneness with the maternal body in which the external object-world is (re)-subsumed into the undifferentiated amorphousness of imaginary plenitude. That fantasy may play a role in gay spectatorships, but this can hardly be the whole story, for such a fantasy would cancel out the differentiated specificity of the mother's position, which is clearly an important organizing principle in the autobiographical accounts of gay spectatorship that I have been discussing. Rather, the structure of maternal relationality that seems to underpin these accounts of gay spectatorial pleasure is primarily one of an *affirming identification* with the position of the mother. As Pendleton puts it in the passage cited above, it is "a verification of my mother's position, there with me before the mirror." Here, cinematic spectatorship acts as a potential site for the repetition of those forms of maternal identification central to the organization of (certain) gay male fantasmatic scenarios. By following the mother's lead and joining her as a spectator before the screen, the gay subject takes up a position of spectatorship that has been defined, prepared, and occupied by the mother before him. Her gaze becomes his gaze, her pleasures, his pleasures, or, as Pendleton puts it elsewhere in his essay, "My desire becomes the desire of the Other, the desire of the mother."[34]

This scenario of maternal identification may explain how it is that the practice of spectatorship can continue to evoke a relatively insistent form of maternal relationality for many gay men long after the actual mother has stopped accompanying them to the cinema — because the act of looking with and from the mother's position of spectatorship has been internalized and translated into an identificatory fantasy that is potentially reactivated and replayed by all subsequent spectatorial engagements. In this way, the space of spectatorship itself becomes the space of a continual repetition and affirmation of the gay subject's fantasmatic identification with the mother.

This notion of spectatorship as a stage for the repetitive declaration of gay fantasies of matrocentric identification is highlighted with particular clarity in several letters I received from men who discuss their personal fascination with classic or vintage Hollywood cinema. One man, for example, claims:

> [I love] these 'older' films [because they] give me a sense of "reuniting" with my dear Mum and Grand-mother, for I know that they lived at this time and may well have viewed these films that I now watch.[35]

In a similar vein, another man writes that

> the greatest influence on my tastes in film was my mother. She introduced me to all of the films of the "golden years of Hollywood" that she had watched and loved when she was growing up. So these films all have a special magic for me, not just because they're great films themselves but because they were so special to my mother as well.[36]

These accounts testify to the influential role of fantasies of maternal identification in the organization of certain gay male spectatorial forms. The subjects of these accounts are explicit about the way they mobilize their spectatorships as the site for a performative articulation of matrocentric desire. When they watch a film that the mother has or may have watched in her capacity as a spectator before them, these subjects are literally playing out a fantasy of maternal identification in which their contemporary position of (gay) spectatorship and desire is aligned with and yoked to that of the mother's historical position of spectatorship before them. When these gay spectators watch a film, they are, fantasmatically speaking, watching through the eyes of the mother.

This type of reading provides a somewhat different approach to questions surrounding the frequently noted gay subcultural popularization and celebration of classic Hollywood film, suggesting that this may, potentially at least, be informed by a fantasmatic scenario of maternal-centered desire and identification. This potential of gay fascinations with classic cinema is highlighted by Jaffe Cohen, Danny McWilliams, and Bob Smith in their recent lighthearted book, *Growing Up Gay:*

> [As protogay children] we were slowly becoming aware of filmdom's more glorious past, often while we were watching television. It was probably some rainy afternoon in front of the TV set when we first become transfixed while watching *Humoresque* with Joan Crawford, or *Niagara* with Marilyn Monroe. . . . And, of course, there was the yearly broadcast of *The Wizard of Oz*, which for young gays was a Rosetta Stone, unlocking the secrets of *an earlier culture which had flowered long before we were born.* . . . Television wasn't the only means by which we were *going back to our futures.* If we were lucky enough to have film buffs for mothers, old *Photoplay* magazines could be dug out of the attic with articles about Jean Arthur and Myrna Loy. . . . And then there were [our mother's] stories, recounted over coffee and cake, about how members of our very own families had brushed up against movie stars, like the time Aunt Grace had seen Claudette Colbert getting gas at the Sinclair Station, or the day Irene Dunne has stepped on Aunt Sylvia's toe.[37]

This passage effects a subtle, but nevertheless central, alignment between gay male cinematic nostalgia and gay matrocentrism. Its shift in focus from a gay interest in the cinematic past to a more specific interest in the mother's past metonymically fuses the two together. The striking use of a rhetoric of the future anterior to mark that shift—"going back to our futures"—suggests the presence of a fantasy of retroactive maternal identification. Thus gay male fascination with classic Hollywood film becomes in this reading not so much a fascination with technological, aesthetic, or even cultural history as a fascination with, specifically, the mother's history.

In writing this I am reminded in particular of Roland Barthes's wonderfully queer (re)definition of "History" as "the time when my mother was alive *before me.*"[38] For Barthes, this definition provides the motivational logic behind his own personal interest in and desire for the visual artifacts of late-nineteenth- and early-twentieth-century history, because this was the period of his own beloved mother's "history," that fantasmatically resonant period of maternal existence that preceded his own. As Barthes reads it, his interest in this period issues from a desire to be with the mother in her past, to position himself with and possibly as the mother in that space of her existence beyond the limits of his own memory, "moving back in time with her, looking for the truth of the face I had loved."[39] Although Barthes makes his remarks in reference to still photographs, a comparable structure of desire is potentially at work in gay male cinematic nostalgia. The gay male popularization of certain Hollywood texts of a previous generation is readable in such a context as a fantasmatic fascination with and reactivation of the past in terms of maternal history. To paraphrase the letter from Ken Schessler cited above, these films have a special magic for the gay spectator because they were so special for the mother before him.

This transgenerational configuration of desire and identification provides a forceful example of the psychoanalytic theory of memory as a space of fantasmatic articulation, for it demonstrates how memories may be organized around scenarios from the past at which the anamnestic subject was not even materially present but that nonetheless provide a real determinative framework for the articulation of his or her desires. By watching Hollywood films from the mother's past, the gay spectator can "recall" in fantasy a structure of desire from the history of the mother's existence that predates his own, taking up her position within this structure and, through an act of identification, making this position his own. In this way, certain forms of gay spectatorship act as a continual "memorialization" of the mother's position that keeps her desire, as well as the gay subject's identificatory attachments to that desire, alive and active within the organizational networks of fantasy life.

The notion of gay spectatorship as an arena for the performative replication of the gay subject's primary modes of maternal identification also provides an alternative access point to issues surrounding the widespread adoration of the female film star in Anglo-American gay subcultures. In the last chapter, I approached this phenomenon primarily through gay camp readings of gender as performative masquerade, arguing that gay spectators recognize and celebrate the potentials for gender disorganization offered by the "excessive" stylization of certain female stars' performances of sexual difference. Within that context, it was suggested that these female star-signs function for gay spectators as topoi of queer identification. More specifically, the female star-image provides a forum for the gay spectator within which to explore and perform the various forms of feminine identification that play such a crucial role in cultural definitions of male homosexuality. In light of the argument being pursued in this chapter, the female star-image may also act as a potential site for the reactivation and exploration of gay male forms of matrocentric identification. So the much vaunted cult of the adored female star among gay men becomes readable in this context as another configuration of gay male fantasies of matrocentrism.

Although the biographical accounts previously cited do not explicitly describe gay male relations to the female star-image in this way, their consistent refraction of gay spectatorial pleasures through an emphatically mother-centered paradigm supports a reading of the gay cult of the female star in terms of matrocentrism. The brief excerpt in which Tony Donnelly mentions that part of his fascination with the star-image of Barbra Streisand comes from the fact that "she reminds me a lot of my mother" certainly suggests the presence of a matrocentric scenario, as does some of the material in Patrick Horrigan's poignant autobiographical history of his gay spectatorship, in which he also represents his own obsession with Streisand as strikingly mother-related. In one section, he recounts:

> I would always want my mom to watch [Streisand movies] with me. At first she would demur, saying that she had some other things to do, she had the wash to fold, and it was such a long movie, tomorrow was a busy day for her. But then, just as the movie was starting, she would come into the den and sit next to me on the sofa, and we would watch the whole thing together, and laugh at all of Barbra's jokes, and then I would race to the kitchen during the commercials to get bowls of chocolate ice cream and orange sherbet mixed, which was one of our favorites.[40]

In my own personal history, my (queer) engagements with certain female stars are subtended by strong fantasmatic currents of maternal desire and identification. My mother loomed large in the formation of my early spectatorship, and from the beginning her central presence become entwined with and made itself felt through the spectacular female star-image on the screen. The very first film my mother ever took me to see was *The Sound of Music* when I was three years old, and it occasioned what has become a lifelong fascination with Julie Andrews. Importantly, this fascination obtains markedly matrocentric resonances. Beyond the fact that a certain image of maternity is central to the Andrews star-persona itself—as exemplified in her two most famous film roles, the governess, Maria, and the magical nanny, Mary Poppins—my obsession with Andrews is firmly tied up with the fact that it was my mother who effectively "gave me" Julie Andrews in the first place. When I try to retrieve that first visit to the cinema from the shadowy depths of my memory, it emerges largely in the form of a single composite image: my mother and I sitting there in rapt delight gazing at the screen as Julie runs up that famous hilltop and encompasses us in her open arms. It is a proto-typical image from my subjective and spectatorial (pre)history that has assumed mythic status in my imagination and that has in many ways been the fantasmatic motor behind much of my fascination with this particular star. I also note that Andrews and my mother share a number of striking similarities—they are both auburn-haired women who exhibit a strong sense of quiet resolve, middle-class respectability and crystal-clear British diction.[41] My mother was also a classically trained mezzo-soprano, and though she only ever performed in amateur musical productions, in my childhood scheme of things, this was tantamount to being a Julie Andrews-like "star." The precise effect of these similarities on my engagements with Andrews may be difficult to pinpoint, but they certainly indicate the presence of an overdetermined maternal dynamic within those engagements. In fact, my mother herself is fond of drawing attention to the matrocentric nature of my devotion to Andrews, remarking on more than one occasion that there seem to be only two women in her gay son's life, herself and Julie Andrews.[42]

My suggestion that gay celebrations of female stars rest on fantasies of maternal identification also finds support in recent essays on cinematic stardom in which the fascination of certain female star-images is theorized in terms of a matrocentric economy of meaning and desire. For example, in her work on Marlene Dietrich, Gaylyn Studlar suggests that much of the power of Dietrich's particular star-image accrues from its potential re-presentation of the omnipotent maternal imago from the pre-oedipal oral phase. She argues that the cold strength and sexual aggressiveness of the Dietrich persona define her as "the authoritative, active pre-oedipal mother" who is "loving, coolly distant, and holding the promise of a fantasmical [*sic*] reunion of unimaginable bliss."[43] As mentioned in chapter 2, Edward Baron Turk reads the star-image of Jeanette MacDonald in a similar vein, arguing that MacDonald's soprano voice has the capacity to invoke in spectators a "regression to an imaginary, pre-Oedipal state of total identification with the mother's voice" and that this is the source of both her pleasures and unpleasures as a star.[44] In relation to the latter, Turk argues that much of the widespread, critical derision of MacDonald stems from male anxieties about maternal relationality and the phallic male spectator's unwillingness "to accept . . . the maternal voice as the agency of acoustic authority" (238).

One of the most explicit examples of this style of reading, however, and one that concentrates on gay male spectatorship, can be found in Peter Matthews's essay on Greta Garbo. Matthews suggests that the characteristic collocation of signs of "legendary grandeur, towering strength and saintly compassion" within the Garbo image endows it with powerful connotations of pre-oedipal, or "phallic," maternity. For Matthews, these distinctive features of the Garbo image have made her a strong candidate for the reactivation of pre-oedipal fantasies of "completion and perfect love in the original dyadic relation of child to maternal body."[45] It is for this reason, he suggests, that Garbo has spoken so powerfully to those groups for whom a fantasy of pre-oedipal nostalgia offers the greatest returns in terms of psychic pleasure, namely women and gay men. Importantly, Matthews is quick to differentiate such readings of Garbo as pre-oedipal, or "phallic," mother from the "much more typical post-Oedipal male fetish of cultic feminine beauty" because, unlike phallic male fantasies of Woman as fetishized other, female and gay male readings of Garbo are underpinned by a "recurrent unconscious reversion to . . . primary maternal desire" relayed through a constitutive mode of "*emotional identification* with her as ego ideal" (23–25).

Although this work on the centrality of maternal-centered desire to certain female star-images and readings of them supports my suggestion that gay spectators mobilize the female star-image to articulate their own fantasmatic forms of maternal relationality and identification, it is unwarranted to think that all gay spectators automatically engage these fantasies in their relationships with film stars or any other cinematic form, or that such fantasies provide a subterranean, concrete "truth" of gay spectatorship. Clearly, the realities of gay spectatorship and how those realities figure and configure maternal relationality are far too complex and multivalent to be reduced to a single meaning. However, the argument offered here does help illuminate a certain potential within gay spectatorships for the performative articulation of highly influential fantasies of maternal-centered desire and identification.

Hollywood Melodrama and Gay Fantasies of Maternal-Centered Desire

Andy Medhurst argues that it "is part of the accumulated folk wisdom of gay male subcultures that the homosexuality of an individual will reveal itself primarily through matters of taste — not good or bad taste but *particular* taste, a fondness for certain cultural artefacts above others, a set of preferences that proclaim one's sexual affiliations as clearly as any sloganeering T-shirt."[46] As I have already suggested, the cinema has been an especially influential cultural site for the articulation of these discourses of "gay taste." Gay male subcultures have long cultivated a popular hierarchization of Hollywood products in which certain films, genres, and star-images are singled out as having special appeal and significance for gay men and are privileged accordingly. In addition to the gay male fascination with and celebration of the Hollywood musical, another cinematic genre has also been popularized in and by Anglo-American gay subcultures: the Hollywood melodrama. As Mark Finch and Richard Kwietniowski write:

Gay men have always been associated with Hollywood melodrama . . . : narratively, not as subjects, but as symptoms, effects of disorder . . . ; in terms of performance, as exaggerated, hysterical, unruly — Dean, Clift; as instrumental off-screen figures of the genre — George Cukor, Tennessee Williams — and, particularly, hairdressers, designers, costumiers — *gossips*; finally, as spectators, in terms of over-identification . . . , imitation . . .—an empathy with melodrama's painful impossibilities, and also an ironic appreciation of the genre's excesses, or camp.[47]

As this passage suggests, the melodrama, like the musical, is widely noted as a genre of excess, and this characteristic is frequently seen as a central reason for its popularity among gay audiences. With its scenarios of sexual and social transgression and its highly stylized mise-en-scène, the melodrama opens a space for queer or otherwise aberrant formations of meaning and desire that "most Hollywood forms have studiously closed off."[48]

The Hollywood melodrama has long been recognized as a privileged site for the cinematic representation of maternal-oriented scenarios of desire. As Naomi Scheman argues, "The presence and dramatic importance of mothers . . . is one of the distinguishing marks of the [melodramatic] genre."[49] Mary Ann Doane goes so far as to claim the melodrama as "the privileged form in the cinema for the investigation of issues associated with maternity."[50] One need only think of the enduring popularity of one of the most important subgenres of the melodramatic form, the maternal melodrama, to gauge the extent to which the Hollywood melodrama foregrounds scenarios of matrocentric desire.

This emphasis on maternal-centered scenarios is an important part of gay preoccupations with the melodrama. The endless tableaux of maternal separation and return offer gay spectators a space to articulate the forms of matrocentric desire and identification that I've been exploring in this chapter. Linda Williams makes a homologous claim in her essay on *Stella Dallas*, in which she argues that the appeal of the maternal melodrama for female spectators lies in its characteristic representation of scenarios of "mother-daughter possession and dispossession." She asserts that female audiences are drawn—and redrawn—to these films because they provide a unique affirmation of "the 'essential female tragedy' of mother-daughter passion, rapture and loss" claimed by theorists like Chodorow as pivotal to feminine psychic development and organization.[51] In a similar way, (some) gay spectators may also be drawn to the melodrama because of its extraordinary centralization of maternal-oriented desire, something that offers fertile scope for the exploration and validation of gay formations of fantasmatic matrocentrism.

To explore this argument I focus on two particular melodramatic films that have achieved a marked cult popularity in Anglo-American gay subcultures: *Sunset Boulevard* (1950) and *Suddenly, Last Summer* (1959). At first glance, these may seem to be peculiar choices. Few critics would classify either one as a maternal melodrama in the strictest sense of the term. Only one of them represents its central female protagonist as a mother within the diegesis, and even here the question of this character's maternity is problematized by the fact that her child is dead before the film begins. Furthermore, the central storylines of these two films do not seem to follow the maternal melodrama's characteristic plot of maternal separation and sacrifice. However, as Mary Ann Doane notes, the "classic" articulation of the maternal melodrama as a story of mother-child separation and maternal self-effacement has a short history confined largely to Hollywood films of the thirties; after this time, the form of the maternal melodrama becomes "witness to a number of aberrations" and "los[es] much of its coherence as a subgenre." Doane contends that, after about 1940, "the maternal becomes a fractured concept" in and for the melodrama and is dispersed across "a number of different types of films."[52] The two texts I have chosen for analysis are products of this "dispersal." Both films present, in one way or another, a sustained attempt to conceive and explore issues of maternal-oriented desire within the closed, intersubjective narratives and rich, baroque styles of the Hollywood melodrama. Thus, although these films do not directly focus on "classic" mother-child scenarios, they feature the concept of the maternal in their narrative concerns and may profitably be read as late examples of the Hollywood maternal melodrama.

That both films date from the fifties is also significant; the postwar era was, for North American culture, a time in which the category of the maternal became a site of extreme ideological struggle and psychocultural obsession. This development is well illustrated by the popularity at the time of Philip Wylie's notorious characterization of America as a culture in the grips of "momism." In Wylie's account, excessive mothering, or "momism," is defined as the root cause of the perceived crisis in American masculinity and patriarchal authority: "Mom is everywhere and everything and damned near everybody, and on her depends all the rest of the U.S. Disguised as good old mom, dear old mom, sweet old mom, your loving mom, and so on, she is the bride at every funeral and the corpse at every wedding. Men live for her and die for her, dote upon her and whisper her name as they pass away."[53] Wylie's reading of "Mom" as the ruination of patriarchal masculinity gripped American culture with astonishing force and led to a widespread reconstruction of maternity as a site and source of social anxiety within popular discourses of the time. In 1946 Edward Strecker claimed that "no nation is in greater danger of failing to solve the mother-child dilemma than our own."[54] By 1950 the discourse of momism had so gripped the public imagination that the psychoanalyst Erik Erikson was impelled to ask if such a mass condemnation might not conceal some sort of "revengeful triumph." "Who is this 'Mom'?" he implored. "How did she lose her good, her simple name? How could she become an excuse for all that is rotten in the state of the nation? Is Mom really to blame?"[55]

The postwar discourse of momism went hand in hand with an equally obsessive discourse of homophobic panic. Given the increasingly widespread penetration of pop Freudianism into American thought at the time, it was almost inevitable that the vision of the powerful mother as the source of social "emasculation" put forward by the discourse of momism would evoke and incorporate psychoanalytic readings of the domineering mother as the "cause" of homosexuality. Wylie, for example, uses Freudian theories to expose the dangers of "mother-love-in-action" and how too close a bond between mother and son can result in "perversion."[56] Similarly, in their 1947 contribution to the momism debate, Lundberg and Farnham extensively allude to Freud's condemnatory descriptions of the mothers of homosexual sons in his study on Leonardo when they characterize American mothers as "overly masculine women" who "strip [their sons] of their male powers" and turn them into "passive echoes."[57] In this way, male homosexuality came to form an increasingly emphatic "subtext" for many of the popular discourses that circulated in and around the category of the maternal in postwar American culture. So much so, that, as Lee Edelman writes, the logic of popular thinking seemed almost to be that if "momism is the theory, then homosexuality is the practice," for homosexuality was "seen as enacting the destabilization of borders, the subversion of masculine identity from within, that momism promote[d]."[58]

The potent reconstruction of the maternal as a site of patriarchal disappropriation and male homosexualization finds voice in the figuration of the maternal as trope in many melodramatic films from this period. Throughout the fifties, the Hollywood melodrama became the site of an increasingly explicit exploration of issues surrounding maternity, male homosexuality, and relations between the two.[59] Both of the films I have chosen for analysis are examples of this tendency, which is why, in part, they obtain such marked gay appeal. Even though gay audiences have long been drawn to the genre of Hollywood melodrama because it uniquely provides for a representation and exploration of the types of matrocentric scenarios central to gay male psychosexual paradigms, this attraction is even further strengthened in certain late melodramas from the fifties and after, wherein the melodramatic representation of matrocentric desire becomes subtly or, on occasions, not so subtly inflected by tropes of male homosexuality.

Given the largely disparaging cast assumed by most of the discourses on momism and homosexuality, it would be naive to think that the Hollywood melodrama's figuration of these issues was somehow different and that the films in question provide gay spectators with a wonderfully affirming celebration of homosexuality and its relations to the maternal. As E. Ann Kaplan argues in her study of the representation of motherhood in Hollywood cinema, most postwar melodramatic films mirror the social anxieties of the time and "manifest what can be described only as a kind of hysteria in relation to the . . . mother."[60] The sense of hysteria is even further pronounced in those films that raise the added specter of homosexuality. Nevertheless, I think it would be equally naive to assume that these texts are all wholly "negative" in their constructions of maternity and homosexuality. Motherhood in the Hollywood melodrama is nothing if not "the site of multiple contradictions."[61] Thus, even though many melodramatic films from this period present extreme representations of the figure of the mother as, in Kaplan's description, "evil," "possessive," "dominating," and "phallic," and, in so doing, repeat and contribute to the widespread demonization of the maternal prevalent in popular social discourses of the time, they also present competing, even contradictory, meanings. Consequently, these films can never be totally exhausted by or reduced to the fixed list of negative meanings identified by critics like Kaplan in their readings of these texts.

Here again I acknowledge the irreducible potential for resistance and negotiation in each act of textual reading. To repeat Christine Gledhill's succinct formulation, meaning in the encounter between text and specta-tor "is neither imposed, nor passively imbibed, but arises out of a struggle or negotiation between competing frames of reference, motivation and experience."[62] This point needs to be borne in mind as we approach the films I have nominated for analysis here. Although these films' inter-related constructions of maternity and homosexuality may, when read from one perspective, seem largely denigrating, they may equally, when read from a different perspective, especially that of a mother-identified gay man, produce a range of alternative meanings.

Suddenly, Last Summer

Suddenly, Last Summer provides the most pressing case for testing out such a hypothesis, for it is arguably the more defamatory and certainly the more explicit of the two in its representations of maternity and male homosexuality.

Set in New Orleans in 1937, the film revolves around the complex re-lations between a young poet, Sebastian Venable, his adoring, wealthy mother, Violet (Katharine Hepburn), and his young cousin, Cathy (Eliz-abeth Taylor). Sebastian has died mysteriously sometime "last summer" while on vacation with Cathy in Europe. The effects of this tragedy have made Cathy insane, and when the film opens, we find that she has been committed to a psychiatric institution. Cathy is allegedly prone to psy-chotic hallucinations and what Violet describes as "dreadful, obscene babblings," most of which assume the form of "hideous attacks on the moral character" of the late Sebastian. Violet, who will brook no tar-nishing of her beloved son's memory, enlists the help of a famed neuro-surgeon, Dr. Cukrowicz (Montgomery Clift), to lobotomize and, thus, silence the loquacious Cathy. Cukrowicz agrees to look into the case, and in a series of encounters with both Cathy and Violet he pieces together the "awful truth" about Sebastian and the reason behind Cathy's "illness." In a final dramatic confrontation on the back terrace of Violet's man-sion, Cukrowicz coaxes Cathy to recall the fateful summer when Sebas-tian died. The story emerges that Sebastian was in fact a homosexual who "used" first his mother and then, when she became "too old," his cousin to help procure young men for his sexual pleasures. In vengeance, the youths of the Spanish town in which Sebastian and Cathy were vacationing pursued the "depraved" Sebastian up to a cliff-top promontory where they killed him in a frenzied attack, ripping his body to pieces and devouring his flesh. The revelation of this secret truth is a catharsis for Cathy, who is restored to "normal" mental health at the end of the film. It proves too much for the doting Violet, however, who is forced to retreat into insanity herself. The film ends with Violet lost in a demented fantasy world in which she thinks Sebastian is still alive with her.

As this brief summary indicates, *Suddenly, Last Summer* voices many of the social fears and anxieties circulating in fifties' America around the image of the domineering mother and the maternal-identified male homosexual. With its potent mix of homosexuality, obsessive mother love, mental illness, and cannibalism, *Suddenly, Last Summer* seems to be, as Vito Russo writes, "the kind of psychosexual freak show that the Fifties almost demanded."[63] Many of the contemporary reviews of the film focused on the issue of maternal-centered male homosexuality as both the site and source of the film's horrific appeal, with *Sight and Sound* calling it a "sickly fantasy . . . of possessive mother domination" and *Time* magazine describing it as "a psychiatric nursery drama, a homosexual fantasy of guilty pleasure and pleasurable punishment [with] the dead hero [as] a perverted Peter Pan."[64] In a similar vein, Henry Hart opined that *Suddenly, Last Summer* "exposes clearly the foremost causes of homosexuality and . . . points to one of the horrible fates that can overtake this particular kind of pervert."[65]

Clearly, for most viewers, *Suddenly, Last Summer* is read as nothing short of contemptuous in its representations of male homosexuality, the maternal, and their interrelations. In fact, *Suddenly, Last Summer* was the first studio-produced film granted "special dispensation" from the Motion Picture Production Code Office to represent homosexuality on screen, because, in the words of the Catholic Legion of Decency, it "illustrates the horrors of such a lifestyle, [and, as such,] can be considered moral in theme even though it deals with sexual perversion."[66]

Given the overwhelmingly homophobic reactions of these mainstream readings of *Suddenly, Last Summer*, why have gay spectators responded to it so enthusiastically and how have they constructed what one would assume are slightly more conciliatory formations of meaning in their engagements of the film? Apart from the fact that all texts, no matter how conservative their implied meanings may seem, can generate different readings, many of the mainstream evaluations of *Suddenly, Last Summer* are disingenuous in their characterization of the film as simply and unproblematically demonizing vis-à-vis the issues of homosexuality and mother-identification that it explores. For a start, far from offering the type of stark, denotative imagery suggested by the Legion of Decency's claim that "the film *illustrates* the horrors" of homosexuality, *Suddenly, Last Summer* is, in fact, extraordinarily circumspect in the representation of its homosexual subject matter. The word *homosexuality* is never once mentioned, and, more curiously perhaps, Sebastian, its homosexual protagonist, is never shown in his entirety. Instead, Sebastian is an abstract presence, someone referred to constantly but only ever represented piecemeal in some of the flashback sequences—a hand or arm piercing the side of the frame, a shadow cast on a wall, a silhouette in profile.[67] Although it could be argued that such an unusual representational practice helps demonize homosexuality even further by defining it as some sort of unrepresentable phantom that "haunts" the diegesis, it also tends to endow the film's constructions of homosexuality with an indeterminacy that is never entirely contained by the film's hegemonic ideological agenda.

As D. A. Miller argues in his influential reading of Hitchcock's *Rope*, although the relegation of homosexuality to "the shadow kingdom of connotation" has been one of "the dominant signifying practices of homophobia" in mainstream film, it also has the "inconvenience of tending to raise th[e] ghost [of homosexuality] all over the place"—something that subverts any notion of a straightforward textual program of homophobic meaning.[68] In the case of *Suddenly, Last Summer,* its curiously abstract representation of homosexuality potentially destabilizes the significatory fixity to which so many mainstream readings seem to wish (symptomatically perhaps) to confine it, opening it instead into the protean semiotic economies of connotation and ambivalence in which it becomes amenable to a wide range of shifting interpretations. In a recent piece published after I first wrote this chapter, D. A. Miller develops a breathtaking critical analysis of *Suddenly, Last Summer* that, though rather different in focus from my own, attests to the profoundly queer dynamics of the film's connotative operations. Addressing how the disallowed visual scene of gay male sex emerges in displaced form in the text as an obsessive metaphorics of queer anality, Miller asserts that the film's "energetic . . . repudiation" of the "spectacle" of homosexuality "does nothing to drive back the genie of homosexual desire into the tiny lamp in which he lay confined; on the contrary, he now expands to such vaporously protean dimensions as enable him to envelop and saturate the very [text] that is, visually speaking, his appointed censor" and, thus, "to steal his still flitty but now far less fleeting pleasures all over the place."[69]

The disruptive multiplication of ostensibly disallowed perverse pleasures can be found equally in *Suddenly, Last Summer*'s construction of the interrelated queer tropes of maternal desire and identification. The figure of the mother plays a pivotal role in the film's networks of meaning and desire. Although it is undeniable that *Suddenly, Last Summer* ultimately seeks to define the figure of maternity that it constructs as monstrous and abject, it nonetheless suggests divergent, even contradictory, meanings for that figure that once again enable spectators to construct alternative formations of meaning in their readings of the film.

The scene in which we first encounter Violet demonstrates how *Suddenly, Last Summer* vacillates between contradictory meanings in its representation of the maternal image. In this scene Dr. Cukrowicz calls to visit Violet at her mansion and is ushered into the entry hall by her secretary. At first, Cukrowicz mistakes the secretary for Violet, and she laughs nervously at his error, informing him that Mrs. Venable will be with him shortly. By preceding Violet's arrival with a rather detailed preamble, the film instates a marked sense of anticipation in the spectator, a desire to see and know the figure of the mother as she is realized in the text. The sense of anticipatory desire is further strengthened when Violet does arrive a few moments later. There is an offscreen noise of machinery whirring into motion, the secretary looks up and, in a hushed, respectful manner, gasps, "She's coming down!" The film then cuts to the reverse visual field, which shows an elevator grille-door, and we hear the unmistakable voice of Katharine Hepburn, who is as yet still out of shot, soliloquizing: "Sebastian always said, 'Mother, when you descend it's like a Goddess from the Byzantine.' It's just like an angel coming to earth as I float, float into view." On the last line Violet does indeed "float into view" as she descends in the elevator and emerges, forceful and self-assured, dressed in a sumptuous gown of white with a matching silk stole draped around her shoulders, her hand outstretched in welcome to the doctor. The exuberant grandiosity of Violet's entrance defines her from the start as a powerful figure who is intensely fascinating and appealing. Cukrowicz clearly thinks so, as he literally cannot take his eyes off her, causing Violet to stop mid-sentence and inquire if something is the matter.

> *Dr. Cukrowicz:* I'm sorry! I had been told that you were a widow.
> *Violet:* I am! I'm in mourning; white was my son's favorite color.

By referring Violet's appearance back to her status as (mourning) mother, the film establishes a significatory economy in which the sense of fascination and appeal woven so carefully around the Violet character is refracted through and anchored within her primary textual function as maternal figure. Any attraction or desire experienced by the spectator for the character of Violet in this sequence would therefore be relayed through an explicit paradigm of matrocentrism.

The film constantly stresses the issue of Violet's maternity, never letting us forget that she is a mother. In the initial sequence with Dr. Cukrowicz, for example, Violet peppers her conversation with endless references to her son, Sebastian, culminating in a lengthy reminiscence in which she explicates the extraordinarily close nature of the bond that they apparently shared:

> We were a famous couple. People never used to speak of Sebastian and his mother or Mrs. Venable and her son. No, they said Sebastian and Violet; Violet and Sebastian are staying at the Lido or they're at the Ritz in Madrid, and every time we appeared attention was centered on us, everyone else eclipsed. My son, Sebastian, and I constructed our days, we would carve each day like a piece of sculpture. Yes, we left behind us a trail of days like a gallery of sculptures until . . . suddenly last summer.

For many — especially, perhaps, for audiences of the fifties and sixties who would have been only too conscious of the dangers of this type of "excessive mothering" — the scenario of extreme maternal intimacy set out in this sequence would be read as shocking or, even, repulsive; there is, in fact, ample textual encouragement for making such a reading. In the scene immediately prior to this soliloquy, Violet takes Cukrowicz out into the back garden — an intricately designed space full of huge, exotic plants gathered from equatorial jungles around the globe — which, she tells him, was built by Sebastian before his death. In a small, glass hothouse in the middle of the garden is a carnivorous plant that Violet refers to as "our lady" and to which she feeds a box full of specially imported flies. As she feeds the plant, she explains to Cukrowicz that "they never get away. The lady exudes this marvelous perfume which attracts them . . . they plunge into a trance and they never come out." The thinly veiled symbolism of this scene, combined with the ominous cello strains and kettle-drum rolls on the soundtrack, clearly seek to introduce a preferred reading of Violet's binding maternity as fatal and devouring. This connection is further emphasized a few moments later when Violet is shown standing in front of a rather grotesque piece of garden statuary in the form of a skeletal angel of death. The quite extraordinary visual framing and composition of this shot produce a stark parallel between the two figures that evokes a blatant metaphoric equation of Violet's maternity with death.

However, given the way the text structures a competing ethos of fascination and attraction around the character of Violet, there is equal room here to negotiate an alternative reading in which the scenarios of maternal potency and bonding crystallized in and around the complex dyadic figure of Violet Venable and her homosexual son can be interpreted as intensely pleasurable rather than threatening. The sense of ambivalence in the film's exploration of maternal desire may be evidenced in one of its key thematic motifs, that of carnivorous violence. I have already suggested that, in the scene of Violet with the Venus flytrap, the film attempts to align Violet's binding maternity with an image of devouring monstrousness. Elsewhere in the film, however, this equation is reversed, and maternal relationality is seemingly recast as a space of gentle nurturance diametrically opposed to, and offering protective refuge from, an external world of danger and threat. In a crucial scene that occurs about midway through the film, Violet recounts a trip she and Sebastian took to the Encantadas to watch the giant sea turtles lay their eggs on the beach. She tells Dr. Cukrowicz that, months later, they returned to the islands at Sebastian's insistence to watch the hatching of the eggs. Apparently, Sebastian knew what would happen and he wanted his mother to see. In a wonderfully overwrought dramatic monologue, Violet recalls how on the night the eggs hatched, the sky filled with birds, "savage, devouring birds" that swooped down and attacked the young turtles, pecking out their eyes and ripping open the soft flesh of their underbellies as they raced furiously down the beach, back to the protection of the sea and their mothers. Violet was horrified and wanted to leave, refusing to believe that "life could be like that," but Sebastian made her stay and watch, claiming grandly that "this was the cruel face of God."

This sequence establishes an explicit opposition between a realm of maternal intimacy and safety and an outside world that threatens to shatter that safety. Given the characterization of this external threat as "God," it is possible to read this sequence as a metaphoric performance of the fears and fantasies attendant on the symbolic father's prohibitive rupture of pre-oedipal maternal bonding. A little later in the same sequence, Violet provides another variation on this theme when she muses: "Millions of years ago, the dinosaurs fed on the leaves of those trees. The dinosaurs were vegetarian, that's why they became extinct, they were just too gentle for their size, and the carnivorous creatures, the ones that eat flesh, the killers, inherited the earth. But then, they always do, don't they?" The whole sequence provides a richly allegorical performance in which the unusually close, pre-oedipal-style relationship between Violet and Sebastian comes to be defined, implicitly at least, as an attempt to stave off the incursion of paternal authority into the "security" of the imaginary dyad. And, inasmuch as the sequence characterizes that paternal intervention in violent and rather horrifying terms, it provides a framework in which Violet and Sebastian's stubborn refusal to cede to patrocentric authority appears both understandable and appealing. Thus, although *Suddenly, Last Summer* tends, on the whole, to define Violet and Sebastian's relationship as perverse and unacceptable, it provides ample textual material from which to construct competing readings and evaluations of that relationship.

Ultimately, a question of spectatorial desire plays the key determinative role here. The ambivalent, even contradictory nature of the film's constructions of maternity, homosexuality, and matrocentric desire leave the field open to competing interpretations, allowing the spectator's own libidinal and cultural proclivities to dictate the meanings and pleasures produced. Given the way in which I have argued for the influential role of matrocentric scenarios in gay male psychosexual paradigms, many gay spectators would have strong subjective motivations for enacting a negotiated reading of *Suddenly, Last Summer* that resists the abjectifying dimensions of the film's construction of matrocentric relationality and embraces, even amplifies, the other more thrilling possibilities of matrocentric celebration.[70]

One could object that this type of reading of *Suddenly, Last Summer* fails to account for the film's ending, which, on the face of things, harshly judges Violet and Sebastian and the "perversity" of their relationship. However, given the overwhelming heteronormativity of most Hollywood endings, resistance to clotural recuperation is a standard feature of gay negotiational readings of popular film. This feature is further overdetermined in the case of the Hollywood melodrama, which is a genre known for the inadequacy of its attempts at restitutive closure. As Laura Mulvey famously puts it: "The strength of the melodramatic form lies in the amount of dust the story raises along the road, a cloud of over-determined irreconcilables which put up a resistance to being neatly settled in the last five minutes."[71]

In *Suddenly, Last Summer,* the closing confrontation on the back terrace of the Venable mansion certainly strives for a final, spectacular demonization of Sebastian and Violet's relationship—by revealing the true horror of that relationship and "punishing" them both, Sebastian with death, Violet with madness, as well as juxtaposing it to a "reassuring" figure of heterosexual normality in the final image of Dr. Cukrowicz and Cathy going back into the house, arm in arm. However, the attempt at clotural restitution is problematized by several elements. For a start, Violet's "flight" into madness is not in itself enough to invalidate the matrocentric economy that she as a character has come to represent in the text. If anything, her turn to insanity actually furnishes Violet with a final opportunity for proclaiming the transgressive pleasures of matrocentric desire. As Cukrowicz leads her back to the elevator in the film's penultimate scene, Violet delivers a delirious monologue in which she apparently assumes Cukrowicz to be Sebastian, alive again:

> Of course, God is cruel, my darling . . . , we've always known about him. The savage face he shows to people and the fierce things he shouts. It's all we ever really see or hear of him now, nobody seems to know why. The difference is we know about him, the others don't. That's where we're lucky! . . . Oh, Sebastian, what a lovely summer it's been, just the two of us, Sebastian and Violet, Violet and Sebas-

tian, just the way it's always going to be. Oh, we are lucky my darling to have one another and need no-one else . . . ever.

Although it would be possible to dismiss this final monologue as the ravings of a madwoman (a dismissal that could be retrospectively extended to all Violet's musings), this scene does open up an opportunity for spectators so disposed to read an oppositional affirmation of matrocentric desire that problematizes any simple restoration of patrocentric heteronormativity at the film's closure.

Similarly, Violet's delusional assumption of Dr. Cukrowicz as Sebastian in this scene may also be read as introducing a tension into the film's cloutral sequence that potentially undercuts the doctor's function therein as an agent of hegemonic, phallic restoration. Given the way the character of Cukrowicz is mobilized as the textual representative of patriarchal stability and authority—like so many other doctor figures in Hollywood melodrama, he is the one charged with discovering, revealing, and rectifying the "problem" in the text—and is, thus, one would assume, meant to act as the very antithesis of Sebastian's form of matrocentric homosexuality, it is surprising the number of times Cukrowicz and Sebastian are actually paralleled in the text. When Violet and Cukrowicz first meet, for example, she is struck by his "beautiful eyes," noting admiringly that they are "just like his." Elsewhere, she refers to something that the doctor has said as "almost poetic" (Sebastian was, remember, a poet) and then goes on to say, "You're very like him, Doctor." At another point, Violet says to Cukrowicz, "You would have liked Sebastian and he would have been charmed by you." Such parallels suggest a rather curious assimilation between the two characters that could work against any easy achievement of heteronormative closure in the final sequence.

Such a reading is further overdetermined by the fact that the character of Dr. Cukrowicz is played by Montgomery Clift. I focus on gay receptions of Clift in some detail in the next chapter, so I do not wish to delve into it too far here. Suffice to note that knowledge of Clift's alleged homosexuality has long formed an integral part of gay responses to and readings of this star and his films. Even in the fifties and sixties, at the time of *Suddenly, Last Summer*'s original release, Clift's homosexuality was the subject of widespread gossip within urban, gay subcultures. Clearly, this "knowledge" would have a profound effect on how gay spectators might read *Suddenly, Last Summer* and would seriously problematize the film's attempts to cast Clift as antithetical opponent to and clotural victor over Sebastian's homosexuality and Violet's matrocentric power.[72]

The use of Clift and Elizabeth Taylor in *Suddenly, Last Summer* as figural representatives of the normative heterosexual couple at the film's end would also be put into question within the context of gay readings, not only by subcultural knowledge of Clift's homosexuality but also by an equally widespread knowledge of the deep, sibling-style relationship that he and Taylor supposedly shared in real life. Indeed, knowledge of Taylor's intimate friendships with Clift and many other gay men has led more than one gay commentator to question the entire premise of *Suddenly, Last Summer*'s demonizing vision of the mother-identified homosexual. Boze Hadleigh writes, "It stretched credulity to believe that such a hip doll as Liz wouldn't know that she was 'being used for evil'. I think Liz would have dragged Sebastian home by his ears and saved them both from considerable embarrassment that summer."[73]

In this way, gay spectators can and do resist the attempts on the part of *Suddenly, Last Summer* to recontain meaning within a clotural paradigm of heteronormativity and focus instead on those parts of the film that seem to allow for the articulation of gay desires. This process of gay resistance and negotiation may, in relation to *Suddenly, Last Summer*, focus in particular on the paradigms of matrocentric desire that form such an integral part of this melodramatic film. Thus, although the film seeks to abjectify the figure of the powerful mother and the maternal-identified homosexual that it represents, gay spectators may negotiate their way around this and produce alternative readings consonant with and receptive to their own queer formations of mother-centered fantasy and desire.

Sunset Boulevard

The other film that I would like to look at briefly in the context of gay matrocentrism is Billy Wilder's 1950 film, *Sunset Boulevard*.[74] Unlike *Suddenly, Last Summer*, *Sunset Boulevard* does not make homosexual relationality with the mother an explicit part of its diegesis. There is in fact no "mother" of which to speak at all in this film. However, with its story of a "perverse" relationship between an aging silent-film star and a much younger man, *Sunset Boulevard* may be read as providing a scenario of

intersubjective desire that is undoubtedly queer and potentially matrocentric in terms of both textual form and libidinal effect. At least, that
is one of the ways in which, as I hope to demonstrate, the film can be
taken up.

Like so many melodramas of this period, *Sunset Boulevard* tells a rather
complex story. The film takes place in Hollywood sometime around 1950.
A young aspiring screenwriter by the name of Joe Gillis (William Holden) stumbles into the home of Norma Desmond (Gloria Swanson), a
once famous but now forgotten film star from the silent era who lives
in virtual seclusion with her German butler, Max (Erich von Stroheim).
Norma tells Joe that she is planning a "return" to the screen in a film for
which she herself has written the script, and she enlists his aid as editorial consultant. Joe moves in to Norma's house to start working with her
and, in return, is showered with affection and expensive gifts. At first, Joe
revels in the ease and luxury of his new existence, but soon starts to feel
stifled by Norma's possessiveness and resents being put in the position of
gigolo that their relationship increasingly implies. To regain some independence, Joe secretly takes on a scriptwriting assignment at night with
Betty Schaefer (Nancy Olson), the young fiancée of one of his friends.
This dual existence seems to work well until Betty and Joe realize that
they have fallen in love with each other. At about the same time, Norma
discovers that the two have been meeting and, in a fit of jealousy, rings
Betty with the intention of telling her the truth about Joe's current lifestyle. Joe overhears Norma and, realizing that there can never be any
future with Betty, decides to leave and return to his hometown in Ohio.
In desperation, Norma grabs a pistol and shoots Joe dead. This final act
drives her insane, and the film closes with Norma believing that she is a
great star once again, back in front of the cameras and her adoring fans.

As suggested, I read *Sunset Boulevard* as a late variation on the Hollywood maternal melodrama. The film foregrounds the same scenarios of
intersubjective possession and dispossession that have been a thematic
hallmark of the maternal melodrama, and the central relationship in the
film between Norma and Joe, though not literally that of mother and son,
is imbued with quite pronounced maternal dimensions. Along these lines,
it is interesting to note how *Sunset Boulevard* situates its central female
character, Norma Desmond, in a series of interactive networks in which
she assumes what is explicitly defined as a symbolic maternal role. When

we first encounter Norma she is "mourning" the death of her pet chim-
panzee. In this scene, Norma mistakes Joe, who has accidentally stumbled
into her house, for the undertaker, and she charges him with taking care
of her "little darling," adding that she wants the pet to be buried in a
white baby coffin. That we are meant to read the chimp as a "surrogate"
child-object for Norma is further emphasized in a later scene when Joe,
watching from his bedroom window, sees Norma and Max bury the animal, commenting in voice-over that it was "as if she were laying to rest
an only child." Norma's possessive approach to the script she has written
is similarly marked with maternal dimensions. When she first discusses
her script with Joe, Norma tells him that she "wrote it with her heart"
and that, as a result, she is fiercely attached to it and could never "let it
out of the house." The implicit maternal dynamics of this exchange are
explicated in a following scene when Joe describes, again in voice-over,
how Norma would hover over him when he was trying to work on the
script, "afraid I'd do injury to that precious brain-child of hers."

It is, however, in the relationship between Norma and Joe that *Sunset
Boulevard* makes the maternal dimensions of the Norma character most
explicit. Several theorists have pointed out that the Hollywood melodrama often presents an intersubjective scenario of heterosexual romance
in which the female character is coded as dominant and in control and the
male character is correspondingly infantilized or feminized.[75] This is certainly the case in *Sunset Boulevard*, in which the "traditional" power dynamics of heterosexuality are inverted, with Norma assuming the dominant, authoritative position and Joe the passive position of infantilized
subordination. The film actively foregrounds this perverse inversion of
orthodox heterosexuality by making it a narrative feature in the opening
scenes when Norma and Joe first meet. Joe reveals in voice-over that he
is hatching a scheme to take advantage of Norma and her wealth by fool-
ing her into thinking that her script is good but in need of some minor
revisions. When Norma invites Joe to do the editorial work, as he had
clearly planned, he feigns initial reluctance, telling her that he is "pretty
expensive" but finally accepting after Norma promises she "will make it
worth his while." Because of the success of his duplicity, Joe thinks he
has Norma firmly in the palm of his hand; as he boasts in voice-over, "I
dropped the hook and she snapped at it." However, his apparent assumption of control is short lived for, after spending the night in her guest

quarters, Joe awakens to find that Norma has arranged for all his possessions to be packed up and brought over to her house during the night. Enraged, he confronts and attacks Norma for her presumptuousness, but his self-righteous indignation is quickly deflated when Norma tells him that she is well aware of his impoverished circumstances and that he can hardly expect to stay on in an apartment where he owes two months in back rent. From this point on, the structure of the relationship is well established, with Norma assuming both economic and emotional control and Joe cast, albeit reluctantly, in the auxiliary position of passive dependency.

That this differentiated power structure is meant to be aligned with a mother-child relationship is spelled out with increasing clarity throughout the film. In one scene, when Norma and her friends are playing bridge, Joe tries to interrupt the game in order to ask for some money but storms off in juvenile petulance when Norma chastises him, much as a mother would a pestering child, by snapping, "Not now dear, can't you see that I'm trying to concentrate?" In a later scene, Norma chides Joe for chewing gum and makes him take it out of his mouth. When they later go shopping for clothes, Norma, much like a doting mother, picks out a wardrobe for him. She assumes a similar parental role in the climactic New Year's Ball sequence, during which she inspects and preens Joe's outfit, straightening his bow tie and putting a carnation in his buttonhole before leading him onto the dance floor, after he has protested that he cannot dance, with the authoritative command "Just follow me!"

Peter Matthews argues that the tendency to infantilize the male character in melodrama complicates and destabilizes phallic male identity and patriarchal authority, and he suggests that this is one reason behind the widespread appeal of the genre for women and gay men. Importantly, Matthews also suggests that this "inverted" power structure may be symptomatic of an underlying libidinal scenario that he correlates to regressive infantile fantasies of Imaginary, maternal *jouissance*. The powerful, idealized female figure of the Hollywood melodrama provides a representational image that potentially reactivates fantasies of the omnipotent, pre-oedipal, or "phallic" mother—the mother "without lack," the mother "at full value," "an imaginary vision of completion and perfect love in the original dyadic relation of child to maternal body." [76]

In relation to *Sunset Boulevard*, several features of Norma's textual construction recommend reading her in terms of a powerful, pre-oedipal maternity. The grandiosity of her appearance and demeanor, the opulence of her lifestyle, and the operatic scale of Gloria Swanson's bravura performance combine to make Norma a cinematic figure who is "larger than life." Everything about Norma is grand. When Joe first arrives at her mansion, his voice-over commentary provides a running description of the place that makes constant recourse to an imagery of grandeur. Norma's garage is described as "a great, big empty garage"; her car, "an enormous, foreign-built automobile"; her house, "a great, big white-elephant of a place." This imagery is extended to apply to Norma herself a few moments later, in that classic exchange when Joe and Norma first meet:

> *Joe:* Wait a minute, haven't I seen you before? I know your face. . . . You're Norma Desmond! You used to be in silent pictures, you used to be big!
> *Norma:* I *am* big, it's the pictures that got small!

From the start, the character of Norma is imbued with a marked sense of grandeur and abundance that aligns her, potentially at least, with subjective fantasies of pre-oedipal maternal plenitude and *jouissance*.

The fact that Norma is a fading silent movie "queen" is also highly significant in this context. By making her a figure whose time of greatness and power is in a bygone era encrusted with popular myth, the film forwards yet another possible point of correlation between Norma and pre-oedipal maternity. The film abounds with references to Norma's fading stardom that can easily be read as elegiac memories of the phallic primal mother. When, after meeting Norma, Joe makes a snide comment about her to Max, the butler retorts by saying, "You're too young, you cannot remember, but there was a time when she was the greatest of them all," and proceeds to recount several stories about the excessive devotion of Norma's fans during her heyday. Similarly, in the scene of Norma and Joe's first encounter, Norma gives vent to a tirade against the "coming of sound" to motion pictures because, as she puts it, it "broke the beautiful dream" and "smashed the idols" of the silent era. Here, Norma's rage against the advent of "talkies" can be read as an allegorical attack on the Symbolic father's disruption and deposition of the matrocentric Imaginary. Given the orthodox Lacanian argument that the subject's entry into the Symbolic—and its consequent refusal of the Imaginary—is achieved largely through the advent of language, such a reading seems almost self-evident. Like the Imaginary mother of the pre-oedipal period, Norma has been superseded by a new order of language, meaning, and desire in which there seems to be no real place for her.

The crux of the film's diegetic economy, however, is the fact that Norma refuses to accept the terms of her deposition from power, refuses to believe that she is no longer a star. In terms of a psychoanalytic reading, this resistance may be translated as a scenario in which the phallic mother refuses to accept the castrated position to which she is reduced in and by the patrocentric Symbolic, stubbornly clinging instead to the position of privilege she enjoyed in the Imaginary. Thus, when Norma tells Joe with quiet indignation that "I *am* big, it's the pictures that got small," she is in fact spelling out the incontrovertible logic of her own desire—a desire that insists on the validity of its existence and refuses to be extinguished in the face of an unaccommodating system.

Read this way, *Sunset Boulevard* becomes a story of the pre-oedipal mother and the paradigms of desire that surround her. Norma, as figural representative of an all-powerful, Imaginary maternity, extends an invitation to the spectator, much as she does to Joe, to enter into a scenario of matrocentric fantasy and desire. That Joe violently refuses this invitation, ultimately choosing death, is an obvious textual cue, if not demand, for spectators to do the same. Indeed, like *Suddenly, Last Summer* and its abjectifying construction of Violet, *Sunset Boulevard* invalidates Norma as a site for the investment of spectatorial desire by making her appear increasingly horrific and, quite literally in the end, murderous. Witness, for example, the widespread use in the film of representational conventions normally associated with the horror or thriller genre, such as screeching violins on the soundtrack, chiaroscuro lighting, and canted camera angles. Such a culturally weighted aesthetic implicitly (re)defines Norma and the paradigm of matrocentric desire she embodies as dangerous and threatening. Similarly, the film's constant use of Joe's sardonic voice-overs as narrational guide belittles Norma and undercuts the presence and authority that she wields. Should these formal cues be lost on the viewer, the film marshalls the character of Max, the butler, as its supreme diegetic indictment of Norma and the dangers of her intimate, binding "mother love." As played by Erich von Stroheim, Max is an enigmatic figure who spends much of the film lurking in the background as an ever-present shadow, silently waiting on Norma and attending to her every need. At first, this servile devotion seems legible as a sign of professional commitment and loyalty, but it becomes progressively encoded in the film as strange and uncanny.[77] The full "queerness" of Max's relation to Norma is finally exposed when, in a climactic scene, it is revealed that he was in fact Norma's director and first husband, but, because he could not bear to be apart from her, he stayed on as her servant even after they divorced. The film thus proffers the figure of Max as the frightening visual embodiment of the effects of unchecked matrocentrism. Remain under the bewitching power of the phallic mother, it seems to suggest, and end up like the pitiable, emasculated Max.

In this way, *Sunset Boulevard* paints a sinister picture of Norma and the paradigms of maternal desire that she so spectacularly represents. However, gay readings of the film tend to resist these textual attempts to demonize Norma and focus instead on the possibilities opened up by the film for an articulation of transgressive matrocentric fantasy. To this end, *Sunset Boulevard* offers a particularly fertile textual arena, for its organizational paradigms bear a striking resemblance to many of the psychocultural scenarios that I have suggested underpin and help organize certain forms of gay male desire. The image of Norma as figural representative of the pre-oedipal mother raging against and rejecting the paternal symbolic's relegation of her to a position of marginal insignificance resonates powerfully with the refusal of maternal castration and devaluation that psychoanalysis posits as integral to gay fantasmatic specificity. Similarly, Norma's stubborn adherence to a position of privilege that she believes is rightfully hers despite dominant views to the contrary corresponds to the unconscious maintenance of Imaginary maternal omnipotence in (some) gay subjectivities and thus provides suggestive scope for queer fantasies of maternal identification.

In reference to this last point, the issue of identification with Norma qua the pre-oedipal maternal image is crucial, and it offers an organizational fulcrum point for queer readings of this film. E. Ann Kaplan has suggested that identification with the mother figure is a critical feature in evaluating the political and libidinal labors of the maternal melodrama. She argues that an identification between spectator and mother makes possible a contestatory site of meaning in which the pleasures of maternal relationality are avowed and in which the "oppressive aspects" of the patriarchal devaluation of the mother are opposed. However, if there is no identification with the mother figure, "the paradigm can look very different; the ideal, self-sacrificing mother threatens to collapse into the evil phallic one" or the mother "may be made object of the text's sadistic urges against her."[78] For Kaplan, the difference between the two is largely a question of representational form, so that, as she sees it, melodramatic films can be evaluated depending on whether they appear to encourage or discourage spectatorial identification with the mother figure at the textual level. Consequently, she proposes a taxonomy of maternal melodramas divided into "complicit" or "resisting" types. However, the effectivity of attempting to determine spectatorial modes of identification on the basis of textual considerations alone is questionable. There are many maternal melodramas that, on the face of things, appear to actively discourage spectatorial identification with the mother but are still amenable to strong identificatory engagements on the part of those spectators prepared—or possibly even impelled—to undertake a certain amount of negotiation.

In the case of *Sunset Boulevard*, though the film clearly strives to invalidate Norma as textual candidate for spectatorial investment and identification by presenting her as abject threat or objectified other, it still provides opportunities for spectators so disposed to seize on the image of Norma qua the omnipotent mother and make her the focus of meaning and desire. There is evidence to suggest that this is the case with many gay engagements of the film. Al LaValley, for example, describes Norma Desmond as a "treasured gaycult" figure and argues that gay spectators identify with Norma in her extravagant difference and her "soaring beyond the limits society and even nature can impose."[79] Similarly, David Clinton describes Norma as "the quintessential gay icon" of Hollywood film, characterizing her, along with what may be defined as Norma's comedic counterpart, Auntie Mame, "as gay men's favorite celluloid alter-egos."[80] Paul Roen writes that "straight men . . . tend to sympathize with the Holden character, wishing that he could break free of stud hustling and lead a normal, productive life (yuck). Old queens like me, however, can't help but identify with Norma all the way through the movie, even up to and including her final, mad writhe toward the camera."[81] By insisting on Norma as the central site for their identificatory investments, these gay spectators actively repudiate the text's attempts to make her a figure of either objectifying curiosity or abjectifying fear, reaffirming instead the validity and appeal of the matrocentric paradigms that Norma as a symbol of an omnipotent, pre-oedipal maternity represents.

Within such a context, the famous final "mad" scene of *Sunset Boulevard* (which, as the preceding comments from gay writers suggest, is something of an iconic moment in many gay receptions of this film) becomes (re)readable not so much as a tragipathetic spectacle of feminine or maternal madness, as seems to be the "preferred" reading, but as an extreme moment of sublime transcendence. Like Violet in *Suddenly, Last Summer*, who is also "doomed" to a clotural insanity, Norma's flight into madness becomes, within a gay matrocentric reading, a final act of rebellion on her part—a further refusal of a patriarchal "reality" that seeks to relegate and confine her to castrated marginality. Like Violet, again, Norma's escape into madness also furnishes her with one last opportunity to affirm and proffer before the spectator a vision of mother-centered desire. As *Sunset Boulevard* closes, Norma, who has just danced her way down the staircase in a compelling display of spectacular stardom, stops and, facing directly into the camera, stares triumphantly out at the spectator. "There's nothing else," she whispers, "just us and the cameras and those wonderful people out there in the audience." At which point, she resumes her hypnotic dance, snaking ever closer toward the camera until she merges into a final blurred, extreme close-up. That this concluding image is "intended" to be read "negatively"—as ominous, threatening, or even just pathetic—is indisputable; but in the context of matrocentric gay engagements, predicated as they are on a resistant maternal identification, this closing sequence may also be seen as a final, triumphal assertion of Norma as pre-oedipal mother filling the space of the screen and, by extension, spectatorial desire with the absolute plenitude of her delirious *jouissance*.[82]

"The most beautiful man in the movies": publicity shot of Montgomery Clift for *The Heiress* (1949) (author's collection)

Chapter Five ∽ PAPA, CAN'T YOU SEE THAT

I'M FLAMING? GAY SPECTATORSHIPS AND

FIGURES OF MASCULINITY

Up till now I have said very little about gay spectatorial relations to and readings of cinematic masculinity, concentrating either on the more general question of gay spectatorial relations to cinematic formations of sexuality or on questions of gay relations to cinematic femininity. The reasons for this are twofold. First, figures of masculinity do not seem to occupy the same central position in histories of gay male spectatorships as figures of femininity. One would be hard-pressed, for example, to find a celebration of male film stars in gay subcultures that would in any way approximate the enduring traditions of gay diva worship. Similarly, there is little evidence to suggest that the conventionally male-oriented genres of mainstream cinema like westerns, war films, and action pictures hold anywhere near the same sort of sustained appeal for gay male audiences as the so-called feminine genres of the musical, the melodrama, and the woman's film. This is not to say that these films and their male stars have not been watched and enjoyed by gay-identifying spectators; rather, with one or two notable exceptions, they do not seem to have been taken up and privileged by gay (sub)cultural discourses/practices in a continuing or systematic way. The second reason for delaying this discussion of gay relations to masculinity is that, by doing so, I hope to have imparted a sense of the distance and ambivalence that are structural features of those relations. Too often the "anatomical fact" of gay and straight men's shared corporeality is used as the grounds for all manner of theoretical conflations. I argue that, far from being continuous, gay and straight forms of masculinity are, in many ways, discontinuous. One of the primary goals of this chapter is to demonstrate that, though gay male subjectivities intersect dominant forms of masculinity in significant ways, they are frequently the site of a thrilling undoing or deconstruction of those forms.

In mounting such an argument, I extend my overarching psychoanalytic reading of gay male desire as a fantasmatic space of sexual/gender disorganization, a point of trouble or excess in the fields of hegemonic sexuality, and develop it in relation to masculinity. In particular, I focus on how gay spectatorships may be seen to disrupt the terms and regulatory effects of phallic masculinity through appropriative reconstructions of masculine images in mainstream cinema. First, I build a theoretical framework for this task by discussing critical writings that address the question of gay relations to masculinity. I then look at how these relations influence gay spectatorial practices, particularly in readings of masculine images in mainstream film. I conclude with a case study of gay spectatorial receptions of the classic film star Montgomery Clift. In all three sections, I emphasize how gay subjectivities/spectatorships perform a fantasmatic "ruination" of phallic masculinity, a simultaneous assumption and de(con)struction of its forms and significances.

By defining my project in these terms, I may appear to be perpetuating homophobic representations of male homosexuality as failed masculinity. There is no gay man who has not at some stage been made aware that, in the eyes of the dominant culture, he is not a "real man." For some this awareness underscores the need to assert the authenticity of gay men's masculinity as an urgent political task. However, I write from the assumption that, far from constituting a political liability, the gay subject's "failure" to meet the demands of "real" dominant masculinity may in fact be his greatest political strength.

Gay Male Subjectivities and the Refusals of Phallic Masculinity

What you must do, son, is become a fucker and not become a fucked. It's as simple as that . . . you've got to remember there's a cock between your legs and you're a man.
—Colin MacInnes, cited in *Male Impersonators: Men Performing Masculinity*

The relations between male homosexuality and masculinity are notoriously fraught with tensions and contradictions. On one side, male homosexuality as an erotics of and between male-sexed bodies clearly depends on the category of masculinity for its very definition. Yet, on the other, male homosexuality is widely represented in cultural discourses as the antithesis of masculinity, its vanishing point, its structural other. Some have argued that this paradox in relations between male homosexuality and masculinity is more apparent than real. Several feminist critics assert that, with their "worship of the phallus," gay men are more like "ardent priests" than "infidels" of patriarchal masculinity and that they have therefore "the very first claim to manhood."[1] I argue, however, that the paradoxical nature of the relations between male homosexuality and masculinity is both real and profound and that it indicates a contradictory logic (potentially) at work in gay male subjectivity itself. In particular, I suggest that phallic masculinity is cast contradictorily in male homosexuality as both an object of desire and an object of denigration. Or, to put it another way, masculinity is for male homosexuality the object of a desire *for* its denigration.

In her study of "marginal male subjectivities," Kaja Silverman argues that of all the subjectivities she explores male homosexuality poses the greatest "libidinal and identificatory challenge to conventional notions of masculinity."[2] She contends that, because male homosexuality turns on a primary psychic identification with the mother rather than the father, "it might be said to negate the most fundamental premise of male subjectivity—an identification with masculinity—and in so doing to obstruct paternal lineality" (362). As Silverman sees it, by refusing to take up paternal identification, the gay subject also refuses to take up the position of phallic masculinity that ideally results from such an identification. This refusal impels the gay subject to "turn away from the phallic legacy" and to recognize and embrace those features of the subjective condition that phallic masculinity rigorously disavows and externalizes, such as lack, specularity, receptivity, and the like; the features, in short, of subjective castration. Given the dominant cultural evaluation of these tropes as inherently feminine, Silverman defines the gay male incorporation of them as a foundational identification with femininity itself, and this assumption largely frames her work on gay male subjectivity. As she describes it, her project is "to demonstrate that femininity inhabits male homosexuality in all kinds of interesting, enabling, and politically productive ways—to show that the subject-positions and psychic conditions which are conventionally designated by that signifier may ultimately be as central to gay identity and erotic practice as are the male genitalia" (387).

As the last clause of this passage may indicate, there is, however, another side to this equation: how maternal identification and the gay male incorporation of castration or femininity that ensues from it work on the formations of masculinity that are inevitably mobilized in and by a gay male psychosocial economy. I say inevitably because, though the psychoanalytic gay male subject may make a foundational identification with psychic femininity — whether by accepting those tropes of castration culturally defined as feminine, or by identifying with the "femininity" of the maternal image — "he" is still required to negotiate a psychocultural relation with the category of masculinity that, by definition, plays a determinative role in the organization of *male* homosexuality. Furthermore, to assert that gay subjectivity is defined largely as a disidentification from phallic masculinity and a repudiation of its constitutive terms does not mean that masculinity is simply absent from a gay psychic economy. The very process of disidentification/repudiation means that masculinity is still inscribed, albeit negatively, in gay male subjectivity as a key element of structural organization.

This last point is an example of what Jonathan Dollimore terms "the paradox of perversion," and it provides an important insight into the particular role assumed by masculinity within gay subjectivities. Because the perverse "inheres within, and is partly produced by, what it opposes," it does not signal a simple erasure of the object it perverts but a representation of it *as an object to be perverted*.[3] In the context of the discussion at hand this means that, even though the gay subject may reject paternal identification and phallic masculinity in preference for maternal identification and a psychic femininity, these former positions still feature centrally in his endopsychic economy, for they are incorporated through the very process of their repudiation. However, the process of incorporation through refusal means that masculinity is present in male homosexuality primarily as a space of repudiation, transgression, and negation.

John Fletcher provides a slightly different take on this argument when he asserts the need for "an erotic or theoretical recognition . . . of the place of the father" in discussions of gay psychosexual organization. Like Silverman, Fletcher avers the primacy of maternal identification in homosexual desire and argues that the gay subject's relationship to paternal lineality and phallic masculinity is essentially one of disidentification. However, he also asserts that the "father cannot just be absent; such an absence is not innocent. He is implied by the threat of castration that converts Oedipal wishes into the maternal identification in the first place. What we might divine in the form taken by desire, an imaginary mother-child relation (whether son or daughter), is an active *refusal* to identify with and take up the place of the father."[4]

Rather than see the gay subject's refusal of paternal identification as a simple erasure of the father, we need to recognize it as a form of active incorporation. The process of paternal disidentification is the grounds on which the father's position, as well as the forms of phallic masculinity predicated on that position, are represented in and for the gay male fantasmatic. This unique inscription of paternal positionality results in an ambivalent, even contradictory, relationship between the gay subject and the symbolic father/masculinity. It is a relationship underscored by desire, inasmuch as the father is still represented as a key player in the libidinal field, but it is a desire to deny and undo the position of the father/phallic masculinity rather than simply identify with it.

Importantly, some psychoanalysts have discussed gay male relations to the paternal position and phallic masculinity in terms that resonate with this argument. In his classic opus, *The Psychoanalytic Theory of Neurosis*, Otto Fenichel asserts that male homosexuality entails not so much a blanket refusal of the paternal phallic position as "an imaginary appropriation of it for other purposes."[5] In Fenichel's schema, the gay subject recognizes and takes on the paternal site but then proceeds to subvert it through an aberrant reconfiguration. Like his theoretical heterosexual counterpart, the gay subject is positioned in a network of desire vis-à-vis the father, but unlike the heterosexual male subject he does not translate that desire into an idealizing incorporation; rather, he plays it out in a transgressive scenario of paternal seduction and subversion in which the father's position is undermined through its appropriative reconstitution as a "passive object" of and for the gay subject's erotic desires. As Fenichel puts it, where the heterosexual male subject takes up the paternal phallic position so as to "learn . . . the secrets of masculinity from the 'master,'" the gay subject does so only in order to "depriv[e] him of them."[6]

The psychoanalyst Francis Pasche makes a similar claim when he argues that the gay subject's relationship with the symbolic father is marked by a contradictory structure of simultaneous desire and hostility. Following Freud's speculations about the role of the inverted or negative oedipus complex in homosexual etiology, Pasche argues that the gay male subject initially recognizes and engages the father through a negative oedipal scenario of "passive desire" but that this desire is subsequently recast as an unconscious wish to displace and undo the father's position of phallic privilege or, as he puts it, "to correct, remake, thwart, parody, and finally destroy . . . the father."[7] Like Fenichel, Pasche also sees this scenario of paternal subversion as articulated most forcefully through a structure of paternal deposition in which the father is robbed of his symbolic claims to phallic status and repositioned in and as a site of receptivity for the gay subject's desires. In male homosexuality, he grandly asserts, "the father is reduced to the level of a sex object" (213).

As utopian as these psychoanalytic readings undoubtedly are, they provide an interesting theoretical frame through which to re-pose the question of gay male relations to masculinity, for they assert the need to reinstate the site of the symbolic father and, by extension, the structures of phallic masculinity organized around that site as important, if contested, elements in gay male fantasmatic organization. They suggest that the forms of gay phallic repudiation identified by theorists like Silverman signify not so much an absolute erasure of masculinity from the arena of gay male subjectivity as the very process and terms by which masculinity is in fact taken up and re-presented within that arena. In this revision, masculinity features as a central object in the libidinal economies of male homosexuality, something that plays a pivotal role in the organization of the gay subject's fantasmatic, his particular mise-en-scène of desire; but the representation of masculinity within male homosexuality is riven by a constitutive contradiction of simultaneous cathexis and repudiation. Phallic masculinity is engaged as an object of desire for the gay subject, but it is a desire to refuse, disrupt, and displace.

This revisionist critical account in turn allows us to read the gay male avowal of subjective castration through the incorporation of such psychocultural categories as passivity, specularity, and lack not simply as an identificatory alignment with femininity, as Silverman suggests, but as a libidinal transgression of the forms and functions of orthodox masculinity. By taking masculinity and opening it up to the marks of castration, gay subjectivity ruptures the foundational myths on which phallic masculinity is founded. It is a fantasmatic scenario of transformative de-phallicization through which masculinity is stripped of its phallic pretensions—or, at least, has those pretensions denaturalized—and is recast anew into perverse or queer (re)configurations.

One issue often identified as central to gay processes of paternal phallic repudiation and one that enables a more specific discussion of those processes is gay anality. Anality is widely conceived in the popular imaginary as "the least dispensable element in defining the true homosexual."[8] More than any other "sign" of male homosexuality, it marks the gay subject's flagrant difference in a phallic economy, that which sets him apart from other men. The scandalous force of gay male anality accrues from diverse factors but arguably no more so than from its blatant transgression of fundamental sociosymbolic taboos. Eve Kosofsky Sedgwick and Michael Moon write: "On the conventional road map of the body that our culture handily provides us the anus gets represented as always below and behind, well out of sight under most circumstances, its unquestioned stigmatization a fundamental guarantor of one's individual privacy and one's privately privatized individuality."[9] This stigmatization is especially acute in relation to male subjectivity, for, according to Freud, the repression of anality is a vital prerequisite for the successful production of phallic masculinity. In part, this is because male phallic identification requires an unchallenged prioritization of the penis as the sole legitimate site of male erotic organization. It is also because the anus has strong psychosexual associations with a "feminine" passivity that is anathema to patrocentric masculinity. Recall that, for Freud, the infantile male subject prototypically imagines sexual intercourse in the fantasy of the primal scene as taking place *a tergo* at the anus.[10] The anal zone thus features psychically as a fundamental symbol of sexual passivity, penetrability, and castration, something that must be disavowed and repressed as part of a cast-off femininity if male phallic identification is to succeed. The relation between the phallic male subject and his own anus tends therefore to be one of profound anxiety. Indeed, the anus functions in many ways as what Mark Simpson terms the "fatal flaw" in phallic masculinity, a flaw "that [men] must constantly repudiate because their anus, much as they might like to pretend otherwise, is always with them . . . , even when they are at their most active, only a few inches from their penis."[11]

Gay male subjectivity forges a very different relation to the anus and therein lies much of its discomfiting scandalousness in a phallic framework. Because gay subjectivity does not prototypically depend on a constitutive denial and projection of its own castration as phallic masculinity does, it can embrace anality and the perverse pleasures of "feminine" passivity it represents. In fact, anality may be one of the primary sociosymbolic ways through which the gay subject assumes the marks of castration that he refuses to project onto the maternal body. Freud was adamant in his belief that anality is central to the homosexual subject's libidinal alignment with a maternal position, arguing that the anus is the organ through which the homosexual subject forges his psychic "identification with women [and] his passive homosexual attitude to men." [12] Anality can thus be seen to function as an important arena for gay subjectivity in its fantasmatic repudiation of phallic masculinity, for if anality works to cement the gay subject's identification with the mother and to corporealize his subsequent acceptance of symbolic castration as Freud suggests, then it surely has a profound effect on the gay subject's psychic relations to masculinity.

According to the logic of (hetero)sexual difference, in which masculinity and femininity are bound to an active/passive division, to be fucked is to be placed in the despised position of femininity and, thus, to lose one's claim to manhood. This is why anal penetration features so prominently in the patriarchal imaginary as the ultimate humiliation of the phallic male subject; something that is exemplified in a string of iconic male texts from the writings of Norman Mailer to the films *Deliverance* (1972) and *Pulp Fiction* (1994). In "Analysis Terminable and Interminable" Freud asserts that one of the most profound sources of castration anxiety for phallic male subjects is the fear of standing in a passive, "feminine" relation to another man and the scenario of psychic "castration" that this inevitably entails.[13] For the gay subject to willingly take up a position of anal passivity then is to enter into a highly charged scenario of masculine castration and denigration. As Brian Pronger notes: "Getting fucked is the deepest violation of masculinity in our culture. Enjoying being fucked is the acceptance of that violation, it is the ecstatic sexual experience in which the violation of masculinity becomes incarnate." [14]

Through anality, the gay subject can take the received image of masculinity as active, impenetrable, and phallocentric and submit it to a violent subversion. In his outrageous Freudian-Marxist theorization of "homosexual desire," Guy Hocquenghem nominates anality as a vital and particularly effective strategy of gay resistance to phallic hegemony. He contends that the gay subject's reclamation of the anus as a pleasurable site of erotic passivity subverts the primacy of the penis on which dominant constructions of masculinity depend, thereby opening up those constructions to the destabilizing effects of a plurality of erotic sites. "To reinvest the anus collectively and libidinally," he writes, "involve[s] a proportional weakening of the great phallic signifier, which dominates us constantly both in the small-scale hierarchies of the family and in the great social hierarchies." This in turn helps contest the patriarchal myth of male phallic equivalence, for if the penis is "dethroned" from its symbolic role as primary signifier of desire and is redefined as simply one erotic signifier among many, the patriarchal conflation of penis and phallus becomes considerably more difficult to sustain. This is why Hocquenghem ultimately defines male homosexuality as the site of a transgressive demolition of phallic masculine identity because "only the phallus dispenses identity; any social use of the anus, apart from its sublimated use, creates the risk of a loss of identity." [15]

Leo Bersani takes this argument even further in his controversial essay "Is the Rectum a Grave?" in which he singles out anality as an important arena for gay men in their deconstructive contestations of phallic masculine identities. Bersani contends that, in the act of anal intercourse, the gay subject avows and embraces a structure of passivity that is antithetical to patriarchal fantasies of male phallic dominance and authority. In fact, he goes so far as to characterize gay male anality as "suicidal" or "murderous" in its effects on phallic masculinity because it "kills"—that is, it negates—the dominant image of masculinity as active and in control.[16] This is why Bersani gives his essay such a provocative title, for in his reading of gay male anality the rectum is reconstituted as a metaphoric grave, a place in which the cultural ideal of phallic masculinity is destroyed and interred.

The Bersani piece is particularly interesting in that it correlates this reading of the potential effects of gay anality to a psychic fantasy-structure of phallic refusal and displacement. For Bersani, the demolition of phallic masculinity is not just a happy by-product of the gay man's incorporation of a libidinal structure of passive anality but the psychocultural impetus and function of that structure. He contends that the practice of gay anality is subtended and fueled by an unconscious desire to depose and "shatter" the structures of phallic masculinity inevitably imbricated to some degree in gay male desire. Through anal passivity, the gay subject engages and plays out a fantasy scenario in which the image of the phallic male body that the gay subject necessarily "carr[ies] within [himself] as [a] permanently renewable source of excitement" is submitted to disintegrative violation (209). Each time the gay subject opens his body to the penetration and possession of another in anal sex he is enacting a delirious act of psychocultural transgression, "a self-shattering and solipsistic *jouissance*" in which the internalized phallic male body is exploded through its fantasmatic re-presentation as an object of endless sacrifice and violation (222).

This provocative reading corresponds to my framing argument that gay male relations to phallic masculinity are organized by a contradictory libidinal structure of desire and refusal. As Bersani suggests, by insisting on a passive desiring use of the male anus, gay subjectivity simultaneously embraces and perverts the phallic male body. The penetrated gay subject desires the male body, submits to its power but, by doing so, violates that body and undermines its power. The subversive capacities of anal passivity makes the anus a highly charged site of male phallic ruination in gay subjectivity, a place in which masculinity encounters its symbolic undoing. Through anality, the gay subject can demolish phallic maleness, thus opening up male subjectivity to embrace the very signs of castration—passivity, receptivity, "femininity"—that it constitutively rejects. It is a dangerous, even "deadly" fantasmatic game (to take up Bersani's metaphor), but it is one that, for the gay subject at least, can occasion important "openings" for psychic pleasure.

Transpositions of Masculinity through Gay Spectatorships

The preceding discussion of anality shows how gay psychic paradigms of paternal disidentification can, as John Fletcher asserts, "indicate a ground or potential in the psychic structure of homosexual men for a *possible* opposition at the level of social and political practice to the dominant forms of [phallic masculinity] and the patriarchal fantasies . . . that fuel them."[17] In the case of anality, the translation of psychic scenarios of paternal repudiation into the realm of the social is played out primarily at the level of the body. Gay recodings of the male body through anality produce a range of meanings and pleasures for that body that differ from and transgress dominant cultural paradigms of male corporeality. Other work, especially that with a sociological perspective, provides evidence that a correlative exchange may also occur at the level of gay style and sartorial practice. Analyses of the rise of macho styles in gay subcultures, for example, frequently conclude that such styles are underwritten by a transgressive camp logic of phallic ironization that works to "mock and ridicul[e] the idea of masculinity." [18] This work provides both precedence and motivation for suggesting that these same fantasmatic scenarios of paternal phallic de(con)struction may also translate into or at least affect gay spectatorial forms. In looking at how gay spectatorship may be informed by queer psychic structures of male phallic transposition, I focus on how gay spectatorships take up certain images or figures of masculinity in film and subject them to psychosexual violation and refiguration.

"According to the principles of the ruling ideology and the psychical structures that back it up," writes Laura Mulvey, "the male figure cannot bear the burden of sexual objectification. Man is reluctant to gaze at his exhibitionist self." [19] This oft-quoted passage spells out the extent to which mainstream film is engaged in what Kaja Silverman terms "male despecularization." Drawing on Lacan's assertion that the "the phallus can play its role only when veiled," Silverman argues that, in a bid to safeguard the shaky myth of male phallic sufficiency, patriarchal cultures engage in a strategic "re-visualization of sexual difference" wherein masculinity is withdrawn from visual scrutiny and femininity is hyperspecularized, offered up as a constant, visible sign of castrated otherness.[20] In relation to film, this process of gendered revisualization gives rise to the "active/passive heterosexual division of labour" theorized so influentially by Mulvey and explored by countless critics after her. Although much of this work has centered on cinematic constructions of femininity, the passage from Mulvey just cited clearly suggests that the gendered organization of cinematic specularity has important implications for how mainstream film envisions masculinity as well.

Steve Neale was one of the first critics to address this issue in his pioneering essay, "Masculinity as Spectacle," in which he argues that, because mainstream cinema is organized around and for a presumed position of male heterosexual spectatorship, "the male body cannot be marked explicitly as the erotic object of" the cinematic gaze.[21] "It is a refusal to acknowledge or make explicit an eroticism . . . in relation to images of men," he asserts, "that tends above all to differentiate the cinematic representation of images of men and women." This "refusal" to sexualize the male figure in mainstream film can be evidenced, Neale suggests, in the paucity of cinematic images of men that are marked out as avowedly erotic spectacles or that are presented in the same fetishized way that female figures and bodies routinely are. One need only think of genre films such as westerns, war films, epics, and action pictures in which, even though the male body is presented as the central focus of textual and spectatorial attention, it is rarely offered as an object of direct erotic contemplation; rather, it is coded as an agent of narrative action, the specular presentation of which is insistently tied to and justified by intradiegetic motivation. "There is no trace of an acknowledgment or recognition of those bodies as displayed solely for the gaze of the spectator," writes Neale. "They are on display, certainly, but there is no cultural or cinematic convention that would allow the male body to be presented in the same way that Dietrich so often is in Sternberg's films" (14–15).

The male image in mainstream film is, thus, constructed very differently from the female image in both form and function and is called to generate equally different effects. Whereas the female image is typically designed to act as a direct object of and for the scopophilic contemplation of the implied male spectator and, as such, features defining elements of passivity and subordination, the male image is typically mobilized to act as the primary point of spectatorial identification, what Neale, following Mulvey, describes as the spectator's "more perfect, more complete, more powerful ideal ego" and is imbued accordingly with characteristic elements of potency and active prowess.[22] In this way, mainstream film engages in and contributes to the wider patriarchal equation of masculinity with phallic agency and control through a strategic process of male "despecularization" and female "hyperspecularization." The cinematic refusal to mark out the male body as scopophilic spectacle bolsters the myth of male phallic sufficiency by shielding masculinity from scrutiny and dissociating the male body from the disempowering possibilities of erotic objectification and passivization.

There are, however, several interrelated points that need to be raised in response to this argument. First, though the process of male cinematic despecularization is certainly widespread, even dominant, in mainstream film production, it is far from universal. There *are* classical Hollywood films in which the male image is offered as a direct, relatively sexualized spectacle for the viewer's contemplation. Some of these have been discussed in earlier chapters, and I examine a few more examples later in this chapter. Furthermore, there are more recent examples of mainstream film that are brazen in their constructions of the male image as erotic spectacle, suggesting that the processes discussed by Mulvey and Neale are historically specific and may currently be undergoing something of a cultural sea change.[23]

Second, as well as being far from universal, these processes of male despecularization and erotic refusal in mainstream cinema are also far from guaranteed. Even in those films in which the eroticism of the male image is seemingly refused, the act of textual and libidinal repression required to produce such a refusal inevitably creates a dynamics of tension within the text that can work against the dominant processes of male phallic support and protection. Following Freud, we may suggest that if anything is certain about repression it is that it is uncertain and that what is repressed may always potentially return to disrupt the stability of those structures founded on the process of repression in the first place. This is something that is, if not directly stated, then at least suggested by Neale at the close of his essay when he argues that male homoerotic desire "is constantly present as an undercurrent, as a potentially troubling aspect of many films and genres, but one that is dealt with obliquely, symptomatically, and that has to be repressed."[24]

Third, precisely because these processes of de-eroticization are neither universally applicable nor guaranteed, there will always be considerable scope for spectators so disposed to circumvent these processes and reconstruct the male image as a central site of and for their own forms of erotic investment. In fact, one major problem with these arguments about the absence of a sustained or conscious eroticism in relation to mainstream cinematic images of men is their apparent assumption of eroticism as a fixed essence that is simply there or not in the filmic image rather than, as is more the case, a variable effect of readings. This textual immanentism tends, as Ian Green notes, "to displace the considerations of representability of the erotic" and what the individual viewer "might be phantasising about as [she or] he watches male images display themselves on the screen."[25] No amount of coaxing on the part of dominant textual structures will prevent individual spectators thus inclined from recognizing within the cinematic male image the potentials for erotic stimulation and subsequently assuming that image as an object of and for their own libidinal cathexes and psychosexual fantasies.

The question of the individual spectator's fantasmatic investment is particularly important to consider in relation to gay male engagements of male cinematic figures because it underscores how the contextual frames of gay male desire impinge on those engagements and the meanings and pleasures they generate. Gay male spectators have a marked interest in and, therefore, considerable motivation for assuming the cinematic male image as a site of erotic investment. Furthermore, given the way in which I have argued for negotiational strategies as an integral component of queer cinematic receptions, they would also seem to be well skilled in the types of interventionist reading required to effect this appropriative reconstruction of the male filmic image as erotic object.

That gay spectators frequently, if not primarily, assume male cinematic figures as erotic objects is a view widely held by most commentators on the relations between gay men and film. Michael Bronski summarizes the "logic" of gay male spectatorship with the succinct formula: "Gay men lust after [cinematic male images] as sexual objects [and] they identify with the women as emotional subjects."[26] The bold universalism of this description clearly requires some tempering, and it turns on a stable polarization of gendered identification and object choice that I suggest is far from stable in the context of gay spectatorships. Nevertheless, it illustrates well the extent to which gay engagements with cinematic images of masculinity are understood to be motivated by and articulated through relations of erotic objectification rather than just through the more conventional modes of narcissistic identification.

The accent on erotic objectification in gay readings of the male image does not mean, however, that the processes of male erotic refusal theorized by Mulvey and Neale are somehow inconsequential or have no impact. It is only when we view gay erotic objectifications of the male image in relation to hegemonic injunctions against such objectifications that we can begin to fathom their status and function, as well as their psychocultural effects. Gay spectatorial reconstructions of the cinematic male image as erotic object rest on the same logic of contravention and transposition that structures gay male relations to paternal authority and phallic masculinity at large. By appropriating the male image as a site of and for an objectifying eroticism, the gay spectator contravenes the cinematic "taboo" against male specularization and thus engages in a structure of transgression similar to the gay fantasmatic dramas of phallic refusal discussed earlier. Within this context, it is worth recalling Pasche's assertion that, unlike the heterosexual male subject who honors and takes up the paternal image as ego-ideal, the homosexual subject refuses and subverts that image by "reduc[ing it] to the level of a sex object." For Pasche, this "reduction" of the father from a position of identificatory ideal to erotic object is a primary way for gay subjectivity to articulate its "rebellious attitude against that which represents the Law."[27] If, as Mulvey and Neale assert, the cinematic male image is defined in accordance with dominant cultural logic as a site solely for male spectatorial identification and self-idealization, the gay spectator's (mis)appropriation of it for purposes of erotic objectification reproduces this fantasmatic logic of "rebellious" phallic transgression in spectacularly literal ways.

Significantly, gay objectifications of the male image are often seen to have strong disorganizational effects on hegemonic masculinity. Mark Simpson argues that much of the anxiogenic status of male homosexuality in patriarchal cultures has to do with the way it occasions "a crisis of looking and looked-at-ness" in phallic masculinity, "a puncturing of 'manly visions.' " Because the male gaze is largely defined in our culture as active, powerful, and penetrative, the homosexual look of desire at the male body places that body in the classic "feminine" role of passive object—a reversal that "traditional heterosexual [masculinity] cannot survive."[28] This is why the gay male look of desire is so troubling to a phallic male economy.[29] Consider, for example, how the recent controversy over gays in the military constantly returned to and became fixated on a single disturbing image: the gay man looking at the naked phallic male body in the shower room.[30] What was represented in this image and what all the nervous jokes about not dropping the soap really pointed to was the intolerability of the idea that the phallic male body might be cast as the passive receptacle of another man's penetrative desire, cast in effect as a "woman." The disgust experienced by straight men at the possibility of gay male voyeurism comes, as Rosalind Coward suggests, from their equating it with "the way that men regularly look at women, that is as objects of desire, desired bodies. It is a disgust based on fear, a fear that you are powerless in the light of someone's active and powerful desire."[31]

Although the gay (re)construction of the male image as object, rather than simply subject, of eroticism is clearly threatening to a male phallic economy, it is perfectly congruent with gay psychocultural pleasures, for it emerges out of and expresses the fantasmatic paradigms of paternal repudiation that structure and work through gay male subjectivities and desire. In the case of film, the gay spectator's insistence on an erotic objectification of the male image in the face of dominant institutional and textual taboos signals a scenario of ecstatic phallic violation. By affirming not only the possibility but also the desirability of male specular passivity, gay spectatorships repudiate dominant equations of the male image with an idealized phallic agency, opening up that image instead to the castrating effects of specular receptivity and objectification. This process of male significatory transposition indicates both the centrality of fantasies of dephallicization to male homosexual desire and how such fantasies may be seen to inform and subtend gay spectatorial practices and effects.

To illustrate and develop this argument further, I examine a cross-section of writings on cinematic male images from gay fanzines. Fanzines are publications that, as the name suggests, are produced by and for fans of a particular cultural form, figure, or text. They range from slickly produced, book-length publications sold in retail outlets around the world to xeroxed newsletters circulated among small fan communities. Fanzines have received much attention in recent media studies because of what is seen as their exemplification of grassroots modes of resistance and negotiation in cultural consumption. As Henry Jenkins notes, fanzines "build upon the interpretive practices of the fan community, taking the collective meta-text as the base from which to generate a wide range of media-related stories." In fanzines, fans actively intervene in and transform the textual object of their devotion; they "treat [it] like silly putty," stretching its boundaries to incorporate their concerns and remolding its elements to better suit their desires.[32] One needs to be careful, however, when dealing with fanzines not to overromanticize them or assume them as some sort of authentic vox populi. This is especially the case in relation to the more "amateur," underground zines that, because of their nonprofit, "communal" publishing basis, are easily idealized as "forms of cultural production and distribution that reflect the mutuality of the fan community" free from the taints of the dominant social, cultural, and economic systems (160). It is important to recognize from the start that fanzines are highly codified textual forms with their own conventions and rule-governed structures, and as such they do not provide an unmediated "reflection" of the real of reception practices. They can, however, provide useful and frequently surprising material from which to speculate about different types of reading relations and the meanings they generate. In the case of gay zines, these publications can illustrate how gay-identifying subjects use popular culture as a forum for their social and erotic investments, as well as indicate specific ways in which they actively engage and transform texts so as to produce specifically queer meanings. Gay zines are often flagrant in their exhibition of queer reading practices. As Matias Viegener argues, "gay 'zines alter and appropriate images . . . , fictionalize (and usually sexualize) histories of the stars, and subvert all the codes of 'pure' desire, breaking down the distance between spectator and performer, reader and text, or audience and star."[33]

Of particular relevance for my purposes, many gay fanzines provide strong evidence of the prevalence of an objectifying eroticism in gay readings of male cinematic figures. Some gay fanzines in fact concentrate on nothing but the eroticization of the male cinematic image. *Movie Buff Checklist*, for example, is a gay zine devoted solely to listing and evaluating those films from the silent era to the present that contain representations of male nudity. The founding editor, Marvin Jones, describes this publication as an "erotic guide for all those moviegoers who secretly looked at Johnny Weissmuller or Steve Reeves with more than just emulative admiration in their hearts."[34] In a similar vein, another gay fanzine titled *Superstars* rates a wide range of male stars in explicitly erotic terms with entries such as the following on the contemporary male film star Rob Lowe: "We swooned at the brief glimpse of him at 19 as he emerged from the shower in *The Outsiders*. And at age 22 in his jockstrap in *Young-blood*, discreetly covering his bulge, then the lingering shot of his oh so very ripe ass as he walks away."[35] Although such examples are admittedly prosaic, they attest to a sustained eroticization in gay spectatorial readings of the male cinematic image. They also suggest that, by placing the male image in such a different interpretive context, these processes of gay objectification radically rupture the traditional phallic semiotics of male cinematic representation.

The disorganizational impulses of queer objectifications of the cinematic male image are exemplified in a series of "film reviews" written by the late Boyd McDonald that originally appeared in North American gay fanzines in the eighties.[36] These reviews proved to be so successful and generated such widespread interest that McDonald "graduated" to writing for more mainstream publications such as the gay magazine *Christopher Street* and the fashionably postmodern culture rag *Art and Text*.[37] In many of his writings, McDonald engages in highly explicit erotic evaluations of the male image as it has been constructed in vintage and contemporary Hollywood films. He then uses these erotic ruminations to construct outrageously gay or otherwise aberrant readings of the various films under discussion. In a "review" of the 1936 film *Mr. Deeds Goes to Town*, for example, McDonald focuses almost solely on its male star, Gary Cooper, appraising his specular appeal with such references as, "He didn't have a nice butt but didn't need one, not with a face like that," and engaging in highly erotic analyses of key scenes in the film, showing how, when read from a gay perspective, these scenes may be seen to "constitute a virtual comic sub-theme of cocksucking."[38] In a discussion of the Elvis Presley vehicle *Love Me Tender* (1956), McDonald constructs a perverse reading of the film that centers on a fantasized homosexual relationship between the Presley character and his on-screen brother played by Richard Egan, who, as McDonald sees it, "could not have remained insensitive to the beauty of Presley's nose . . . of his full lips, of his mascara . . . and of his substantial and authoritative rear end" (70).

McDonald is well aware of the transgressive dynamics of this brash style of queer erotic objectification, often playing on them to the point at which his writing assumes the status of an aggressive assault on the phallic male image. In a review of the 1979 film *North Dallas Forty*, for example, McDonald submits its male star, Nick Nolte, to a scathing specular examination. Using what he terms "the same harshly sexist and ageist standards that are applied to women in pictures," McDonald comments on how, in this film, Nolte's "butt had swollen almost closed," "his hips had lost their flatness," and "he had the beginnings . . . of a soft belly" and "a double-chin." He goes on to argue that when "Nolte got out of bed wearing Jockey shorts in this picture and wandered around long enough for the viewer to subject his body to analysis, he ended his era as a piece of eating stuff and entered a new, lower rank as just a plain fuck." McDonald concludes by claiming that, in this film, Nolte is "almost lardy enough to play Pope John Paul II," adding that "the Holy Father's body, in all probability, is dreadfully soft and white" (98).

What I find so interesting about this particular piece of writing and why I highlight it here is that it spectacularly explicates how gay objectifications of the cinematic male image frequently respond to and express the logic of male phallic violation that structures gay fantasmatic relations to masculinity. By submitting the particular film image of Nick Nolte to a derisive specular evaluation here, McDonald reproduces a similar scenario to that posited by Pasche in which the psychic and cultural authority of the symbolic father (and, by extension, phallic masculinity) is challenged by the gay subject through an aberrant process of erotic subordination—a "reduction" of the father/phallic masculinity from his/its idealized site of supreme Subjecthood to the subordinated level of a "sex object." The libidinal charge of this particular piece, its erotic *frisson*, comes not so much from the appeal of the male image per se but from the exhilarating performance of an illicit scenario of paternal refusal and phallic devalorization. This is crystallized in McDonald's suggestive comparison of the body of Nick Nolte with that of the pope. It is a curious, even shocking, analogy that is used by McDonald to show up the insistently transgressive nature of gay practices of male cinematic objectification, their breaking of certain dominant cultural taboos (it is difficult to think of another male figure that is so emphatically barred in Western cultures from erotic objectification than the pope). However, more specifically, the irreverent comparison between the (devalued) body of an objectified male film star and that of the pope suggests that what is being transgressed and subverted in and by gay erotic objectifications of the male image may, at a certain level at least, be the image of the symbolic father itself—something that is emphasized by McDonald's reference to the pope as "the Holy Father."

Even when McDonald is openly appreciative in his erotic appraisals of the cinematic male image, there is still a discernible undercurrent of devalorization, a recognition that the very processes of objectification to which the male image is being so thrillingly subjected signal an inevitable denigration of that image. Thus, in one of his many erotic panegyrics to the cinematic image of Elvis Presley, McDonald writes that, "unlike straights, I have no qualms about defiling the image of the King with all manner of perverse ruminations."[39] Once again the overdetermined (anti-)oedipal resonances of McDonald's reference to Presley as "the King" strongly suggest that the particular pleasures generated in this act of queer erotic objectification stem not merely from the sexual appeal of the male image itself but from the disorganizational effects that objectification has on that image and the patrocentric masculinity it represents. In this way, McDonald's readings suggest that gay male objectifications of the cinematic male image may be underscored by similar impulses of paternal/phallic devalorization to those operative within the grander scenarios of gay male psychocultural organization.

The violative dimensions of gay readings of the cinematic male image are foregrounded in many of the more "hardcore" gay fanzines. Apart from the fact that their "underground" status endows them with ready-made connotations of illicitness, these zines actively aim for and trade on an aggressive iconoclasm, something often highlighted by their titles, for example, *Homocore* and *Starfuckers*.[40] This sense of illicit iconoclasm often assumes a central role in many of the letters and stories themselves. One gay fan, for example, writes:

> I have now acquired a video machine and *I put the stars through the most degrading explorations*. For example, Roger Daltrey bares his magnificent globes in *McVicar* when he jumps out of bed and slips on his trousers. After viewing the sequence in slow motion, stopping at a point where the buttocks are parted just enough to hint at a sweaty crack, I then ran it forward and backward repeatedly so that Daltrey was like a prick-teasing hooker, lowering his pants off his buttocks a split second after pulling them up. I had him doing this for me while I played with myself and came.[41]

The writer of this letter demonstrates how far some gay spectators go in order to appropriate the cinematic male image as an erotic object. He also underscores how this appropriation is frequently understood and experienced by the gay spectator as a thrilling violation of the phallic male image. Note the writer's characterization of his activities as a "degrading exploration" and his implicit suggestion that this effects a "feminiza-tion" of the male image (turning the male star-image into "a prick-teasing hooker").

In a slightly different vein, an essay in *Starfuckers* titled "Schw-arse-enegger" engages in a comical "perversion" of the macho star-image of Arnold Schwarzenegger. In this essay, a gay fan writer relates a reverie he had while "watching Arnie swagger his way across the screen" in *Ter-minator 2: Judgment Day* (1991) wherein he imagines "shov[ing] one of the sub-machine guns that Arnie brandishes so proudly right up his de-licious, right-wing arse." This act causes the robotic character played by Schwarzenegger to become "re-programmed" into "a champion crusader for faggots and dykes all over the world."[42] Here again gay male read-ings of the cinematic male image are explicitly described as the space of a transgressive violation of that image and the phallic economy it repre-sents.

Although not as self-consciously mocking as these preceding exam-ples, other entries in gay fanzines exhibit similar scenarios of phallic vio-lation. One of the more popular forms of fan writing in gay zines is a style of erotic fiction that works to sexualize certain male homosocial relation-ships in mainstream film texts. Thus, for example, one gay fan builds an elaborate sexual fiction around the two male characters played by Keanu Reeves and Patrick Swayze in the 1991 film *Point Break;* another describes fantasized gay orgies he imagines taking place among the gang of male teenage vampires in *The Lost Boys* (1987).[43] This style of gay fan discourse is not unlike the far more publicized form of "slash" fiction that origi-nated among *Star Trek* fan communities and that fantasizes about homo-erotic relationships between male costars in TV series.[44] But whereas "slash" is largely a form of female heterosexual fan discourse that tends to insist, sometimes even homophobically, on the nonhomosexuality of the characters or stars about whom it fantasizes, gay erotic fan writing ex-plicitly aims to homosexualize the male star-image. In the essay on *Point Break*, for example, the writer imagines the characters played by Reeves and Swayze as men who are fully aware of their homosexuality but who are forced to pass as straight because of the homophobic social contexts within which they move, the FBI and professional surfing, respectively. On one level, this process of explicit homosexualization simply signi-fies the potential sexual availability of these star-images in and for gay erotic fantasy, but it also works at another level to fundamentally violate and transform the phallic male significations of these images. Thus the writer of the essay on *Point Break* takes a key scene from this film in which Johnny Utah (Keanu Reeves) jumps out of a plane without a parachute in his pursuit of Bodhi (Patrick Swayze) and rewrites it as a scenario of male phallic subversion through gay anality. In the film Utah grabs on to Bodhi and the two descend safely to earth. In his fantasy, this gay fan writer imagines the two engaging in free-fall anal intercourse part of which he describes as follows:

> Bodhi felt a flash of blinding pain as Utah lunged into him. It seemed to rip apart his very soul . . . but slowly his body started to tingle. . . . "If only the ex-presidents [the name of Bodhi's gang] could see me now," he thought, "legs spread wide, being fucked to kingdom come." . . . With each thrust Bodhi imagined his macho facade smashing open wider and wider. It made him groan with delight and push back even harder onto Utah's invading cock. His entire body seemed to be melting away. He had never felt so free. No longer body, no longer man, he was becoming a void, a hole filled with nothing but pleasure plummeting towards earth and destruction.[45]

Although there is no easy correspondence between fantasy writings such as this and the actual practices of gay spectatorship, this fiction highlights the centrality of a logic of male phallic violation to gay spectatorial readings of the cinematic male image. This gay fan engages in a breathtaking fantasy scenario wherein he imagines the macho male image being subjected to and transformed by the transgressive ecstasy of passive anality. It is a fantasy far beyond the limits of the actual cinematic text in question, but it is a fantasy that still emerges out of and builds on this particular gay spectator's reading of the text.[46] As such, this erotic scenario may be taken as a metaphor for the violative processes of gay specular objectification themselves. Just as the act of anal intercourse shatters the phallic identification of the macho male star in this particular fantasy, so too the act of male specular objectification in gay spectatorship subverts the phallic moorings of the cinematic male image, "freeing" that image into the pleasurable possibilities of male passivity, receptivity, and powerlessness.

This discussion of the disorganizational effects of gay specular objectification provides an interesting point of access into questions of gay identifications with the cinematic male image. Despite the fact that many commentators argue that gay spectators prefer to identify with female rather than male cinematic figures, it is important to acknowledge that gay spectators obviously can and do forge identificatory alignments with male images. Indeed, the masculinist bent of mainstream filmic enunciation and the fact that, in many films, male figures are often the only sites of identification made available demand an inevitable degree of identification on the part of the gay spectator with the privileged male figure of the mainstream film-text.[47] However, these forms of identification are very different from the more orthodox forms of idealizing narcissistic identification described by critics like Mulvey and Neale as standard for straight male spectatorship. The figures of masculinity operative in gay cinematic engagements, and the figures of masculinity with which, therefore, the gay spectator would identify, are figures that have been subjected to and transformed by the disorganizational processes of gay sexual objectification. That is, they are figures of masculinity that have been placed by the eroticizing desires of the gay spectator in the non- or even antiphallic position of "feminine" passivity.[48] Consequently, when the gay spectator does identify with the cinematic male image, it is an identification with an image that has been reconstructed through an objectified, "dephallicized" masculinity and not with an image of masculinity understood in the more "conventional" terms of phallic agency and control.

This point highlights once again the transgressive potentials of gay spectatorship. Steve Neale argues that male spectators will only identify with cinematic images of masculinity that have been idealized or lionized. In "Masculinity as Spectacle," he contends that male spectatorial identification in film is articulated solely in terms of an idealizing narcissism; the male spectator assumes the male image as his "more perfect, more complete, more powerful ideal ego." This is one reason why mainstream film works so obsessively to bar the male image from erotic objectification, because objectification compromises the male image's idealized status as phallic subject. Neale argues that on the rare occasions when the male image is "presented . . . as the object of an erotic look" in mainstream film (he cites the musical and some melodramas as examples) that image is effectively "feminized" and therefore "disqualified" from serving as a site of male identificatory investment.[49] In the case of gay spectatorship, however, "feminization" of the male cinematic image does not automatically negate the identificatory appeal of that image; indeed, it may even serve as the very grounds on and through which identificatory engagements with the male image are made. Not only do many gay spectators not reject those elements of the male image conventionally defined as "feminine" (passivity, receptivity, specularity, and the like), but they actively mobilize such elements as privileged points of signification in and for their engagements of the male image.

Here again, many of the writings in gay fanzines support this argument that gay spectatorships effect an identification with a masculinity that has been feminized or dephallicized through erotic objectification. The film reviews of Boyd McDonald, for example, frequently mobilize the various elements of passivity that inevitably circulate around the male image within the context of gay objectification as central sites for identificatory investment. In his discussion of Gary Cooper alluded to earlier, McDonald makes extensive use of what can only be called a rhetoric of castration to describe his pleasures in this particular male star. At one point, McDonald comments on an accompanying still from one of Cooper's very early pictures in which the star is apparently wearing lipstick, noting that "lipstick was . . . optional, and in *submitting* to it . . . Cooper looks *abandoned* in the best sense: *desirable, available*. A man who wears lipstick is *open* to a lot of things." He then goes on to wonder: "For what other *surrender* than lipstick was young Cooper, fresh out of Helena, Montana . . . , *available* in the fancy world of Hollywood?"[50] The recurring imagery in this passage attests to the central status accorded issues of passivity in the context of gay readings of the cinematic male image. McDonald's adoration of the particular male image of Gary Cooper is motivated by a reading of it not as powerful male ego-ideal but as wonderfully powerless and objectified. For McDonald, it is the receptivity of the Cooper image, its dimensions of passivity, of openness and feminine allure that fuels both his desire and his admiration. Thus, if McDonald may be said to identify with Cooper here, it is an identification with a male image defined and celebrated as passive and dephallicized.

In a similar vein, many of the more hardcore articles in gay fanzines discussed earlier stress how identification with the passivized male image functions in gay spectatorships as a potential site of psychocultural pleasure. Some of these writings seem to indicate that it is only through the dephallicizing process of passivization that the male image can emerge as a site of and for a sustained identificatory investment for many gay spectators. Thus, in the article on *Terminator 2*, the writer uses the imagined scenario of sodomizing Arnold Schwarzenegger with his submachine gun as a way to claim, albeit tongue-in-cheek, this particular male image as a figure of queer identification or what he describes as "a champion crusader for faggots and dykes." In the erotic fantasy of the gay viewer of *Point Break*, the violation and disintegration of the macho star-image through gay anality similarly functions as an organizational pivot for gay identificatory pleasures. By refiguring the male image in a fantasized scene of sexual objectification and symbolic dephallicization, this gay viewer reconstructs that image as a site for his own specifically gay identifications.[51]

However, these examples also suggest that by discussing identification and objectification as relatively coherent, self-identical terms, we are perhaps missing the most important point. That is, in the context of gay engagements with the male image, identification and desire are frequently incoherent terms, indistinguishable from each other. In the three instances of gay engagements with the male star-image just cited, it is difficult, even impossible, to determine where desire ends and identification begins. The gay spectators of these accounts desire the male image, assume it as a sexual object, yet at the same time and as part of the same process they also identify with that desired image. Gay receptions of cinematic masculinity may thus provide one of the strongest exemplifications yet of my argument that gay subjectivities/spectatorships refuse and disorder dominant gender binarisms and the polarization of identification and object-choice through which they are articulated. The notion of the gay spectator identifying with the very male image that he desires provides a wonderfully literal exemplification of the gay fantasmatic refusal of the symbolic injunction to (hetero)sexual difference characterized by John Fletcher as "you cannot be what you desire, you cannot desire what you wish to be."[52] In his engagement with the male image, the gay spectator can in fact have it both ways, he can be the male image through projective identification and have the male image through erotic objectification.

Gay Engagements with the Dephallicized Male Image:
The Case of Montgomery Clift

To further explore this fascinating complex of dephallicizing desire, identification, and fantasy operative in gay engagements with cinematic masculinity I focus on gay receptions of the classic Hollywood star Montgomery Clift. Clift was—and, to a certain extent, still is—one of the most enduringly popular male stars in postwar, Anglo-American gay subcultures. John Stubbard claims that "no other male star captured the hearts and minds of gay men like Montgomery Clift."[53] He thus seems to be the ideal candidate for a critical case study of gay spectatorial receptions of cinematic masculinity. In large part, the queer popularity of the Clift star-image stems from its unique receptivity to gay identificatory investments. Clift introduced a radically different, even aberrant, style of male gender and sexual performance into the semiotic economy of mainstream film that stressed such nonphallic attributes as sensitivity, powerlessness, and masochism. As such, he represents one of the few sustained examples in mainstream cinema of what I would term a dephallicized masculinity. This is why gay spectators have been drawn to Clift and how they have been able to reconstruct him as a uniquely gay subcultural icon.

In his devotional article on gay popularizations of Clift—an article summarily titled, "Our Monty"—John Stubbard writes: "Even before news of Clift's sexual preferences became widely publicised, we knew deep down that Monty was one of us" (23). As the insistent use here of the first-person plural suggests, gay engagements with Clift's star-persona frequently assume the status of a rather intense narcissistic identification. Many gay spectators have long recognized in the star-image of Clift a particularly receptive site for the projection of their own self-images. This was especially true, no doubt, for gay audiences in the fifties and early sixties, when Clift was at the height of his popularity, but this current of narcissistic identification has continued to inform gay subcultural receptions of Clift to the present day, with the result that he has emerged as something of a privileged identificatory ideal, a queer cinematic semblable, within gay spectatorial reading formations.

As the quote from Stubbard also suggests, the issue of Clift's alleged homosexuality has played a pivotal role in the construction of these relations of symbolic gay auto-identification. For many gay men, it is Clift's supposed real-life homosexuality that has made him such a powerful candidate for their own forms of identificatory fantasy. Andrea Weiss argues that rumored knowledges about certain stars' homosexuality have long played an important part in shaping lesbian and gay responses to film. Following Patricia Meyer Spacks's influential theorization of gossip as an alternative form of discourse used by certain marginalized social groups to produce some of their own self-identified meanings, Weiss argues that lesbian and gay spectators have frequently mobilized the knowledges available through subcultural gossip about various stars' homo- or bisexuality to claim these stars for and reconstruct them within frameworks of gay signification.[54] As an example, she looks at how lesbian spectators of the thirties and after often used subcultural gossip about the alleged homosexuality of female stars like Garbo and Dietrich to assume them as privileged figures of and for a specifically lesbian identification, as well as to renegotiate alternative formations of meaning for these stars and their texts. Even today, the discourses of gay gossip are still used to reconstruct certain star-images within a framework of gay or lesbian meaning and desire, as the much publicized "outing" campaigns targeted against many contemporary media figures attest.[55] Although it is difficult, if not impossible, to ascertain if any of these stars were or are homosexual in "real life," Weiss points out that this is, in many ways, "less relevant than how their star personae were perceived by lesbian [and gay] audiences."[56]

In the case of Montgomery Clift, knowledges about his homosexuality have long been used by gay spectators in their (re)constructions of Clift as a specifically queer figure of identificatory investment or, as Stubbard puts it above, as "one of us." In the fifties and sixties these knowledges circulated primarily through the discursive networks of gay gossip in which they functioned as privileged modes of subcultural capital, "insider information" mobilized as a conduit of identificatory exchange between gay men through which they could articulate their shared membership of a homosexual identity formation while arrogating the star-image of Clift to and for that formation. With the demise of the studio system and its regulatory regimes of control over the production and dissemination of star discourse, revelations about Clift's queer sexuality started to appear increasingly in more public fora such as the popular press, critical commentaries, and biographies. Indeed, the publication in the seventies and after of a series of popular biographical exposés that "lifted the lid" on Clift's sexuality have ensured a widespread reconstruction of him as "gay Hollywood star," effectively cementing homosexuality as the primary hermeneutic code through which Clift's star-image is engaged and read by many, if not most, contemporary spectators, gay or otherwise.[57]

By itself, the issue of Montgomery Clift's biographical homo- or bisexuality is not enough, however, to account for the intensity or durability of gay engagements with the Clift star-sign. There are other male stars who have also been constructed as "homosexual" by the discourses of gossip, yet they have not been taken up and celebrated by gay audiences with anywhere near the same level of sustained affection that Clift has. The reason for this, I think—and the reason why Clift in particular has been so privileged by gay subcultures/audiences—has to do with the types of images presented by Clift in his star-persona and, by extension, his films. Whereas other male stars whose biographical homosexuality has also been the subject of (gay) gossip—Randolph Scott, Clint Eastwood, or Tom Cruise, for example—tend to limit the signifying potentials of such gossip by presenting what are, on the whole, emphatically phallic heterosexual images at both the general level of star-persona and the specific level of film-text, Montgomery Clift offers a range of alternative images that, if not explicitly homosexual, provide marked elements of sexual and gender irregularity that can be read as queer. The capacity of Clift's persona for queer effect in turn offers additional support for gay knowledges about Clift's biographical homosexuality, but it also provides crucial openings in the various films themselves through which these extratextual knowledges may be introduced into and brought to bear upon intratextual networks of meaning and desire.

The receptivity of his textual images to queer investments has already been suggested in my earlier reference to Clift as a cinematic figure of aberrant masculinity. Throughout his career, Clift acquired a marked reputation for bringing a new, previously unseen style of masculinity to the screen. As Graham McCann writes, "Clift's movie image is, in the context of Hollywood iconography, an exquisite mistake. It breaks all the old rules concerning what a male sexual symbol should look like. . . . He wore his masculinity at an angle; it nearly fitted, but not quite." Indeed, McCann nominates Clift as "one of the great promissory icons of 1950s male sexuality," arguing that Clift, along with Marlon Brando and James

Dean, were the archetypal "rebel males" of fifties' cinema, all working to "subvert . . . the traditional masculine solidity of their predecessors."[58]

The correlation of Clift with other "rebel male" figures of the time like Dean and Brando is a fairly common move in film criticism and commentary. It tends, however, to gloss over the specificity of the Clift star-image and its extraordinary challenge to dominant structures of gender and sexuality. For where the "rebelliousness" of the star-personae of Dean and the young Brando is largely articulated through a (sub)cultural vocabulary of youthful male angst, aggression, and violence, the "rebelliousness" of Clift's star-persona, by opposition, is signaled through a rather different set of cultural terms. In many ways, the difference or nonconformity of the Clift persona is expressed precisely through a rejection of those conventions of social behavior like action, aggression, and physical prowess that are defined in our culture as key signs of phallic masculinity and a concomitant incorporation of those conventions ordinarily disavowed by and antithetical to phallic masculinity like passivity, interiority, specularity, and nurturance. Consider, for example, the following descriptions of the Clift persona taken almost at random from broadly popular sources:

> [Montgomery Clift's] gift was a unique . . . sensitivity that made him different and kept him dancing on the lip of a volcano. . . . he displayed a vulnerable, sensitive quality.[59]

> The image consistently represented by Montgomery Clift . . . was that of the fragile and sensitive man for who [sic] love is, by its very nature, ambiguous, filled with problems and pratfalls. The weakness that he so effectively portrayed seemed to be channelled through him from some great reserve of essentially manly disability.[60]

> Montgomery Clift . . . was apparently as tortured in his private life as he usually was in his screen performances but this inwardness gave an intensity to his acting which has rarely been equalled. His screen persona was a mixture of suffering, ambition and thwarted desire. . . . He was usually a loner, victimised . . . , passive and vulnerable.[61]

The language used in these passages is very different from that generally used in discussions of other "rebel" male stars like Brando and Dean. The recurring adjectives in these passages—"sensitive," "vulnerable," "tender," "passive," "fragile," "weak," "victimised"—approach what I referred to earlier in this chapter as a rhetoric of castration. As such, they provide a possible insight into what it is about the Clift star-image that makes it so "different," so nonconforming. The nature and source of the Clift persona's challenge to or "rebellion" against the received structures of male gender and sexuality lies in its constitutive representation of a "castrated" or "dephallicized" masculinity—a masculinity that is "opened up" to the thrillingly aberrant possibilities of subjective castration. As Jane Fonda puts it in a highly memorable response to an interviewer's question about Clift: "No one had ever seen an attractive man who was so vulnerable. *He was like a wound.*" [62]

A dynamics of male dephallicization is evident in many features of the Clift persona and films. His unique and rather unconventional acting style is a good case in point. As is well known, Clift was a key proponent of the so-called Method form of acting that emerged with great éclat in postwar American film and theater. This style of acting was named after the post-Stanislavskian method taught by Lee Strasberg and others at the influential Actor's School in New York, which sought to infuse an actor's performance with a heightened degree of realism by amplifying elements of a character's psychology, particularly as these pertained to forms of emotional struggle or turmoil. The accent in Method acting was on revealing a character's "inner life," bringing his or her deep-seated feelings and conflicts to the surface and playing these out, not only through speech but through facial expressions, body language, and gestural movement.[63] Such an approach signaled a radical departure from conventional performance styles, especially in relation to cinematic images of masculinity in which the stress had largely been—and, in many instances, continues to be—on concealing a male character's interiority and focusing instead on external forms of action and physical mastery. The emphasis in method acting on "opening up" and exposing male interiority ruptured these orthodox modes of masculine performance, constituting a potential subversion of traditional structures of phallic masculinity as powerful and in control. Virginia Wright Wexman argues that the Method style of performance used by Clift and other young male actors of the period occasioned a veritable "crisis in masculinity" that both reflected and contributed to "contradictions in the culture of 1950s America concerning male roles." The "neurotic qualities" of Method acting such as "emotional confusion, irrationality, and violent behaviour" foregrounded "the tenuousness of [these actors'] commitment to a heterosexual regime" and "the conflicted nature of their gender identifications," thereby articulating in coded form "the deep strains that existed in gender relations" throughout the postwar period.[64] Certainly, the brooding intensity and nervous motility of Clift's Method acting imbues his star-image with a strong current of gender and sexual ambivalence. The repertoire of shifting gazes, quirky tics, and restless movements that largely constitutes the Clift style evokes a decided sense of corporeal and psychical unease that disrupts the traditional stillness and assuredness of hegemonic modes of masculine performance while positioning the Clift star-persona in opposition to—or, at least, in excess of—those modes.

Another interrelated issue fundamental to the queer dynamics of Clift's acting style is its promotion of a certain ideological discourse of youthful transgressiveness. Wexman notes that the personae of Method actors like Clift tend to trade on a central image of youthful rebellion articulated largely in terms of generational contest. This articulation extends the neurotic gender conflicts represented in Method acting techniques, she suggests, expressing those conflicts "in terms of a division between youth and age" while also referring the star-personae of Method actors to—and further energizing their semiotic productivity through—the disruptive ideological significations of postwar youth cultures (169). Steven Cohan develops this argument further in his recent book-length study of fifties cinematic masculinities in which he reads the star-image of Clift, and some of his contemporaries such as the young Brando and Paul Newman, through the ideological sign of "boyishness." The anti-hegemonic rebelliousness of these stars, he contends, "was interpreted, both on film and in the fan discourse, through the trope of boyishness which mainstream American culture repeatedly drew upon after the war when representing deviations from hegemonic masculinity as a boy's impersonation of manhood, as a performance that always falls short of the original."[65] In the case of Clift, Cohan suggests that the unabashed beauty of his youthful star-image, combined with what he terms the "feminine, neurotic, bisexual qualities . . . of his distinctive performance style," connotes a central "boyishness" that has the effect of producing a performative, though quite "deliberate criticism of . . . machismo" and traditional heterosexual masculinities more generally (220). These

correlations between Clift's star-image and postwar discourses of boyishness are especially significant within the context of gay receptions.
Given hegemonic representations of male homosexuality as a deviation
from (straight) manhood, the ideological figure of "the boy who is not
a man" evokes a ready semiotics of queerness that speaks to gay audiences in potent, if variable, ways, as does the discursive correlation of
this figure to the historical emergence of postwar youth cultures. In relation to the latter, though homosexual subcultures have existed in Euro-
American cities from at least the late nineteenth century, they developed
an increasing public visibility and a markedly stronger social and economic importance in the extended postwar era.[66] Inevitably linked with
the spectacular emergence of youth cultures that developed during this
same period, gay subcultures have consequently assumed various discursive codings that impute to them—even if only symbolically and, often,
erroneously—the status of "transgressive youth counterculture." All of
the above add inestimably to the queer resonances and appeals of the Clift
persona that, with its key signs of boyish sexual ambiguity, youthful social rebellion, and generational conflict, parallels and personifies many
of the discourses and images that were and continue to be so central to
postwar and contemporary formations of gay identity.[67]

Beyond but in direct concert with the queer transgressiveness of his
general persona are the actual roles that Clift played in his films. The
essential Clift character tended, as Patricia Bosworth writes, "to be a
loner, outside the mainstream, isolated—intense but always struggling
against conformity."[68] Significantly, this sense of "nonconformity" is
frequently tied to issues of dephallicized or otherwise unconventional
male gender forms. From early roles like the sensitive, nurturing soldier
in *The Search* (1948) and the soft, introverted cowboy in *Red River* (1948),
through later ones such as the emotional idealist in *Lonelyhearts* (1958)
and the masochistic drifter in the suggestively titled *The Misfits* (1961),
Clift played marginal male characters whose phallic statuses were problematized, even disendowed through an incorporation of those tropes
of subjective experience conventionally classified and negated by phallic
masculinities under the sign of feminine castration. As Clift himself put
it: "[My screen characters] all seem to have a skin missing."[69] This predilection for playing dephallicized male characters reaches a literal and
fairly self-referential apotheosis in one of Clift's last films, *Judgment at*

Nuremberg (1961), in which he plays the part of Rudolph Petersen, a mentally incompetent middle-aged man who has been physically castrated by the Nazis during the Second World War.[70]

This representation of male dephallicization is further enhanced perhaps through Clift's physical appearance. Though certainly not "unmanly," Clift had what Graham McCann refers to as "an odd physical fragility which contradicted his conventional masculine beauty."[71] It is interesting to note that Clift's good looks are nearly always described in traditionally feminine terms such as "beautiful" and "gorgeous"—he was, for example, widely dubbed by fan magazines "the most beautiful man in the movies" or, another popular epithet, "the male Garbo"—rather than in standard masculine adjectives like "handsome" or "striking." In his discussion of Clift's 1948 film *Red River*, Anthony Easthope argues that, with "his arched dark eyebrows, wide eyes, long eyelashes, delicate nose [and] slim body," Clift presents a style of corporeal beauty that is decidedly "feminine," especially in comparison to the "rugged masculinity," "rocky face," and "sardonic smile" of his costar, John Wayne.[72] Furthermore, Clift frequently carried his body in a loose, "effeminate" fashion. Patricia Bosworth, for example, argues that Clift often walked with "an androgynous swagger" in his films, which she claims seemed to be "telling the millions of women who swooned over him—'You think you're beautiful? Well, I'm beautiful too, more beautiful than you.'"[73] Angela Allen, the script adviser on Clift's 1962 film *Freud*, claims that several scenes in that film had to be reshot because Clift's walk was, as she puts it, "too camp."[74]

The "effeminacy" of the Clift persona is further underscored by the way in which he is often shot and presented in his films. There are, for example, many instances when Clift's face or body are fetishized—when they are "glamorized" through the use of extreme close-ups and soft-focus lighting—in a way that is ordinarily only used in mainstream film to construct female images. Clift's body is thus frequently coded through the cinematic conventions of female representation and, as such, assumes markedly feminine connotations. In some films, this equation between Clift's specularized body and that of the traditional female image is so marked as to appear almost self-conscious. At the very beginning of *A Place in the Sun* (1951), for example, there is an extraordinary sequence in which Clift is shown hitchhiking alongside a busy freeway. At first Clift is facing away from the camera, walking backward, but as he approaches, he suddenly turns around, at which point the music on the soundtrack swells to a crescendo and the camera zooms in to an extended erotic close-up of his face. The film then cuts to a long shot that reveals Clift standing in front of a large billboard featuring an image of a woman lying supine in a classic pose of female erotic objectification. This sequence seemingly constructs an explicit parallel between the specularized image of the "beautiful" Clift and that of the objectified female form.

Interestingly, though not surprisingly, this insistent incorporation of such "feminine" features as interiority, emotionalism, passivity, and specularity has tended to split audience responses to Clift along gendered lines. He was, as Mary Burton writes, "essentially a woman's star. Women loved him and flocked to see him in droves but he had difficulty attracting male audiences. Men found him too soft, too effeminate."[75] However, if straight male spectators found and possibly still find Clift's images of dephallicized masculinity alienating, many gay spectators have found them appealing, even compelling. In particular, gay spectators have long recognized in Clift's extraordinary performance of aberrant masculinity an image broadly homologous to their own self-images of (homo)sexual difference. As John Stubbard writes, "Monty was always different from the other men in his films, he was softer, gentler, more 'feminine' and this became a beacon for every one of us who had ever been called 'sissy boy' . . . and [it] gave us something that we could all relate to."[76] This queer identification with the "sissiness" of the Clift image would undoubtedly have been more intense for gay spectators of the fifties and sixties when cultural discourses enforced an almost mandatory reading of male homosexuality in terms of gender dysphoria; however, given the more than residual hold such discourses still exercise on the cultural imaginary and, by implication, on many gay men's own subjectivities and auto-representations, it would continue as a central dynamic of contemporary gay receptions and readings as well. Certainly, recent gay or queer discussions of Clift still cite and celebrate the gender aberrance of his star-persona as a central element in the gay appeal of this star. A recent article on Clift in the national Australian gay magazine, *Outrage*, for example, explicitly attributes his iconic status in gay subcultures to his "subversion of traditional masculine styles" and the "strong queer resonances" of his "sexually ambivalent persona."[77] In this way, the various signs of male dephallicization that circulate through the Clift persona have provided gay audiences across several decades with a strong foundation on which to build specifically gay identifications.

This reconstruction of Clift as gay star-image has also provided gay spectators with a rather different purchase on many of Clift's films, enabling them to read such films "queerly," as it were. At a fairly immediate level, gay spectatorial assumptions of and identifications with Clift as a queer filmic image provide a very different perspective from which to read and evaluate many of the intermale relationships in Clift's films. The close relationship between Clift's character of Prewitt and that of the other "misfit," Maggio (Frank Sinatra), in *From Here to Eternity* (1953), for example, can appear startlingly homosexual rather than just homosocial if one reads this film from the perspective of a queer identification with Clift; and the famous scene in this film of Prewitt, tears streaming down his face as he plays taps for Maggio after he has been killed, becomes readable as a gay man's grieving for his lost lover.[78] Similarly, Prewitt's subjection to a barrage of abuse from his fellow soldiers who despise him for his softness and his refusal to act like other men can also be interpreted within this context as a scenario of male homophobic intolerance. Just as Prewitt's ultimate explosion in the celebrated scene where he screams at his male tormentors, "We may all *look* alike but we *ain't* all alike," can very easily be taken as a liberatory moment of "coming out," a vindication of a gay man's right to sexual and gender difference.

In a similar vein, the relational networks between the male characters in *Red River* can be queerly reinterpreted if one assumes a gay identification with Clift's character of Matthew Garth. Vito Russo argues that the presence of Clift in this famous Western works for the gay spectator to throw the frequently noted homoerotic potentials of the Western genre film into high relief, asserting that "the Clift screen persona do[es] for the young Matthew what Garbo's did for Queen Christina."[79] Indeed, I can recall attending a public screening of *Red River* with a predominantly gay male audience, most of whom laughed "knowingly" at the many scenes in this film of mutual gunplay between Clift and the other male characters.[80]

Furthermore, a reading of *Red River* from the position of a queer identification with Clift provides a rather different gloss on this film's dominant narrative concerns. Many critics have pointed to *Red River* as a prime example of the phallocentric, patriarchal cast of the classic

Western. Anthony Easthope argues that, with its central story of rivalry and contest between an older man, Thomas Dunson (John Wayne), and his young foster son, Matthew Garth, *Red River* plays out an "archetypal" scenario of male heterosexual oedipal development. In particular, Easthope contends that the film's resolution of this father-son conflict, through a conciliatory arrangement in which the father agrees to "share" his power and wealth with the young Garth in exchange for his identificatory allegiance, mirrors how male heterosexual identity and phallic authority are transmitted and secured in a patriarchal culture.[81] Such a reading is persuasive, and it is possible that it is the dominant or preferred reading encouraged by the text. It does, however, depend on an unquestioned assumption of the young Garth as unproblematically heterosexual. In the context of gay readings, the heterosexual masculinity of the Clift character is far from assured, with profound ramifications on the film's narrative meanings. For example, by (re)interpreting the Clift character of Garth as queer, gay readings shift this film's dominant narrative scenario of father-son conflict out of the more traditional arena of male heterosexual oedipal contest and into the potentially anti-oedipal arena of gay patriarchal refusal and devalorization. Within such a reading, Matthew is in conflict with his father-figure of Dunson not because he covets his power and wishes to take over his position of phallic dominance but because he rejects the type of social and psychic system that Dunson represents and demands. Thus Matthew's "mutiny" in the film against the increasingly tyrannical rule of Dunson and his breaking away with a maverick group of like-minded cowboys to create an alternative cattle run becomes readable as or, at least, resonates with the type of gay fantasmatic scenario discussed earlier in which the "tyranny" of patrocentrism is refused and an "alternative" order of identification and desire is instated in its place.

Like most leading male stars, Clift is nearly always engaged at some point in his films in a romantic relationship with a female character. Several of his films in fact focus their entire narratives on a central heterosexual romance. Although I do not think it is necessary to deny or repress the heterosexual elements in order to read these films queerly, gay identificatory engagements with Clift still have significant transformative bearings on the male-female relationships in his films.[82] In some ways, the transformation or "queering" of the heterosexual relationships is facilitated by the fact that many of these relationships are problematized in the films to begin with. In *The Heiress* (1949), for example, in which he plays the part of Morris Townsend, Clift's romantic relationship with Catherine Sloper (Olivia de Havilland) is under a constant cloud of doubt and suspicion, as Catherine is increasingly forced to question the sincerity and motivation of his desires. In *I Confess* (1953), Clift's character of Father Michael Logan is the object of Ruth Grandfort's (Anne Baxter) longtime (hetero)sexual desire, but it is a desire Michael cannot reciprocate because of his priestly vows. Similarly, in *Indiscretion of an American Wife* (1953), Vittorio DeSica's "notorious" reworking of *Brief Encounter*, Clift's character of Giovanni is caught in an illicit affair with an older married woman, Mary (Jennifer Jones), that ends in disaster and social disgrace. In *Raintree County* (1957), the relationship between Clift's character of John Shawnessy and Susanna (Elizabeth Taylor) careens almost out of control through much of the film across such rocky melodramatic territory as infidelity, insanity, and miscegenation. Thus, although heterosexual relationships figure centrally in many of Clift's films, they are frequently marked by a profound sense of tension that destabilizes their significatory fixity, potentially placing their heterosexuality under question.

Even in the films in which the heterosexual romantic liaisons engaged in by Clift's characters are rather less disturbed, an ambivalence still seems to circulate around and trouble their diegetic and libidinal functions. Much of this has to do with Clift's distinctive performance style, which tends to amplify certain elements of psychological turmoil in his characters. In particular, the aura of withdrawal and introversion that is a standard feature of Clift's acting style and that is frequently achieved with pained expressions and long, vacant stares imbues his characterizations with strong elements of uncertainty and detachment. In reference to the heterosexual romances in his films, this detachment can strike a rather unsettling note, suggesting that the Clift character is not fully engaged with them but has retreated instead to some "other" place deep inside his psyche. The sense of withdrawal from heterosexuality is even highlighted in some of the films themselves. In a key scene in *Red River*, for example, Tess (Joanne Dru) is perplexed by Matthew's brooding introspection and lack of response to her romantic overtures, eventually asking him what the problem is. He simply replies by murmuring, "I've always been kinda slow making up my mind." Similarly, in *A Place in the Sun*, Angela (Elizabeth Taylor) looks down at George during one of their romantic scenes and, noticing his vacant, withdrawn stare, comments, "You seem so distant, so alone and far away."

The air of detachment in the Clift performance style also tends to effect a marked disorganization of the "orthodox" forms of male-female relationality in many of his films. In *Wild River* (1960), Clift's character of Chuck is supposed to be courting Carol (Lee Remick), the granddaughter of an elderly woman whose land he is trying to repossess for the government, but Clift plays the role, in general, and the love scenes, in particular, with such sensitivity and passive reserve that the traditional structures of heterosexual desire are forced awry. As his costar, Lee Remick, comments: "Insofar as Monty was incapable of being the dominant partner in a male-female relationship, my character always ended up literally above him. In every love scene, his head would end up on my shoulder. It was the way he was . . . I think in the end, the film showed a very different kind of relationship than one usually sees."[83] The type of scenario identified by Remick here is a standard feature in many of Clift's films. Both *A Place in the Sun* and *The Misfits* feature famous love scenes in which Clift rejects the conventional male role of heterosexual aggressor and ends up passive and supine in the laps of Elizabeth Taylor and Marilyn Monroe, respectively. These moments all point to a strong sense of ambiguity that circulates around and destabilizes the heterosexual coding of these films. This ambiguity, in turn, provides strong opportunities for gay spectators to question the sexual identity of Clift's characters, enabling a queer (re)reading of the apparent heterosexuality of these characters as little more than a performance, a thin façade concealing the hidden "truth" of their "real" (homo)sexuality. Such a rereading could also fuel the type of intensely personal identifications that seem to characterize (some) gay engagements with Clift because it could be readily interpreted by many gay spectators as homologous to their own experiences of heterosexual performance or "passing for straight."[84] More generally, however, the potential ambiguation of the heterosexual coding of Clift's films highlighted here enables a fundamental rereading or reevaluation of the "status" of the male-female relationships in these films, shifting their meanings away from orthodox forms of intergenital heterosexuality to other "unorthodox," even queer, forms of male-female relationality.

On one level, the inversion of traditional heterosexual power structures produced by Clift's passive performance style endows the male-female relationships in his films with unmistakably maternal resonances. Many films actually play on this potential by foregrounding issues of maternal desire within their diegeses. Thus, in *A Place in the Sun* and *The Misfits*, Clift's characters are shown to have unusually strong attachments to their mothers, and the female characters are defined as fairly obvious mother-substitutes—to wit, the classic moment in *A Place in the Sun* when Angela (Elizabeth Taylor) embraces George to her, cooing, "Tell Mama all." Similarly, *Indiscretion of an American Wife* draws on the matrocentric dynamics of the romantic melodrama to represent Clift as the infantilized Giovanni struggling with an illicit love for the older, motherly—and rather suggestively named—Mary. Although the "maternal" aspect of the male-female relationships in Clift's films is potentially compatible with traditional heterosexuality, it unsettles the heterosexual fixity of these relationships, suggesting the presence of other, potentially "perverse" desires. In particular, this "maternalization" offers, in the case of gay spectatorships, strong textual support for reading the Clift characters as queer, as well as providing a potential scenario of maternal-centered desire and identification that corresponds with the structures of matrocentrism discussed in the last chapter.

On another level, these formations of "unconventional" male-female exchange in Clift's films may also de-eroticize these relationships entirely. Although there is certainly strong emotional communication and rapport between the male and female characters in these films because of the way Clift plays his roles, the dynamics of heterosexual passion or lust seem noticeably muted, even absent. Consequently, the relationships can appear startlingly desexualized at times, with the two characters bonded together and relating through a mode of male-female exchange that is evidently nongenital and possibly even nonsexual. At least, this is how these relationships can be interpreted. In the case of gay spectatorships this reading is widely pursued. Most gay commentaries on Clift underscore what they see as the essentially "platonic" nature of his relationships with women by describing them in terms of a "sibling-like" bond. "Monty developed a very special relationship with his female co-stars both on the screen and off," asserts John Stubbard. "Unlike other male stars before and after, he never tried to dominate or possess these women, rather he responded to them with a tenderness and a respect that was more like brother and sister than anything sexual."[85] Similarly, in a review of a recent biography of Clift, Ian Baintree and Bob Burns take the author, Bob Hoskyns, to task for what they see as "a smug tone of homophobia under the otherwise generous writing." In particular, they claim that "Hoskyns misreads Liz Taylor's unwavering love for Monty, proscribing it to the lifelong obsession of a jilted suitor rather than the real sibling-like kinship between them, an intimacy that lasted Monty's entire life."[86]

As these examples indicate, gay readings of the male-female relationships in Clift's films frequently refer to and incorporate extratextual knowledges about the types of "offscreen" relationships Clift enjoyed with his female colleagues, thereby crossing and blurring the division between film and biography. They do this, I think, to undergird their readings of these textual relationships as essentially nonsexual. As is widely known, particularly within gay subcultures, Clift enjoyed extraordinarily strong, platonic relationships with several of his female costars in "real life." He is reputed to have said of Marilyn Monroe, for example, "Maybe Marilyn and I would have gotten together one day if we weren't so much alike. As it is, it's too much like brother and sister getting together." Monroe is alleged to have remarked, "I look at him [Clift] and see the brother I never had and feel stronger and get protective." Similarly, Elizabeth Taylor is on record as saying of Clift, "He was the kindest, gentlest, most understanding man I have ever known. He was like my brother. He was my dearest, most devoted friend."[87] Obviously, these quotes refer to the actors' "real" relationships and not their textual relationships, but these types of comments can be and, indeed, have been widely used by gay spectators as extratextual supports for their readings of the male-female relationships in the films of Montgomery Clift as something other than simply heterosexual.[88]

An exploration of queer engagements with Montgomery Clift would be incomplete without a discussion of Clift's "tragic" death at age forty-five from a heart attack brought on by years of chronic substance abuse. It is a central feature of the whole Clift legend, and, consequently, it plays a major role in how Clift's persona and films are read and evaluated. It has, for example, helped endow the Clift persona with a mythic status, placing him in a long line of Hollywood stars who died "too young." It has also helped secure one of the more enduring images often associated with Clift, namely that of the sad and doomed young man. This is an image widely presented in many of Clift's films, including *A Place in the Sun, I Confess, From Here to Eternity*, and *Lonelyhearts*, and the apparent reflection of it in his personal biography has effectively crystallized this image as one of the central signs of the Clift repertoire. This image raises something of a problem for gay identificatory engagements with Clift, for the trope of the sad and doomed young man is also a popular and enduring staple of mainstream homophobic iconography, which uses it to maintain dominant cultural readings of the gay man as a melancholic "victim" of his own suicidal desires.[89] This homophobic tradition has played a central role in most biographical commentaries on Clift, which forge connections of varying degrees of explicitness between Clift's homosexuality and his "tragic" but inevitable path of self-destruction. Thus Gerold Frank describes Clift's life as "the passage through Hell of a gifted actor, a man maddened by his homosexuality even as he was driven to live with the truth"; Rex Reed characterizes it as a "soap opera of pills, booze and perversion"; and Robert LaGuardia writes that Clift's life was a "slow, painful process of self-destruction," "a journey into darkness . . . and perversion . . . which reduce[d] into clinical terms [would read]: Hebephrenic schizophrenia. Oedipal breakdown. Death wish."[90] Even the most recent Clift biography, Maurice Leonard's 1997 entry, sells itself through a reading of Clift as "a tortured spirit who harboured a dark secret. Lonely, vulnerable, and homosexual, he was forced to hide his true nature behind a veneer of normality."[91] The metonymic logic at work in all these representations clearly seeks to represent homosexuality as the direct correlative, if not source, of Clift's alleged self-destructive impulses. As a result, for a gay spectator to identify with Clift as queer star-image is to identify in some way with an "oppressive" stereotype of the homosexual as suicidal victim.

This type of argument is, in fact, forwarded with some frequency in gay discourses. In an article titled "Death Wish," Mark Robbins attacks what he sees as the "morbid tradition" of "gay preoccupations with tragic, martyr figures" like Montgomery Clift but also other gay cult icons such as Judy Garland, Oscar Wilde, Marilyn Monroe, and even St. Sebastian.[92] As Robbins sees it, this gay fascination with "doomed" martyr figures is one of the more "unhealthy" aspects of gay culture,

Papa, Can't You See That I'm Flaming? 239

an example of gay self-loathing fueled by internalized homophobia and "dangerous masochis[m]." He argues that this tradition within gay culture repeats and plays into preexisting stereotypes of the homosexual as essentially melancholic, self-destructive, and moribund and that, therefore, it should be resisted and denounced. Although arguments like this can provide a forceful and frequently persuasive critique of potentially damaging tendencies within gay cultural practices, they paint a rather monolithic picture of what is in effect an exceedingly complex and multifaceted issue. In particular, such arguments tend to assume that gay men take up cultural images of the sad and doomed martyr in a fixed, homogeneous manner, whereas I suggest that gay engagements with these images, as indeed with any cultural image or text, are plural and multivalent.

Richard Dyer has attempted to reclaim gay identificatory readings of the image of the sad young man by arguing that this image is not the static "stereotype" that so many critics assume but a dynamic textual structure that draws on a wide range of representational traditions. He argues that this complexity gives the image "rich possibilities of connotation and use and enables it to be read in a multiplicity of ways."[93] Gay readers in particular, he suggests, engage the image of the sad young man in ways qualitatively different from other readers because they inhabit different social and cultural relations to this image. As he writes, "Stereotypes mean differently for different groups, and especially for those who are members of the stereotyped group compared to those who are not. It is partly a matter of how you see it." In the case of gay readings of the stereotype of the sad young man, Dyer suggests that gay readers use their own "knowledges" of oppression to counter mainstream interpretations of the "sadness" of the young man as an inherent or inevitable property of his gayness, rereading it instead as an effect of an intolerant society—"if [the sad young man] is unhappy it is not because of himself but because of social oppression" (94). This potential reading strategy may also be used by gay spectators to engage with the representational currents of tragedy and melancholy in the Clift persona as well. Indeed, in his article on Clift, gay critic Richard Lippe castigates mainstream critical evaluations for their failure to recognize that the primary source of Clift's tragedy was not his sexuality per se but "the degradation and mental anguish he experienced as a gay person living and working in a homophobic society."[94]

Another way in which gay readers have "recuperated" the image of the sad young man is by engaging it as what Dyer terms "a figure of romance/pornography." Gay readers have, he contends, long used the image of the sad young man as a figure on which to project and through which to articulate their own erotic desires. Far from anathematizing gay desire, the image of the sad young man is thus mobilized in gay contexts to express that desire and construct what Dyer terms "a celebration of homosexual love." He writes: "If we are turned on by the men he is turned on by, that means we share and, if only during the reading/viewing, endorse his desire; and if we think he is desirable because handsome and admirable because sensitive, then we also endorse being him. For all the bad feelings he has about himself, we could feel pretty good about him." [95]

Although it is not made explicit or even seemingly recognized, Dyer's argument here that gay engagements with the figure of the sad, doomed young man contain important sexual forms and functions has the effect of highlighting what may be one of the central pleasures of those engagements, namely, erotogenic masochism. In the case of gay spectatorial engagements with Montgomery Clift, they obtain unavoidably strong masochistic dynamics, even if for no other reason than that masochism is such an emphatically vital subtext of the fantasmatic economy of male dephallicization that I have suggested structures both the Clift star-sign and its gay subcultural receptions. As Richard Lippe claims, the Clift persona exhibits a central "compulsion to experience suffering" and other such "masochistic impulses" that work "to intensify [its] identification with the 'feminine', women having been traditionally associated with victimization and masochism." [96] This precise issue, however, is often raised by those critics who oppose gay fascinations with Clift or other such cultural figures of suffering specifically because they are, to repeat Mark Robbins's contention, "dangerously masochistic." The primary problem here is that masochism is generally assumed to be "bad." Critics who refute certain formations of gay cultural reception because of their masochistic potentials are laboring under the popular misconception that masochism is pathological, that it signals a dysfunctional mode of libidinal activity that is negative and disabling. From a psychoanalytic perspective, however, though masochism may be defined as a "perversion," it is generally seen to be a formation of desire engaged, in varying degrees, by all subjects. As Freud writes, "Masochism accompanies the libido through all its developmental phases." [97] Furthermore, several psychoanalytic critics have recently attempted to demonstrate that, far from being a disabling impediment, masochism may in fact be a liberating paradigm of libidinal organization.[98] These theorists argue that masochism provides subjects, especially male subjects, with a psychic strategy for renegotiating oedipal systems of gender and sexuality. Most of these arguments take as their starting point Freud's assertion that masochism prototypically entails the assumption of a psychic position of passive femininity. In his 1924 paper "The Economic Problem of Masochism," he writes, "if one has an opportunity of studying cases in which the masochistic phantasies have been especially richly elaborated, one quickly discovers that they place the subject in a characteristically female situation; they signify, that is, being castrated, or copulated with, or giving birth to a baby."[99] Although such a scenario is hardly radical for women—indeed, it is, as Kaja Silverman notes, an "accepted," even "requisite . . . element of 'normal' female subjectivity, providing a crucial mechanism for eroticizing lack and subordination"—it is profoundly disruptive for male subjectivity, in which it subverts the fundamental moorings of an active phallic identification.[100] Freud argues that masochism in male subjectivity explicitly depends on a "deviant" structure of negative oedipality, placing the male subject in a "homosexual" relation of passive desire for the father. Thus, in relation to the all-important beating fantasy, which Freud defines as prototypical of masochism, he identifies a nucleus of homosexual desire in which the manifest scenario of "a child is being beaten" translates into the latent scenario, "I am being beaten/loved by my father."[101]

Freud does not make the claim, but his representation of male masochism through the negative male oedipus complex suggests that not only is the male subject of masochism positioned in a relation of passive or "feminine" desire to the father, he is positioned in a relation of active identification with the mother as well. As Silverman notes:

> The . . . position . . . of (passive) male homosexuality . . . is the position into which the male subject inserts himself in the masculine version of the beating fantasy, and there it has an emphatically maternal significance; Freud maintains that it is "derived from a feminine attitude toward the father", i.e. from the negative Oedipus complex. The male subject thus secures access to femininity through identification with the mother.[102]

The subversive dynamics of this reading of male masochism have been most forcefully highlighted by Gilles Deleuze in his retheorization of masochism as a site of male psychic transgression. Deleuze argues that, unlike sadism, which originates in the oedipus complex, masochism belongs to the pre-oedipal phase and refers to a structure of desire organized around the imaginary bonds between the pre-oedipal mother and the subject-as-child. In the case of male subjectivity, masochism thus signals a radical psychic restructuration, for it reinstates a matrocentric economy. Indeed, Deleuze goes so far as to claim that male masochism effects a libidinal "contract" between the masochistic male subject and the pre-oedipal mother that writes the father out almost entirely and re-creates the male masochist as "a new, sexless man."

> The [male] masochist tries to exorcise the danger of the father and . . . [create a] symbolic order in which the father has been abolished for all time. . . . [He does this by] ensur[ing] that he will be beaten . . . what is beaten, humiliated and ridiculed in him is the image and likeness of the father, and the possibility of the father's aggressive return. . . . The masochist thus liberates himself in preparation for a rebirth in which the father will have no part.[103]

This reading of masochism strikingly accords with the libidinal scenarios of paternal refusal and maternal identification that I have argued form potential structures of and for the gay fantasmatic, and hence it suggests that "masochism" can provide a source of strong psychic appeal and pleasure for (some) gay subjects. Indeed, much of the discussion presented earlier in this chapter about the violative (re)figurings of masculinity/male corporeality in gay subjectivities is underwritten by a fairly obvious subtext of masochism.[104] I have preferred not to highlight that subtext before now, however, because I wanted to underscore the specificity of gay male psycholibidinal paradigms and thus avoid any overhasty conflation of those paradigms with masochism. As the work just discussed indicates, there are strong elements of potential homology between gay male psychosocial organization and male masochism, but this does not mean that they are one and the same, or that there is an inevitable link between them. It simply suggests that male homosexuality and masochism share similarities in terms of their psychocultural profiles and that masochism may therefore provide gay subjects with a resonant site through which to articulate their own fantasmatic scenarios of phallic divestiture.

In reference to gay readings of the masochistic dynamics of Montgomery Clift, this argument challenges those critics who dismiss such readings on the grounds that they are at heart masochistic and therefore "bad," demonstrating that masochism can be potentially useful, even empowering, for gay men. In particular, this argument recuperates potential engagements between gay spectators and the masochistic elements of the star-image of Montgomery Clift, suggesting that such engagements are not necessarily identifications with an oppressive stereotype but that they may in fact be "channels" for gay erotic and fantasmatic articulation.

The star-image and texts of Montgomery Clift provide significant possibilities for gay spectators to make and explore their own investments in formations of masochistic desire. In general, the extensive performances of masculine dephallicization in the Clift persona attest to the central presence of a logic of masochism in that persona. In particular, many of Clift's most famous films feature important moments of masochism—moments that play out the transgressive fantasmatic scenarios identified by Freud and Deleuze with extraordinary candor. In *From Here to Eternity*, for example, Clift's character, Prewitt, is subjected to a barrage of physical and verbal abuse at the hands of his fellow soldiers. He is humiliated, tripped, kicked, stomped on, and forced to do all manner of torturous labor. Far from fighting against this abuse, Prewitt seems to accept it with a sense of perverse pleasure. At one point he even invites his tormentors to subject him to ever greater feats of sadistic punishment: "You guys want to put the screws on, go right ahead. I can take anything you can dish up." The reason for the abuse is, significantly, Prewitt's refusal to conform to the other men; he refuses to "play ball," as one of the other characters puts it. Specifically, Prewitt refuses to join the platoon's boxing team. Years previously, he had blinded an opponent in a boxing match and, because of this, renounced physical aggression. Thus, whereas the other men take up and delight in a position of active sadism, Prewitt refuses to do this, opting for a passive masochism instead. And it is this assumption of masochistic passivity that signals Prewitt/Clift's "difference," most notably, his difference from the other men.

Similar scenes are also featured in other Clift films such as *The Young Lions* (1958), in which Clift's character of Noah Ackerman is repeatedly taunted and beaten by his fellow soldiers; *The Misfits*, in which Clift plays a disaffected, alcoholic drifter, who takes pleasure in getting battered in cheap rodeos; and *Red River*, which is particularly interesting in the context of the present discussion because of this film's previously noted oedipal dynamics. At the very end of *Red River*, there is a highly charged scene in which Clift's character of Matthew Garth is violently attacked by his foster father, Dunson (John Wayne). For much of the scene, Matthew refuses to fight back. He simply stands there in passive silence allowing Dunson to shoot at and then punch him. Significantly, Matthew's display of masochistic passivity here is defined in the film as "feminizing." In a highly symbolic act, Dunson steals Matthew's gun out of his holster and tosses it aside, shouting, "You once told me never to take your gun off you." He then repeatedly screams at Matthew to "fight back" and "be a man," not, by implication, a "woman." This assumption of a "feminine" relation to the father places Matthew in a fairly obvious negative oedipal scenario of homosexual desire similar to that identified by Freud as a primary subtext of male masochism. The homosexual dynamics of the sequence are highlighted in the film when the two male characters are forced apart by Tess (Joanne Dru), who yells at them, "Why don't you two recognize that you really love each other?" Yet this sequence also plays out the other side of the negative oedipal subtext of male masochism: the disavowal of paternal identification highlighted by Deleuze. By refusing to fight with Dunson and willingly submitting to an extended beating by him, Matthew is in effect denying his likeness to Dunson qua the father, denying any form of equivalence or identification. To repeat Deleuze's formulation, "what is being beaten, humiliated and ridiculed" in Matthew/Clift in this sequence is, on one level at least, "the image and the likeness of the father." [105] The transgressive enactment of paternal refusal through masochism is, of course, only temporary. Matthew does fight back and is, thereby, reconciled to Dunson and, by extension, patrocentric masculinity. Nevertheless, this sequence in *Red River* is a good example of how the recurrent performances of male masochism in Clift's films function as points of sexual disorganization and, thus, as receptive avenues for gay fantasmatic investment and articulation.

The image of Clift as self-debasing masochist offers the ultimate crystallization of those fantasmatic scenarios of paternal deposition and dephallicization that I have been arguing structure not only gay engagements with that particular star-persona but gay engagements with the cinematic male image at large. What more forceful vision of dephallicization could there be than that of the masochist submitting the male body and the phallic subjectivity of which that body is always a psychocultural symbol to the castrating effects of "feminizing" passivity and self-shattering subjugation? As such, this might be a fitting image with which to conclude both my discussion of queer identificatory (re)constructions of Clift and the chapter on gay spectatorships and figures of masculinity.

It's long been a truism of both popular and academic thought that cinema, the "dream factory," operates as one of our culture's key institutions for the production of desire in fantasy. Although cinema's capacity for fantasmatic production has predominantly been theorized within the contexts of heterosexual presumption—so much so that heterosexual desire is frequently represented as the natural condition and effect of film—my concern has been to address how cinema supports gay male desires and gay male fantasies. In this chapter, I have attempted to profile the process of gay cinematic fantasy production through a reading of queer spectatorial engagements with cinematic masculinities. Drawing on psychoanalytic theories of gay male subjectivities as invested in libidinal scenarios of phallic disruption, or what I have been calling male dephallicization, I have suggested that gay spectatorships receive and (re)figure male images within a contradictory fantasmatic economy of desire and disavowal through which the hegemonic male image is simultaneously engaged as an object of erotic investment and stripped of its phallic pretensions and reconstructed as a "perverse" figure of queer identification. Although I argue that this scenario of phallic ruination is a central, possibly even typical, dynamic of gay spectatorial formations, it is obviously not an essential or universal property of them. The relations of gay spectatorship—as, indeed, of any form of cultural reception—are necessarily complex and heterogeneous, formed in and across an almost infinite range of shifting contingencies. The most any theorization of those relations can provide, therefore, is a provisional and inevitably partial representation of their potentialities, the possible forms gay spectatorships may assume and the possible effects they may generate in certain contexts.

   This is precisely why I nominated psychoanalytic fantasy theory and, in particular, the notion of the fantasmatic as a governing paradigm for my explorations of gay spectatorships. With its central reading of fantasy as constituted through the simultaneous pull of transindividual psychocultural structure and contingent instance, the fantasmatic offers a bifocal framework that recognizes the determinative functions of "gayness" as a psychosocial formation of subjective meaning and desire and enables a critical analysis of those functions while also acknowledging that they may be realized in vastly different ways depending on the multiple variables that constitute both the individual fantasizing subject and the fantasmatic event. Within such a context, gay spectatorship emerges as a complex configuration produced in and through competing registers. It is part libidinal formation (the networks of fantasy and desire that constitute and govern the psychic profiles of male homosexualities), part sociohistorical construct (the framing discourses of gay subcultural identities, practices, and knowledges), and part textual figure (the exchange and interactions of both the above with the narrative scenarios and formal dynamics of film, the production of gay desires in cinematic textuality). How this composite formation is realized — or not — in material instances is itself (over)determined by the further panoply of particularities that frame individual acts of cinematic reading, the precise forms and effects of which remain almost entirely beyond analytic apprehension or even knowability.

The critical complex created in the preceding pages under the sign of gay spectatorship is thus little more than a theoretical chimera, a fabricated fiction of epistemological desire. It is, however, a fiction that seeks to furnish — and hopefully delivers — a useful and critically enabling way to think about gay spectatorships and the real values, significances, and pleasures that they produce. To "envision" the gay spectator as I have here is to assert that, though the "realities" of gay cinematic reception will always and necessarily exceed any attempt at representation or analysis, spectatorship performs a range of generative operations in and for gay male subjectivities and cultures that are vital, substantive, and worthy of critical recognition. The primary aim of this study has been to offer such a recognition and to begin the difficult but long overdue task of affirming the diverse productivities of gay spectatorships and the thrilling possibilities for queer fantasmatic production afforded by their spectacular passions.

Notes

Introduction *At First Sight: Definitions, Clarifications, and Assorted Prolegomena*

1 Joe Morella and Edward Epstein, *Judy: The Films and Career of Judy Garland*, 2d ed. (New York: Citadel Pess, 1974).

2 The term *open secret* was coined by D. A. Miller, who uses it to refer to the paradoxical construction of homosexuality in modern cultures as a site of simultaneous knowing and unknowing; a construction that functions, he suggests, as a central strategy of homophobic discipline. By relegating homosexual desires and relations to the twilight status of an "open secret," something known but unspoken, mainstream culture can "construct a homosexuality held definitionally in suspense on no less than a question of its own existence" while "produc[ing] in the process homosexual subjects doubtful of the validity and even the reality of their desire, which *may only be, does not necessarily mean*, and all the rest" (D. A. Miller, "Anal *Rope*," in *Inside/Out: Lesbian Theories, Gay Theories*, ed. Diana Fuss [New York: Routledge, 1991], 125).

3 Henry Jenkins, *Textual Poachers: Television Fans and Participatory Culture* (New York: Routledge, 1992), 15–19. See also the essays by Joli Jenson, John Fiske, and Lawrence Grossberg in *The Adoring Audience: Fan Culture and Popular Media*, ed. Lisa A. Lewis (London: Routledge, 1992).

4 The phrase belongs to Mary Ann Doane, who uses it to describe the status of the femme fatale. (*Femmes Fatales: Feminism, Film Theory, Psychoanalysis* [New York: Routledge, 1991], 1).

5 Judith Mayne, "Discussion," in *How Do I Look? Queer Film and Video*, ed. Bad Object-Choices (Seattle: Bay Press, 1991), 143.

6 Raymond Bellour, "Alternation, Segmentation, Hypnosis," in *Feminism and Film Theory*, ed. Constance Penley (New York: Routledge, 1988), 88; Laura Mulvey, "Afterthoughts," in *Visual and Other Pleasures* (London: Macmillan, 1989), 29.

7 Ellis Hanson, introduction to *Out Takes: Essays on Queer Theory and Film*, ed. Ellis Hanson (Durham: Duke University Press, 1999), 8.

8 Vito Russo, *The Celluloid Closet: Homosexuality in the Movies*, rev. ed. (New York: Harper and Row, 1987), 322.

9   Paul Burston and Colin Richardson, introduction to *A Queer Romance: Lesbians, Gay Men, and Popular Culture*, ed. Paul Burston and Colin Richardson (London: Routledge, 1995), 1-2.

10 Hanson, *Out Takes*, 7.

11 Diana Fuss, *Essentially Speaking: Feminism, Nature, and Difference* (New York: Routledge, 1989), 28.

12 Caroline Evans and Lorraine Gamman, "Reviewing Queer Viewing," in Burston and Richardson, *Queer Romance*, 35-40.

13 Michel Foucault, *The History of Sexuality: An Introduction*, trans. Robert Hurley (Harmondsworth: Penguin, 1981), 78.

14 Teresa de Lauretis, *The Practice of Love: Lesbian Sexuality and Perverse Desire* (Bloomington: Indiana University Press, 1994), xvii.

15 Evans and Gamman, "Reviewing Queer Viewing," 39-40.

16 Jonathan Keane, "AIDS, Identity, and the Space of Desire," *Textual Practice* 7.4 (1993): 382.

17 Robert Stam, Robert Burgoyne, and Sandy Flitterman-Lewis, *New Vocabularies in Film Semiotics: Structuralism, Post-Structuralism, and Beyond* (London: Routledge, 1992), 123-24.

18 Jacqueline Rose, *Sexuality in the Field of Vision* (London: Verso, 1986), 90-91.

19 Jane Gallop, *Feminism and Psychoanalysis: The Daughter's Seduction* (London: Macmillan, 1982), xii.

20 Mary Ann Doane, "Response," *Camera Obscura* 20-21 (1989): 143.

21 D. N. Rodowick, "Response," *Camera Obscura* 20-21 (1989): 269.

22 Eve Kosofsky Sedgwick, *Tendencies* (Durham: Duke University Press, 1993), 73-74. For similar critiques of the alleged heteronormativity of psychoanalysis see Michael Warner, "Homo-Narcissism, or Heterosexuality," in *Engendering Men: The Question of Male Feminist Criticism*, ed. J. A. Boone and M. Cadden (New York: Routledge, 1990); and John Brenkman, *Straight Male Modern: A Cultural Critique of Psychoanalysis* (New York: Routledge, 1993).

23 Hanson, *Out Takes*, 13-14.

24 Sigmund Freud, "Three Essays on the Theory of Sexuality," in *On Sexuality*, vol. 7 of *The Pelican Freud Library*, trans. J. Strachey (Harmondsworth: Penguin, 1977), 56.

25 Tim Dean, "On the Eve of a Queer Future," *Raritan* 15.1 (1995): 132-34.

26 Stephen Heath, "Difference," *Screen* 19.3 (1978): 61.

27 For an excellent overview of the histories and genealogies of *queer* see Annamarie Jagose, *Queer Theory* (New York: New York University Press, 1997).

28 Sedgwick, *Tendencies*, 8.

Chapter One *Something a Little Strange: Theorizing Gay Male Spectatorships*

1   Leonard Maltin, *Leonard Maltin's TV Movie and Video Guide, 1997 Edition* (New York: New American Library, 1996), 595.

2   "Screen Kiss: An Interview with Hector Babenco," *Campaign* (February 1986): 23.

3   J. P. Telotte, "Beyond All Reason: The Nature of the Cult," in *The Cult Film Experience: Beyond All Reason*, ed. J. P. Telotte (Austin: University of Texas Press, 1991), 5.

4   Roland Barthes, *Mythologies*, trans. Annette Lavers (London: Granada, 1973), 157.

5   Richard Dyer, introduction to *Gays and Film*, ed. Richard Dyer, rev. ed. (New York: Zoetrope, 1984), 1.

6   Judith Mayne, *Cinema and Spectatorship* (London: Routledge, 1993), 159-66.

7   Mark Finch, "Gays and Lesbians in the Cinema," in *The Political Companion to American Film*, ed. Gary Crowdus (Chicago: Lake View Press, 1994), 122.

8   George Chauncey, *Gay New York: Gender, Urban Culture, and the Making of the Gay Male World, 1890-1940* (New York: Harper Collins, 1994), 194.

9   Dyer, *Gays and Film*, 1.

10 Miriam Hansen, *Babel and Babylon: Spectatorship in American Silent Film* (Cambridge: Harvard University Press, 1991), 12. Although Hansen makes her argument about film as an alternative space for marginalized subjects specifically in relation to early cinema, claiming that this was largely repressed with the subsequent development of classical narrative cinema, other critics have stressed cinema's continued potential as a productive site for the identificatory investments of marginalized social groups. See, for example, Jacqueline Bobo, *Black Women as Cultural Readers* (New York: Columbia University Press, 1995); and Jackie Stacey, *Star Gazing: Hollywood Cinema and Female Spectatorship* (New York: Routledge, 1994).

11 Dick Hebdige, *Subculture: The Meaning of Style* (London: Methuen, 1979).

12 Sarah Thornton, *Club Cultures: Music, Media, and Subcultural Capital* (Middletown: Wesleyan University Press, 1996).

13 Andrea Weiss, *Vampires and Violets: Lesbians in the Cinema* (London: Jonathan Cape, 1992), 50.

14 Although this study focuses on gay male spectatorship alone, it would be interesting to chart the homologies and interrelations between gay and lesbian histories of spectatorship. Most commentators agree that gay male subcultures seem to have developed a much more spectacular set of relations to and uses of Hollywood cinema than lesbian subcultures, though one can't help but wonder how much of this is historical fact and how much is simply the result of gendered imbalances in representation and research. Recent critical work suggests

that there is a very rich, if undertheorized, history of significant spectatorial practices in lesbian subcultures that is only now beginning to be documented. See Weiss, *Vampires and Violets*; Tamsin Wilton, ed., *Immortal Invisible: Lesbians and the Moving Image* (New York: Routledge, 1995); and Clare Whatling, *Screen Dreams: Fantasising Lesbians in Film* (Manchester: Manchester University Press, 1997).

15   Michael Bronski, *Culture Clash: The Making of Gay Sensibility* (Boston: South End Press, 1984), 92.

16   See Chauncey, *Gay New York*, 287ff.

17   John Lestrange, letter to author, Sydney, Australia, 15 April 1994.

18   For an overview of some of the cinematic practices, at least in terms of production and exhibition, that have emerged in contemporary gay, lesbian, and queer subcultures see Martha Gever, Pratibha Parmar, and John Greyson, eds. *Queer Looks: Perspectives on Lesbian and Gay Film and Video* (New York: Routledge, 1993); and Samantha Searle, *Queer-ing the Screen* (Sydney: Moving Image, 1997).

19   Al LaValley, "The Great Escape: Gays and Film," *American Film* 10.6 (1985): 28.

20   Elizabeth Ellsworth, "Illicit Pleasures: Feminist Spectators and *Personal Best*," *Wide Angle* 8.2 (1986): 46.

21   Telotte, *Cult Film Experience*, 13.

22   Daniel Harris, *The Rise and Fall of Gay Culture* (New York: Hyperion, 1997), 10.

23   Searle, *Queer-ing the Screen*, 80. For an analysis of the performative functions of other gay subcultural media practices such as community television see Alan McKee, "Do You Believe in Fairies? Creating Fictional Identities in Bent TV," *Media International Australia* 79 (February 1996); and Eric Freeman, "Producing (Queer) Communities: Public Access Cable TV in the USA," in *The Television Studies Book*, ed. Christine Geraghty and David Lusted (London: Arnold, 1998).

24   Eve Kosofsky Sedgwick, *The Epistemology of the Closet* (Berkeley: University of California Press, 1990).

25   Tamsin Wilton, "On Not Being Lady Macbeth: Some (Troubled) Thoughts on Lesbian Spectatorship," in *Immortal Invisible*, 146.

26   Cited in Bronski, *Culture Clash*, 95–96.

27   Telotte, *Cult Film Experience*, 11. See also the essays by Corrigan, Grant, and Studlar in the same collection.

28   Diana Fuss, *Essentially Speaking: Feminism, Nature, and Difference* (New York: Routledge, 1989), 102–3.

29   Steven Seidman, *Difference Troubles: Queering Social Theory and Sexual Politics* (Cambridge: Cambridge University Press, 1997), 132.

30   David Herkt, "Being Gay," *RePublica* 3 (1995): 46.

31   Caroline Evans and Lorraine Gamman, "The Gaze Revisited, or Reviewing

Queer Viewing," in *A Queer Romance: Lesbians, Gay Men, and Popular Culture*, ed. Paul Burston and Colin Richardson (London: Routledge, 1995), 14.

32 Mayne, *Cinema and Spectatorship*, 97.

33 David Halperin, *Saint Foucault: Towards a Gay Hagiography* (New York: Oxford University Press, 1995), 62.

34 Evans and Gamman, "Reviewing Queer Viewing," in Burston and Richardson, *Queer Romance*, 40.

35 Alexander Doty, *Making Things Perfectly Queer: Interpreting Mass Culture* (Minneapolis: University of Minnesota Press, 1993), 2–3.

36 Halperin, *Saint Foucault*, 64.

37 Leo Bersani, *Homos* (Cambridge: Harvard University Press, 1995), 56.

38 Seidman, *Difference Troubles*, 135.

39 Bersani, *Homos*, 6.

40 Shane Phelan, *Getting Specific: Postmodern Lesbian Politics* (Minneapolis: University of Minnesota Press, 1994), 8.

41 Judith Butler, *Gender Trouble: Feminism and the Subversion of Identity* (New York: Routledge, 1990), 147.

42 Judith Butler, *Bodies That Matter: On the Discursive Limits of "Sex"* (New York: Routledge, 1993), 93ff.

43 See Mayne, *Cinema and Spectatorship*, 31ff.; Robert Lapsley and Michael Westlake, *Film Theory: An Introduction* (Manchester: Manchester University Press, 1988); and Graeme Turner, *British Cultural Studies: An Introduction* (London: Unwin Hyman, 1990).

44 See Robert Stam, Robert Burgoyne, and Sandy Flitterman-Lewis, eds. *New Vocabularies in Film Semiotics: Structuralism, Post-Structuralism, and Beyond* (New York: Routledge), 142ff.

45 Tony Bennett, introduction to *Popular Culture and Social Relations*, ed. Tony Bennett, Colin Mercer, and Janet Woollacott (London: Open University Press, 1986), xvi.

46 Simon During, introduction to *The Cultural Studies Reader*, ed. Simon During (New York: Routledge, 1993), 7.

47 Christine Gledhill, "Developments in Feminist Film Criticism," in *Re-vision: Essays in Feminist Film Criticism*, ed. Mary Ann Doane, Patricia Mellencamp, and Linda Williams (1978; rpt., Frederick, Md.: University Publications of America, 1984), 40.

48 Christine Gledhill, "Pleasurable Negotiations," in *Female Spectators: Looking at Film and Television*, ed. E. Deirdre Pribram (London: Verso, 1988), 64.

49 Stuart Hall, "Encoding/Decoding," in *Culture, Media, Language*, ed. Stuart Hall et al. (London: Hutchinson, 1980).

50 Gledhill, "Pleasurable Negotiations," 67–68.

51 Ellsworth, "Illicit Pleasures."

52 Richard Dyer, *Heavenly Bodies: Film Stars and Society* (New York: St. Martin's Press, 1986), 162.

53 Janet Staiger, *Interpreting Films: Studies in the Historical Reception of American Cinema* (Princeton: Princeton University Press, 1992), 210.

54 See, for example, James Donald, "On the Threshold: Psychoanalysis and Cultural Studies," in *Psychoanalysis and Cultural Theory: Thresholds*, ed. James Donald (London: Macmillan, 1991).

55 See, for example, Stuart Hall, "Recent Developments in Theories of Language and Ideology: A Critical Note," and David Morley, "Texts, Readers, Subjects," in Hall et al., *Culture, Media, Language*.

56 Staiger, *Interpreting Films*, 71.

57 Constance Penley, *The Future of an Illusion: Film, Feminism, Psychoanalysis* (Minneapolis: University of Minnesota Press, 1989), xix.

58 Significantly, an increasing amount of work emerging out of a cultural studies problematic attempts to do just that. Much of this work acknowledges that the problem is not psychoanalysis itself but the reductive, universalizing ways it has been used by certain traditions of cultural analysis. This work has started to look at how a careful reading of psychoanalysis may be used to supplement and extend cultural studies projects. The recent work of Stuart Hall is exemplary in this respect. Despite previously being a staunch opponent of psychoanalysis, Hall draws quite extensively on psychoanalytic theory in many of his recent writings. See, for example, Stuart Hall, "New Ethnicities," in *Black Film, British Cinema*, ed. Kobena Mercer (ICA: London, 1988); and Stuart Hall and Paul du Gay, eds., *Questions of Cultural Identity* (London: Sage, 1996).

59 John Fletcher, "Freud and His Uses: Psychoanalysis and Gay Theory," in *Coming on Strong: Gay Politics and Culture*, ed. Simon Shepherd and Mick Wallis (London: Unwin Hyman, 1989), 95.

60 Mayne, *Cinema and Spectatorship*, 38.

61 Janet Bergstrom and Mary Ann Doane, "The Female Spectator: Contexts and Directions," *Camera Obscura* 21–22 (1989): 12.

62 Stephen Frosh, *For and against Psychoanalysis* (New York: Routledge, 1997), 156.

63 James Donald, general introduction to *Fantasy and the Cinema*, ed. James Donald (London: British Film Institute, 1989), 8.

64 Jean Laplanche and Jean-Bertrand Pontalis, "Fantasy and the Origins of Sexuality," in *Formations of Fantasy*, ed. Victor Burgin, James Donald, and Pat Caplan (London: Methuen, 1986): 5–34.

65 Slavoj Žižek, *Looking Awry: An Introduction to Jacques Lacan through Popular Culture* (Cambridge: MIT Press, 1991), 6.

66 Laplanche and Pontalis, "Fantasy and the Origins of Sexuality," 27.

67 Like so much of Lacan's work, his theorization of the concept of deferred action is found in several different texts. For relatively thorough discussions of it see

"Function and Field of Language in Psychoanalysis," in *Ecrits: A Selection*, trans. Alan Sheridan (London: Tavistock, 1977); and "The Nucleus of Repression," in *The Seminar of Jacques Lacan Book I: Freud's Papers on Technique, 1953–54*, trans. John Forrester (Cambridge: Cambridge University Press, 1988).

68   In his celebrated case study of a female paranoiac, for example, Freud uses the notion of deferred action to suggest that the paranoid delusions this woman had about being watched and photographed during sex were in fact a deferred reactivation of fantasies of the primal scene (i.e., of watching parental coitus) from the woman's infancy, which were interwoven in and articulated through her contemporary fantasies of lovemaking. It was only through the framework of her later fantasies that the "earlier" primal fantasy was given shape. Thus, in this case, the constitutive role of the primal fantasy is inextricably tied up with the equally constitutive role of the contemporary fantasmatic event. In fact, neither form of fantasy could, in Freud's estimation, be effectively apprehended on its own (Freud, "A Case of Paranoia Running Counter to the Psychoanalytic Theory of the Disease," in *On Psychopathology*, vol. 10 of *The Pelican Freud Library* [Harmondsworth: Penguin, 1979]).

69   This dialectical reading of fantasy as determined by the mutual interactions of transindividual structure and contingent event is not specific to Laplanche and Pontalis alone. Jacques Lacan mounts a similar argument in his theorizations of fantasy. Like Laplanche and Pontalis, Lacan asserts that fantasy assumes a structural role as "the support of desire" but that its structuring dimensions are neither one-sided nor absolute. Lacan's celebrated algebraic formulation for fantasy, $\$ \Diamond a$, makes this explicit. Here the subject's ($\$$) access to the object of fantasy—represented as *a: objet petit a*—is not direct but relayed through the field of the Other, represented by the lozenge ($\Diamond$), which is also the field of the subject's desire. Desire is never a given for any subject, Lacan proposes, but is produced for him or her in the place of the Other, which is also the field of the symbolic, the significatory network of law and social regulation. Importantly, however, the field in which fantasy is enounced moves in a circular fashion, the lozenge is not a unidirectional arrow but flows in either direction both to and from the subject, to and from the fantasmatic object. This figures the same constitutional simultaneity in fantasy as that posited by Laplanche and Pontalis, both a producing and a production of the subject. Clearly, the setting of the subject's desire in fantasy is determined by the structure of the originary fantasy molded by the sociocultural symbolic of which the subject is an heir, but the particular form the fantasy assumes, its fleshing out, as it were, depends on the highly variable social, historical, and psychic specificity of the subject, a specificity capable of articulating dominant fantasmatic scenes in varied, even subversive ways. See Jacques Lacan, *The Four Fundamental Concepts of Psychoanalysis*, trans. Alan Sheridan (Harmondsworth: Penguin, 1979), 185ff.

70 Laplanche and Pontalis, "Fantasy and the Origins of Sexuality," 22.

71 Rose, *Sexuality in the Field of Vision*, 5.

72 Elizabeth Cowie, "Fantasia," *m/f* 9 (1984): 80.

73 Donald Greig, "The Sexual Differentiation of the Hitchcock Text," in *Fantasy and the Cinema*, ed. James Donald (London: British Film Institute, 1989), 175–76.

74 Teresa de Lauretis, *The Practice of Love: Lesbian Sexuality and Perverse Desire* (Bloomington: Indiana University Press, 1994), 140.

75 Cowie, "Fantasia," 102, 91.

76 Lapsley and Westlake, *Film Theory*, 91.

77 De Lauretis, *Practice of Love*, 77.

78 Sigmund Freud, "The Dynamics of Transference," in vol. 12 of *The Standard Edition of the Complete Psychological Works*, trans. James Strachey (London: Hogarth Press, 1959), 100.

79 Jean Laplanche and Jean-Bertrand Pontalis, *The Language of Psychoanalysis*, trans. David Nicholson-Smith (London: Karnac Books, 1988), 317.

80 Kaja Silverman, *Male Subjectivity at the Margins* (New York: Routledge, 1992), 354.

81 Laplanche and Pontalis, *Language of Psychoanalysis*, 317. In a similar vein, Freud, in his essay "The Dynamics of Transference," claims that the "stereotype plate" of unconscious fantasies is "constantly reprinted afresh" in accordance with the subject's "external circumstances" (100).

Chapter Two *Fantasmatic Escapades: Gay Spectatorships and Queer Negotiations of the Hollywood Musical*

1 Alexander Doty, *Making Things Perfectly Queer: Interpreting Mass Culture* (Minneapolis: University of Minnesota Press, 1993), 14.

2 Judith Mayne, *Cinema and Spectatorship* (London: Routledge, 1993), 124.

3 Tony Bennett and Janet Woollacott, *Bond and Beyond: The Political Career of a Popular Hero* (London: Macmillan, 1987), 64.

4 Teresa de Lauretis, *The Practice of Love: Lesbian Sexuality and Perverse Desire* (Bloomington: Indiana University Press, 1994), 130.

5 Al LaValley, "The Great Escape," *American Film* 10.6 (1985): 31.

6 Phillip Brett, "Musicality, Essentialism, and the Closet," in *Queering the Pitch: The New Gay and Lesbian Musicology*, ed. Phillip Brett et al. (New York: Routledge, 1994), 11. See also Wayne R. Dynes, *Homoplexis: A Historical and Cultural Lexicon of Homosexuality* (New York: Gay Academic Union, 1985).

7 Wayne Koestenbaum, *The Queen's Throat: Opera, Homosexuality, and the Mystery of Desire* (New York: Poseidon, 1993), 11.

8 John Thurfitt, "Show Queens," *Outrage* 156 (May 1996): 34.

9   D. A. Miller, *Place for Us: Essay on the Broadway Musical* (Cambridge: Harvard University Press, 1998), 16.

10 Richard Dyer, *Only Entertainment* (London: Routledge, 1992), 18.

11 LaValley, "Great Escape," 29–32.

12 Peter Kemp, "Secret Love (or Gays and Musicals: An Attractive Connection)," in *The Bent Lens: A World Guide to Gay and Lesbian Film*, ed. C. Jackson and P. Tapp (Melbourne: Australian Catalogue Co., 1997), 18.

13 Neil Weiss, letter to the author, San Francisco, 13 April 1994.

14 Jonah Satoa, letter to the author, Sydney, Australia, 2 June 1994.

15 Michael Bronski, *Culture Clash: The Making of Gay Sensibility* (Boston: South End Press, 1984), 92.

16 Take, for example, a recent article by Larry Galbraith wherein he attacks what he loosely terms *camp culture*, that "eclectic . . . instantly recognisable gay culture which can include off-Broadway shows, Hollywood movies (often the older the better), Broadway blockbusters and supper club cabaret." Such a culture is, he suggests, moribund in its "total reliance on nostalgia" and apolitical in its promotion of escapism. He writes: "In a world where gay men can be themselves and live their lives, openly and proudly, there is little need to live their lives through Judy Garland, Hollywood movies or Broadway musicals" ("The Slow Demise of Camp Culture," *Outrage* 146 [1995]: 64).

17 Patricia Mellencamp, "Spectacle and Spectator: Looking through the American Musical Comedy," in *Explorations in Film Theory: Selected Essays from Cine-Tracts*, ed. Ron Burnett (Bloomington: Indiana University Press, 1991), 5; Steve Neale, *Genre* (London: British Film Institute, 1980), 23.

18 Rick Altman, *The American Film Musical* (Bloomington: Indiana University Press, 1989), 35.

19 Mayne, *Cinema and Spectatorship*; and Rhona J. Berenstein, *Attack of the Leading Ladies: Gender, Sexuality, and Spectatorship in Classic Horror Cinema* (New York: Columbia University Press, 1996).

20 Elizabeth Ellsworth, "Illicit Pleasures: Feminist Spectators and *Personal Best*," *Wide Angle* 8.2 (1986): 45–56.

21 LaValley, "Great Escape," 29.

22 Andy Medhurst provides a rather more personal example of these types of gay negotiational practices in his essay on possible gay readings of the British melodrama *The Spanish Gardener*. He recalls how, as a protogay child, he constructed a patently queer reading of this film by focusing on a brief, homoerotically charged scene between Nicholas and José. Medhurst writes: "It's only a fragment, an instant, far too tiny to bear all the weight I want to load on to it, but it's exactly the kind of shred that queer eyes will identify, memorise and cherish" (" 'It's as a Man That You've Failed': Masculinity and Forbidden Desire in *The Spanish Gar-*

dener," in *You Tarzan: Masculinity, Movies, and Men*, ed. Pat Kirkham and Janet Thumim [London: Lawrence and Wishart, 1993], 100).

23 See Kristin Thompson, "The Concept of Cinematic Excess," in *Narrative, Apparatus, Ideology: A Film Theory Reader*, ed. Phil Rosen (Princeton: Princeton University Press, 1986).

24 Stephen Heath, *Questions of Cinema* (London: Macmillan, 1981), 52.

25 Jane Feuer, *The Hollywood Musical* (1982; rpt., Bloomington: Indiana University Press, 1993), 68–69.

26 Mellencamp, "Spectacle and Spectator," 11.

27 See, for example, Teresa de Lauretis, *Alice Doesn't: Feminism, Semiotics, Cinema* (Bloomington: Indiana University Press, 1984).

28 Dana Polan, *Power and Paranoia: History, Narrative, and the American Cinema, 1940–1950* (New York: Columbia University Press, 1986), 302, emphasis added.

29 Sigmund Freud, "A Child Is Being Beaten," in *On Psychopathology*, vol. 10 of *The Pelican Freud Library* (Harmondsworth: Penguin, 1979), 178–79; and "A Case of Homosexuality in a Woman," in *Case Histories II*, vol. 9 of *The Pelican Freud Library* (Harmondsworth: Penguin, 1978), 395.

30 Doty, *Making Things Perfectly Queer*, 3.

31 See, for example, Tim Dean's two essays on queer theory and psychoanalysis: "On the Eve of a Queer Future," *Raritan* 15.1 (1995): 116–34; and "Sex and Syncope," *Raritan* 15.3 (1996): 64–86. See also Christopher Lane, "Psychoanalysis and Sexual Identity," in *Lesbian and Gay Studies: A Critical Introduction*, ed. A. Medhurst and S. R. Munt (London: Cassell, 1997).

32 Altman, *American Film Musical*, 85.

33 Linda Williams, *Hard Core: Power, Pleasure, and the "Frenzy of the Visible"* (Berkeley: University of California Press, 1989), 133.

34 Doty, *Making Things Perfectly Queer*, 10–11.

35 Steve Neale, "Masculinity as Spectacle," *Screen* 24.6 (1983): 14–15.

36 Steven Cohan, " 'Feminizing' the Song-and-Dance Man: Fred Astaire and the Spectacle of Masculinity in the Hollywood Musical," in *Screening the Male: Exploring Masculinities in Hollywood Cinema*, ed. Steven Cohan and Ina Rae Hark (New York: Routledge, 1993).

37 As Les Solomon notes when explaining his own fascination with the musical, "there were a lot of gay overtones in the old MGM musicals of the '50s. It was often quite unbelievable to see these supposedly straight men leaping about the place doing some very effeminate things in some cases" (cited in Phillipe Cahill, "Heavenly Knowledge," *Campaign* 227 [1995]: 66).

38 Annette Kuhn, *The Power of the Image: Essays on Representation and Sexuality* (London: Routledge, 1985), 50.

39 Altman, *American Film Musical*, 290.

40 Carol J. Clover, "Dancin' in the Rain," *Critical Inquiry* 21 (summer 1995): 738–39.

For a broader reading of the history of white cinematic appropriations of African American cultural forms, and one to which Clover's own analysis is indebted, see Michael Rogin, *Blackface, White Noise: Jewish Immigrants in the Hollywood Melting Pot* (Berkeley: University of California Press, 1996).

41 Marjorie Garber, *Vested Interests: Cross-Dressing and Cultural Anxiety* (Harmondsworth: Penguin, 1992), 16.

42 Adrienne L. McLean provides an interesting reading of possible queer investments in the musical's formations of racial otherness in her recent article on the "orientalist" choreography of Jack Cole. Cole was a gay choreographer who worked on a string of Hollywood musicals in the forties and fifties such as *Moon over Miami* (1941), *Kismet* (1955), and *Gentlemen Prefer Blondes* (1953). Heavily influenced by the "oriental dance" tradition of the twenties and thirties, Cole incorporated Middle Eastern and Asian motifs and movements in his choreography. Although recognizing the problematical "orientalism" undergirding Cole's work, McLean argues that Cole mobilized "his Orientalist dance practice as a Camp discourse" through which he was able to express his queer sexuality and articulate a satirical critique of "the hegemony of the great white fathers by emphasizing the physical power and spiritual authority of Arabs, Asians, and women" (Adrienne L. McLean, "The Thousand Ways There Are to Move: Camp and Oriental Dance in the Hollywood Musicals of Jack Cole," in *Visions of the East: Orientalism in Film*, ed. Matthew Bernstein and Gaylyn Studlar [New Brunswick: Rutgers University Press, 1997], 151).

43 On the complex relations between gay cultures, gay men (both black and white), and representations of blackness see Kobena Mercer and Isaac Julien, "Race, Sexual Politics, and Black Masculinity: A Dossier," in *Male Order: Unwrapping Masculinity*, ed. R. Chapman and J. Rutherford (London: Lawrence and Wishart, 1988); and Kobena Mercer, "Skin Head Sex Thing: Racial Difference and the Homoerotic Imaginary," in *How Do I Look? Queer Film and Video*, ed. Bad Object-Choices (Seattle: Bay Press, 1991).

44 Guy Rosolato, cited in Kaja Silverman, *The Acoustic Mirror: The Female Voice in Psychoanalysis and Cinema* (Bloomington: Indiana University Press, 1988), 84–85.

45 Julia Kristeva, *The Revolution of Poetic Language*, trans. M. Waller (New York: Columbia University Press, 1984).

46 Brett, "Musicality, Essentialism, and the Closet," 12. See also Susan McClary, *Feminine Endings: Music, Gender, and Sexuality* (Minneapolis: University of Minnesota Press, 1991); and Renee Cox, "Recovering *Jouissance:* An Introduction to Feminist Musical Aesthetics," in *Women and Music: A History*, ed. Karen Pendle (Bloomington: Indiana University Press, 1991).

47 Edward Baron Turk, "Deriding the Voice of Jeanette MacDonald: Notes on Psychoanalysis and the American Film Musical," *Camera Obscura* 25–26 (1991): 237–45.

48 Miller, *Place for Us*, 90.

49 Koestenbaum, *Queen's Throat*, 32–33.

50 See Martin Rubin, *Showstoppers: Busby Berkeley and the Tradition of Spectacle* (New York: Columbia University Press, 1993).

51 Harold Beaver, "Homosexual Signs," *Critical Inquiry* 8.1 (autumn 1982): 105.

52 See, for example, Peter Stallybrass and Allon White, *The Politics and Poetics of Transgression* (Ithaca: Cornell University Press, 1986).

53 Mellencamp, "Spectacle and Spectator," 11.

54 Feuer, *Hollywood Musical*, 68.

55 LaValley, "Great Escape," 31. Several commentators have used the notion of camp to explain and evaluate the appeal of the musical for gay spectators. I have preferred to bracket out the notion of camp in my own discussions here, as camp is the focus of the next chapter. However, my own readings of gay engagements with the musical in terms of queer excess offer significant correspondences with readings of the musical as camp. For a fascinating take on the question of camp, musicals, and gay appeal see Matthew Tinkcom, "Working Like a Homosexual: Camp Visual Codes and the Labor of Gay Subjects in the MGM Freed Unit," *Cinema Journal* 35.1 (1996): 24–42.

56 Feuer, "Postscript," 141.

57 Ted Sennett, *Hollywood Musicals* (New York: Henry H. Abrams, 1981), 229–32.

58 Richard Dyer, *Heavenly Bodies: Film Stars and Society* (New York: St. Martin's Press, 1986), 142–43.

59 Janet Staiger, *Interpreting Films: Studies in the Historical Reception of American Cinema* (Princeton: Princeton University Press, 1992), 165.

60 Bruce Babington and Peter William Evans, *Blue Skies and Silver Linings: Aspects of the Hollywood Musical* (Manchester: Manchester University Press, 1985), 205–6. See also Thomas Elsaesser, "Vincente Minnelli," in *Genre: The Musical*, ed. Rick Altman (London: RKP, 1981).

61 Dyer, *Heavenly Bodies*, 142ff.

62 D. N. Rodowick analyzes the enunciative structures of the opening scene of *The Pirate* in "Vision, Desire, and the Film-Text," *Camera Obscura* 6 (1980): 54–89.

63 Although the erotic specularization of Serafin achieves its most obvious instance in the rotunda dance, the whole sequence tends to frame Serafin within a marked economy of specularization. Much of this is a direct result of the sequence's cinematographic form, for it is played out entirely in a series of very elaborately choreographed long takes, with a mobile camera weaving around the set as it follows Serafin. Although there are several cuts, they are minimal and generally unobtrusive. The whole sequence thus has a decidedly "stagey" feel, which in turn heightens the sense that Serafin is on show, there to be looked at. This overt spectacular framing of Serafin reoccurs in the later "Pirate" dream sequence.

64 Polan, *Power and Paranoia*, 293.

Chapter Three *Camping under the Stars: Gay Spectatorships,*
Camp, and the Excessive Female Star Image

1 Pierre Bourdieu, *Distinction: A Social Critique of the Judgement of Taste*, trans. Richard Nice (Cambridge: Harvard University Press, 1984), 466.

2 For an overview of cultural configurations of camp taste in nongay contexts see Andrew Ross, "Uses of Camp," in *No Respect: Intellectuals and Popular Culture* (New York: Routledge, 1989).

3 Susan Sontag, "Notes on Camp," in *A Susan Sontag Reader* (1964; rpt., Harmondsworth: Penguin, 1983), 106.

4 See, for example, Sontag, "Notes on Camp"; Mark Booth, *Camp* (New York: Quartet, 1983); and Phillip Core, *Camp: The Lie That Tells the Truth* (New York: Delilah, 1984).

5 Andrew Britton, *Katharine Hepburn: Star as Feminist* (London: Studio Vista, 1995), 87.

6 Sontag, "Notes on Camp," 107.

7 Britton, *Katharine Hepburn*, 40. See also Andrew Britton, "For Interpretation: Notes against Camp," *Gay Left* 7 (winter 1978–79): n.p.

8 This slippage endangers my own discussions. Although, as my framing proposition that we read camp as a discourse of gay taste suggests, I view camp less as an essential property of objects or texts than as a constructed effect of particular ways of reading, I am still well aware that occasionally in this chapter I speak of various texts as if they were essentially camp in and of themselves. This is a direct result of the performative nature of camp being discussed here.

9 Sontag, "Notes on Camp," 109–15.

10 George Burnett, "The ABC of Camp," *I-D* (January–February 1986): 42.

11 Jonathan Dollimore, *Sexual Dissidence: Augustine to Wilde, Freud to Foucault* (Oxford: Oxford University Press, 1991), 311–12.

12 Sontag, "Notes on Camp," 109.

13 Jack Babuscio, "Camp and the Gay Sensibility," in *Gays and Film*, ed. Richard Dyer (London: Zoetrope, 1984), 46.

14 Michael Bronski, *Culture Clash: The Making of Gay Sensibility* (Boston: South End Press, 1984), 46.

15 Babuscio, "Camp and the Gay Sensibility," 44–45.

16 That the argument here refers to both gay and lesbian formations of camp is an important point. Even though most studies of gay camp—my own included—concentrate on gay male contexts, camp has a rich, if undertheorized, tradition within lesbian contexts as well. For recent attempts to locate and analyze the histories of camp in lesbian cultures see Sue-Ellen Case, "Towards a Butch-Femme Aesthetic," *Discourse* 11.1 (1988–89): 55–73; Andrea Weiss, *Vampires and Violets: Lesbians in the Cinema* (London: Jonathan Cape, 1992); and Paula Graham,

"Girl's Camp? The Politics of Parody," in *Immortal Invisible: Lesbians and the Moving Image*, ed. Tamsin Wilton (London: Routledge, 1995).

17   Cynthia Morrill, "Revamping the Gay Sensibility: Queer Camp and *dyke noir*," in *The Politics and Poetics of Camp*, ed. Moe Meyer (London: Routledge, 1993), 119.

18   Bourdieu, *Distinction*, 466–67.

19   Richard Dyer, *Only Entertainment* (New York: Routledge, 1992), 135.

20   Jean Laplanche and Jean-Bertrand Pontalis, *The Language of Psychoanalysis*, trans. David Nicholson-Smith (London: Karnac Books, 1988), 28.

21   John Fletcher, "Freud and His Uses: Psychoanalysis and Gay Theory," in *Coming on Strong: Gay Politics and Culture*, ed. Simon Shepherd and Mick Wallis (London: Unwin Hyman, 1989), 101.

22   Sigmund Freud, *On Psychopathology*, vol. 10 of *The Pelican Freud Library* (Harmondsworth: Penguin, 1979), 206.

23   Sigmund Freud, *Introductory Lectures on Psychoanalysis*, vol. 1 of *The Pelican Freud Library* (Harmondsworth: Penguin, 1973), 345.

24   Kenneth Lewes, *The Psychoanalytic Theory of Male Homosexuality* (London: Quartet, 1989), 77.

25   Irving Bieber, *Homosexuality: A Psychoanalytic Study of Male Homosexuals* (New York: Basic Books, 1962), 113.

26   Mark J. Adair, "A Speculation on Perversion and Hallucination," *International Journal of Psycho-Analysis* 74 (1993): 81.

27   Julia Kristeva, "The Other of Sex," in *The Kristeva Reader*, ed. Toril Moi (Oxford: Blackwell, 1986), 145. Judith Butler provides an incisive critique of these and other homophobic formulations in Kristeva in *Gender Trouble: Feminism and the Subversion of Identity* (London: Routledge, 1990), 84ff.

28   Jane Gallop, *Thinking through the Body* (New York: Columbia University Press, 1988), 110–13.

29   Fletcher, "Freud and His Uses," 105.

30   As Freud himself continuously—if not always coherently—stressed, "from the point of view of psychoanalysis" heterosexuality is "not a self-evident fact" grounded in biology but a cultural construct that is, thus, as much "a problem that needs elucidating" as any of the so-called perverse forms of sexuality ("Three Essays," in *On Sexuality*, vol. 7 of *The Pelican Freud Library* [Harmondsworth: Penguin, 1976], 57).

31   Fletcher, "Freud and His Uses," 104.

32   See Juliet Mitchell's description of hysteria as "the woman's simultaneous acceptance and refusal of the organization of sexuality under patriarchal capitalism. It is simultaneously what a woman can do both to be feminine and to refuse femininity, within patriarchal discourse" (*The Longest Revolution* [London: Virago, 1984], 289).

33 This is where my framing concept of the fantasmatic can provide an important safeguard. By defining gay psychocultural specificity through a radically unlocalizable field of variable elements whose articulation in and for any specific "instance" (in this case, any individual subject) can never be determined or known in advance, the notion of the fantasmatic ensures that no single model of or statement about gayness can ever be assumed as universal or absolute. If read through the notion of the fantasmatic, psychoanalytic speculations about the etiology or psychodynamics of male homosexuality such as those outlined here emerge as analytic reconstructions that bear no necessary relation to the organization of homosexuality as either a "whole" or in any of its diverse configurations in the contingent performances of individual gay subjectivities.

34 Ann Cvekovitch, "The Powers of Seeing and Being Seen: *Truth or Dare* and *Paris Is Burning*," in *Film Theory Goes to the Movies*, ed. Jim Collins et al. (London: Routledge, 1993), 158.

35 David Bergman, introduction to *Camp Grounds: Style and Homosexuality*, ed. David Bergman (Amherst: University of Massachusetts Press, 1993), 11.

36 Butler, *Gender Trouble*, 31, 137–38.

37 Judith Butler, "Imitation and Gender Insubordination," in *Inside/Out: Lesbian Theories, Gay Theories*, ed. Diana Fuss (New York: Routledge, 1991), 23.

38 David Carroll, "Narrative, Heterogeneity, and the Question of the Political: Bakhtin and Lyotard," in *The Aims of Representation: Subject/Text/History*, ed. M. Krieger (New York: Columbia University Press, 1989), 95.

39 Babuscio, "Camp and the Gay Sensibility," 46.

40 Sontag, "Notes on Camp," 107. See also Carol-Ann Tyler, "Boys Will Be Girls: The Politics of Gay Drag" in Fuss, *Inside/Out*. Later in this chapter I address in further detail critiques of gay camp.

41 David Bergman, "Strategic Camp: The Art of Gay Rhetoric," in *Camp Grounds*, 106.

42 Butler, *Gender Trouble*, 31.

43 The single most comprehensive analysis of the signifying structures of Hollywood stardom is Richard Dyer's *Stars* (London: British Film Institute, 1979); see also the essays collected in Christine Gledhill, ed., *Stardom: Industry of Desire* (London: Routledge, 1991).

44 Annette Kuhn, *The Power of the Image: Essays on Representation and Sexuality* (London: Routledge, 1985), 52.

45 Dyer, *Stars*, 16.

46 Sontag, "Notes on Camp," 109.

47 Babuscio, "Camp and the Gay Sensibility," 45–46; Bronski, *Culture Clash*, 97–99.

48 Ross, *No Respect*, 159.

49 Recent examples of explicitly queer camp readings of male stars as gender perfor-

mative can be found, however, in Jonathan Goldberg, "Recalling Totalities: The Mirrored Stages of Arnold Schwarzenegger," *differences* 4.1 (1992): 172–204; and Chris Holmlund, "Masculinity as Multiple Masquerade: The 'Mature' Stallone and the Stallone Clone," in *Screening the Male: Exploring Masculinities in Hollywood Cinema*, ed. Steven Cohan and Ina Rae Hark (New York: Routledge, 1993). Although these essays are written by a gay male and a lesbian critic who actively foreground their queer identifications, they tend to cast their readings more in the spirit of academic camp than popular gay or lesbian camp. Holmlund, in fact, acknowledges that her kind of "perverse interrogation" is largely motivated by academic and political interests and that the heterosexual male genre films and star-images she deconstructs would have limited appeal for gay- or lesbian-identifying spectators.

50   Paul Roen, *High Camp: A Gay Guide to Camp and Cult Films*, vol. 1 (San Francisco: Leyland Publications, 1994), 18.

51   Kaja Silverman, *Male Subjectivity at the Margins* (New York: Routledge, 1992), 353.

52   Alexander Doty, *Making Things Perfectly Queer: Interpreting Mass Culture* (Minneapolis: University of Minnesota Press, 1993), 6.

53   Bronski, *Culture Clash*, 95–96.

54   In addition to the works discussed below, see also Julie Burchill, "Homosexuals' Girls," in *Girls on Film* (New York: Pantheon, 1986); Tyler, "Boys Will Be Girls;" Sheila Jeffries, "The Queer Disappearance of Lesbians; Sexuality in the Academy," *Women's Studies International Forum* 17.5 (1994): 459–72; and Caryl Flinn, "The Deaths of Camp," *Camera Obscura* 35 (1996): 53–84.

55   Britton, *Katharine Hepburn*, 88.

56   Marilyn Frye, *The Politics of Reality: Essays in Feminist Theory* (Trumansburg, N.Y.: Crossing Press, 1983), 137–38.

57   Butler, *Gender Trouble*, 21.

58   Doty, *Making Things Perfectly Queer*, 84.

59   Butler, *Gender Trouble*, 122.

60   Michael Moon, "Flaming Closets," in *A Small Boy and Others: Imitation and Initiation in American Culture from Henry James to Andy Warhol* (Durham: Duke University Press, 1998), 86.

61   Wayne Koestenbaum, *The Queen's Throat: Opera, Homosexuality, and the Mystery of Desire* (New York: Poseidon, 1993), 18.

62   This is a reference to John Fletcher's characterization of the oedipal law of sexual polarity discussed earlier as "you cannot be what you desire, you cannot desire what you wish to be" ("Freud and His Uses," 101).

63   Molly Haskell, *From Reverence to Rape: The Treatment of Women in the Movies* (New York: Holt, Rinehart and Winston, 1974), 214.

64   Ross, *No Respect*, 139.

65   Roen, *High Camp*, 14.

66   See Marybeth Hamilton, *The Queen of Camp: Mae West, Sex, and Popular Culture* (London: Pandora, 1995), 120ff.

67   Esther Newton, *Mother Camp: Female Impersonators in America* (Chicago: University of Chicago Press, 1972).

68   George Eells and Stanley Musgrove, *Mae West: A Biography* (London: Paladin, 1986), 177.

69   See, for example, Hamilton, *Queen of Camp;* Maurice Leonard, *Mae West: The Empress of Sex* (London: Fontana, 1992); June Sochen, *Mae West: She Who Laughs Last* (New York: Harlan Davidson, 1992); Ramona Curry, *Too Much of a Good Thing: Mae West as Cultural Icon* (Minneapolis: University of Minnesota Press, 1996); Pamela Robertson, *Guilty Pleasures: Feminist Camp from Mae West to Madonna* (Durham: Duke University Press, 1996); and Emily Wortis Leider, *Becoming Mae West* (New York: Farrar, Straus and Giroux, 1997).

70   Curry, *Too Much of a Good Thing*, 4.

71   Cited in Hamilton, *Queen of Camp*, 136.

72   See Bronski, *Culture Clash*, 98; and Kenneth Anger, *Hollywood Babylon* (San Francisco: Straight Arrow Books, 1975). Many of her biographers claim that West actually copied much of her style from gay female impersonators of her acquaintance, especially Bert Savoy and Julian Eltinge, when she was developing her famous persona in New York during the teens and twenties. See, for example, Leonard, *Mae West*, 70ff.

73   Joan Mellen, *Women and Their Sexuality in the New Film* (New York: Horizon, 1973), 243.

74   Robertson, *Guilty Pleasures*, 29.

75   Parker Tyler, *Screening the Sexes: Homosexuality in the Movies*, rev. ed. (New York: Da Capo, 1993), 353.

76   That contemporary camp readings of West are still predicated on a central logic of idealizing gay identification is clearly illustrated in Paul Roen's recent series of best-selling books, *High Camp: A Gay Guide to Camp and Cult Films*, vols. 1, 2 (San Francisco: Leyland Publications, 1994, 1997). Like Tyler, Roen is an obvious fan of West, whom he describes as "one of the catalytic gay icons," and his appraisals of her and her films are, to say the least, enthusiastic. Roen is the author of the statement cited earlier in this chapter that Mae West is "like a gay man trapped in a woman's body" (*High Camp*, 1:14).

77   Robertson, *Guilty Pleasures*, 29–33.

78   Roen, *High Camp*, 2:19.

79   Kaja Silverman, *The Acoustic Mirror: The Female Voice in Psychoanalysis and Cinema* (Bloomington: Indiana University Press, 1988), 61.

80   Cited in Hamilton, *Queen of Camp*, 176.

81 William Stewart, *Cassell's Queer Companion: A Dictionary of Lesbian and Gay Life and Culture* (London: Cassell, 1995), 269.

82 Robertson, *Guilty Pleasures*, 26–27.

83 Curry, *Too Much of a Good Thing*, 114, 121.

84 Molly Haskell, "Mae West's Spirit Spans the Gay 90s," *New York Times*, 15 August 1993, sec. 2, 15.

85 Robertson, *Guilty Pleasures*, 53.

86 Mary Russo, *The Female Grotesque: Risk, Excess, and Modernity* (New York: Routledge, 1994), 56ff.

87 Al LaValley, "The Great Escape: Gays and Film," *American Film* 10.6 (1985): 32.

88 Both LaValley ("Great Escape," 33) and Babuscio ("Camp and the Gay Sensibility," 42) discuss horror as an important genre for gay camp readings. On the female grotesque in contemporary cinematic horror see Barbara Creed, *The Monstrous-Feminine: Film, Feminism, Psychoanalysis* (London: Routledge, 1993).

89 A discourse of the female grotesque has been central to West's persona and performance style from the very beginning. This is even true of the more specific trope of the aging female grotesque. It is often forgotten that West was already forty years old by the time she made her first film and was fifty when she starred in the last of her classic studio films in 1943. Although not old by conventional standards, it is by those of Hollywood, especially for a female star who, like West, was playing the role of the sexually attractive woman, often opposite men many years younger. In this sense, *Myra Breckinridge* and *Sextette* are simply continuing the same concerns, strategies, and effects of West's earlier persona, albeit taking them to new extremes.

90 Curry, *Too Much of a Good Thing*, 138.

91 Cited in Boze Hadleigh, *The Lavender Screen: The Gay and Lesbian Films* (New York: Citadel, 1993), 109–10.

92 Anonymous, "Some Sort of Nadir," *Time*, 6 July 1970, 70.

93 Vincent Canby, "Screen: Mae West, 87, Does an Encore," *New York Times*, 8 June 1979, sec. 3, 10.

94 The grotesque figure of the monster in the horror film, for example, is often metaphorically associated with the "excessive" sexualities of both women and homosexuals. See Linda Williams, "When the Woman Looks," in *Re-Vision: Essays in Feminist Film Criticism*, ed. Mary Ann Doane, Patricia Mellencamp, and Linda Williams (Frederick, Md.: University Publications of America, 1984); and Rhona J. Berenstein, *Attack of the Leading Ladies: Gender, Sexuality, and Spectatorship in Classic Horror Cinema* (New York: Columbia University Press, 1996). This latter work is particularly interesting because it mounts an explicit argument for the grotesque as a site of identification for gay and lesbian spectators.

95 Madonna Kolschenblag, "The Female Grotesque: Gargoyles in the Cathedrals of Cinema," *Journal of Popular Film* 6.4 (1978): 329.

96 Roen, *High Camp*, 1:183.

97 Tyler, *Screening the Sexes*, 1.

98 Michael Moon and Eve Kosofsky Sedgwick, "Divinity: A Dossier, a Performance Piece, a Little Understood," *Discourse* 13.1 (1990–91): 27.

Chapter Four *Mommie Dearest: Gay Spectatorships and Formations of Maternal-Oriented Desire*

1 On the significance of *Brief Encounter* for gay spectatorships and gay male subcultures see Andy Medhurst, "That Special Thrill: *Brief Encounter,* Homosexuality, and Authorship," *Screen* 32.2 (1991): 197–208.

2 Eve Kosofsky Sedgwick, *The Epistemology of the Closet* (Berkeley: University of California Press, 1990), 41.

3 Teresa de Lauretis, *The Practice of Love: Lesbian Sexuality and Perverse Desire* (Bloomington: Indiana University Press, 1994), xiv.

4 Sigmund Freud, "Three Essays," in *On Sexuality,* vol. 7 of *The Pelican Freud Library* (Harmondsworth: Penguin, 1977), 56n.

5 Sigmund Freud, "Leonardo da Vinci and a Memory of his Childhood," in *On Art and Literature,* vol. 14 of *The Pelican Freud Library* (Harmondsworth: Penguin, 1985), 191.

6 Madelon Sprengnether, *The Spectral Mother: Freud, Feminism, and Psychoanalysis* (Ithaca: Cornell University Press, 1990), 75.

7 Freud, "Leonardo da Vinci," 209.

8 Monique Plaza, "The Mother/The Same: The Hatred of the Mother in Psychoanalysis," *Feminist Issues* 2.1 (1982): 77.

9 See Henry Abelove, "Freud, Male Homosexuality, and the Americans," *Dissent* 33.1 (1985–86): 59–69; and Thomas Domenici and Ronnie C. Lesser, eds., *Disorienting Sexuality: Psychoanalytic Reappraisals of Sexual Identities* (New York: Routledge, 1995).

10 Freud, "Three Essays," 57.

11 Malcolm Bowie, *Lacan* (London: Fontana, 1991), 127.

12 Jacques Lacan, "Intervention on Transference," *Female Sexuality: Jacques Lacan and the Ecole Freudienne,* ed. Juliet Mitchell and Jacqueline Rose (London: Macmillan, 1982), 69.

13 John Fletcher, "Freud and His Uses: Psychoanalysis and Gay Theory," in *Coming on Strong: Gay Politics and Culture,* ed. Simon Shepherd and Mick Wallis (London: Unwin Hyman, 1989), 112–13.

14 Leo Bersani, *Homos* (Cambridge: Harvard University Press, 1995), 61.

15 Kaja Silverman, *Male Subjectivity at the Margins* (New York: Routledge, 1992), 362.

16 Linda Williams, " 'Something Else besides a Mother': *Stella Dallas* and the Maternal Melodrama," in *Home Is Where the Heart Is: Studies in Melodrama and the Woman's Film*, ed. Christine Gledhill (London: British Film Institute, 1987), 316.

17 Richard Friedel, *The Movie Lover* (Boston: Alyson, 1981); Dick Scanlan, *Does Freddy Dance* (Boston: Alyson, 1995).

18 David Pendleton, "My Mother, the Cinema," *Wide Angle* 15.2 (1993): 40.

19 Patrick E. Horrigan, *Widescreen Dreams: Growing Up Gay at the Movies* (Madison: University of Wisconsin Press, 1999), xv.

20 This brief letter appeared in mid- to late 1994 in *Outrage, Campaign, Queensland Pride, The Advocate.* The letter was purposefully broad, patterned largely after Ien Ang's exemplary model in *Watching Dallas: Soap Opera and the Melodramatic Imagination* (London: Methuen, 1985). In keeping with Ang's strategy of minimal guidance, my letter stated simply that I was developing a research project on the relations between gay men and cinema, and that I was interested in hearing from any gay men who would like to share their views on film. I suggested that I was especially interested to hear about their various likes and dislikes in terms of films, stars, genres, and so on, and any special memories that they may have of film and/or filmgoing.

21 Ken Schessler, letter to author, Brisbane, Australia, 2 August, 1994.

22 Tony Donnelly, letter to author, Brisbane, Australia, 26 August 1994.

23 Mike Stein, letter to author, Seattle, Wash., 14 February, 1995.

24 Paul Lawrence, letter to author, San Diego, Calif., 11 January 1995; Phillip Bell, letter to author, Sydney, Australia, 28 June 1994. Michael Lambert, letter to author, Maryborough, Australia, 11 April 1994.

25 Sigmund Freud, "Some Notes on the 'Mystic Writing-Pad,' " in *On Metapsychology*, vol. 11 of *The Pelican Freud Library* (Harmondsworth: Penguin, 1984), 429–34.

26 Sigmund Freud, *The Origins of Psychoanalysis: Letters to Wilhelm Fliess, 1887–1904*, trans. and ed. Jeffrey Masson (Cambridge: Harvard University Press, 1985), 173.

27 Michel de Certeau, *Heterologies: Discourse on the Other*, trans. Brian Massumi (Minneapolis: University of Minnesota Press, 1986), 4.

28 This is the process of "nachträglichkeit," or "retroactivity," the concept used by Freud and Lacan to explain the nonlinear temporality of psychic reality. As I introduced this concept in chapter 1, as a model for (re)thinking the structural relations of the fantasmatic, the concept of retroactivity represents the structure of psychic reality as one that turns on the constitutive logic of the future anterior, the continuous inscription and reinscription of the past as determinative of the present.

29 Pendleton, "My Mother, the Cinema," 40–41.

30 Jean-Louis Baudry, "The Apparatus," *Camera Obscura* 1 (1976): 97–126; and Christian Metz, *The Imaginary Signifier: Psychoanalysis and the Cinema*, trans. Celia Britton et al. (Bloomington: Indiana University Press, 1982).

31 Laura Mulvey, "Visual Pleasure and Narrative Cinema," *Screen* 16.3 (1975): 6–18.

32 Jacqueline Rose, *Sexuality in the Field of Vision* (London: Verso, 1986), 53.

33 E. Ann Kaplan, *Motherhood and Representation: The Mother in Popular Culture and Melodrama* (New York: Routledge, 1992), 28.

34 Pendleton, "My Mother, the Cinema," 44.

35 Graeme Loyer, letter to author, Maryborough, Australia, 11 April 1996.

36 Schessler, letter to author.

37 Jaffe Cohen, Danny McWilliams, and Bob Smith, *Growing Up Gay: From Left Out to Coming Out* (New York: Hyperion, 1995), 156–57, emphasis added.

38 Roland Barthes, *Camera Lucida: Reflections on Photography*, trans. Richard Howard (London: Fontana, 1984), 65. For a reading of the potential queer resonances of Barthes in terms of both his work and his biography as a gay man see D. A. Miller, *Bringing Out Roland Barthes* (Berkeley: University of California Press, 1992).

39 Barthes, *Camera Lucida*, 67.

40 Horrigan, *Widescreen Dreams*, 73.

41 These physical characteristics are shared by two other female stars with whom I have a particularly strong personal fascination, Deborah Kerr and Greer Garson.

42 I am not alone in my queer matrocentric adoration of Julie Andrews. Both Patrick Horrigan and Wayne Koestenbaum suggest the presence of a similarly maternal-centered fantasmatic scenario at work in their queer responses to her. Horrigan devotes an entire chapter of his spectatorial memoirs to *The Sound of Music*, a film that, he writes, "my mother and I both love." He argues that his "childhood obsession" with the film turned on a fantasy structure involving "a trinity of female mentors, liberators, and role models — Maria von Trapp, as played and sung by Julie Andrews; my piano teacher, Mrs. Hasbrouck; and my mother," all of whom, he claims, "helped me find my place in the world" (*Widescreen Dreams*, 21, xviii). In his book on gay subcultural relations to opera, Koestenbaum writes that "Julie Andrews prepared me for opera and homosexuality . . . because she was a nanny in *Mary Poppins* and a governess in *The Sound of Music*, because her haircut was short and mannish, like my mother's, and because her voice, like my idea of opera, confidently checkered the air with summary, silver, emotionless bellicosity" (*The Queen's Voice: Opera, Homosexuality, and the Mystery of Desire* [New York: Poseidon, 1993], 11).

43 Gaylyn Studlar, "Masochism, Masquerade, and the Erotic Metamorphoses of Marlene Dietrich," in *Fabrications: Costume and the Female Body*, ed. Jane Gaines and Charlotte Herzog (New York: Routledge, 1990), 238. See also Gaylyn Stud-

lar, *In the Realm of Pleasure: Dietrich, Von Sternberg, and the Masochistic Aesthetic* (New York: Columbia University Press, 1988).

44 Edward Baron Turk, "Deriding the Voice of Jeanette MacDonald: Notes on Psychoanalysis and the American Film Musical," *Camera Obscura* 25–26 (1991): 245.

45 Peter Matthews, "Garbo and Phallic Motherhood: A 'Homosexual' Visual Economy," *Screen* 29.3 (1988): 22.

46 Medhurst, "That Special Thrill," 198.

47 Mark Finch and Richard Kwietniowski, "Melodrama and *Maurice:* Homo Is Where the Het Is," *Screen* 29.3 (1988): 73.

48 Geoffrey Nowell-Smith, "Minnelli and Melodrama," in Gledhill, *Home Is Where the Heart Is,* 74. For complementary readings of the melodrama as a genre of excess see the essays by Thomas Elsaesser and D. N. Rodowick also in this collection.

49 Naomi Scheman, "Missing Mothers/Desiring Daughters: Framing the Sight of Women," *Critical Inquiry* 15 (1988): 77.

50 Mary Ann Doane, *The Desire to Desire: The Woman's Film of the 1940s* (Bloomington: Indiana University Press, 1987), 71.

51 Williams, "Something Else besides a Mother," 320. Joan Copjec produces a rather different, but nevertheless complementary, reading of the melodrama as a genre with constitutive feminine psychic resonances in her recent essay "More! From Melodrama to Magnitude," in *Endless Night: Cinema and Psychoanalysis, Parallel Histories,* ed. J. Bergstrom (Berkeley: University of California Press, 1999): 249–72.

52 Doane, *Desire to Desire,* 78.

53 Philip Wylie, *A Generation of Vipers* (New York: Farrar, 1942), 185. Although Wylie's book was actually published during the war, it was not until the late forties and fifties that the reading of "momism" it presents penetrated the public imagination in any real sense, which is why I read it as a contribution to and symptom of postwar discourses of the maternal.

54 Cited in Lucy Fischer, "Mama's Boy: Filial Hysteria in *White Heat,*" in *Screening the Male: Exploring Masculinities in Hollywood Cinema,* ed. Steven Cohan and Ina Rae Hark (New York: Routledge, 1993), 81. Fischer's essay provides a brief but incisive reading of the rise of debates over "momism" in postwar America.

55 Cited in Fischer, "Mama's Boy," 81.

56 Wylie, *Generation of Vipers,* 43.

57 Cited in Fischer, "Mama's Boy," 81.

58 Lee Edelman, "Tearooms and Sympathy, or, The Epistemology of the Water Closet," in *The Lesbian and Gay Studies Reader,* ed. Henry Abelove, Michele Aina Barale, and David M. Halperin (New York: Routledge, 1993), 568.

59 Other melodramatic films from this period that explore issues surrounding the

maternal and male homosexuality, either by way of direct diegetic focus or indirect thematic subtext, include *A Streetcar Named Desire* (1951), *My Son John* (1952), *Indiscretion of an American Wife* (1953), *All That Heaven Allows* (1955), *Tea and Sympathy* (1956), *The Roman Spring of Mrs. Stone* (1961), *Sweet Bird of Youth* (1962), *Five Finger Exercise* (1962), and *Of Love and Desire* (1963).

60 Kaplan, *Motherhood and Representation*, 115.

61 Doane, *Desire to Desire*, 81–82.

62 Christine Gledhill, "Pleasurable Negotiations," in *Female Spectators: Looking at Film and Television*, ed. E. Dierdre Pribram (London: Verso, 1988), 68.

63 Vito Russo, *The Celluloid Closet: Homosexuality in the Movies*, rev. ed. (New York: Harper and Row, 1987), 116.

64 Cited in Boze Hadleigh, *The Lavender Screen: The Gay and Lesbian Films* (New York: Citadel, 1993), 28.

65 Cited in Russo, *Celluloid Closet*, 117–18.

66 Cited in ibid., 116. For an account of the "history" of the censorship of homosexual subject matter in classic Hollywood film production see Chris Noriega, "'Something's Missing Here!': Homosexuality and Film Reviews during the Production Code Era, 1934–1962," *Cinema Journal* 30.1 (1990): 20–41.

67 Vito Russo suggests that this rather unusual approach was a result of the Production Code's caveat to the filmmakers that they could "infer" but not "directly show" homosexuality (*Celluloid Closet*, 116). Boze Hadleigh, however, argues that it was more likely the result of writer Tennessee Williams's conviction that Sebastian was "too stunning to be portrayed by an actor, that his presence would be felt more strikingly via his absence"—an argument that is lent further credence by the fact that Williams's original one-act play from which the film was adapted similarly refrains from ever showing Sebastian on stage (*Lavender Screen*, 27).

68 D. A. Miller, "Anal *Rope*," in *Inside/Out: Lesbian Theories, Gay Theories*, ed. Diana Fuss (New York: Routledge, 1991), 125.

69 D. A. Miller, "Visual Pleasure in 1959," in *Out Takes: Essays on Queer Theory and Film*, ed. Ellis Hanson (Durham: Duke University Press, 1999), 103.

70 Notably, Vito Russo was widely criticized by many gay readers of his best-selling study, *The Celluloid Closet*, for his unquestioning dismissal of *Suddenly, Last Summer* as a "denigrating," "tortured view" of homosexuality. Many readers felt that he was being "too literal-minded in his approach" and that he "wilfully ignored the poetry and symbolism" of the film. See Paul Roen, *High Camp: A Gay Guide to Camp and Cult Films*, vol. 1 (San Francisco: Leyland Publications, 1994), 209.

71 Laura Mulvey, "Notes on Sirk and Melodrama," in Gledhill, *Home Is Where the Heart Is*, 76.

72 In relation to the issue of matrocentrism, Clift was widely reputed to have had an extraordinarily close relationship with his own mother, Sunny. Nearly all the

available biographies of Clift focus on this relationship as an influential one in his life and career. Indeed, biographer Patricia Bosworth writes that Clift felt rather uncomfortable at times during the making of *Suddenly, Last Summer,* as it seemed, in many ways, "like a case of art imitating life" (*Montgomery Clift: A Biography* [New York: Harcourt Brace Jovanovich, 1978], 342).

73 Hadleigh, *Lavender Screen,* 28.

74 On the gay popularization of *Sunset Boulevard* see Al LaValley, "The Great Escape: Gays and Film," *American Film* 10.6 (1985): 28–34; Devon Clayton, "Put the Blame on Mame: The Movie Characters That Made Us Gay," *The Advocate,* 7 November 1988, 47–51; and Roen, *High Camp,* 1:212–14.

75 See, for example, Matthews, "Garbo and Phallic Motherhood"; and Tania Modleski, "Time and Desire in the Woman's Film," in Gledhill, *Home Is Where the Heart Is.*

76 Matthews, "Garbo and Phallic Motherhood," 22.

77 Significantly, the film produces this uncanny coding of Max through many of the same generic elements of cinematographic horror referred to earlier. Indeed, Max's representation seems styled after the classic vampire film figure of the "faithful retainer" who does the monstrous "master's" bidding, right down to a thick, middle-European accent and a penchant for playing pipe organs.

78 Kaplan, *Motherhood and Representation,* 77.

79 LaValley, "Great Escape," 34.

80 David Clinton, "Gayzing at the Screen," *Different Fruits* 3 (1987): 16.

81 Roen, *High Camp,* 1:213–14.

82 In the reading I am advancing here, this final blurred close-up of Norma is particularly significant, for it may be seen to replicate the "blurred" gaze at the mother's face of the young infant in its prefocus stage.

Chapter Five *Papa, Can't You See That I'm Flaming?
Gay Spectatorships and Figures of Masculinity*

1 Marilyn Frye, *The Politics of Reality: Essays in Feminist Theory* (Trumansburg, N.Y.: Crossing Press, 1983), 138. Similar arguments have also been made by other feminist critics from Luce Irigaray and Julia Kristeva to Jane Gallop. For an overview and a respectful gay critique of these arguments see Craig Owens, "Outlaws: Gay Men in Feminism," in *Men in Feminism,* ed. Alice Jardine and Paul Smith (London: Methuen, 1987).

2 Kaja Silverman, *Male Subjectivity at the Margins* (New York: Routledge, 1992), 344.

3 Jonathan Dollimore, *Sexual Dissidence: Augustine to Wilde, Freud to Foucault* (Oxford: Oxford University Press, 1991), 33.

4 John Fletcher, "Freud and His Uses: Psychoanalysis and Gay Theory," in *Coming*

on Strong: Gay Politics and Culture, ed. Simon Shepherd and Mick Wallis (London: Unwin Hyman, 1989), 112.

5 Cited in ibid., 112.

6 Cited in ibid., 113.

7 Francis Pasche, "Symposium on Homosexuality (ii)," *International Journal of Psycho-analysis* 45 (1964): 211.

8 D. A. Miller, "Anal *Rope*," in *Inside/Out: Lesbian Theories, Gay Theories*, ed. Diana Fuss (New York: Routledge, 1991), 134.

9 Michael Moon and Eve Kosofsky Sedgwick, "Divinity: A Dossier, a Performance Piece, a Little Understood Emotion," in *Tendencies*, Eve Kosofsky Sedgwick (Durham: Duke University Press, 1993), 246–47.

10 Sigmund Freud, "On the Sexual Theories of Children" and "Character and Anal Erotism," in *On Sexuality*, vol. 7 of *The Pelican Freud Library* (Harmondsworth: Penguin, 1977).

11 Simpson, *Male Impersonators*, 81.

12 Sigmund Freud, *Case Histories II*, vol. 9 of *The Pelican Freud Library* (Harmondsworth: Penguin, 1979), 315.

13 Sigmund Freud, "Analysis Terminable and Interminable," in vol. 23 of *The Standard Edition of the Complete Psychological Works of Sigmund Freud*, trans. James Strachey (London: Hogarth Press, 1986), 252.

14 Brian Pronger, *The Arena of Masculinity: Sports, Homosexuality, and the Meaning of Sex* (New York: St. Martin's Press, 1990), 139.

15 Guy Hocquenghem, *Homosexual Desire*, trans. D. Dangoor (London: Allison and Busby, 1978), 87–89.

16 Leo Bersani, "Is the Rectum a Grave?" *October* 43 (1987): 212.

17 Fletcher, "Freud and His Uses," 114.

18 Gregg Blachford, "Male Dominance and the Gay World," in *The Making of the Modern Homosexual*, ed. Ken Plummer (London: Hutchinson, 1981), 196. See also Jack Nichols, "Butcher Than Thou: Beyond Machismo," in *Gay Men: The Sociology of Male Homosexuality*, ed. M. P. Levine (New York: Harper and Row, 1979); and Martin Humphries, "Gay Machismo," in *The Sexuality of Men*, ed. Andy Metcalf and Martin Humphries (London: Pluto, 1985).

19 Laura Mulvey, "Visual Pleasure and Narrative Cinema," *Screen* 16.3 (1975): 12.

20 Kaja Silverman, *The Acoustic Mirror: The Female Voice in Cinema and Psychoanalysis* (Bloomington: Indiana University Press, 1988), 24.

21 Steve Neale, "Masculinity as Spectacle," *Screen* 24.6 (1983): 8.

22 Ibid., 5; Mulvey, "Visual Pleasure and Narrative Cinema," 11.

23 On the increasing specularization of the male body in contemporary Hollywood cinema see Yvonne Tasker, *Spectacular Bodies: Gender, Genre, and the Action Cinema* (London: Comedia, 1993).

24 Neale, "Masculinity as Spectacle," 15.

25 Ian Green, "Malefunction," *Screen* 25.4–5 (1985): 47.

26 Michael Bronski, *Culture Clash: The Making of Gay Sensibility* (Boston: South End Press, 1984), 95.

27 Pasche, "Symposium on Homosexuality," 213.

28 Simpson, *Male Impersonators*, 4–6.

29 It is also why the female look of desire at the male body is less threatening. Women are not generally defined in patriarchal cultures as active or powerful; consequently, their look is not perceived in and by the phallic male imaginary as the same as another man's look. This may explain why the female look of desire at the male body has started to emerge with relative ease in recent popular cultural forms from advertising to film. The exception to this—and it is, perhaps, the one that proves the proverbial rule—is the look of the "phallic woman," the classic femme fatale.

30 For an overview of the controversy—at least in the United States—see Randy Shilts, *Conduct Unbecoming: Gays and Lesbians in the U.S. Military*, rev. ed. (New York: Ballantine, 1994).

31 Rosalind Coward, *Female Desire: Women's Sexuality Today* (London: Paladin, 1984), 229. Brian Pronger makes a similar claim in his study on male homosexuality and that other bastion of phallic masculinity, sport. He cites one straight male athlete as saying that the disgust most straight men feel at the thought of a gay man looking at them comes from "equating it with what they do to women" (*Arena of Masculinity*, 197).

32 Henry Jenkins, *Textual Poachers: Television Fans and Participatory Cultures* (New York: Routledge, 1992), 156.

33 Matias Viegener, "Kinky Escapades, Bedroom Techniques, Unbridled Passion, and Secret Sex Codes," in *Camp Grounds: Style and Homosexuality*, ed. David Bergman (Amherst: University of Massachusetts Press, 1993), 234–35. Other analyses of gay fanzines can be found in Mark Fenster, "Queer Punk Fanzines: Identity, Community, and the Articulation of Homosexuality and Hardcore," *Journal of Communication Inquiry* 17.1 (1993): 73–94; and Bruce LaBruce, "The Wild, Wild, Wild World of Fanzines," in *A Queer Romance: Lesbians, Gay Men, and Popular Culture*, ed. Paul Burston and Colin Richardson (London: Routledge, 1995).

34 Marvin Jones, *Movie Buff Checklist: Male Nudity in the Movies*, 3d ed. (Los Angeles: Campfire Video Productions, 1990), 5.

35 From the anthology *The Best of the Superstars: The Hottest Men in Their Best Roles*, ed. J. Patrick (Tampa: Starbooks, 1989), 81.

36 Some of these articles have been anthologized in Boyd McDonald, *Cruising the Movies: A Sexual Guide to "Oldies" on TV* (New York: Gay Presses of New York, 1985).

37 Boyd McDonald, "Art from the Post-Heterosexual Age," *Art and Text* 20 (1986).

38 McDonald, *Cruising the Movies*, 90–91.

39 Boyd McDonald, "Presley-a-Go-Go," *Outrage* 17 (1983): 6.

40 Underground fanzines are notoriously vague in terms of publishing details. *Homocore* is edited by Todd Jennings in San Francisco. *Starfuckers* is produced out of Sydney. The only copy I have of the latter was sent to me by a friend who picked it up in an Oxford Street nightclub in August 1993. It has no number and no address, so I am unable to determine if it is part of a continuing series.

41 Anonymous letter reprinted in McDonald, *Cruising the Movies*, 157, emphasis added.

42 Anonymous, "Schw-arse-enegger," *Starfuckers* (1993): n.p.

43 Dick Master, "In Bed with Keanu"; and Anonymous, "Sucking the Boys," *Starfuckers* (1993): n.p.

44 On "slash" see Henry Jenkins, *Textual Poachers: Television Fans and Participatory Culture* (New York: Routledge, 1992), 185–222; and Constance Penley, "Feminism, Psychoanalysis, and the Study of Popular Culture," in *Cultural Studies*, ed. Larry Grossberg et al. (New York: Routledge, 1992).

45 Master, "In Bed with Keanu."

46 As Henry Jenkins notes in relation to "slash" fiction, this type of erotic fan writing, "like other genres of fan fiction, represents *a mode of textual commentary.*" Writers of erotic fan fiction are "reflecting something they have found within the broadcast material," something "apparent both in the scripted action of th[e] characters and also in the nuances of the actors' performances (ways they look at each other, ways the actors move in relation to each other)" (*Textual Poachers*, 202, emphasis added).

47 However, as stated earlier, those types of films dominated by male characters and male concerns such as westerns, war films, action pictures, etc. have not really been taken up or popularized in any notable way by gay subcultures. This suggests that, though they may not be able to avoid some form of identification with the dominant male figure of mainstream film, many gay spectators tend to avoid or at least marginalize those films that require a sustained or exclusive identification with phallic masculinity.

48 Not every single cinematic male image will automatically be submitted to an erotic objectification on the part of the gay spectator. However, within the context of gay spectatorship, the male image is rendered amenable to the possibility of erotic objectification with the result that the male image is always marked with a structural potential for objectification in gay spectatorships that fundamentally alters its signifying status and effects.

49 Neale, "Masculinity as Spectacle," 14–15.

50 McDonald, *Cruising the Movies*, 86, emphasis added.

51 Anonymous, "Schw-arse-enegger"; and Master, "In Bed with Keanu."

52 Fletcher, "Freud and His Uses," 101.

53 John Stubbard, "Our Monty," *Out/Takes* 3 (1984): 23.

54 Patricia Meyer Spacks, *Gossip* (New York: Knopf, 1985).

55 See David Ehrenstein, *Open Secret: Gay Hollywood, 1928–1998* (New York: William Morrow, 1998).

56 Andrea Weiss, *Vampires and Violets: Lesbians in the Cinema* (London: Jonathan Cape, 1992), 33.

57 Some of the more significant and popular biographies of Clift include Robert LaGuardia, *Monty: An Intimate Biography of Montgomery Clift* (New York: Arbor House, 1977); Patricia Bosworth, *Montgomery Clift: A Biography* (New York: Limelight, 1978); Barney Hoskyns, *Montgomery Clift: Beautiful Loser* (London: Bloomsbury, 1991); and Maurice Leonard, *Montgomery Clift* (London: Hodder and Stoughton, 1997).

58 Graham McCann, *Rebel Males: Clift, Brando, and Dean* (London: Hamish Hamilton, 1991), 28–32.

59 Rex Reed, "Montgomery Clift," in *The National Society of Film Critics on the Movie Star,* ed. Elizabeth Weis (Harmondsworth: Penguin, 1981), 170–71.

60 Donald Spoto, *Camerado: Hollywood and the American Man* (New York: New American Library, 1978), 135.

61 Ken Wlaschin, *The Illustrated Encyclopedia of the World's Great Movie Stars* (Hong Kong: Salamander Books, 1979), 34.

62 Cited in McCann, *Rebel Males,* 47, emphasis added.

63 For discussions of method acting in film see Richard Dyer, *Stars* (London: British Film Institute, 1979); and James Naremore, *Acting in the Cinema* (Berkeley: University of California Press, 1988).

64 Virginia Wright Wexman, *Creating the Couple: Love, Marriage, and Hollywood Performance* (Princeton: Princeton University Press, 1993), 167.

65 Steven Cohan, *Masked Men: Masculinity and the Movies in the Fifties* (Bloomington: Indiana University Press, 1997), 203.

66 See John D'Emilio, *Sexual Politics, Sexual Communities: The Making of a Homosexual Minority in the United States, 1940–1970,* 2d ed. (Chicago: University of Chicago Press, 1998).

67 This is part of the reason, perhaps, why the figure of the "rebellious youth" is so privileged in contemporary gay (sub)cultures. Other than Clift, one can cite in this context the star-images of actors like James Dean, Joe Dallesandro, and River Phoenix, or, in a slightly different vein, "rock goddesses" such as Janis Joplin, Deborah Harry, Madonna, and Courtney Love, all of whom embody a central representation of countercultural youthful rebellion and have achieved a strong iconic status in Anglo-American gay cultures.

68 Bosworth, *Montgomery Clift,* 134.

69 Cited in McCann, *Rebel Males,* 24.

70 The significance of this particular role in and for the Clift persona is high-

lighted by both the widespread critical acclaim that this part drew—it earned Clift his fourth and final Academy Award nomination, for example—and the much-publicized "behind-the-scenes" story that Clift actually turned down the leading role of the prosecuting attorney in this film, offering his services for free if he could play the part of Petersen instead, because, as Clift himself put it, he felt this particular role offered him "something important to say." See Bosworth, *Montgomery Clift*, 359.

71 McCann, *Rebel Males*, 39.

72 Anthony Easthope, *What a Man's Gotta Do: The Masculine Myth in Popular Culture* (London: Paladin, 1986), 20.

73 Bosworth, *Montgomery Clift*, 213.

74 Cited in McCann, *Rebel Males*, 74.

75 Mary Burton, *Stars of the Forties and Fifties* (Sydney: Endeavour Books, 1983), 97.

76 Stubbard, "Our Monty," 24.

77 Keith Howes, "Montgomery Clift: Icon," *Outrage* (March 1998): 33–34.

78 This scene has perhaps assumed added resonances for gay audiences in more recent years with the AIDs crisis. The New Zealand queer filmmaker Scott Trunger quotes this scene in his short video about AIDS and mourning, *Saraband for Dead Brothers* (1991).

79 Vito Russo, *The Celluloid Closet: Homosexuality in the Movies*, rev. ed. (New York: Harper and Row, 1987), 78.

80 Contrary to Steven Cohan's assertion that "most viewers of *Red River* instantly recognize that the shooting match between Matthew and Cherry is homoerotic" (*Masked Men*, 212), I argue that such an interpretation is largely dependent on the ability or willingness of the viewer to entertain a fantasmatic homosexualization of phallic homosociality—something that is far from universal. That many straight viewers fail, if not refuse, to make such an illicit reading is highlighted by an experience the gay filmmakers Rob Epstein and Jeffrey Friedman had when they approached the Corporation for Public Broadcasting about using scenes from *Red River* in their 1995 documentary on gays and film, *The Celluloid Closet*. They screened a couple of choice excerpts for the mainly male heterosexual members of the corporation, who failed to understand the point. Friedman relates: "I'll never cease to insist that it's homoerotic. . . . But the funding body couldn't see [it]" (cited in Leigh Raymond, "Gays Step Out from behind the Screen," *Weekend Australian*, 30 July 1994, 11).

81 Anthony Easthope, *What a Man's Gotta Do: The Masculine Myth in Popular Culture* (London: Paladin, 1986), 17–23.

82 As was pointed out in chapter 2, the "logic" of negotiational readings is not necessarily one of uniformity or even of coherence. Negotiational readings can and often do proceed in the most fragmentary and haphazard manner, weaving marginal or aberrant textual features with more dominant patterns of signification

in ways that may seem patently illogical, even contradictory, but that nonetheless enable the articulation of alternative meanings. In the case of gay negotiational readings of the films of Montgomery Clift, this means that it is perfectly possible for a gay spectator to identify queerly with Clift's characters in these films while accepting the heterosexuality assigned to these characters and their relationships.

83 Cited in LaGuardia, *Monty*, 207.

84 As Steven Cohan notes, the "masquerading" of heterosexual masculinity *"was* a constant factor in the lives of fifties gay men, as Clift's biography dramatizes [and, it should be added, in the lives of many contemporary gay men, as well], and it helps to explain why his star persona . . . so readily yields a queer subtext" (*Masked Men*, 227). Interestingly, the publicity campaign for one of Clift's final films, *Freud* (1962) seems to play knowingly with this type of reading potential with the suggestive tag line: "Alone he fought against his own dark passions . . . knowing that the shocking truth could ruin his career."

85 Stubbard, "Our Monty," 26.

86 Ian Baintree and Bob Burns, "Book Reviews," *Inches* (May 1993): 16.

87 Cited in McCann, *Rebel Males*, 74–76.

88 There is evidence to suggest that this type of reading is not limited to gay spectators alone. Many female spectators have also pursued a reading of Clift's relationships with women as something other than the standard scenario of intergenital heterosexuality. The female novelist Caryl Rivers, for example, recalls that an important part of Clift's appeal for her as a young woman in the fifties was his representation of a nonthreatening, nonphallic mode of male-female relationality. "I think every girl who saw him in the quiet dark of a movie theater of a Saturday afternoon fell in love with Montgomery Clift, his dark eyes like the deep water of a cavern pool, holding promise of worlds of tenderness. . . . At the same time I was in love with Montgomery Clift, I found the growing awareness of how people 'did it' pretty revolting: all that touching and pinching and groping about. . . . With me and Montgomery, it wasn't that way at all. Love with him would be long, languorous sighs, pressing close against his manly chest and telling each other all those secrets we had never told anybody, and gazing eyeball-to-eyeball, and he wouldn't think of putting his hand on my thigh" (cited in LaGuardia, *Monty*, 67). On the appeal of nonphallic male starimages for adolescent girls see Gael Sweeney, "The Face on the Lunch Box: Television's Construction of the Teen Idol," *Velvet Light Trap* 33 (spring 1994): 50–59.

89 This is, of course, a reading that has reached precipitous proportions in recent years with the AIDS crisis. See Jeff Nunokawa, " 'All the Sad Young Men': AIDS and the Work of Mourning," in *Inside/Out: Lesbian Theories, Gay Theories*, ed. Diana Fuss (New York: Routledge, 1991).

90 Bosworth, *Montgomery Clift*, back cover; Reed, "Montgomery Clift," 171; La-Guardia, *Monty*, 4–5.

91 Leonard, *Mae West*, back cover.

92 Mark Robbins, "Death Wish," *Out/Takes* 3 (1984): 17.

93 Richard Dyer, *The Matter of Images: Essays on Representation* (London: Routledge, 1993), 77.

94 Richard Lippe, "Montgomery Clift: A Critical Disturbance," *CineAction!* 17 (summer 1989): 37.

95 Dyer, *Matter of Images*, 90.

96 Lippe, "Montgomery Clift," 38.

97 Sigmund Freud, "The Economic Problem of Masochism," in *On Metapsychology*, vol. 11 of *The Pelican Freud Library* (Harmondsworth: Penguin, 1984), 419.

98 See, for example, Parveen Adams, "Per Os(cillation)," *Camera Obscura* 17 (1988): 7–29; Gaylyn Studlar, *In the Realm of Pleasure: Von Sternberg, Dietrich, and the Masochistic Aesthetic* (New York: Columbia University Press, 1988); Linda Williams, *Hard Core: Power, Pleasure, and the "Frenzy of the Visible"* (Berkeley: University of California Press, 1989); and Silverman, *Male Subjectivity at the Margins*.

99 Freud, "Economic Problem of Masochism," 416.

100 Silverman, *Male Subjectivity at the Margins*, 189.

101 Sigmund Freud, " 'A Child Is Being Beaten,' " in *On Psychopathology*, vol. 10 of *The Pelican Freud Library* (Harmondsworth: Penguin, 1979).

102 Silverman, *Male Subjectivity at the Margins*, 204.

103 Gilles Deleuze, *Masochism: An Interpretation of Coldness and Cruelty*, trans. J. McNeil (New York: Harper and Row, 1971), 58.

104 The work on gay anality, for example, discussed earlier effectively defines masochism as a privileged libidinal mode for gay men in their performative "refusals" of phallic identity. By subjecting their male bodies to a recurrent process of debasement and "sacrifice" through the act of passive anal intercourse, gay men engage and reproduce a "delirious shattering" of the phallic significations of those bodies, an argument that entails an unavoidable logic of masochism.

105 Deleuze, *Masochism*, 58.

Filmography

Adventures of Priscilla, Queen of the Desert, The, 1994, Village-Roadshow, Stephan
  Elliott.
All That Heaven Allows, 1955, Universal, Douglas Sirk.
Apartment Zero, 1988, Summit, Martin Donovan.
Babes on Broadway, 1941, MGM, Busby Berkeley.
Band Wagon, The, 1953, MGM, Vincente Minnelli.
Beautiful Thing, 1996, Channel Four Films, Hettie MacDonald.
Belle of the Nineties, 1934, Paramount, Leo McCarey.
Billy's Hollywood Screen Kiss, 1998, Trimark Pictures, Tommy O'Haver.
Boys in the Band, The, 1970, National General, William Friedkin.
Brief Encounter, 1945, Rank, David Lean.
Broadway Melody of 1936, 1935, MGM, Roy Del Ruth.
Cabaret, 1972, Allied Artists, Bob Fosse.
Calamity Jane, 1953, Warner Bros., David Butler.
Easter Parade, 1948, MGM, Charles Walters.
Farmer Takes A Wife, The, 1953, 20th Century–Fox, Henry Levin.
Five Finger Exercise, 1962, Warner Bros., Daniel Mann.
Footlight Parade, 1933, Warner Bros., Lloyd Bacon.
For Me and My Gal, 1942, MGM, Busby Berkeley.
42nd Street, 1933, Warner Bros., Lloyd Bacon.
Freud, 1962, Universal, John Huston.
From Here to Eternity, 1953, Columbia, Fred Zinnemann.
Fruit Machine, The, 1988, Goldcrest, Philip Saville.
Gold Diggers of 1933, 1933, Warner Bros., Mervyn LeRoy.
Go West, Young Man, 1936, Paramount, Henry Hathaway.
Grease, 1978, Paramount, Randal Kleiser.
Head, 1968, Columbia, Bob Rafelson.
Heiress, The, 1949, Paramount, William Wyler.
Hello, Dolly! 1969, 20th Century–Fox, Gene Kelly.
I Confess, 1953, Warner Brothers, Alfred Hitchcock.
Indiscretion of an American Wife, 1953, Columbia, Vittorio DeSica.

Judgment at Nuremberg, 1961, United Artists, Stanley Kramer.

Kiss Me Kate, 1953, MGM, George Sidney.

Kiss of the Spider Woman, 1985, Columbia, Hector Babenco.

Klondike Annie, 1936, Paramount, Raoul Walsh.

Lonelyhearts, 1958, United Artists, Vincent J. Donehue.

Long Day Closes, The, 1992, BFI, Terence Davies.

Lost Boys, The, 1987, Warner Bros., Joel Schumacher.

Love Me Tender, 1956, 20th Century–Fox, Robert D. Webb.

Magnificent Obsession, 1954, Universal, Douglas Sirk.

Mary Poppins, 1964, Disney, Robert Stevenson.

Misfits, The, 1961, United Artists, John Huston.

Mr. Deeds Goes to Town, 1936, Columbia, Frank Capra.

Music Man, The, 1962, Warner Bros., Morton Da Costa.

My Little Chickadee, 1940, Universal, Edward Cline.

Myra Breckinridge, 1970, 20th Century–Fox, Michael Sarne.

My Son John, 1952, Paramount, Leo McCarey.

North by Northwest, 1959, MGM, Alfred Hitchcock.

North Dallas Forty, 1979, Paramount, Ted Kotcheff.

Of Love and Desire, 1963, 20th Century–Fox, Richard Rush.

Oklahoma! 1955, 20th Century–Fox, Fred Zinnemann.

On a Clear Day You Can See Forever, 1970, Paramount, Vincente Minnelli.

Pajama Game, The, 1957, Warner Bros., George Abbott and Stanley Donen.

Pink Flamingos, 1972, New Line Cinema, John Waters.

Pirate, The, 1948, MGM, Vincente Minnelli.

Place in the Sun, A, 1951, Paramount, George Stevens.

Pleasantville, 1998, New Line Cinema, Gary Ross.

Point Break, 1991, 20th Century–Fox, Kathryn Bigelow.

Raintree County, 1957, MGM, Edward Dmytryk.

Red River, 1948, United Artists, Howard Hawks.

Rocky Horror Picture Show, The, 1975, 20th Century–Fox, Jim Sharman.

Roman Spring of Mrs. Stone, The, 1961, Warner Bros., José Quintero.

Rosalie, 1937, MGM, W. S. Van Dyke.

Royal Wedding, 1951, MGM, Stanley Donen.

Saraband for Dead Brothers, 1991, Taurus, Scott Trunger.

Search, The, 1948, MGM, Fred Zinnemann.

Seven Brides for Seven Brothers, 1954, MGM, Stanley Donen.

Seven Sinners, 1940, Universal, Tay Garnett.

Sextette, 1978, Warner Bros., Ken Hughes.

She Done Him Wrong, 1933, Paramount, Lowell Sherman.

Singin' in the Rain, 1952, MGM, Stanley Donen and Gene Kelly.

Sound of Music, The, 1965, 20th Century–Fox, Robert Wise.

South Pacific, 1958, 20th Century–Fox, Joshua Logan.

Star! 1968, 20th Century–Fox, Robert Wise.

Star Is Born, A, 1954, Warner Bros., George Cukor.

Stella Dallas, 1937, Goldwyn, King Vidor.

Strait-Jacket, 1964, Columbia, William Castle.

Streetcar Named Desire, A, 1951, Warner Bros., Elia Kazan.

Strike Up the Band, 1940, MGM, Busby Berkeley.

Suddenly, Last Summer, 1959, Columbia, Joseph L. Mankiewicz.

Sunset Boulevard, 1950, Paramount, Billy Wilder.

Sweet Bird of Youth, 1962, MGM, Richard Brooks.

Sweet Charity, 1969, Universal, Bob Fosse.

Tea and Sympathy, 1956, MGM, Vincente Minnelli.

Terminator 2: Judgment Day, 1991, Tri-Star, James Cameron.

Thoroughly Modern Millie, 1967, Universal, George Roy Hill.

Till the Clouds Roll By, 1946, MGM, Richard Whorf.

Twenty Million Sweethearts, 1934, First National, Ray Enright.

Victor/Victoria, 1982, MGM, Blake Edwards.

What Ever Happened to Baby Jane? 1962, Warner Bros., Robert Aldrich.

Wild River, 1960, 20th Century–Fox, Elia Kazan.

Wizard of Oz, The, 1939, MGM, Victor Fleming.

Yellow Submarine, 1968, United Artists, George Dunning.

Yolanda and the Thief, 1945, MGM, Vincente Minnelli.

Young Lions, The, 1958, 20th Century–Fox, Edward Dmytryk.

Bibliography

Abelove, Henry. "Freud, Male Homosexuality, and the Americans." *Dissent* 33.1 (1985–86): 59–69.

Abelove, Henry, Michele Aina Barale, and David M. Halperin, eds. *The Lesbian and Gay Studies Reader.* New York: Routledge, 1993.

Adair, Mark J. "A Speculation on Perversion and Hallucination." *International Journal of Psycho-Analysis* 74 (1993): 81–91.

Ang, Ien. *Watching Dallas: Soap Opera and the Melodramatic Imagination.* London: Methuen, 1985.

Angelides, Steven. "The Queer Intervention: Sexuality, Identity, and Cultural Politics." *Melbourne Journal of Politics* 22 (1994): 66–88.

Anger, Kenneth. *Hollywood Babylon.* San Francisco: Straight Arrow Books, 1975.

Babuscio, Jack. "Camp and the Gay Sensibility." In Dyer, ed. 1977.

Babington, Bruce, and Peter William Evans. *Blue Skies and Silver Linings: Aspects of the Hollywood Musical.* Manchester: Manchester University Press, 1985.

Bad Object-Choices, eds. *How Do I Look? Queer Film and Video.* Seattle: Bay Press, 1991.

Baintree, Ian, and Bob Burns. "Book Reviews." *Inches* (May 1993): 16.

Barthes, Roland. *Mythologies.* Translated by Annette Lavers. London: Granada, 1973.

———. *Camera Lucida: Reflections on Photography.* Translated by Richard Howard. London: Fontana, 1984.

Baudry, Jean-Louis. "Ideological Effects of the Basic Cinematographic Apparatus." *Film Quarterly* 28.2 (1974–75): 39–47.

———. "The Apparatus." *Camera Obscura* 1 (1976): 97–126.

Beaver, Harold. "Homosexual Signs." *Critical Inquiry* 8.1 (autumn 1982): 99–119.

Bennett, Tony, Colin Mercer, and Janet Woollacott, eds. *Popular Culture and Social Relations.* London: Open University Press, 1986.

Bennett, Tony, and Janet Woollacott. *Bond and Beyond: The Political Career of a Popular Hero.* London: Macmillan, 1987.

Berenstein, Rhona J. *Attack of the Leading Ladies: Gender, Sexuality, and Spectatorship in Classic Horror Cinema.* New York: Columbia University Press, 1996.

Bergman, David, ed. *Camp Grounds: Style and Homosexuality.* Amherst: University of Massachusetts Press, 1993.

Bergstrom, Janet, and Mary Ann Doane. "The Female Spectator: Contexts and Directions." *Camera Obscura* 20–21 (1989): 5–27.

Bergstrom, Janet, ed. *Endless Night: Cinema and Psychoanalysis, Parallel Histories.* Berkeley: University of California Press, 1999.

Bersani, Leo. "Is the Rectum a Grave?" *October* 43 (1987): 197–222.

———. *Homos.* Cambridge: Harvard University Press, 1995.

Bieber, Irving. *Homosexuality: A Psychoanalytic Study of Male Homosexuals.* New York: Basic Books, 1962.

Blachford, Gregg. "Male Dominance and the Gay World." In Plummer, ed. 1981.

Bobo, Jacqueline. *Black Women as Cultural Readers.* New York: Columbia University Press, 1995.

Booth, Mark. *Camp.* New York: Quartet, 1983.

Bourdieu, Pierre. *Distinction: A Social Critique of the Judgement of Taste.* Translated by Richard Nice. Cambridge: Harvard University Press, 1984.

Bosworth, Patricia. *Montgomery Clift: A Biography.* New York: Harcourt Brace Jovanovich, 1978.

Bowie, Malcolm. *Lacan.* London: Fontana, 1991.

Brett, Phillip, et al., eds. *Queering the Pitch: The New Gay and Lesbian Musicology.* New York: Routledge, 1994.

Britton, Andrew. "For Interpretation: Notes against Camp." *Gay Left* 7 (winter 1978–79).

———. *Katharine Hepburn: Star as Feminist.* London: Studio Vista, 1995.

Bronski, Michael. *Culture Clash: The Making of Gay Sensibility.* Boston: South End Press, 1984.

Burchill, Julie. *Girls on Film.* New York: Pantheon, 1986.

Burnett, George. "The ABC of Camp." *I-D* (January–February 1986): 40–44.

Burnett, Ron, ed. *Explorations in Film Theory: Selected Essays from Cine-Tracts.* Bloomington: Indiana University Press, 1991.

Burston, Paul, and Colin Richardson, eds. *A Queer Romance: Lesbians, Gay Men, and Popular Culture.* London: Routledge, 1995.

Butler, Judith. *Gender Trouble: Feminism and the Subversion of Identity.* London: Routledge, 1990.

———. *Bodies That Matter: On the Discursive Limits of "Sex."* New York: Routledge, 1993.

Cahill, Phillipe. "Heavenly Knowledge." *Campaign* 227 (1995): 19–21, 66–67.

Carroll, David. "Narrative, Heterogeneity, and the Question of the Political: Bakhtin and Lyotard." In Krieger, ed. 1989.

Case, Sue-Ellen. "Towards a Butch-Femme Aesthetic." *Discourse* 11.1 (1988–89): 55–73.

Chauncey, George. *Gay New York: Gender, Urban Culture, and the Making of the Gay Male World, 1890–1940.* New York: Harper Collins, 1994.

Clayton, Devon. "Put the Blame on Mame: The Movie Characters That Made Us Gay." *The Advocate,* 7 November 1988, 47–51.

Clinton, David. "Gayzing at the Screen." *Different Fruits* 3 (1987): 16.

Clover, Carol J. "Dancin' in the Rain." *Critical Inquiry* 21 (summer 1995): 722–47.

Cohan, Steven. *Masked Men: Masculinity and the Movies in the Fifties.* Bloomington: Indiana University Press, 1997.

———, and Ina Rae Hark, eds. *Screening the Male: Exploring Masculinities in Hollywood Cinema.* New York: Routledge, 1993.

Cohen, Jaffe, Danny McWilliams, and Bob Smith. *Growing Up Gay: From Left Out to Coming Out.* New York: Hyperion, 1995.

Collins, Jim, et al., eds. *Film Theory Goes to the Movies.* New York: Routledge, 1993.

Copjec, Joan. "More! From Melodrama to Magnitude." In Bergstrom, ed. 1999.

Core, Phillip. *Camp: The Lie That Tells the Truth.* New York: Delilah, 1984.

Coward, Rosalind. *Female Desire: Women's Sexuality Today.* London: Paladin, 1984.

Cowie, Elizabeth. "Fantasia." *m/f* 9 (1984): 70–105.

Cox, Renee. "Recovering Jouissance: An Introduction to Feminist Musical Aesthetics." In Pendle, ed. 1991.

Creed, Barbara. *The Monstrous-Feminine: Film, Feminism, Psychoanalysis.* London: Routledge, 1993.

Curry, Ramona. *Too Much of a Good Thing: Mae West as Cultural Icon.* Minneapolis: University of Minnesota Press, 1996.

Cvekovitch, Ann. "The Powers of Seeing and Being Seen: *Truth or Dare* and *Paris Is Burning.*" In Collins et al., eds. 1993.

Dean, Tim. "On the Eve of a Queer Future." *Raritan* 15.1 (1995): 116–34.

———. "Sex and Syncope." *Raritan* 15.3 (1996): 64–86.

de Certeau, Michel. *Heterologies: Discourse on the Other.* Translated by Brian Massumi. Minneapolis: University of Minnesota Press, 1986.

de Lauretis, Teresa. *Alice Doesn't: Feminism, Semiotics, Cinema.* Bloomington: Indiana University Press, 1984.

———. *The Practice of Love: Lesbian Sexuality and Perverse Desire.* Bloomington: Indiana University Press, 1994.

de Lauretis, Teresa, ed. *Feminist Studies/Critical Studies.* Bloomington: Indiana University Press, 1986.

Deleuze, Gilles. *Masochism: An Interpretation of Coldness and Cruelty.* Translated by J. McNeil. New York: Harper and Row, 1971.

D'Emilio, John. *Sexual Politics, Sexual Communities: The Making of a Homosexual Minority in the United States, 1940–1970,* 2d ed. Chicago: University of Chicago Press, 1998.

Doane, Mary Ann. *The Desire to Desire: The Woman's Film of the 1940s.* Bloomington: Indiana University Press, 1987.

———. "Response." *Camera Obscura* 20–21 (1989): 142–47.

———. *Femmes Fatales: Feminism, Film Theory, Psychoanalysis.* New York: Routledge, 1991.

Doane, Mary Ann, Patricia Mellencamp, and Linda Williams, eds. *Re-Vision: Essays in Feminist Film Criticism.* 1978. Reprint, Frederick, Md.: University Publications of America, 1984.

Dollimore, Jonathan. *Sexual Dissidence: Augustine to Wilde, Freud to Foucault.* Oxford: Oxford University Press, 1991.

Domenici, Thomas, and Ronnie C. Lesser, eds. *Disorienting Sexuality: Psychoanalytic Reappraisals of Sexual Identities.* New York: Routledge, 1995.

Donald, James, ed. *Fantasy and the Cinema.* London: British Film Institute, 1989.

———, ed. *Psychoanalysis and Cultural Theory: Thresholds.* London: Macmillan, 1991.

Doty, Alexander. *Making Things Perfectly Queer: Interpreting Mass Culture.* Minneapolis: University of Minnesota Press, 1993.

During, Simon. *The Cultural Studies Reader.* New York: Routledge, 1993.

Dyer, Richard. *Stars.* London: British Film Institute, 1979.

———. *Heavenly Bodies: Film Stars and Society.* New York: St. Martin's Press, 1986.

———. *Only Entertainment.* New York: Routledge, 1992.

———. *The Matter of Images: Essays on Representation.* London: Routledge, 1993.

Dyer, Richard, ed. *Gays and Film.* Rev. ed. London: Zoetrope, 1984.

Dynes, Wayne R. *Homoplexis: A Historical and Cultural Lexicon of Homosexuality.* New York: Gay Academic Union, 1985.

Easthope, Anthony. *What a Man's Gotta Do: The Masculine Myth in Popular Culture.* London: Paladin, 1986.

Edelman, Lee. "Tearooms and Sympathy, or, The Epistemology of the Water Closet." In Abelove, Barale, and Halperin, eds. 1993.

Eells, George, and Stanley Musgrove. *Mae West: A Biography.* London: Paladin, 1986.

Ehrenstein, David. *Open Secret: Gay Hollywood, 1928–1998.* New York: William Morrow, 1998.

Ellis, John. *Visible Fictions: Cinema, Television, Video.* London: RKP, 1982.

Ellsworth, Elizabeth. "Illicit Pleasures: Feminist Spectators and *Personal Best.*" *Wide Angle* 8.2 (1986): 45–56.

Elsaesser, Thomas. "Vincente Minnelli." In Altman, ed. 1981.

Evans, Caroline, and Lorraine Gamman. "The Gaze Revisited, or Reviewing Queer Viewing." In Burston and Richardson, eds. 1995.

Fenster, Mark. "Queer Punk Fanzines: Identity, Community, and the Articulation of Homosexuality and Hardcore." *Journal of Communication Inquiry* 17.1 (1993): 73–94.

Feuer, Jane. *The Hollywood Musical.* Rev. ed. Bloomington: Indiana University Press, 1993.

Finch, Mark. "Gays and Lesbians in the Cinema." In *The Political Companion to American Film*, ed. Gary Crowdus. Chicago: Lake View Press, 1994.

Finch, Mark, and Richard Kwietniowski. "Melodrama and *Maurice:* Homo Is Where the Het Is." *Screen* 29.3 (1988): 72–80.

Fischer, Lucy. "Mama's Boy: Filial Hysteria in *White Heat.*" In Cohan and Hark, eds. 1993.

Fletcher, John. "Versions of Masquerade." *Screen* 29.3 (1988): 43–70.

———. "Freud and His Uses: Psychoanalysis and Gay Theory." In Shepherd and Wallis, eds. 1989.

Flinn, Caryl. "The Deaths of Camp." *Camera Obscura* 35 (1996): 53–84.

Foucault, Michel. *The History of Sexuality: An Introduction.* Translated by Richard Hurley. Harmondsworth: Penguin, 1981.

Freeman, Eric. "Producing (Queer) Communities: Public Access Cable TV in the USA." In *The Television Studies Book*, edited by Christine Geraghty and David Lusted. London: Arnold, 1998.

Freud, Sigmund. "The Dynamics of Transference." In vol. 12 of *The Standard Edition of the Complete Psychological Works of Sigmund Freud*, trans. James Strachey. London: Hogarth Press, 1959.

———. *The Pelican Freud Library.* 15 vols. Translated by James Strachey. Edited by Alan Richards. Harmondsworth: Penguin, 1973–1986.

———. *The Complete Letters of Sigmund Freud to Wilhelm Fliess, 1887–1904.* Translated and edited by Jeffrey Masson. Cambridge: Harvard University Press, 1985.

———. "Analysis Terminable and Interminable." In vol. 23 of *The Standard Edition of the Complete Psychological Works of Sigmund Freud*, trans. James Strachey. London: Hogarth Press, 1986.

Friedel, Richard. *The Movie Lover.* Boston: Alyson, 1981.

Frosh, Stephen. *For and against Psychoanalysis.* New York: Routledge, 1997.

Frye, Marilyn. *The Politics of Reality: Essays in Feminist Theory.* Trumansburg, N.Y.: Crossing Press, 1983.

Fuss, Diana. *Essentially Speaking: Feminism, Nature, and Difference.* New York: Routledge, 1989.

Fuss, Diana, ed. *Inside/Out: Lesbian Theories, Gay Theories.* New York: Routledge, 1991.

Gaines, Jane, and Charlotte Herzog, eds. *Fabrications: Costume and the Female Body.* New York: Routledge, 1990.

Galbraith, Larry. "The Slow Demise of Camp Culture." *Outrage* 146 (1995): 64–66.

Gallop, Jane. *Feminism and Psychoanalysis: The Daughter's Seduction.* London: Macmillan, 1982.

———. *Thinking through the Body.* New York: Columbia University Press, 1988.

Garber, Marjorie. *Vested Interests: Cross-Dressing and Cultural Anxiety.* Harmondsworth: Penguin, 1993.

Gever, Martha, Pratibha Parmar, and John Greyson, eds. *Queer Looks: Perspectives on Lesbian and Gay Film and Video.* New York: Routledge, 1993.

Gledhill, Christine. "Developments in Feminist Film Criticism." In Doane, Mellencamp, and Williams, eds. 1984.

———. "Pleasurable Negotiations." In Pribram, ed. 1988.

Gledhill, Christine, ed. *Home Is Where the Heart Is: Studies in Melodrama and the Woman's Film.* London: British Film Institute, 1987.

———, ed. *Stardom: Industry of Desire.* London: Routledge, 1991.

Goldberg, Jonathan. "Recalling Totalities: The Mirrored Stages of Arnold Schwarzenegger." *differences* 4.1 (1992): 172-204.

Graham, Paula. "Girl's Camp? The Politics of Parody." In Wilton, ed. 1995.

Green, Ian. "Malefunction." *Screen* 25.4-5 (1985): 36-48.

Greig, Donald. "The Sexual Differentiation of the Hitchcock Text." In Donald, ed. 1989.

Grossberg, Larry, et al., eds. *Cultural Studies.* New York: Routledge, 1992.

Hadleigh, Boze. *The Lavender Screen: The Gay and Lesbian Films.* New York: Citadel Press, 1993.

Hall, Stuart. "New Ethnicities." In *Black Film, British Cinema,* ed. Kobena Mercer. London: ICA, 1988.

Hall, Stuart, and Paul du Gay, eds. *Questions of Cultural Identity.* London: Sage, 1996.

Hall, Stuart, Dorothy Hobson, Anne Love, and Paul Willis, eds. *Culture, Media, Language.* London: Hutchinson, 1980.

Halperin, David. *Saint Foucault: Towards a Gay Hagiography.* New York: Oxford University Press, 1995.

Hamilton, Marybeth. *The Queen of Camp: Mae West, Sex, and Popular Culture.* London: Pandora, 1995.

Hansen, Miriam. *Babel and Babylon: Spectatorship in American Silent Film.* Cambridge: Harvard University Press, 1991.

Hanson, Ellis, ed. *Out Takes: Essays on Queer Theory and Film.* Durham: Duke University Press, 1999.

Harris, Daniel. *The Rise and Fall of Gay Culture.* New York: Hyperion, 1997.

Haskell, Molly. *From Reverence to Rape: The Treatment of Women in the Movies.* New York: Holt, Rinehart and Winston, 1974.

Heath, Stephen. "Difference." *Screen* 19.3 (1978): 51-112.

———. *Questions of Cinema.* London: Macmillan, 1981.

Hebdige, Dick. *Subculture: The Meaning of Style.* London: Methuen, 1979.

Herkt, David. "Being Gay." *RePublica* 3 (1995): 36-50.

Hocquenghem, Guy. *Homosexual Desire.* Translated by Daniella Dangoor. London: Allison and Busby, 1978.

Holmlund, Chris. "Masculinity as Multiple Masquerade: The 'Mature' Stallone and the Stallone Clone." In Cohan and Hark, eds. 1993.

Horrigan, Patrick E. *Widescreen Dreams: Growing Up Gay at the Movies*. Madison: University of Wisconsin Press, 1999.

Hoskyns, Barney. *Montgomery Clift: Beautiful Loser*. London: Bloomsbury, 1991.

Howes, Keith. "Montgomery Clift: Icon." *Outrage* (March 1998): 33–34.

Humphries, Martin. "Gay Machismo." In Metcalf and Humphries, eds. 1985.

Jackson, Claire, and Peter Tapp, eds. *The Bent Lens: A World Guide to Gay and Lesbian Film*. Melbourne: Australian Catalogue Company, 1997.

Jagose, Annamarie. *Queer Theory*. New York: New York University Press, 1997.

Jardine, Alice, and Paul Smith. *Men in Feminism*. London: Methuen, 1987.

Jeffries, Sheila. "The Queer Disappearance of Lesbians: Sexuality in the Academy." *Women's Studies International Forum* 17.5 (1994): 459–72.

Jenkins, Henry. *Textual Poachers: Television Fans and Participatory Culture*. New York: Routledge, 1992.

Jones, Marvin. *Movie Buff Checklist: Male Nudity in the Movies*. 3d ed. Los Angeles: Campfire Video Productions, 1990.

Kaplan, E. Ann. *Motherhood and Representation: The Mother in Popular Culture and Melodrama*. New York: Routledge, 1992.

Keane, Jonathan. "AIDS, Identity, and the Space of Desire." *Textual Practice* 7.4 (1993): 379–411.

Kemp, Peter. "Secret Love (or Gays and Musicals: An Attractive Connection)." In Jackson and Tapp, eds. 1997.

Kirkham, Pat, and Janet Thumim, eds. *You Tarzan: Masculinity, Movies, and Men*. London: Lawrence and Wishart, 1993.

Koestenbaum, Wayne. *The Queen's Throat: Opera, Homosexuality, and the Mystery of Desire*. New York: Poseidon, 1993.

Kolschenblag, Madonna. "The Female Grotesque: Gargoyles in the Cathedrals of Cinema." *Journal of Popular Film* 6.4 (1978): 325–31.

Krieger, Mark, ed. *The Aims of Representation: Subject/Text/History*. New York: Columbia University Press, 1989.

Kristeva, Julia. *The Revolution of Poetic Language*. Translated by M. Waller. New York: Columbia University Press, 1984.

———. *The Kristeva Reader*. Edited by Toril Moi. Oxford: Basil Blackwell, 1986.

Kuhn, Annette. *The Power of the Image: Essays on Representation and Sexuality*. London: Routledge, 1985.

LaBruce, Bruce. "The Wild, Wild, Wild World of Fanzines." In Burston and Richardson, eds. 1995.

Lacan, Jacques. *Ecrits: A Selection*. Translated by Alan Sheridan. London: Tavistock, 1977.

———. "Intervention on Transference." In Mitchell and Rose, eds. 1982.

————. *The Seminar of Jacques Lacan Book I: Freud's Papers on Technique, 1953–54.* Translated by John Forrester. Cambridge: Cambridge University Press, 1988.

LaGuardia, Robert. *Monty: An Intimate Biography of Montgomery Clift.* New York: Arbor House, 1977.

Lane, Christopher. "Psychoanalysis and Sexual Identity." In Medhurst and Munt, eds. 1997.

Laplanche, Jean, and Jean-Bertrand Pontalis. "Fantasy and the Origins of Sexuality." In *Formations of Fantasy*, ed. Victor Burgin, James Donald, and Pat Caplan. London: Methuen, 1986. First published in English in *International Journal of Psychoanalysis* 49 (1968): 5–34. Originally published as "Fantasme originaire, fantasmes des origines, origine du fantasme." *Les Temps modernes* 19. 215 (1964).

————. *The Language of Psychoanalysis.* Translated by David Nicholson-Smith. London: Karnac Books, 1988.

Lapsley, Robert, and Michael Westlake. *Film Theory: An Introduction.* Manchester: Manchester University Press, 1988.

LaValley, Al. "The Great Escape: Gays and Film." *American Film* 10.6 (1985): 28–71.

Leider, Emily Wortis. *Becoming Mae West.* New York: Farrar, Straus and Giroux, 1997.

Leonard, Maurice. *Mae West: The Empress of Sex.* London: Fontana, 1992.

————. *Montgomery Clift.* London: Hodder and Stoughton, 1997.

Levine, Mark P., ed. *Gay Men: The Sociology of Male Homosexuality.* New York: Harper and Row, 1979.

Lewes, Kenneth. *The Psychoanalytic Theory of Male Homosexuality.* London: Quartet, 1988.

Lewis, Lisa A., ed. *The Adoring Audience: Fan Culture and Popular Media.* London: Routledge, 1992.

Lippe, Richard. "Montgomery Clift: A Critical Disturbance." *CineAction!* 17 (summer 1989): 36–42.

Matthews, Peter. "Garbo and Phallic Motherhood: A 'Homosexual' Visual Economy." *Screen* 29.3 (1988): 14–39.

Mayne, Judith. *Cinema and Spectatorship.* London: Routledge, 1993.

McCann, Graham. *Rebel Males: Clift, Brando, and Dean.* London: Hamish Hamilton, 1991.

McClary, Susan. *Feminine Endings: Music, Gender, and Sexuality.* Minneapolis: University of Minnesota Press, 1991.

McLean, Adrienne L. "The Thousand Ways There Are to Move: Camp and Oriental Dance in the Hollywood Musicals of Jack Cole." In *Visions of the East: Orientalism in Film*, ed. Matthew Bernstein and Gaylyn Studlar. New Brunswick: Rutgers University Press, 1997.

McDonald, Boyd. "Presley-a-Go-Go." *Outrage* 17 (1983): 16–17.

————. *Cruising the Movies: A Sexual Guide to "Oldies" on TV.* New York: Gay Presses of New York, 1985.

—————. "Art from the Post-Heterosexual Age." *Art and Text* 20 (1986): 44–49.

McKee, Alan. "Do You Believe in Fairies? Creating Fictional Identities in Bent TV." *Media International Australia* 79 (February 1996): 115–18.

Medhurst, Andy. "That Special Thrill: *Brief Encounter*, Homosexuality, and Authorship." *Screen* 32.2 (1991): 197–208.

—————. "'It's as a Man That You've Failed': Masculinity and Forbidden Desire in *The Spanish Gardener*." In Kirkham and Thumin, eds. 1993.

Medhurst, Andy, and Sally R. Munt, eds. *Lesbian and Gay Studies: A Critical Introduction*. London: Cassell, 1997.

Mellen, Joan. *Women and Their Sexuality in the New Film*. New York: Horizon, 1973.

Mellencamp, Patricia. "Spectacle and Spectator: Looking through the American Musical Comedy." In Burnett, ed. 1991.

Mercer, Kobena. "Skin Head Sex Thing: Racial Difference and the Homoerotic Imaginary." In Bad Object-Choices, ed. 1991.

Mercer, Kobena, and Isaac Julien. "Race, Sexual Politics, and Black Masculinity: A Dossier." In Chapman and Rutherford, eds. 1988.

Merck, Mandy. *Perversions: Deviant Readings*. London: Virago, 1993.

Metcalf, Andy, and Martin Humphries, eds. *The Sexuality of Men*. London: Pluto, 1985.

Metz, Christian. *The Imaginary Signifier: Psychoanalysis and the Cinema*. Translated by Celia Britton et al. Bloomington: Indiana University Press, 1982.

Meyer, Moe, ed. *The Politics and Poetics of Camp*. London: Routledge, 1993.

Miller, D. A. *The Novel and the Police*. Berkeley: University of California Press, 1988.

—————. "Anal *Rope*." In Fuss, ed. 1991.

—————. *Bringing Out Roland Barthes*. Berkeley: University of California Press, 1992.

—————. *Place for Us: Essay on the Broadway Musical*. Cambridge: Harvard University Press, 1998.

—————. "Visual Pleasure in 1959." In Hanson, ed., 1999.

Millot, Catherine. *Horsexe: Essay on Transsexuality*. New York: Autonomedia, 1990.

Mitchell, Juliet. *The Longest Revolution*. London: Virago, 1984.

Mitchell, Juliet, and Jacqueline Rose, eds. *Feminine Sexuality: Jacques Lacan and the Ecole Freudienne*. London: Macmillan, 1982.

Moon, Michael. *A Small Boy and Others: Imitation and Initiation in American Culture from Henry James to Andy Warhol*. Durham: Duke University Press, 1998.

Moon, Michael, and Eve Kosofsky Sedgwick. "Divinity: A Dossier, a Performance Piece, a Little Understood Emotion." *Discourse* 13.1 (1990–91): 12–39.

Morella, Joe, and Edward Epstein. *Judy: The Films and Career of Judy Garland*. New York: Citadel Press, 1974.

Morrill, Cynthia. "Revamping the Gay Sensibility: Queer Camp and *dyke noir*." In Meyer, ed. 1993.

Mulvey, Laura. "Visual Pleasure and Narrative Cinema." *Screen* 16.3 (1975): 6–18.

———. "Notes on Sirk and Melodrama." In Gledhill, ed. 1986.

———. *Visual and Other Pleasures*. London: Macmillan, 1989.

Naremore, James. *Acting in the Cinema*. Berkeley: University of California Press, 1988.

Neale, Steve. *Genre*. London: British Film Institute, 1980.

———. "Masculinity as Spectacle." *Screen* 24.6 (1983): 2–16.

Newton, Esther. *Mother Camp: Female Impersonators in America*. Chicago: University of Chicago Press, 1972.

Nichols, Jack. "Butcher Than Thou: Beyond Machismo." In *Gay Men: The Sociology of Male Homosexuality*, edited by M. P. Levine. New York: Harper and Row, 1979.

Noriega, Chris. " 'Something's Missing Here!': Homosexuality and Film Reviews during the Production Code Era, 1934–1962." *Cinema Journal* 30.1 (1990): 20–41.

Nowell-Smith, Geoffrey. "Minnelli and Melodrama." In Gledhill, ed. 1987.

Nunokawa, Jeff. " 'All the Sad Young Men': AIDS and the Work of Mourning." In Fuss, ed. 1991.

Olivier, Christiane. *Jocasta's Children: The Imprint of the Mother*. Translated by G. Craig. London: Routledge, 1989.

Owens, Craig. "Outlaws: Gay Men in Feminism." In Jardine and Smith, eds. 1987.

Pasche, Francis. "Symposium on Homosexuality (ii)." *International Journal of Psycho-Analysis* 45 (1964): 211–14.

Patrick, J. *The Best of the Superstars: The Hottest Men in Their Best Roles*. Tampa: Starbooks, 1989.

Peary, Danny. *Cult Movies*. London: Vermilion, 1982.

Pendle, Karen, ed. *Women and Music: A History*. Bloomington: Indiana University Press, 1991.

Pendleton, David. "My Mother, the Cinema." *Wide Angle* 15.2 (1993): 40–47.

Penley, Constance. *The Future of an Illusion: Film, Feminism, and Psychoanalysis*. Minneapolis: University of Minnesota Press, 1989.

———. "Feminism, Psychoanalysis, and the Study of Popular Culture." In Grossberg et al., eds. 1992.

Phelan, Shane. *Getting Specific: Postmodern Lesbian Politics*. Minneapolis: University of Minnesota Press, 1994.

Plaza, Monique. "The Mother/The Same: The Hatred of the Mother in Psychoanalysis." *Feminist Issues* 2.1 (1982): 75–99.

Plummer, Ken, ed. *The Making of the Modern Homosexual*. London: Hutchinson, 1981.

Polan, Dana. " 'Above All Else to Make You See': Cinema and the Ideology of Spectacle." *boundary 2* 11.1–2 (1982–83): 129–44.

———. *Power and Paranoia: History, Narrative, and the American Cinema, 1940–1950*. New York: Columbia University Press, 1986.

Pribram, E. Deirdre, ed. *Female Spectators: Looking at Film and Television*. London: Verso, 1988.

Pronger, Brian. *The Arena of Masculinity: Sports, Homosexuality, and the Meaning of Sex.* New York: St. Martin's Press, 1990.

Raymond, Leigh. "Gays Step Out from behind the Screen." *Weekend Australian,* 30 July 1994, 11.

Reed, Rex. "Montgomery Clift." In Weis, ed. 1981.

Robertson, Pamela. *Guilty Pleasures: Feminist Camp from Mae West to Madonna.* Durham: Duke University Press, 1996.

Rodowick, D. N. "Vision, Desire, and the Film-Text." *Camera Obscura* 6 (1980): 54–89.

———. "Response." *Camera Obscura* 20–21 (1989): 269–74.

Roen, Paul. *High Camp: A Gay Guide to Camp and Cult Films.* Vol. 1. San Francisco: Leyland Publications, 1994.

———. *High Camp: A Gay Guide to Camp and Cult Films.* Vol. 2. San Francisco: Leyland Publications, 1997.

Rogin, Michael. *Blackface, White Noise: Jewish Immigrants in the Hollywood Melting Pot.* Berkeley: University of California Press, 1996.

Rose, Jacqueline. *Sexuality in the Field of Vision.* London: Verso, 1986.

Rosen, Phil, ed. *Narrative, Apparatus, Ideology: A Film Theory Reader.* New York: Columbia University Press, 1986.

Ross, Andrew. *No Respect: Intellectuals and Popular Culture.* New York: Routledge, 1989.

Rubin, Martin. *Showstoppers: Busby Berkeley and the Tradition of Spectacle.* New York: Columbia University Press, 1993.

Russo, Mary. *The Female Grotesque: Risk, Excess, and Modernity.* New York: Routledge, 1994.

Russo, Vito. *The Celluloid Closet: Homosexuality in the Movies.* Rev. ed. New York: Harper and Row, 1987.

Rutherford, Jonathan, ed. *Identity: Community, Culture, Difference.* London: Lawrence and Wishart, 1990.

Ryman, Geoff. *Was.* London: Flamingo, 1993.

Scanlan, Dick. *Does Freddy Dance.* Boston: Alyson, 1995.

Scheman, Naomi. "Missing Mothers/Desiring Daughters: Framing the Sight of Women." *Critical Inquiry* 15 (1988): 68–82.

Searle, Samantha. *Queer-ing the Screen.* Sydney: Moving Image, 1997.

Sedgwick, Eve Kosofsky. *The Epistemology of the Closet.* Berkeley: University of California Press, 1990.

———. *Tendencies.* Durham: Duke University Press, 1993.

Seidman, Steven. *Difference Troubles: Queering Social Theory and Sexual Politics.* Cambridge: Cambridge University Press, 1997.

Sennett, Ted. *Hollywood Musicals.* New York: Henry H. Abrams, 1981.

Shepherd, Simon, and Mick Wallis, eds. *Coming on Strong: Gay Politics and Culture.* London: Unwin Hyman, 1989.

Shilts, Randy. *Conduct Unbecoming: Gays and Lesbians in the U.S. Military.* Rev. ed. New York: Ballantine, 1994.

Silverman, Kaja. *The Acoustic Mirror: The Female Voice in Psychoanalysis and Cinema.* Bloomington: Indiana University Press, 1988.

———. *Male Subjectivity at the Margins.* New York: Routledge, 1992.

Simpson, Mark. *Male Impersonators: Men Performing Masculinity.* New York: Routledge, 1994.

Sochen, June. *Mae West: She Who Laughs Last.* New York: Harlan Davidson, 1992.

Sontag, Susan. *A Susan Sontag Reader.* Harmondsworth: Penguin, 1983.

Spacks, Patricia Meyer. *Gossip.* New York: Knopf, 1985.

Spoto, Donald. *Camerado: Hollywood and the American Man.* New York: New American Library, 1978.

Sprengnether, Madelon. *The Spectral Mother: Freud, Feminism, and Psychoanalysis.* Ithaca: Cornell University Press, 1990.

Stacey, Jackie. *Star Gazing: Hollywood Cinema and Female Spectatorship.* New York: Routledge, 1994.

Staiger, Janet. *Interpreting Films: Studies in the Historical Reception of American Cinema.* Princeton: Princeton University Press, 1992.

Stallybrass, Peter, and Allon White. *The Politics and Poetics of Transgression.* Ithaca: Cornell University Press, 1986.

Stam, Robert, Robert Burgoyne, and Sandy Flitterman-Lewis. *New Vocabularies in Film Semiotics: Structuralism, Post-Structuralism, and Beyond.* London: Routledge, 1992.

Stewart, William. *Cassell's Queer Companion: A Dictionary of Lesbian and Gay Life and Culture.* London: Cassell, 1995.

Straayer, Chris. "The She-man: Postmodern Bi-Sexed Performance in Film and Video." *Screen* 31.3 (1990): 262–80.

Stubbard, John. "Our Monty." *Out/Takes* 3 (1984): 23–26.

Studlar, Gaylyn. *In the Realm of Pleasure: Von Sternberg, Dietrich, and the Masochistic Aesthetic.* New York: Columbia University Press, 1988.

———. "Masochism, Masquerade, and the Erotic Metamorphoses of Marlene Dietrich." In Gaines and Herzog, eds. 1990.

Sweeney, Gael. "The Face on the Lunch Box: Television's Construction of the Teen Idol." *Velvet Light Trap* 33 (spring 1994): 49–59.

Tasker, Yvonne. *Spectacular Bodies: Gender, Genre and the Action Cinema.* London: Comedia, 1993.

Telotte, J. P., ed. *The Cult Film Experience: Beyond All Reason.* Austin: University of Texas Press, 1991.

Thompson, Kristin. "The Concept of Cinematic Excess." In Rosen, ed. 1986.

Thornton, Sarah. *Club Cultures: Music, Media, and Subcultural Capital.* Middletown: Wesleyan University Press, 1996.

Thurfitt, John. "Show Queens." *Outrage* 156 (May 1996): 32–35.

Threadgold, Terry, and Anne Cranny-Francis, eds. *Feminine/Masculine and Represen-tation.* Sydney: Allen and Unwin, 1990.

Tinkcom, Matthew. "Working Like a Homosexual: Camp Visual Codes and the Labor of Gay Subjects in the MGM Freed Unit." *Cinema Journal* 35.1 (1996): 24–42.

Turk, Edward Baron. "Deriding the Voice of Jeanette MacDonald: Notes on Psycho-analysis and the American Film Musical." *Camera Obscura* 25–26 (1991): 224–49.

Turner, Graeme. *British Cultural Studies: An Introduction.* London: Unwin Hyman, 1990.

Tyler, Carol-Ann. "Boys Will Be Girls: The Politics of Gay Drag." In Fuss, ed. 1991.

Tyler, Parker. *Screening the Sexes: Homosexuality in the Movies.* Rev. ed. New York: DaCapo, 1993.

Viegener, Matias. "Kinky Escapades, Bedroom Techniques, Unbridled Passion, and Secret Sex Codes." In Bergman, ed. 1993.

Warner, Michael. "Homo-Narcissism, or Heterosexuality." In *Engendering Men: The Question of Male Feminist Criticism,* ed. J. A. Boone and M. Cadden. New York: Routledge, 1990.

Weis, Elizabeth, ed. *The National Society of Film Critics on the Movie Star.* Harmonds-worth: Penguin, 1981.

Weiss, Andrea. *Vampires and Violets: Lesbians in the Cinema.* London: Jonathan Cape, 1992.

Wexman, Virginia Wright. *Creating the Couple: Love, Marriage, and Hollywood Perfor-mance.* Princeton: Princeton University Press, 1993.

Whatling, Clare. *Screen Dreams: Fantasising Lesbians in Film.* Manchester: Manches-ter University Press, 1997.

Williams, Linda. " 'Something Else besides a Mother': *Stella Dallas* and the Maternal Melodrama." In Gledhill, ed. 1987.

———. "When the Woman Looks." In Doane, Mellencamp, and Williams, eds. 1984.

———. *Hard Core: Power, Pleasure, and the "Frenzy of the Visible."* Berkeley: University of California Press, 1989.

Wilton, Tamsin, ed. *Immortal Invisible: Lesbians and the Moving Image.* New York: Routledge, 1995.

Wlaschin, Ken. *The Illustrated Encyclopedia of the World's Great Movie Stars.* Hong Kong: Salamander Books, 1979.

Wylie, Phillip. *A Generation of Vipers.* New York: Farrar, 1942.

Žižek, Slavoj. *The Sublime Object of Ideology.* London: Verso, 1988.

———. *Looking Awry: An Introduction to Jacques Lacan through Popular Culture.* Cam-bridge: MIT Press, 1991.

Index

escapism, 75–77; and gay subcultures, 73–76, 175; and heteronormativity, 77–79, 101–102; and homoeroticism, 85–86; and queerness, 84–98; and racial difference, 87–90, 259n 42

Music Man, The, 98

Musicology, 90

My Foolish Heart, 31

Myra Breckinridge, 143–148

My Sister Eileen, 98

Nachträglichkeit (deferred action, retro-activity), 55–56, 65–66, 71, 255n 68

Neale, Steve, 78, 79, 209–210, 212, 221–222

Negotiation, 45, 179–180, 277–278n 82; and gay spectatorship, 46–48, 71, 79–81, 94–96, 181–189

Newman, Paul, 229

Newton-John, Olivia, 98

Nolte, Nick, 216–217

North Dallas Forty, 216–217

Oedipality, 83; and homosexuality, 83–85, 91–92, 117–122, 154–161, 201–204, 242–246; and narrative, 83–85

Oklahoma!, 86, 98

Olson, Nancy, 190

On a Clear Day You Can See Forever, 98

On the Town, 85

Outsiders, The, 215

Pagan Love Song, 88

Pajama Game, The, 93

Parton, Dolly, 133

Pasche, Francis, 203–204, 217

Peggy Sue Got Married, 135

Pendleton, David, 162, 166

Performativity, 41–42, 113; and cinema, 124–126; and gender, 114, 122–123; identificatory, 29–32, 49, 171–172

Personal Best, 46–47, 80

Phelan, Shane, 41

Pirate, The, 99–109

Place in the Sun, A, 231–232, 236–237, 239

Plaza, Monique, 156

Pleasantville, 135

Point Break, 219–220, 223

Polan, Dana, 83, 109

Porgy and Bess, 87

Porter, Cole, 109

Poststructuralism: anti-identitarian, 33–35

Powell, Eleanor, 87, 97

Pre-oedipal, the, 90–91, 155–161, 167–168, 174, 192–197

Presley, Elvis, 86, 216, 218

Pronger, Brian, 206

Psychoanalysis, 12–15, 40, 49–53; and heteronormativity, 13–14; and homosexuality, 13, 83–84, 154–161, 201–204; and memory, 165–166, 171; social, 52; and subjectivity, 50–51; and teleology, 157. *See also* Fantasy; Freud, Sigmund; Lacan, Jacques; Laplanche, Jean, and Jean-Bertrand Pontalis

Pulp Fiction, 206

Queer, 15, 84–85, 195; critique of, 16, 37–38; spectatorship, 35–37; theory, 15, 35–38

Race, 87–90, 259n 42

Raintree County, 235

Raye, Martha, 145

Red River, 230–235, 245

Reed, Rex, 239

Reeves, Keanu, 219–220

Reeves, Steve, 114, 215

Remmick, Lee, 236

Robbins, Mark, 239–240

Robertson, Pamela, 137, 139, 144

Robinson, Bill, 87

Rocky Horror Picture Show, The, 87

Brett Farmer is Lecturer in Cultural Studies in the
Department of English at the University of Melbourne.

Library of Congress Cataloging-in-Publication Data
Farmer, Brett
Spectacular passions : cinema, fantasy, gay male
spectatorships / Brett Farmer.
p. cm.
Includes bibliographical references and index.
ISBN 0-8223-2559-4 (alk. paper)
ISBN 0-8223-2589-6 (pbk. : alk. paper)
1. Motion pictures and gay men. 2. Motion picture
audiences—Psychology. I. Title.
PN1995.9.H55 F37 2000
791.43'75'086642—dc21   00-028829